DIARY OF AN MP'S WIFE

DIARY OF AN MP'S WIFE

Inside and Outside Power

Sasha Swire

Little, Brown

LITTLE, BROWN

First published in Great Britain in 2020 by Little, Brown

3 5 7 9 10 8 6 4

A CIP catalogue record for this book is available from the British Library.

Hardback ISBN 978-1-4087-1341-9
Trade Paperback ISBN 978-1-4087-1340-2

Typeset in Baskerville by M Rules
Printed and bound in Great Britain by Clays Ltd, Elcograf S.p.A.

Papers used by Little, Brown are from well-managed forests
and other responsible sources.

Little, Brown
An imprint of
Little, Brown Book Group
Carmelite House
50 Victoria Embankment
London EC4Y 0DZ

An Hachette UK Company
www.hachette.co.uk

www.littlebrown.co.uk

To Hugo
Sorry!

Contents

Preface

I have been a secret journal writer since childhood. For anyone born with the compulsion to write, the journal-writing process has many benefits, from releasing emotions to trying to create a historical record of some value, to honing observational skills. The only discipline required is an ability to regularly capture your impressions. Mostly, my diaries felt like a safe space for critical reflection, but also a place to unload my own personal and political perspectives. At no time did I write with the intention of publication. I have never felt any need for self-vindication (pre- or posthumous) or the desire to profit from them. I can't say the thought didn't exist at the back of my mind, but I always pushed it away because I thought my family, my husband's colleagues and my friends would see it as an act of betrayal.

What changed? When my husband decided to quit the political stage in 2019, I, out of curiosity, and somewhat foolishly, showed the agent Caroline Dawnay some extracts, and before I knew it, I was swept up into a publishing tornado. As a result, I have decided to negotiate all the hazards that come with publishing memoirs, particularly political ones, not only because I much enjoy reading diaries but because I think it is rare indeed to read a female perspective on what is still a very male-dominated and secret world. As my great friend Kate Fall once told me, 'It's always the men that write history.'

I have been immersed in politics my whole life. I was brought up between London and Cornwall where my father, Sir John

Nott, was Member of Parliament for St Ives from 1966 to 1983. He was Economic Secretary to the Treasury under Ted Heath and served as Secretary of State for Trade when Thatcher won the 1979 general election. He was Secretary of State for Defence during the Falklands War. My mother, Lady (Miloska) Nott, is of Slovenian descent. During the Second World War, she was hidden on a farm in Maribor after her father's internment in Dachau as a Slav partisan, where he died. She met my father at Cambridge, at her engagement party to another man, and they married three weeks later. When I asked her why she had made such a rash decision, she said, 'Your father was always going places and I thought I would enjoy the ride.' I must have held on to those words. I can't remember the number of times I have been asked, 'So what's it like being an MP's wife, then?' My reply is usually: 'I'm an MP's daughter, so my life hasn't changed much.'

I married my husband, Hugo Swire, in 1996. He was then a director of Sotheby's. He became MP for East Devon in 2001 and I gave up my journalism career to support him. I raised our two daughters, Saffron and Siena, and because I could work from home, I became his part-time political researcher doing most of his writing work, including several newspaper columns under his name and all his press releases, and in more modern times I managed his social media accounts. Employing family members is now prohibited for new MPs.

Of course, there is something about the phrase 'political wife' that still evokes an image of a passive, helmet-haired, jam-making woman standing silently behind her husband, either smiling admirably as he asks for votes or frowning firmly as he admits to abusing his power or marriage. When my husband was first elected as an MP, I remember being invited to join a Westminster Wives group. The first event planned was a trip to the Aga Centre for a cookery demonstration. Back then there was still very much an attitude that you got 'two for the price of one', both at Westminster and more importantly in the constituency. I and my fellow MPs' wives, such as Samantha Cameron and Frances Osborne, were very determined not to play that traditional role and to hold on to our own jobs and identities. I think anyone reading this book will note that I have never been a political 'pushover'.

As for my diary-writing, it was not until my husband entered politics that a consistent narrative seemed to weave itself through my journals. They appeared to match an emerging and probably genetic obsession with the activities associated with governance and especially the debate between parties in the fight for power. The entries slowly evolved into a detailed record of what it was like to be a couple at the beating heart of politics during two tumultuous political decades.

When I finally decided to publish my diaries, the next task was to cut them down, which was a massive undertaking as there were nearly a million words to choose from. My editor, Richard Beswick, detached nine years' worth, the period from 2010 to 2019, and again shrank them down to a manageable range.

The volume here starts when my husband becomes a Minister of State for Northern Ireland after the 2010 general election, and ends in December 2019, when he left the political stage. It is an informal account of that period, from someone watching in the corner of the room. Extracts were not written to throw light on historic events, or to justify my husband's or party's positions – after all, I was not the elected one. I was also never restricted in my commentary or my observations or by any sense of professional legacy. I regret if I have offended anyone but, in my defence, I only tried to memorialise how I saw things at the time, so I imagine some entries might offend without meaning to do so. If so, I apologise. Re-reading the diaries also reminded me how politics not only brings friends together, even old ones, but how it wrenches them apart when they become passionate and partisan; Brexit, a case in point, which, at the time, even threatened to detonate the entire British party system. But then it also divided couples and country, and politics is designed to reflect the ebbs and flows of the national mood as well.

Last, I have to say that the hero of this book is absolutely not me, but Hugo, who is renowned in political circles for his charm and his humour. Many of the stories he has told me over the years have found their way into these diaries and I hope I have done them justice. He rode the political tiger, mostly unknown, working diligently for his departments and his constituents. He is an archetypal English gentleman, an old-style British politician, who never sought fame or legacy; in fact, he often found it positively distasteful, and in that he was almost unique amongst his peers. What happens between these pages is just one story, about one couple, in one extraordinary political decade, and how we navigated, with love and humour, the exhilarating but often choppy waters of a political life together.

2010

12 May

Still waiting to hear whether H has a job. Wake up in foul mood. I have been a member of a whole constituency of political thought since the age of about six, dedicated to ensuring that these people are locked out of the parliamentary process and now we are in bed with them! Five to be in cabinet and one in every department, apparently. Unbelievable. Particularly when they came third and lost seats. Has David sold his party down the river? Given too much away? Is this really the government the people voted for? Oh, I know the arguments: tie them in, let them share the hit on these difficult austerity-style decisions, but surely I'm not the only one experiencing deep and unsatisfying unease about this new alliance and its long-term political implications. How are we going to fight them when we have to?

Of course, the novelty will keep the show on the road for a few weeks; the gullible of the centre left will call it the new politics, as if coming from different ideological positions is so 'yesterday', but ideas and values are what this game is all about. New Labour suffered from its extreme pragmatism, and we will as well because you can't please all the people all the time. I have a boundary and so do the people in my party. Careful, David, how far you push us and how quickly. And can a fiercely Eurosceptic party with deeply held convictions about tax, public spending and the role of the state work for very long with a pro-European party? One that stages an annual party conference that has been known to career to the left of Labour? I don't know, but I don't think so.

My dad, Sir John, always complained about David, that he was a wishy-washy liberal, but I would herd Letwin and Hague into this pen as well; it does not surprise me that they were both members of the negotiating team that has given so much away for a chance to govern. It just feels like an experiment, a route to medical tests. I know it's not exactly Porton Down, but it still feels uncomfortable. Or is it just that age-old equation: Men + power = whores?

13 May

7.30 a.m. Walk into the bedroom with tea, and *The Times* tucked into my armpit. H barks, 'Don't give me that paper if it has a picture of that revolting couple on the front.' True enough, pic of Nick (Clegg) and Dave (Cameron) in civil partnership.

5 p.m. Downing Street rings while we are in an antique shop on Lillie Road in Fulham, trying to distract ourselves. Can H take a call from the PM, they ask. We do rushed and whispered negotiations about what he will or will not take behind a Victorian screen as we wait for him to come on the line. First, the usual bollocks about how everyone has been squeezed because of the Lib Dems, then it comes: will he take Minister of State in the Northern Ireland Office? H says he would be honoured. DC sounds shocked: 'God, I wish everyone was as easy as you. Hugo Swire stock is definitely on the rise.'

We are both pleased. H was on the Northern Ireland Defence Select Committee, so he knows a little bit about the place and its issues. He also knows David is very keen to strengthen every part of the UK, democratically, socially and economically; the Conservative position has always been pro union. But we also wonder whether it's the keep-Hugo-quiet slot, casting him out into the wilderness. ('I will leave you in the desert, you and all the fish of your streams. You will fall on the open field and not be gathered or picked up. I will give you as food to the beasts of the earth and the birds of the sky.' Ezekiel 29:5)

Hell, at least it's an MoS!

Ring Kate Fall, who is in terrible state; overwhelmed by her new responsibilities in No. 10 and wondering how she can cope with her two young children as a single mother. She has already had a run-in with the civil servants, who excluded her from a meeting. I just think she is exhausted after a long election campaign on the road. She told me she didn't dare leave the room, there was such a scramble for MoS jobs, because apparently the Chief Whip had tried to sew everything up for his mates; had even promised the ruddy-faced, clipped and military MP Andrew Robathan MoS at the Northern Ireland Office. *PLEASE!* George (Osborne), Dave and Kate had wrestled it back for Hugo. Kate added that the turf wars have been a complete nightmare. As it turns out, DC has had to carry out a series of brutal demotions of senior colleagues after the coalition left him with far fewer places than he anticipated.

H rings me later from his mobile as he is strolling down Whitehall. 'I would just like to say I have spoken to my private secretary, who called me Minister. I thought you should know that because I liked it very much, and I will be expecting a new and similar deference when I come home.' Then the No. 10 switch-board calls to find out where he is so they can make a car available to him. He rings back to tell me this as well.

When he comes home, a black rather than a red box is delivered. I ask H what the main issues are; he is cagey, but basically says the Bloody Sunday report, the continued funding of public services, the relationship between Northern Ireland and the Justice Department.

Until we collapse into bed, he keeps asking me to say 'Yes, Minister'. He likes its tone.

14 May

6.15 a.m. H flies to Belfast. He is met by security then taken straight to his armoured car, then on to Stormont House, where he meets all his staff and is shown his private office, which he tells me is 'the size of several tennis courts'. Stormont has recently been refurbished in the most tasteless of fashions by the female Head of the Northern Ireland Office, Hilary Jackson. H has accommodation there if he wants it but decides to take up a berth at Hillsborough Castle instead. Much more his style. He is then given his security briefing level, which is very high. He joins Owen (Paterson, Secretary of State) in meetings all day, with ministers and the Chief Constable etc. H's responsibilities are mainly to support the Secretary of State, but he also has control over elections, including the impact of political reforms on NI, human rights and the NI Human Rights Commission (including NI Bill of Rights), and day-to-day security case work as well as liaison with the Parades Commission. Together they then go to meet defeated Conservative candidates before moving on to Hillsborough for dinner and the night.

He texts Randal Dunluce:* 'Forget your castle, come to my castle!'

Greg (Barker) texts from the Climate Change Department: 'Do I like all this, or do I like this? Certainly beats being in opposition.' H replies he is sitting in Hillsborough Castle with two bodyguards. '*Oooh!* So you!' Greg replies.

16 May

Stay at the Old Parsonage Hotel in Oxford to celebrate Saffron's birthday. George O rings H for a gossip; says his negotiations with the Lib Dems are not a patch on those he is currently conducting with his wife, who refuses to move into No. 11. Good for Frances! He says he still has to pinch himself that he is Chancellor. They gossip about colleagues who have missed out, particularly Keith Simpson, who has been threatening a by-election because he didn't get a job.

---

* Viscount Dunluce, son of the Earl of Antrim, owner of Glenarm Castle.

18 May

Ashcroft kicking off, angry at not getting a job. George and Clegg fighting for Dorneywood, but then George just drives down there to plant his flag – well, toothbrush to be more precise. Wins the battle and Clegg ends up sharing Chevening with Hague.

Frances texts: 'You must come and stay at Dorneywood.'

I text back, 'And you must come to Hillsborough, darling!'

We are like kids in a sweet shop.

I sign off: 'Rejoice, for tomorrow we die.'

Then Kate: 'Gosh, he can really waffle for Britain, that man Clegg, never draws breath.'

H accosted in Portcullis House by Peter Luff, who is waving a piece of paper in the air. 'Looks like you are the only one who has been rehabilitated. I have the list, I have the list,' he booms jealously. H replies meekly that he was also the only one unceremoniously dumped from the shadow cabinet because of the school he went to.

'There is no such thing as fairness in politics, Peter.'

'Only one on the list,' repeats Luff, walking off in disgust.

The Conservative Home website also points this out and adds that it is clearly because H is a lifelong friend of Dave's, which of course is utter rubbish; he only met him when they went into politics together. A lot of them are spitting blood. H has an awkward conversation with Andrew Robathan, who says he and his lovely wife have not slept for three days. He's going round saying how he feels utterly let down by DC. He believes he was shafted by the Chief Whip, which is not quite the truth, and he is altogether furious. He makes it sound like a drive-by shooting.

20 May

H in Ireland to receive DC on his first visit. Has meeting with Gerry Adams, Peter Robinson and more. Before the roundtable discussion starts, Cameron rather surprisingly gives H a huge plug. 'I'd like to tell you that the only reason I am sitting here is because of Hugo Swire, who happened to run my leadership campaign.' This comes as news to Hugo, who did nothing of the sort. Afterwards all household staff at Stormont are gathered to be introduced to him; there is some joking about looking after the new minister.

'He's easy, but wait till you meet his ferocious wife.'

'Yes,' chips in H. 'That's why you will be seeing rather more of me than you probably expected.'

6 June

Gurning horror ...

'I'm not wearing a hat!'

'It's a royal garden party, you have to wear a hat.'

'I hate wearing hats. I'm not going to wear one. I mean, what's the purpose of it? It's not occupational, is it? A garden party?'

'Sasha, please don't be difficult, it's royal protocol.'

'Well, it's outdated. I'm going to make a stand.'

Of course, I don't. I nip down to John Lewis, where I opt for a fascinator. It's a small act of rebellion because in hat land, such as Royal Ascot, they are frowned upon, but it makes me feel better as it's less of a statement than a wide brim – and, more importantly, it's dirt cheap. I am flying to Belfast tomorrow for my first visit.

8 June

Sitting in our apartment at Hillsborough Castle watching the groundsmen outside drawing white lines to segregate the public from royalty. Beyond them, clipped yews descending to a pond and a temple in the woods. Beautiful. Now I know how power corrupts.

Here for the Secretary of State's garden party. Some 2500

invited, including Prince Edward and Sophie Wessex, who we will be having dinner with afterwards. Looks as if it is going to be a washout.

Hillsborough far more stunning than I had anticipated, a low-lying eighteenth-century mansion in the middle of an attractive village. It was the seat of the Marquesses of Downshire for well over two hundred years, but is now the official residence of the Secretary of State for Northern Ireland (and his Minister! And his wife!) It is used generously for official functions and acts as a motel for passing VIPS and royals.

I tour the castle when I arrive. Nice anecdote about the recent reconciliation talks that took place here. The DUP were the first to appear, and took over the long blue drawing room. When Sinn Féin showed up, they were put in the room opposite, the throne room, which to this day contains no furniture as it is used for state occasions such as dinners and investitures. As the talks dragged on, hour after hour, day after day, Gerry Adams was found asleep on the floor by the throne. So incensed were Sinn Féin that the Unionists had a better room, with furniture in it, they staged a sit-in when the DUP made a brief exit. The idea that these two groups were going to go into a power-sharing deal was getting remoter by the minute. The long and short of it was that a whole round of sub-talks had to open to remove Sinn Féin from squatting in the drawing room. It was agreed that the quickest way out of this was for soft furnishings to be brought to the throne room to accommodate their wishes. This was promptly done, Sinn Féin finally moved across the corridor and talks resumed.

Our apartment is small, rather like a suite in a five-star hotel: all Molton Brown shampoos and Heal's dressing gowns. All laundry is taken away and washed. All beds made and fridges stocked to requirements. Cloudy Bay, no less. It's less grand than Owen's but cosier because it is compact; Owen's rooms are in the royal section of the castle.

As I'm unpacking my washbag Dave is on telly against his chosen backdrop of happy, shiny, smiley, perfect people; this time in Milton Keynes. He's saying it's really bad, really, really bad and suddenly the people behind him don't seem to be smiling any more. Dave is saying our debt is massive, colossal, mind-blowing; it's so terrible that the lot behind him owes him nearly £1 trillion and if they don't give it to him now – he says NOW! – the total will be £1.4 trillion in five years. But the people do get it, because most of them have racked up something similar on their M&S store cards. Still, they really don't look happy any more, not at all. I wait for him to get to the nitty gritty: defence? NHS? Northern Ireland Office? Cuts delayed for a year. But it is bad, we know that; the country is suffering the worst recession since the Second World War, banks are being nationalised, businesses are going under and unemployment is rising. A stable government has never felt more important.

Sue Lawley and her husband Hugh Williams taxi over from Belfast to have dinner with us at the Parson's Nose, a lovely restaurant in Hillsborough village. We talk about *It's a Royal Knockout*, which Hugh produced for the BBC after being approached by Edward and Anne and Fergie. Hugh is hilarious, imitating Andrew and Edward mincing around deciding what ye olde English lavish costumes they were going to deck themselves out in before lending themselves to a custard-pie TV game show. We agree most of their time is spent dipping into the dressing-up box anyway, so it would have come naturally to them.

Yesterday taken on a political tour of Belfast by Patrick Lynch, an amiable Scot from the political unit. Patrick studied at Aberdeen and did his masters in conflict resolution at Queen's here in Belfast. He takes me to most of the flashpoints, starting in east Belfast, notably the Short Strand, a mainly Catholic and Irish Nationalist enclave in a six thousand-strong Protestant area. For decades, Protestants and Catholics regularly clashed at its edges. We then drive down Cluan Place, a cul-de-sac; wooden crates are stacked up here, ready to light for the 12 July parade bonfire. This is a

Protestant working-class street and it sits on the peace line. Fifteen years ago, this would have been a no-go zone for anyone as extraneous as myself, and although windows have wire grilles, front gardens are often filled with children's toys and it is surprisingly neat. In fact, I am really struck by the tidiness and cleanliness of these areas, much more so than their equivalents on the 'mainland'. (I'm not meant to call it that any more.) We pass St Matthew's Roman Catholic Church, and I'm told of a gun battle fought between the IRA and loyalist paramilitaries back in June 1970.

On into the Catholic heartland, the Falls Road. It's long and busy, and overlooked by the lone Divis Tower.

The road is illustrated with a series of murals, blossoms on walls, some part of the information machine, others expressions of the community's current cultural and political concerns. I'm particularly drawn to those that pay tribute to other international liberation movements, particularly Palestine. I will see them everywhere here, across divides, naive artistic portrayals that are passionate, angry, how art should be, direct from the heart, art of the street, Banksy-style. When this is all over there will be temptations to strip this art down, to sanitise the streets, to help grease the peace process, but war graffiti leaves such an enduring document of pain shared. They are sacred expressions about common sentiments and cultures and should be left to history.

Back to Hillsborough. Get the lowdown on Shaun Woodward from one of the staff. When he came here, he brought his own retinue: cook, butler, probably nannies. He also insisted on having extra security in the UK; a huge black Range Rover with stacks of security guards following his already bulletproof Jaguar. Outriders even. Altogether more prime ministerial than Secretary of State.

2.30 p.m. Hugo is unable to attend the garden party. Stuck in Downing Street with the heads of the UK's devolved assemblies, it seems.

He is due to fly back for dinner with the royals after the meeting.

2.45 p.m. Summoned to be in a line-up with Rose Paterson to greet the Wessexes. She has the right hat on and a nice neat boxy suit, naturally. Rose is uptight English: lean as a thoroughbred racehorse; if she smelt – which she doesn't – it would be of hay and saddle soap. She has owned point-to-pointers and event horses. She is also a Cambridge bluestocking and clearly the more clever of the pair. Ever vigilant, she watches Owen closely and blunts his edges. But then that's the thing about women and horses: it's all about power and powerlessness, to be in control, or out of control. And power can only be accessed by persuasion because of the differences in strength, a gift we political wives share. Despite this, she makes me feel mildly inadequate as a political consort.

The Secretary of State is running late because of low-lying dense cloud over a lough near Belfast airport, but he and his gang all arrive safely, if not a little agitated.

I follow the royal party's procession through to the state rooms. It's all very formal. Rigid, even. From there we proceed into the garden and full pelt into a rainstorm. It feels as if the entire region's average annual rainfall is about to be deposited on my flimsy fascinator.

I look out at a sea of umbrellas, under which are serving PSNI officers and their guests, and a bevy of service personnel based in the province all stand looking miserable. Up goes the national anthem, played by the band of the Northern Ireland Fire & Rescue Service, into the ground goes a nice new tree courtesy of a spade and a prince. I turn to Belinda, my chaperone for the afternoon, and groan, 'Come on then, let's do a circuit.' As I walk, I have to clench my thighs and pull my heels out of the sodden ground; it's like drawing the cork out of a cheap bottle of wine. I have this ridiculous fascinator on my head and I'm shivering in my spotty silk L.K. Bennett dress. Green with envy, I look over at Rose in her neat little tweed suit, laughing with the guests. Truth is, I'm not remotely interested in laughing or talking to anyone. I only meet Belinda's mum, though that's partly because Belinda can't see anyone's faces under their umbrellas. We immediately strike up a deal and shake on it; she won't tell my husband anything and I scarper as fast as my long legs will carry me to the soft, dry confines of the flat, where I text H, who is in Downing Street: 'Unbearable. Pissing torrential rain. You fucking owe me.' He rings me half an hour later and asks why I'm answering the telephone. *Oh God, he's rumbled me.* And he is furious, then I get furious that he's furious, abandoning me to the rain and the small talk. And he puts the phone down on me.

7 p.m. H rings: 'I'm not going to make it over for dinner. They keep delaying the flight. I would get in at ten and the dinner will almost be over. It's not worth it.'

'Bloody hell, you're joking. That means there's only six of us for dinner.'

'Well, you better turn up this time then.'

'I didn't sign up for this, you know.'

'I pay you, don't I?'

'No, darling, the taxpayer pays me as your political researcher, this grin-and-curtsy shit does not fall under my job description. I can show you my contract if you like.'

'It falls under a wife's job description.'

'You forget, my darling, I am something of a republican.'

'You dare—'

'Ta-ta.'

7.45 p.m. I make my way down to the drawing room. The Patersons and I are soon standing to attention, listening to the Countess of Wessex in full sail as she bangs on about farming matters. She justifies her forthright views in her capacity as vice-patron of the Bath and West Show, but as she makes some fatuous comment about dairy farmers I can no longer contain myself. I explain that in my part of the world (Devon), if a dairy farm goes to the wall (as they have been) a yuppie comes in and buys the property and the farm is sold off, which is a tragedy for the countryside. Owen also pitches in as he has a rural constituency as well. Then she moves on to ramblers and rights of access. Again, I feel I have to interject. I say it would be political suicide for the Conservative Party to reverse legislation on this. As we walk into dinner Rose whispers, 'Well done! Very brave of you.' Gosh!

At dinner I sit next to Sophie and opposite Prince Edward, who spends the entire dinner talking across the table to me, completely ignoring Rose and Owen on either side of him. I don't suffer from a case of the vapours around the royals and I don't feel particularly deferential towards them so I'm quite relaxed. To be honest, even though I am not actually a republican, which I said to wind H up, I'm no ardent monarchist, although I would not want the alternative, which would be a Boris Johnson or, God forbid, a Ken Livingstone type. Or Simon Cowell? The point is, what we would have imposed on us would be downright worse than what we have now.

It comes as a surprise that I like Prince Edward; he is friendly, over-excitable like a puppy and, like his wife, highly opinionated about political matters. We talk about MPs' expenses, the media (I am very damning about the *Telegraph*), the House of Lords. At one point I say, 'I think I like you – you are agreeing with everything I say. That's a very good principle: my husband will tell you that!' He seems overwhelmed with relief that the Conservatives have got in.

So, we are back in the drawing room for coffee and I'm on the sofa with the Countess, wondering how the hell I am going to loosen this woman up.

'So, bet he didn't tell you he was a royal when he married you.'

She looks at me, puzzled. 'I knew he was a royal, of course I did. What do you mean by that?'

'It was a joke!'

'Oh.'

We move on to discuss her royal duties. There is a long moan about how she dislikes doing functions with Edward (she is usually on her own) because she gets frozen out. 'Well, I suppose he's the royal one,' she sighs. She tells me that she had been slighted that day, by some woman who refused to acknowledge her, instead fixing all her beady concentration on the Prince, and I reply by saying it happens to me all the time as an MP's wife, and that as a result I carry revenge in my heart until my dying day – but that is because I have Slav blood and wanting to kill people all the time comes naturally to me. A smile finally emerges from her pale, milky face and she says thinks she must have Slav blood in her as well.

She talks about how she still worked at her PR company after her wedding, under the name Sophie Wessex, but was quickly forced to give it up because she came in for criticism for appearing in public with clients and was accused of using her royal status to promote her business. As she tells me this there is real regret in her eyes, and sadness that this part of her life is gone and not allowed to return. The conversation moves on to the fake sheikh affair, which I barely remember. I said did she remember what he looked like, the fake sheikh, aka *News of the World* undercover reporter Mazher Mahmood?

'No, I couldn't pick him out in a line-up of one.'

'Pity, you could have warned Fergie, because that was always going to happen.'

(In May, Fergie was stung by the tabloids when she was caught offering something called 'access' to Prince Andrew for half a million big ones, with the promise that he might be able to help industrialists because of some grand title he holds. Personally, I'd pay half a million to avoid seeing him, but then that's me.)

'Did you see it?' she asks me.

'Yes.'

'What was it like?'

'Excruciating. No wriggle room. Embarrassing beyond belief.'

After they go to bed I reflect on how sorry for her I feel. I recall how in 2001 she was rushed to hospital with an ectopic pregnancy, and how she had to undergo a massive life-saving operation, losing a lot of blood. It's as if she has never recovered, she is still pale, drained, tired and it feels to me, and I could be wrong, most definitely sad. I can't help thinking, when I think of all these royal women – Fergie, Diana and now Sophie – how the monarchy swallows them up whole and probably retains its strength by doing so. As an institution it seems to have an uncanny ability to destroy or weaken everything near it; its weapons of choice a whispered aside, a cold shoulder, a dropped title, a small divorce settlement, a reduction of identity. Of course, the Palace is run mostly by men, who want women to be seen, decoratively so, but not heard.

14 June

H in Downing Street with D, preparing the Bloody Sunday statement. They are drafting and re-drafting. The Saville report, out tomorrow, comes down heavily against the Paras. DC wants to be very apologetic. Owen is there, of course, and Liam Fox. K is taking notes. David exits to go to a dinner with Andy Feldman but leaves everyone in his office. He calls H on his mobile from his car. 'What do you think? Am I doing the right thing?'

'Yes,' says H reassuringly, 'absolutely the right thing. It's right to be apologetic.' They both express their amazement at how compliant Fox is being about it all.

K will tell me later that both she and David were deeply moved by the summary of the report. And appalled by the disgraceful way the paratroopers behaved.

15 June

DC brilliant in the House of Commons, at his absolute best.

All in all, an important day in our political history because what this report and inquiry have demonstrated is how the state must always be held accountable, however difficult that may be. It must set the standard so that others can follow. As D commented, 'openness and frankness about the past, however painful, do not make us weaker; they make us stronger'. And he couldn't have been clearer: 'No government I lead will ever put those who fight to defend democracy on an equal footing with those who continue to seek to destroy it, but nor will we hide from the truth that confronts us today.'

But the time has also come to move forward. Owen and H and the people of Northern Ireland must come together to resolve injustices in non-violent ways to ensure a peaceful and prosperous, and shared, future. That is now the job in hand.

When people out of politics ask me now what the job in Northern Ireland involves, I respond by saying it's rather like carrying a huge Ming vase that can break at any moment.

21 June

Philippa, my beloved mother-in-law, aka the Dowager Marchioness Townshend, rings my mother. 'Thank you so much for asking me to Cornwall. I will be bringing my butler, Keith, and my dog.'

Silence. Gulps. 'Did you say your dog?' my Slovenian mother, Miloska, asks.

'Don't worry, he can sleep with me.'

'In four-poster room? No, darlink, our dogs are kept outside in shed. I suppose we could put a basket in kitchen.'

'Oh, he's not really a dog, Miloska, he's a human and I have to have him with me. I absolutely insist, otherwise I will have to decline your generous invitation.'

Philippa's adored dog Merlin, an aristocratic blue whippet, mostly sits sphinx-like by her side, including as a sleep-sitter beside her bed. When he is released from his quivering bug-eyed station, which is rare, he is prone to bouts of snarling, saliva-dripping aggression. We think her affection is down to her belief that the dog is in some way the reincarnation of her recently deceased husband George, whom she worshipped, and who is guarding her during her time left on earth.

I tell H, who is incensed by the grandeur of it all.

'She's only got the butler for a year, for God's sake. She needs to get used to life without him.'

'Stuff the butler, it's the dog they are getting worked up about. I'm nearly fifty and I've only been allowed to sleep in that room once in my life. A dog, believe me, is way down the pecking order as regards entry.'

'Leave it to me,' says H.

28 June

Dinner hosted by my old friend Martha Fiennes at the Westbury Hotel. An eclectic bunch: Martina Navratilova, Patti Smith, Michael Barrymore, Sigrid Rausing, Ralph Fiennes, Sabrina Guinness, Julie Myerson, Nicky Haslam. I'm placed next to Marc Quinn, of YBA (Young British Artist) fame.

We get talking and I'm immediately alarmed by his low calcium intake: apparently, he eats no dairy products, and I tell him I'm scared his bones might dry out and he'll be unable to paint. Mind you, from what I can establish, his assistants do a lot of the work.

'So did Caravaggio, you know. And Michelangelo,' he protests. Michelangelo he ain't.

I ask him if it's a Primrose Hill thing, being averse to the bovine. Only today, another resident, Gwynnie (Paltrow) announced she had the early stages of osteoporosis because she had been following a macrobiotic diet since the nineties, and had cut out dairy and never put her face in the sun.

'Oh, I do that, I get sun – I'm building a house in Majorca. I just find the idea of lactation disgusting.'

We also have an interesting conversation about tax. I've ceased to be surprised by how people become more focused on such matters when they start making tons of money. His wife, Lady Georgia Byng, daughter of the Earl of Strafford, is flirting mercilessly with the actor Ben Chapman, which I also can't help teasing him about.

Then he shows me some of his artwork on his iPhone. Vague memories of a head made from his own blood, a marble statue of a limbless woman in Trafalgar Square, but the ones he is showing me now are more beautiful; exotic flowers in photographic colour, orchids, very sexual; the flower petals resembling vaginas, nature mirroring itself back on itself type of thing. They would look great on a hedge fund manager's wall, which is probably where they all are, since no one else can afford them.

1 July

DC at Norman Lamont's last night: 'You have to be nice to me now, Sasha, I've given your husband a castle and a butler, for goodness sake, and he's even got more bloody security than me.'

'Oh, all right then.'

He then asks H whether he wants to come in on prep for PMQs; he says he needs him for the jokes. I butt in, saying that H will be crap at it, he's more off the cuff, but secretly I'm thinking he also knows sod all about what's going on outside his brief.

H has very good Irish questions in the House, so much so he shows up Owen. A colleague whispers afterwards: 'Not a good idea to upstage the Secretary of State, Hugo.'

The Dowager rings me: 'He is an absolute genius, isn't he, darling, brilliant, just brilliant and you are brilliant for getting him to marry you.'

'Excuse me, Philippa, may I remind you that it is me who has made him brilliant.'

'Yes, yes, darling, of course you have.'

She'll be dining out on his brilliance for months to come, telling her crusty old aristocratic guests he is clearly heading for the portals of No. 10. Not.

7 July

To Christopher Moran's Chelsea palace on the Thames. The core of Crosby Hall is an original Tudor house which was moved from the City of London in 1908 to Thomas More's old garden in Chelsea, and eventually incorporated, rather like a smaller Russian doll, into a hostel for the British Federation of University Women.

Enter Christopher Moran, with a thin cheque for the lease (a mere £100,000) and the old biddies are booted out. He subsequently spent £25 million to turn it into a thirty-bedroom mansion. Moran, who Hugo has known for quite a while, gives the appearance of having it all – which he does, up to a point. But of course that which is most desirable is proving the most elusive – that being 'recognition', or in layman's terms, a peerage.

What he has done at Crosby Hall is deeply impressive, though he doesn't exactly restrain his ego: his initials and crest are freely displayed all over it, as are casts of his and his children's heads. Incidentally, his first wife ran off with a flower-seller on the Fulham Road. At the time she said, 'He doesn't say things in jest – ever. When he wants something, he will stop at nothing to get it. He wants people to remember what he has achieved and he's very persuasive.'

Anyway, we walk into this black-tie dinner he is hosting in the courtyard designed by the irrepressible Mollie Salisbury (she is there, still looking beautiful, but even older and whiter than usual) and I'm already looking for an exit strategy. H has to vote so I'm terrified he is going to leave me stranded. As it turns out, it's one of those unexpectedly fun evenings where the company just gels. On our small table: Moran, Owen and Rose Paterson, a Prince of Wales flunkey on the charitable side, Francis Maude, Hugo and me, and the portly and cheery Jonathan Marland, who is on hilariously good form. The humour commences when Moran gets up with a microphone, practically giving it a blow job, it's that close to his lips. He starts rambling on about his esteemed guests, most of whom listen, bored and silent. No such respect is demonstrated at our table. When he starts to pick people out of the crowd, which is his way, Marland and Hugo throw in asides, which he unwittingly starts to incorporate into his verbal evocations. When he comes to Hugo:

'And we have Hugo Swire here, new Minister of State for Northern Ireland. Formerly an auctioneer, Hugo is—'

'A great shot!' calls Marland.

'A great shot,' echoes Moran.

'And a great lover,' I shout.

'A great lover ... Is he, now? And you are?'

When the speech is over, H is still on a roll and turns to another target at our table, this time the Fagin-like Francis Maude, all villainous-looking with his tight little weasel eyes. He currently spends his days bent over the books in the Cabinet Office, counting the money, or more precisely the lack of it.

'You know how no one has ever seen him smile? Now we get one with a cut in the morning, one with a cut at lunchtime, and even one in the evening, when another slash is planned for the next day.' Maude smiles back with his customary blend of wariness and cunning.

Hugo and Marland then turn to the subject of Moran, who is sitting down again, and start digging into the tar pit of his past. H, with huge doses of embellishment, relays a tale of when Moran tried to clear the local 'wee free' out of the church on his Scottish estate. H, who was in the passenger seat at the time, says Moran insisted on revving the accelerator of his Range Rover as they came out of church. 'Terrified they would be mown down, the poor wee free were left flat and scattered in the hedgerows.' Moran smiles and jokingly says that a few of his tenants were something of an irritation to him and as result he refused to put baths in their properties. We don't believe this is actually true. Another story is recounted by Marland, of a man who had two barns within view of Moran's window. He promptly threw money at the problem and discovered that one was illegal so sent in a digger and knocked it down overnight. 'The view was vastly improved after that,' Moran chuckles.

Afterwards, we offer to give Esther McVey and Charlotte Leslie, newly elected MPs, a lift in the government Prius to get to the vote. They are both refreshingly normal (for members of the political class). Charlotte is wearing a tight shoulder-less red satin dress, and as soon as she is outside the heavy oak doors of Crosby Hall she kicks off the most amazingly high red satin heels and runs down the street barefoot. 'My mum says wear them while you can, but they are so bloody high.' I love her sense of mischief, though she makes me feel suddenly very old.

Esther McVey, who is perfectly groomed with a pretty face and a strong Scouse accent, follows behind. In the car she is more ladette than lady, telling us she will tell the whips to 'piss off' if they make her stay too late. Wonderful. But this new bunch of Tories should not be underestimated: many of them believe they were elected despite David Cameron, not because of him. Many even whisper that they could have doubled their majority if he hadn't been such a liberal wimp. Dave, in his PR way, picked them because they ticked the right boxes, but they in turn picked the party, and they picked it because they are reform-minded, resolutely Eurosceptic and right wing. They are also acutely aware that to be cool is to be independent – look no further than the election of Graham Brady as chairman of the 1922 Committee. David's whips have got their work cut out.

A fun evening.

16 July

H asks his driver to take me home after an event as he expects to be in the Commons until late – as it turns out, he will be there until 4 a.m. This request is, however, strictly against the rules. I say to the driver, as we purr along electrically in his Prius, do they really expect me to find my own way, in a long dress and painful heels, to some excruciatingly dull public function, sit next to some God-awful bore, pay for the taxi to get there, and then get left stranded on some dark corner trying to find a non-existent taxi home because the driver is taking my husband in completely the opposite direction to vote? The government needs to be gently reminded that they do not get two for the price of one! Those days are well and truly over. I do them a favour, they do me one back. Simple.

When DC came in as leader, he vowed to get rid of ministerial cars, following a long campaign orchestrated by arch-moderniser Ed Vaizey. Any minister who does not have security implications can use a pool car or make do with public transport. We all groaned: token politics again. In his usual mad PR dash, the oily Jeremy Hunt was the first to give up his car, much to the annoyance of little Hugh Robertson: 'It's all right for him, he's rich. He just gets a bloody taxi home.' Ed Vaizey can now be found, night after night, loitering outside the Members' Entrance, trying to cadge a lift from a chauffeured colleague. His problem is that most of the drivers object to giving him passage, in retaliation for having endangered their livelihoods. Another one hoisted by his own petard!

There are ways and means in politics, and H has pretty much worked these out. He keeps Sid, his driver, for 'security reasons', but another way around this, as others are working out, is to become friends with the red box. As long as you have that arrogant little upstart beside you in the Prius, you have a ticket to ride. The box, you see, is the important passenger: it represents the office of state, whereas the politician is not only replaceable but irrelevant.

But the whole system is in chaos, partly because the Government Car Service and its drivers are devoted to maximising use of the car. Drivers are paid a low basic wage and are therefore heavily reliant on overtime. They are happy to be kept hanging around at all hours of the day and night. The PM's call to use pool cars is causing all-out civil war between the regular drivers and the pool drivers; the regulars loathe the pool drivers for stealing their jobs. They simply don't talk to each other.

27 July

Answering to the new middle-class glamping trend, we spent three nights at Port Eliot Festival; the four of us under a tepee, which I hire at huge expense because I think the only way to get through it is to throw money at it.

The trouble with tepees is that they are constructed around three or four bamboo poles, which, as a rule, meet at the top through a hole in the canvas. This is not a bricks-and-mortar, air- and watertight type of affair, and as a shelter is not entirely suited to bad weather conditions. Having said that, the indoor shower with Hugo's bed as a rain tray was a somewhat unexpected feature.

H gets his chance to have his Victor Meldrew moment. In a raging monsoon of a wet Cornish evening he storms over to the reception tent to find a group of laddish men spaced out around a log-burning stove. The mere sight of their comfort makes him go off on one. Forget Victor Meldrew, he is turning into Derrick Bird, the madman who shot some perfectly innocent people up in Cumbria last month. H picks up one of them, drags him by the collar over to our tepee and forces him to lie down on his wet mattress.

'Yeah, OK, man, I get the message. I'll go and get a ladder and fix the leak.'

I bark after him, 'And a new mattress, duvet, pillow and sheet.'

'It's all gravy, ladies.' (We *think* that means don't worry, it's all cool.)

He returns ten minutes later with a mattress even damper than the one I foisted on him in the first place. He looks crestfallen when I reject this one as well. He understands, and rightly so, that this incident is proving to be a direct challenge to his cosy existence back at reception, where his mates were last heard laughing uncontrollably about the Luft Wafter, a famous topless German techno fan with body odour issues. He goes on to tell us that the dry mattresses are in some camper van but his boss has the key and he doesn't know where his boss is.

He goes off to get the ladder but of course doesn't return. Hugo storms over again and has another rant. He grabs the one he knows and drags him back to our tepee.

By now our tent supervisor is being subjected to an insurmount-able tide of abuse from this entitled middle-aged Tory couple who clearly have had no experience whatsoever of camping and are clearly not very chilled people.

'You're stoned, aren't you?' I say.

'No, I don't drink or take drugs, I'm just laid back.'

Liar. I was young once, you know.

'Well, that's not normal. Why don't you drink?' H asks.

''Cause I don't like stress.'

He goes off again to get the ladder, muttering 'It's all gone Pete Tong . . .'

After he's left Hugo says, 'Fuck's sake, Sasha, why did you accuse him of being stoned? You have completely destroyed our legal case now.'

'What legal case is that, exactly? It's in the contract, babe. Tepees leak.'

'Shower?'

'Leak.'

H throws his hands in the air, exasperated. 'I'll have to sleep with you.'

'You are not bloody sleeping with me. You stink.'

'Siena, move over, darling, I'm coming in.'

'OK, Dad, but please don't snore.'

Wake up bleary-eyed and lift the tent flap, to be greeted by the beaming face of a camp tramp. Except that H knows this one; he is a double-barrelled old family friend. This is a posh festival, after all – in fact, at times it feels more like an Etonian reunion. William Sieghart and James Studholme, who was in the same class as H, are also here. Anyway, our uninvited visitor clearly hasn't washed, hasn't changed his clothes for three days and is moon burnt from too much clubbing. Now here he is, begging for toothpaste. When he sticks out his tongue to demonstrate why, it is a rather strange shade of RAF blue. He actually seems remarkably happy, unnaturally happy in fact, for one who has been out for the last two nights, passing out in other people's tents and not quite knowing how he got there. The children think he is marvellous, rather like a white-faced circus clown. I think he's out of his head and need to shrug him off, but he keeps offering to help me carry gear to the car.

Saffron goes off with her friend Io. She's loving it in her festival gear – mascara (H hasn't noticed), short shorts and wellingtons. Only thirteen and she'll probably be in 'beefa next year, doing the big fish little fish cardboard box, speakers hoofing it and mum 'n' bass with her ounce bounce friends (oh yes, I know all the lingo now) . . . Then again, hopefully we have got a few years left.

Hugo comes back from the crapocalypse, the festival club toilet, which is in another league of horror, and without any paper, but when desperation calls . . .

6 August

Cornwall

My mother has signed over her field and pond to me. As a war child she is determined that I have a patch of ground to grow vegetables, should the time come. It has caused difficulty in my relationship with my brother, which is already strained. He expected to cop the lot, but unluckily for him (not so for me) we share a foreign mother who does not understand or comply with the concept of primogeniture. Everything has been signed over to him for tax reasons, everything except Barn Cottage (situated inconveniently in his courtyard), and one field and one pond.

It is simply the most wonderful gift I have ever received.

I walk down through my field, golden and high with barley, with swallows flying low overhead on this sunny August day, to the pond. The jarring noises of husband and children left behind. The pond is large and fringed by dense common reed with occasional reedmace and lots of yellow iris. To the south the reed becomes overshadowed by grey willow and grades into wet woodland, and to the north a marshy area along by the fringe of reeds surrounding the pond. There are moorhens here and a pair of mute swans; snipe and reed bunting are also resident, nesting close to the ground in the dense tangled brambles and tall grass tussocks. I stand for a moment intoxicated by the smell of water mint, the sound of grasshoppers, the calls of song thrush and linnet and, most of all, the colours of the flowers: meadowsweet, bird's foot trefoil, the dominating great willowherb, common fleabane and valerian and purple loosestrife. The teasel is particularly tall and commanding, with its green armour and its big, brutish electric lilac flowerheads shaped like eggs, which also contain sharp prickles. Where the leaves clasp the stem, a little bowl is formed that holds rainwater, like a moat; it's there to keep the aphids from climbing up. They look so grand against the sky, which today is very clear and very blue.

I walk along the riverbank and again the vegetation at this time of year is luxuriant and diverse. The river is slow-flowing and unglamorous as far as rivers go but there are many tall water-loving plants including wild angelica, hemlock water dropwort and more meadowsweet and heather interspersed, and abundant sweet vernal grass and cock's foot, Yorkshire fog, even. The butterflies are out and so are the dragonflies and damselflies, the small red damselfly that is nationally scarce can be found here, as well as the keeled skimmer.

Why would anyone want to be anywhere else than beside water, be it river or pond, in this English summer month? Roger Deakin says 'water provides a metaphor of space ... of mental space, of freedom, of free-floating. All water – river, sea, pond, lake – holds memory and the space to think. Water levels the spirit too ... It is the only opportunity we have in the landscape to see a truly level *flatness*; the rest of the landscape, especially in Britain, is always spiky, full of virtual lines – grass, trees, hills, buildings, people themselves ... '

My spirit is certainly calm after this visit. Walk back home.

14 August

Lincombe Farm

State visit by the Prime Minister and his family. First, security sniff out the place before the arrival. Cards are exchanged with details of all David's close protection team, access routes are discussed, exit routes, security of the building itself and those surrounding it. Panic buttons and alarms are located. Siena is watching it all very closely; she has recently read *Harriet the Spy* and has taken to careful and close observation of all activity around her, and is writing down everything in a black notebook in preparation for a future career in the security services. To encourage her in her efforts I have given her an enormous pair of black-rimmed glasses with clear panes which make her look decidedly serious about her spying endeavours as she pops out from behind numerous bits of furniture around the house. The security officers talk over her as she sits at the kitchen table pretending to write a story, when in fact, in a treacherous act of espionage, she is writing down the entire conversation, which contains secret and confidential information about the security detail.

Later, she is out hiding in the bushes, preparing to monitor behaviour and activities at the arrival, which involves convoys of Range Rovers, two Mercedes-Benz people carriers, the official Jag, guns, walkie-talkies, lots of security men. I don't think our little old country lane has seen so much activity in its life. Even the neighbour rings up to inform us there are some very dodgy men sitting outside our house in black vehicles.

The Camerons swan in with children, relaxed, Sam heavily pregnant, not remotely grand.

'Whatever you do, David, if you see Siena acting oddly around you, don't say anything to her. She has recently morphed into an undercover agent and wishes that her endeavours remain invisible,' says H.

Ten minutes later Siena walks into the kitchen and Dave

immediately says, 'Hello, Harriet,' at which Siena has a complete meltdown, bursts into tears and runs out the room with me following in her sobbing slipstream, but not before I throw my head over my shoulder, eyes blazing at him: 'Christ, David!'

The weather is appalling and I'm not sure what I am going to do with them all. 'We'll have to get drunk,' I say, which is what we do, over marinated mozzarella, vongole, chocolate brownies with shredded beetroot and strawberry fool. Dave irritatingly tells me not to put lemon on the cheese because it will curdle it; irritatingly, because he is right.

After lunch H takes the Camerons and the children and the security guards down to Branscombe beach, but Dave is mobbed every five steps for a picture and the weather is foul, so they retreat.

'I know, let's go for a run, Hugo,' says the Prime Minister. He is clearly proud of his honed physique courtesy of a new personal trainer, but which H privately maintains is more the result of a prolonged and vigorous period of trying to get Sam pregnant again. So, after a manoeuvre not unlike Montgomery moving the whole of the Eighth Army, the presidential-style convoy of black four-by-fours with their darkened windows powers up to East Hill Strips, where the ground is level and the running is discreet. In the car H tries to persuade Dave of a rather shorter route but he typically overrules him and issues orders as if he knows the place backwards, which of course he doesn't. To well up some enthusiasm Hugo tells the flunkies that the place they are going to run to is well known to the locals as a top dogging spot, which greatly amuses them, but of course no one is more amused by it than the Prime Minister himself, who starts to make lots of dogging jokes.

They set off at a killing pace accompanied by two security men who were born to run, physically. H not so. He has taken the precaution of popping two Nurofen, two deep inhalations of his Symbicort Turbohaler and a quick puff of his Ventolin Evohaler for good measure, causing even his heart to race ahead of him. After a few yards he is feeling distinctly queasy but still manages to keep up with D. After about ten minutes one of the security men mutters in H's ear, 'Go your own pace, sir, it's not a race.' H replies, 'If you think I'm going to be beaten by the PM on my own ground, you have got to be bloody joking,' and forges on. H, who was thinking tactically, as in the tortoise and the hare, had planned to sprint ahead in the last three hundred yards, but on account of the swirling sea mist unfortunately misjudged how close he actually was to the finish. To his absolute horror, as he pulled past the PM, panting and groaning horribly, he saw the road continue into the mist with no apparent end. It was a matter of minutes before the PM overtook him again, with two monster back-up cars in his wake. The security man jogging alongside H says reassuringly, 'Don't worry, sir, we've got a defibrillator in the back.'

When they eventually get to White Cross, Dave does lots of stretching exercises, then claps his hands together and exclaims, 'Marvellous! Now let's run back.' H by this stage is trying to disguise the fact that he is at the point of collapse and had been eyeing up the back seat of the Range Rover with some lust. He says rather weakly, 'Fine,' and they set off again. That was the last he saw of the Prime Minister and all the security for the next twenty-five minutes, other than the second back-up car, which insisted on bringing up the rear. H, who by this stage is running like Norman Wisdom, gets increasingly angry and keeps beckoning them to go past him, which they don't; they are also having great difficulty keeping their high-powered vehicle turning over at such a slow speed. When H finally re-joins the party, the Prime Minister, smug as hell, is making caustic remarks about his minister's suitability for high office on account of his poor health. H replies curtly, 'If there had been a proper handicap in place, given that I am eight years older, I would have technically won. So there.'

After dinner, chat about Dave's Big Society. 'It's really starting to take off,' he says. I sit on the sofa and ask difficult questions. He is trying hard to convince me; he clearly wants this to be the defining theme of his government. I listen, but to me the Big Society already exists, it is quiet, unassuming, what we have here is just a slogan, a political ideology, a rhetoric, and how are ministers actually going to establish what the programme involves? 'What will the budget be,' I ask, 'when local councils are making such huge savings? Where is the Green or White Paper? Where is the legislation?'

DC's main concern is to carry the coalition through its full five-year term. He intends to go low key during the Alternative Vote campaign because he is desperate not to rock the boat. He needs the boundaries redrawn because he is convinced that is the only way we can ever win an election outright, and he reckons this redrawing will only happen if the coalition sticks together. He says he has given up on Scotland, thrown everything at it, and now has no expectations of ever winning more seats there. We will fight the next election with the Lib Dems as enemies. My concern, again, is how he is going to carry his party with him, especially if he gives more concessions to the coalition.

As for his own personal game plan, he tells us seven years, then a return to the back benches, some outside interests, and then leave all together, but also adds he would quite like to be Foreign Secretary one day. I have a similar game plan for H; whether they fall on their swords before that is anyone's guess, but the probability is high. Who did he think would take over? 'I don't know, someone like Jeremy Hunt, I suppose.'

I groan. 'No! Please, far too wet. It's only because he sucks up to you and tells you what you want to hear.'

They leave after breakfast the next day and all H and I want to do is put wet tea towels on our heads and lie down. Later, he writes me a thank-you letter saying all the eating and drinking had brought on the birth of his fourth child.

3 September

Gay rumours come to the surface again for Hague. He finally responds to them and somewhat foolishly puts out an uncomfortable statement about the gynaecological secrets of his wife. If my husband had done the same, I would have decapitated him.

16 September

H rings from Hillsborough: he is off to meet the Pope in Edinburgh. No. 10 had been in a panic about the visit and decided to field the regional ministers, hence Owen and H having to travel to Edinburgh at short notice. They fly up there and are met at the steps of the plane by Owen's armoured Jaguar, which has been driven up overnight doing an average of about five miles to the gallon. Much to their surprise, there are also police outriders with flashing lights to smooth their passage to Holyrood Palace, where the day's events are to take place. Apparently, they climb into the Jag and H asks what time they are supposed to be at Holyrood. 'Not for an hour and half,' Owen says.

'Well, we can't drive round and round Edinburgh as the police will get giddy and fall off their motorbikes and the Jag will soon run out of fuel.'

H arranges a quick tour of the local branch of Sotheby's, which is run by a former colleague, Ant Weld-Forester.

The day goes well, and in the evening they return to the airport to fly back to Belfast. There is another armoured car in front of them on the runway. H gets competitive and asks their policemen to go and check out who is in the other car. They return saying it belongs to Ian Paisley. It turns out his lordship has been having a right old time of it, up early with a large delegation from his Free Presbyterian Church of Ulster and beginning the day's excitements with a service in Edinburgh's Magdalen Chapel, where that other firebrand John Knox also preached against Catholicism. *Plus ça change.* The Big Man then howled at the Pope's convoy with chants of 'Go Home, the Bishop of Rome', 'The whore of Babylon is not welcome here' and so forth in his always-helpful ecumenical way.

Suddenly, the door swings open and the Big Man emerges wearing a large black fedora and a massive billowing black cape, looking the spitting image of Hilaire Belloc. By the time Owen and Hugo get on the plane he is sitting squeezed between his two policemen, chuckling away. H greets him warmly and asks if he's had a good day.

'A greeaaat daaaagh,' the old lion roars back.

H asks him mischievously if he'd managed to get a glimpse of the Holy Father. Paisley, in faux outrage, heaves his shoulders and bellows, 'SEE HIM? SEE HIM? DIDN'T EVEN SMELL HIM!'

Pope Benedict had in fact been well received in Scotland; that is, until he sermonised about the evils of drugs, money, sex, pornography and alcohol, which, judging by their nonplussed expressions, didn't go down at all well with the young Catholics gathered around him.

18 September

In Greek mythology, September is when the goddess Persephone returns to the underworld to be with her husband Hades. It is a good time to enact rituals for protection and security as well as reflect on successes or failures from the previous months. Now the children are back at school and before the new parliamentary session begins, we think a long walk will help us restore our equilibrium. H is now spending three days a week in Northern Ireland, coming back to vote in the House late on a Wednesday, then disappearing to the constituency. Our only time spent together now is often that precious four hours when we drive back to London on a Sunday night. Politics is almost carnivorous in its greed; it is not one for relationships.

We have decided to tackle the South West Coast Path, which runs from Minehead, on the Somerset coast, to Poole Harbour in Dorset. We suspect it will take us many years to complete all 630 miles of the path, so our intention is to do it in stages and, like migratory birds, return every year to the spot we left off from. The plan is to walk for eight hours a day, from the blushing of dawn mornings to the fine grey of nights moving in. Walking will,

I hope, help us find a centre of strength during this temporary upheaval in our marriage. It will improve our brains and our bodies, our moods and our clarity of thinking, our creativity; it will connect us back to the people and the land and to nature, but mostly to each other. What our society needs is not always new ideas and inventions, important as these are, and not geniuses and supermen, but persons who can just 'be'. In an age of media scrutiny this is becoming increasingly rare.

19 September

The direction is important. South West, the words split on a spherical coordinate system: an azimuth. Like a crossword, down five towards the heat, across five to eternity. To go west you need to set a bearing of 270 degrees. West is the opposite direction to the earth's rotation on its axis. To go west feels right; it is to arrive at a beautiful sunset. To move west has always been to gain freedom: in Chinese Buddhism it was the route towards Buddha and enlightenment; for the Aztecs, it was the dominion of water, mist and maize; but most appropriately it was the Celts, the early inhabitants of this leg of land, who saw the western sea off the edges of all maps as the Otherworld, or Afterlife.

We take a bus from our hotel to Minehead, down a boulevard of trees to the seafront. There, a sculpture of a pair of hands gripping an open Coast Path map emerges from the ground to mark the official start of the path. We set off, under a hyacinth-blue sky, leaves still green but with the slightest of autumn tints, past pensioners idling away their time in a wind shelter, a man fixing his boat, two men and a pram between them talking about fishing, following the tarmac path beside the pebble beach up to the end of a wide grass lawn. And on and up North Hill we go.

7 October

Owen and H have a meeting with Gerry Adams and some representatives of those killed at the Ballymurphy Massacre in 1971. The meeting at Stormont House starts well enough, until Adams spots that Owen is wearing a green wristband supporting the Royal Irish Regiment. He glares at him from across the table, and in those deep growling vowels banished for so long from the airwaves Adams says that it is 'unbelievable' and the 'height of discourtesy', an insult 'to those that lost their lives to the British state', that the Secretary of State is wearing a wristband glorifying the British Army that murdered so many. H was rather taken aback, as up until then he had been grinning in a friendly manner at Adams and he thought that, behind his heavy spectacles and greying beard, Adams had been smiling back at him. It was only on closer inspection that he realised Adams's stony cold eyes were devoid of any emotion and that his gleaming outsized teeth had been something of a distraction, and that he was not smiling at all. Owen, meanwhile, was visibly stiffening, muttering that he had a connection with the Royal Irish as they were based at Tern Hill in his Shropshire constituency and was perfectly entitled to show his support. Officials were shifting nervously in their seats behind as the mood inside the room spiralled. H says he now thinks Adams is one of the most sinister and unpleasant people he has ever had the misfortune to come across. He much prefers Martin McGuinness on a personal level, although he is not blind to what McGuinness has done in the past.

11 October

Shooting weekend with John and Suzy Lewis at Shute House in Donhead St Mary, Dorset. Other guests include Julian Fellowes and the rather eccentric Mrs Fellowes. Julian is quite puffed up at the moment and rightly so; he has written and created *Downton*

Abbey, which is currently drawing in millions of viewers on ITV. Basically, it's *Upstairs, Downstairs* with knobs (and nobs) on, but like so many costume dramas it is a backward glance, a *then* better than *now* piece of entertainment. Julian is eloquent and intelligent but faintly ridiculous; his entire conversation, in one form or another, concerns his obsession with social hierarchy and nostalgia. We have a discussion at dinner about hereditary peerages and their technicalities, and in particular primogeniture and whether his wife should have legally challenged the Kitchener title, which was due to die out. 'We decided not to, because I would have become a laughing stock in the industry,' he tells me. He's probably right, mainly because of the way he presents himself. But this must have been something of a conflict for him; on the one hand a belief in an old system, and on the other the unfairness of it and his own sense of entitlement. Julian has had quite a meteoric rise. He was a jobbing actor when Robert Altman pulled him in as an adviser on *Gosford Park*. He was only meant to tell them how one holds a knife and fork, but then he muscled in on the scriptwriting. An actress I know, who worked on a film with Fellowes, told me he directed her in plus fours.

His wife Emma is easily recognisable in that she always wears a turban. Her fingers are long and thin and manicured, and she uses them in actressy Gloria Swanson-type displays, often propping up the end of her eyebrows, which looks as if she is calming a headache. She is very much Julian's add-on and sticks up her hand to seek permission from him to interrupt. If this request is denied because he is in full sail, her hand starts revolving in the air in fast propeller motions until her husband finally permits her a gap in the conversation.

K tells me later Julian may be considered for a peerage. 'They think he has done a lot for the party and that it is good to have someone from the arts in the Lords.' We agree the arts cognoscenti are mostly left-leaning and we need some of our own in there. I imagine it's a Frances/George Osborne push, but will find out next month when I go to Dorneywood.

*

Also shooting is Jonathan Rothermere. On first viewing, and from a distance, he affects the air of a man with status and money, but a giant, twinkle-eyed, curly-mopped bear soon emerges. I enjoy taking the piss out of his new tweed suit, which has clearly arrived straight from his tailor. You want to disapprove of him, *Daily Hate Mail* and all that, but he's too pleasant and polite, and he takes my teasing with good humour. We talk about the future of regional newspapers at dinner. It's a serious conversation; he tells me he thinks the industry is heading towards free sheets and websites.

The day after the shoot we drive over to Ferne House, the Rothermeres' Palladian-style mansion designed by Quinlan Terry, which has been erected in the Wiltshire countryside at a rumoured cost of £40 million, for a tour. I say 'their' house, but of course Jonathan is some sort of non dom so it's actually Claudia's, which she takes great pleasure in telling us. Despite its grand scale, it is as discreet as a military base on an Ordnance Survey map; land was purchased all around it to protect their privacy. Ironic, I know. Only one hill remains out of their possession and is clearly quite an irritation to them. Claudia shows us around at breakneck speed, as she is heading off to church, with Hugo skipping gaily behind making flattering comments. Each time there is a stop or an explanation, he's like a faithful poodle sitting up on its hind legs, begging or saying please, as he gazes up at her adoringly, tongue hanging out, panting. I'd have given him a doggy treat, if I'd had any in my pocket.

It is a common reaction: men of a certain class are known to swoon over her immense power. I can only judge her from the surface, as that is all she reveals in this brief encounter, but I come away thinking that I have just been in the controlled scene of a *Town & Country* photoshoot where the illusion of minimal effort but striking elegance is presented. With Claudia, you are only allowed to tread the path of perfection, yet somehow there is something absent in every tidy space you move through. I come away exhausted and yearning for some discord. An overturned boot or a stray sock, maybe.

14 October

H notches up another enemy. This time Nick Boles; he is wearing cord trousers and a jumper, and is called over by H as he leaves the chamber: 'Er, don't you own a suit, Nicholas?'

'Of course I bloody well own a suit.'

'I know you are a moderniser but really, we are Conservatives, you know. Don't you think you should wear one?'

Nicholas goes ballistic, 'I'll wear what I fucking well want, now fuck off.' And he sashays off all steamy and red.

(Letters of profuse apologies have since been exchanged between both parties.)

DC, Greg Barker and H walking down the corridor to vote. DC has always, much to his own amusement, called Siena and Saffron 'Sauvignon' and 'Chardonnay', the implication being that their names are mildly ridiculous, akin to those of footballers' wives. H raises this as they walk, and reminds the PM of our younger daughter's real names: Siena, Rose and Senara (after our favourite Cornish church, St Senara in Zennor). H then suggests DC will have to source his jokes elsewhere since he has named his new daughter Florence Rose Endellion (the last after Betjeman's favourite Cornish church).

'Are you accusing me of plagiarism, Hugo?' asks the PM.

'Well, not exactly.' They walk on a little further and the MP Claire Perry comes into view. H says, 'What I'm really interested in: is Claire Perry the incorrigible crawler they are making her out to be?'

DC's face goes into full flush mode, which can be quite sudden and embarrassing for him, as it involuntarily advertises his emotions.

What H can't see is that the formidable Mrs Perry has spotted the PM through concrete walls and around Pugin corners, has been licking her lips and bouncing her curls to make one of her famous beelines towards him, and is now standing right behind him.

'Ah, Hugo, I don't think you know Claire.'

She completely ignores him, practically screwdriving a stiletto heel into his foot as she elbows the Minister of State for Northern Ireland out of the line-up. Greg chuckles beside them.

H watches them walk away together, with her chatting animatedly. The last thing he sees is Claire's eyes gleaming with adoration, resting upon our sainted leader as he finally manages to get a word in.

He walks on a bit and next up is George, who is on his phone.

'Just reading my congratulatory texts,' he says smugly.

'Can't be your phone, then.'

George looks rather crestfallen. No one can pull him down quite like Hugo. 'But it *is* my phone. Do you want to come for a drink?'

'No, I'm going to do my box.'

And off H goes, exhausted by all the bruised and competing egos that this place brews up so well.

21 October

Dash back to Hillsborough for another royal visit. This time it is the Queen and Phil the Greek. Siena flies over as it's half term. She is to present a posy, which H has organised. She is still physically attached to her little black spying book and clings on to it, next to her heart.

God, what a fuss it all is. Siena and I are sitting quietly in the flat the night before the arrival when about nine security officers with all kinds of terrorist-busting machinery with flashing red lights come over to check the place out – dogs, even, jumping onto the sofa, sniffing around in my knicker drawer. Siena is of course scribbling it all down, hiding behind the sofa.

In the morning I take Siena into central Belfast for a pizza before the Queen arrives at Hillsborough. In the car back to the castle I say, 'You have got your little black book, haven't you?' Siena knits her brow and purses her lips, then rummages through her bag.

'I think I left it behind in the pizza restaurant.'

Oh fuck! Oh fuck! Please God, say you have it.

'Where? Where?'

'On the table, Mummy. In the restaurant.'

Oh no! Oh no!

'Did you write anything down about the Queen in it?'

'Yes, I did.'

'What . . . what did you write?'

'What time she was coming in, what door, what time her plane lands. Those sorts of things. What her policemen are called.'

I almost drive the car into the hedge. Rummaging manically through my own bag to find my phone, I ring H's private secretary, Deborah. 'I think we have a problem.' I explain what's in the book, most notably details about the Queen's upcoming visit but also all David's own security detail, which Siena wrote down from the cards they gave us back in the summer. Deborah says, 'Leave it with me.'

Within minutes of the call, it feels like the entire anti-terrorist squad has been dispatched to central Belfast and a rolling pandemonium ensues. Shoppers are shoved aside, streets are roped off, routes are retraced, a phalanx of policemen moves like a tide into the pizza restaurant, where I expect the purely innocent and dopy Italian waiter who served us earlier raises both his hands, surrendering to the crime he has absolutely no idea he committed. 'Got it!' says one of the policemen. Phone calls are made. The squad scoops up the team, armoured vehicles are mounted and the little black book is winging its way back to Hillsborough, where we decide that it is best we shred it. Siena is so traumatised by the ordeal she willingly agrees.

Panic over.

*

When I get to meet the Queen, I feel about two inches tall, irrelevant. She fixes her beady eyes on me briefly then swans past, not saying a word. She is telling me I am just a plus-one, not a player or a heroine. But she is charming to Siena, who inspires a smile as she does her wobbly bob before her.

There is a dinner in the throne room for Northern Ireland businesspeople. Hugo is next to the Duke of Edinburgh. An awkward moment occurs when he savages the businessman two away from him for pulling out his BlackBerry at the table.

'What are you doing?' he asks, angrily waving his finger at the hapless Ulsterman.

'I'm only checking my emails, sir,' he pleads in mitigation.

It was an *off-with-your-head* moment, with the rest of the table watching on with amazement, even embarrassment, at the mauling. As all the blood came into bloom in the man's face, the Duke ranted on about some royal banquet where the guests got out their laptops and how appalled he and the Queen were.

The other negative was Rose Paterson's comment to H that she didn't think it was appropriate that Siena wore trainers to present a posy to the Queen. (Actually, Rose, trainers are not the frowned-upon footwear of the past, but I don't suppose the trend has reached Shropshire yet.)

22 October

Saffron joins us at Hillsborough. We all go for a tour: to the Giant's Causeway and a walk in the Mountains of Mourne. Unlike Siena, who is now completely blasé about the security and bodyguards, Saffron is a little taken aback by the machine guns lying by her feet in the people carrier. Out walking there also appear to be helicopters hovering overhead. 'Are those for us?' she asks. 'Probably,' says H.

The next day we take the girls on a tour bus around Belfast. H and I have a routine of booking ourselves on tour buses in a new city. It is a great way to orientate oneself and it's always surprising what can be seen from a bird's eye view, things that would be missed just walking down the street.

When H first proposed this Belfast tour to his private office his security team had a meltdown and ruled it out. H persisted. After some days there was a compromise, a careful plan hatched whereby two of the team would be on the bus with us, H's armoured Land Rover would shadow us and H would get off in the 'difficult' areas such as the Lower Falls Road and Andersonstown, and get back on in the safer bits – in other words, the Shankill Road and the Protestant areas.

We go up to the top deck of the bus and two of Hugo's team, to whom he's become very close, are sitting huddled together in the seat behind us, looking extremely uncomfortable but attempting to blend in. What they actually look like is PSNI officers trying to blend in. The bus is full of tourists eager to photograph the murals on the peace walls and to learn more about the Troubles. H turns around rather laconically and asks his lads if they are on their honeymoon. They murmur 'No, Minister,' the 'Minister' said very quietly, with a grimace. The bus sets off, but instead of turning right onto our expected route, it turns immediately left, heading for west Belfast; the badlands as far as the PSNI are concerned. H is delighted by this turn of events and is rather cruelly enjoying their discomfort. We look over the side of the bus and the large, heavily armoured Land Rover is shadowing us so closely it almost looks as if it's kissing our bumper. H asks jocularly, 'Would you like me to get off now?' The pair are raising their mournful eyes to the heavens in sudden despair.

'No, Minister. Please, Minister. Not here.'

They look utterly relieved when the bus moves on with H still on it and we continue the tour perfectly normally. This episode is not forgotten and is the subject of much joshing later.

5 November

Jonathan Caine, Northern Ireland special adviser, sends H an email entitled 'Wanted: XL Flak Jacket for Lord Maginnis'. It appears that two of Northern Ireland's politicians are spitting nails after a trip to visit troops in Afghanistan was called off because they were too portly for standard-issue flak jackets. Lord Maginnis and David Simpson of the DUP had been due to fly out to meet soldiers from the Royal Irish and the Irish Guards, but the Army couldn't find flak jackets large enough to fit them.

'To be told at the last minute that the British Army has not got two flak jackets with a 54″ chest was just a bit thick,' said Ken Maginnis, who must weigh about eighteen stone.

Shortly afterwards, a flunkey from high command issues a statement along the lines that correctly fitting body armour is a prerequisite for any trip to the Islamic Republic of Afghanistan and although their resources covered a diverse range of sizes, on this occasion they were unable to find one suitable for a body of such dimensions.

Jonathan sends an email to H, saying: 'It's hilarious. You couldn't invent it.'

Hugo replies: 'Couldn't they try and have squeezed him into a Hercules, or at least underslung him under a Chinook?'

28 November

To Dorneywood, where George and Frances are now in occupation. This moderately large Queen Anne-style house is a typically tired government mansion, set down in now-frosty countryside half an hour from London. Oddly enough, the atmosphere is still steeped in the Prescotts. The fragrant Pauline clearly had a run at our bathroom (we are in the Prescott suite), judging from the tiles in differing degrees of pink, including a swirly border – think Barbara Cartland, then think bathroom. And in the visitors' book lots of jokes like 'son of Two Jags' and Prescott's first entry, where he writes: 'John Prescott, Deputy Prime Minister!!!' It seems half of his family moved in here at some point, and why not? Then there was the outcry over photographs of him playing croquet here when Tony Blair was out of the country and the Deputy PM was supposed to be in charge. George says he doesn't dare take out the croquet set, which now sits rather famously in the loggia.

George, in typical shit-stirring form, causes me a little grief. I make some throwaway comment that an invitation to Chequers has, to date, not winged its way over to me and that I had been feeding that bloke for nigh on ten years and my husband was one of his earliest supporters and the world and his wife seems to have been there except me and how sore I am. Within the hour he is on the phone to David: 'Sasha is here, whingeing that she has not been asked to Chequers yet.' Embarrassingly, just twenty-four hours after that an invitation is sent via Samantha to me, saying it is very important for them, the Camerons, to keep up with the Osbornes, and would we both like to stay the weekend before Christmas?

The sweetest thing, which excites the Chancellor most, is stumbling across a book given as a school prize to a young pupil by the name of Kenneth Grahame, author of *The Wind in the Willows*. I have long suspected that, like me, George is a frustrated writer, and deeply admires those who have achieved success in this field. After Oxford he had wanted to pursue a career in journalism but didn't make the *Times* trainee scheme, and he was rejected for a job on *The Economist* as well. When he speaks of Frances's trips to New York, promoting her books, he is glowing with pride.

4 December

Big fights between Coulson and Hilton; they're now not on speaking terms. Kate Fall is left to sort it out. As a result, a new beefed-up policy unit has been set up to tighten 10 Downing Street's grip on government and act as an engine for ideas for the coalition in the second half of this parliament. Well, that's the official line anyway. Truth is, crazy ideas courtesy of Mr Hilton are not going through any filtering before reaching David, which is driving everyone else nuts. This new 'strong but tight' unit is designed to bring everything out from under Steve's control, and to reflect more of a coalition philosophy rather than a Steve Hilton philosophy. K is appalled when I tell her how I'd heard at Dorneywood that Steve had said Coulson was on the way out. 'He didn't really say that, did he?' she exclaims. We agree he might be dropping this to hacks as well.

Coming up this week we have Hilton's 'relationship' agenda. George, Kate and Coulson are despairing. Kate even says to me, 'I don't understand why David loves all this Steve/marriage/police stuff.'

Steve is actually suggesting putting ten top tips on relationships in IKEA flat packs, which he's identified as being a moment of extreme stress. He's probably right about that bit, at least.

I suggest maybe it's Samantha, but no, she insists D genuinely gets excited by it all. K is concerned it's too 'smug married', that people's lives are more complicated than that, as her own is – she has recently split from her husband, Ralph. Exasperated, she writes David a note and warns him that he is 'in danger of looking like Prince Charles talking to his plants while George is out there saving the economy'.

On the subject of G, we discuss over supper how there has been a change in him. We agree he is for the first time looking at succession, whereas before it was always 'I'm off to Goldman Sachs next to make some money'. Now there is a different tone. He certainly said to me at the weekend how well he was now placed with the right-wingers of the party, the implication being should he want to make a bid the support would be there. K and I agree it might not work out for him anyway; she thinks he may be too intrinsically linked to David, that they are more likely to go down together in the end. Maybe he could become Foreign Sec, she says. I point out he would be absolutely useless at that because he can't handle

people at all and is actually quite shy. We both agree that the problem is – and it happened with Brown as well – that the Treasury is
such a fiefdom, as all big departments are: it is running the country.
It is hard to give up. And George has huge numbers of courtiers
and yes-people, and the power side of things is greatly appealing
to him. In contrast, Downing Street is physically small in all its
operations. It's no wonder these chancellors spiral out of control.

18 December

Chequers

Worst snow in twenty years. Leave London at 11 a.m. and arrive
at 3 p.m. on what should be a forty-minute journey. All along the
route a necklace of abandoned vehicles and overturned lorries.
Dave rings every five minutes: where are we? What's happening
now? Should he advise Sam's sister Emily to turn around?

'Blimey,' Hugo tells him, 'I've spoken to you more in the last
hour than I have in three years.'

'Oh, fuck off, Hugo,' says Dave, who is concerned the bullshots
he's made will go to waste.

In between Dave's check-up calls, H and I are having a monumental row about the cold air blowing in my face. He bought a
'new' ten-year-old Jeep Cherokee for image reasons but is clueless
about how it works – which is not helpful in twelve inches of snow.
Knobs are turned and switched off, and expletives issued, culmi-
nating in me landing a left hook under my husband's chin. Well,
not really. More like a punch to the upper arm.

'Where are you now?' texts D in the midst of this.

'Look, David, it's like North and South Korea in here at the
moment. I'll call you when I know what junction we are at.
All right?'

'Hope there's no low-level firing!'

Within minutes another text flies in about the war breaking

out in the Jeep, this time from Ed Llewellyn, Dave's chief of staff. You'd think they would both have better things to do. I mean, the snow has brought the entire country to a halt and is developing into something of a national crisis.

'Do you need me to send in a peacekeeping force?' asks Ed.

'I don't think even the good Dr Kissinger can help on this one.'

Still not speaking, we drive down a discreet side lane to a heavily guarded gatehouse where we wait to be given the once-over by armed guards before a bomb-proof barrier is lifted and we are waved through. We are greeted by a rather stiff Mrs Danvers-style housekeeper who says, 'Welcome to Chequers, Mr and Mrs Swire.' And we are shown through to the great hall where the others are gathered.

The first thing you realise is that you are, for a brief moment, embedded in layers of history. Apart from all its famous political inhabitants, it was here, after all, that Churchill broadcast to the nation during the tense days of the Second World War. Here that a potential claimant to the English throne had been kept prisoner for two years in a garret by Elizabeth I. Here that Cromwell's death mask resides amongst other memorabilia (his grandson married the owner of Chequers).

A sixteenth-century house built of mellow russet brick with tall chimneys, gables and mullioned windows, Chequers is situated in a fold of the Chiltern Hills. It's difficult, however, to get a real take on it because we are in a winter wonderland; all the hedgerows and stately beech woods covered in snow, as is the open parkland. On Saturday we do little but sit around talking (not much politics), the children, including my two, screeching and laughing in the indoor heated swimming pool, then on Sunday before lunch climb the rising ground of Beacon Hill and Coombe Hill, the highest point of the Chilterns, where we are treated to snow-dusted views of seven counties, taking in the Berkshire Downs, Salisbury Plain and the Cotswolds. David, Hugo and Samantha, and Catherine Powell (also staying with husband Hugh, who being a Powell has a genetic assumption of divine rule and is wondering when and how he is ever going to get into Downing Street) toboggan down, either on bin liners or trays or sledges, watched on by D's security men and somewhat surprised villagers. Catherine is charming; she is high up in the Disney Corporation and presents herself like one of their smiley blonde princesses. Hugo pulls Sam back to Chequers on one of the sledges while the rest of us hum the theme from *Dr Zhivago*.

I sit next to Dave at dinner and discuss the student riots. We calculate the next political decade will be defined by the Baby Boomers versus the students, that mainstream parties will need to get these young voters on side if they are to survive politically. He tells me that I should join his political unit. I groan and say, 'Oh God, don't ask me to do that – I wouldn't be able to say no.'

He gives us wonderful vignettes of the Sarkozys' fake marital displays and of being given a tour around Rome's equivalent of No. 10 by Berlusconi: when they come to his bedroom he points at a Renaissance two-way mirror above the bed and with his characteristic grin says, 'Well, they didn't have porn channels in those days, did they?'

The snow is so thick on the ground we all decide to stay Sunday night and head off early Monday morning. As David's pleasures are very simple (family and TV) we are treated to a disgusting meal of RAF catering cheese toasties and a particularly unchallenging episode of *Poirot*. D is not a man of surprises or even secrets, not nearly as multi-layered as GO. I go to bed and D stays up with H to admire Keira Knightley's nipples when she comes out of the fountain in *Atonement*. Not for him the greater complexities of Ian McEwan's work, it seems.

2011

10 January

H has a drink with the Chief Whip, Patrick McLoughlin, who is miserable: 'I've got ten who are complete nutters. Around seventy, including the new lot, who think what the hell am I doing here, moaning about pay and conditions, the failings of IPSA, the coalition, Europe etc. Then I've got the lot that were in the last parliament who have seen their jobs dished out to the Lib Dems and are really pissed off about it' (i.e. Bernard Jenkin). He's right, of course, this bunch are desperate to retain their own distinct identity, and they share a sense that Liberal Democrat concerns are more important to Downing Street than their own. It explains, at least in part, the recent rebellions and discontent.

The poor man is exasperated. An alternative whipping operation has now been put in place at Downing Street to target the new intake, under the auspices of Stephen Gilbert. I ask H whether this has pissed Patrick off. 'Not at all, he's grateful for the help.'

At Chequers, DC told me how much effort he has put in to chatting up these groups. Apparently, they are in and out of Downing Street the whole time. 'I know you think I'm doing nothing, Sasha, but I promise you it's really not the case.' He was even in the tearoom this week before a vote, said H, but he looked lost and no one was rushing up to him to speak.

Meanwhile, the dark arts have been left to the master. GO has been on manoeuvres again with the new MPs. *Do you really want to spend your entire political career on the back bench?*

2 February

Article by Sarah Vine (aka Mrs Michael Gove) entitled 'Stand by your man – but not his politics'. Her argument: that a woman automatically waives all rights to independence the moment she utters her marriage vows to a politician is, in this day and age, 'preposterous'. She says unfortunately what is expected is 'such old-fashioned acquiescence from one of the most well-informed and naturally outspoken group of women in the world: those at the sharp end of politics'. *Mmm, that bit I can go with!* She even defends Sally Bercow for constantly making her husband the butt of ridicule. The trouble with the Bercow/Vine argument is that people are only really interested in our statements or opinions in the context of our husbands' jobs. Sally Bercow is invited on to *Have I Got News for You* because she is the Speaker's wife. If she wasn't, she would not be there. The same of Vine's and my opinion: people ask it because they think we have inside knowledge via our husbands, which of course we do. No, we are not the property of our husbands, but this is their job, not ours, and we cannot expect the same entitlements.

4 February

Having quiet dinner with K in a nice Notting Hill Italian eatery when the equivalent of a human tornado comes over to harangue her about the proposed disposal of the Public Forest Estate. It is one Rachel Johnson, she of the self-publicising clan that is the Johnsons. She completely ignores me of course, except for the brief second when she turns and says 'I love your husband; he's such a good auctioneer,' then back to Kate. She tries, with journalistic muster, to trick her into saying that George O is up in arms about it. K looks puzzled by this, and so do I, as we both know rural matters are way down the agenda of our favourite metrosexual male. Her lobbying continues; a violent, dangerous, rotating column of air that is in such close proximity we think we might be lifted from our seats.

I ask her why she is so interested. Does she live up a tree? But she's not amused. *Look, it was only to break the path.*

'It's just a consultation, Rachel,' K says forlornly.

'No, it's not,' she replies. 'That's a complete lie, Kate. You know it and I know it.'

I'm keeping quiet but really, this whole issue has been completely hijacked by the chattering classes. Since when did we start elevating the role of the Forestry Commission, probably one of the biggest despoilers – after pylons – of our landscape in this country? Why should a nationalised body be more inventive about access and the environment than a local community is? It seems the idea of wood making profit is repulsive to the likes of Ms Johnson, Tracey Emin, Ken Livingstone, Vivienne Westwood et al. Quite frankly, that bunch alone just makes you want to call your stockbroker to buy the stuff – which is also silly, because if people want to use it they also want to renew it.

'Look, Rachel,' I say, interrupting her flow, 'you are defending the Forestry Commission as being the protector of our forests. Why, then, did they sell off twenty-five thousand acres of forestry land with no protections?' What I really meant to say was that over the last thirteen years it was the Labour government that sold off all the land, whereas we were guaranteeing all kinds of safeguards ... but hell, it worked: it completely shut her up, it deflated her balloon and she walks away saying she must attend to her husband. (Poor bloke!)

'Thank God you had a killer fact,' says K, 'she would have been here all night.'

Following on from this, watched Boris being interviewed by Paxman. Everything is just a bit of a joke to him. In fact, he just came across as a complete idiot, which of course he isn't. Is he really prime minister material? K says she thinks he might lose the next mayoral election. The irony is, of course, that it is Boris who considers Dave the political lightweight, Dave who has stolen the crown that is rightfully his. Dave a mere fee-paying squit to Boris's King's Scholar status back at school. At the core of this, I suspect, is the fact that DC refused to put Boris in his first shadow cabinet; considered him too much of a liability.

There is no doubt in anyone's mind that Boris harbours leadership ambitions. If he does win re-election next year, there is now speculation that he will try to re-enter parliament straight away and not wait for his term of office to expire. DC, who despite himself can't help but like the man, needs to watch out. Or should that be George, a much more formidable enemy for Boris to be up against?

8 March

H stands in for Owen at the National Security Council. Afterwards he tells me Gove went off on one again, about Libya. I said what the hell was he doing there, he's Education. 'No idea!' replies H. 'And I'm actually starting to think he is ever so slightly bonkers.' Hague, H says, had that exasperated look every time Michael spoke.

H does manage to throw him a comment after the meeting: 'This democracy idea of yours – you are happy to impose it in Saudi Arabia as well, are you? And all the Gulf States?'

I speak to someone who is in the know about MG; he says there is a feeling inside No. 10 that he is exhausted, that he cannot continue at this pitch. He is also surrounded by young yes-people who are encouraging him to become the voice of neoconservatism. Later, I talk to H about it. Is he really interested in foreign affairs, I ask. 'Oh yes,' comes the reply, 'he desperately wants one of the top jobs, Chancellor, Foreign or PM.' But there is a view he might well blow himself out before then.

20 March

Lincombe Farm

Last night, on the way out to a Masonic Ladies dinner in Exmouth, we were treated to an extraordinary moon. Right there, in our faces. It was the largest and brightest and certainly the closest I have ever seen. A beautiful pale orange. It was not until later that I learnt quite what an event it was: the moon in its orbit was a mere 221,567 miles away – the closest full moon for twenty years. Today also happens to be the spring equinox, when the hours of day and night are roughly equal and the sun is directly over the equator at noon. The doomsayers saw this as quite a coincidence and were predicting a number of godly events to occur: earthquakes, freak tides – they were right in some respects, given the horrors of Fukushima – but nothing obviously unnatural seemed to happen last night.

21 April

Boy George comes to lunch at Lincombe with his PA, Poppy. He is doing H a favour, opening the Flybe Training Academy at Exeter.

H and George toddle off to Flybe's £12 million training centre where they each have a turn in the flight simulator. George's efforts are interesting. When asked what airport he would like to fly into he says Manchester, which is the one he uses to get to his constituency. He commences his descent, with H looking decidedly queasy as the aircraft makes its erratic progress towards the airport.

His first attempt is poor, so much so the instructor shouts 'ABORT! ABORT!' Then he turns to George and says, 'Oh dear, we better not let that one get out, Chancellor.'

Boy George is looking rather cross as H fake vomits out the window. He asks to have another go. Soon enough, the 'plane' is put into emergency measures and prepares itself for what is commonly known in the industry as a crash landing. Apparently, it would have caused considerable casualties after the plane, having cleared the perimeter fence, pancakes onto the runway and comes to a halt, having destroyed the entire terminal building, which subsequently explodes in a ball of fire, hell and damnation.

'George, you have just taken out your constituency!' says H.

Boy George turns to H wearing his trademark impish grin and says, 'But that terminal building is not in my half of the constituency!'

Let's hope, for all our sakes, his steering of the economy out of recession is a little bit better.

1 May

Royal wedding went off without a hitch. David and George a bit pissed off, though, as they were invited to the ceremony but not to the reception afterwards. G says they all sat in Westminster Abbey for about three hours and then went home without a single drink. G jokes at lunch that he is feeling revengeful, that he might tell Her Maj he is slashing her budget when he sees her next week. Dave and Sam throw a street party at Downing Street to compensate, with a hundred revellers chosen by local charities and Save the Children.

Speaking of sitting in the Abbey for a long time, the great national debate in the end was how did the heavily pregnant Victoria Beckham sit from 9.15 a.m. to 12.15 p.m. with a human time bomb pressed up against her bladder? It almost made me run to the facilities in gratitude. Maybe that's why her frock was a nice midnight blue. In case she sneezed or coughed or something . . . Anyway, we are all in love with the Middletons now. Such middle-class dignity. They have diluted those royals and probably saved them for another couple of decades.

10 May

Just back from Hillsborough, where I have been fuming about Mrs Paterson's removal of two sets of curtains from our flat. She decided that ours would be better suited to her sitting room and promptly took them without a by your leave. We now have a frothing Colefax and Fowler floral confection which is completely out of keeping with our interiors. I rant at H.

'Calm down, dear! She is the Secretary of State's wife,' he replies.

'I don't care who she is, it's bloody bad manners. I'm going straight to the top on this one!'

And I do. The Prime Minister is informed via his gatekeeper. There is much chortling in No. 10 about the curtain spat, apparently.

Truth is, those Patersons really piss me off.

On this recent trip, we spent Saturday night at Baronscourt in County Tyrone, the home of the Duke of Abercorn. His wife, Sacha, has part Russian heritage (a direct line to Pushkin) and is sister-in-law to the Duke of Westminster – the real McCoy, in other words. Oh, my husband so loves a castle creep, and with a duke thrown in! H looked like the cat that got the cream all weekend. More so because James not only held rank in the Grenadier Guards as H did but served as an Ulster Unionist MP. All in all, an intoxicating cocktail, and believe me there were plenty of those on offer as well.

The interior of the house was designed by their great friend David Hicks – there is a Mountbatten family connection as well. The look – all those bright colours and mixing antiques with modern furniture – is so dated it's having its second coming – very now, in other words. The four of us go for a long stroll in the grounds flanked by security guards; the rhododendrons are in full sail and the lake looks calm and peaceful. We see Sacha's turf maze, which is a similar idea to that in Chartres Cathedral: you walk the maze as a substitute for a pilgrimage to Jerusalem, or shuffle along on your knees as a penance. Sacha says it's very calming, very peaceful, so H hangs back with his heavies and starts to walk it. He reappears thirty minutes later not remotely calm, sweating from exhaustion, the heavies chuckling behind his back.

I'm rather intrigued by Sacha. She has an edge of mystery, or is it unhappiness? Boredom? I can't quite put my finger on it, but I know there is a tale to be told. He, on the other hand, is everything a duke should be: tall, confident, charming, gracious and accommodating and friendly to the 'little people'. For two days after the visit H seems intimately tied up with the ducal personality. He not only adopts his catchphrase: 'Sasha, come on *frew* ...' but makes me and everyone bask in glory by saying, as James does, 'Yes, that is an excellent thought – why did I not think of it? How *very* clever of you.'

26 May

Fulham

3 a.m. Woke up with a start, thinking Irish dissidents were climbing up the scaffolding. Staring out the window, no assassins but a fat, mottled orange-grey fox lying like a Roman emperor in the middle of the road, moon bathing. Its partner, meanwhile, was nosing through the rubbish sacks selecting items between the discarded cream cartons and chicken bones, coming back every now and then to report its finds. When it's quiet, and the city is down, you often see foxes about, but this one sprawled in the middle of road without a care in the world makes me realise how arrogant they have become.

8 June

Peter Robinson in a meeting for the Big Society leans over to H and whispers, 'From high society to Big Society, eh, Hugo?'

*

H discovers that Lord Shutt has been sleeping in his bed at Hillsborough. The final straw. A smelly Lib Dem in his bed, for God's sake. That's taking the coalition a step too far! H has words with the manager, Matthew: 'I don't want any more people in my bed, particularly Lib Dems.'

Can't think why he was put there when there are about six thousand other beds in the joint.

H has a habit of referring to the Lib Dem spokesman for Northern Irish matters in the Lords as Lord Shuttupyourface, which does cause his civil servants to cock a few eyebrows.

19 June

Email from Sir John about impending visit to Hillsborough:

No reply required to sitrep sent to your spouse on 25 May. We return to London on Thurs evening one day before depart for ulster orgy. What time is flight and which airport? I will order car and can take Dowager Marchioness if you inform her. Presumably will need an accompanying pantechnicon to carry luggage of 2 titled ladies. And what about couture for men? I normally bring Gandhi loincloth for such events but should my valet lay out a suit? What other equipment is required? Please refer to other queries in my original message to you about quality of chambermaids etc. (after Strauss-Kahn). Is there a spinning machine to keep me busy or has a programme of distractions been arranged for your Balkan guests? Yours rt hon sir nott

Reply from H:

Dear Nott the Nine O'Clock News
    Thank you for your communication with the Minister who is

only now arising from his four poster as he and his good lady
wife danced all night at Dorneywood. Huge fun. I will send
details of flights. Couture should be as for weekend in Scotland.
Wet weather gear and good shoes as expedition is planned for
Saturday weather permitting. Smart casual for Saturday night
i.e. I shall probably wear dark suit sans tie. Sasha picking up Two
Fat Ladies (oops sorry I mistyped should have read Two Titled
Ladies) from airport. I am picking you up in heavily armoured
vehicle to go straight to vicinity of Belfast Castle. Am off to Paris
tomorrow for Air Show but will let you have all details before I go.
Love from The Privy Counsellor en route to the Privy.

George's fortieth birthday party at Dorneywood last night. Not
a big fan of Hague's, but his speech about our mutual friend was
side-splittingly funny. He just got him down to a T. As Hague
rattled off George's four laws of political success the birthday
boy stood by with that delightful sneer of his while the rest of us,
including David, fell about the place with laughter. We started with
Osborne's Law One, which is basically work out, ahead of anyone
else, who will be the next leader, stick to them like glue and become
indispensable. Hague recalled how, shortly after he became Tory
leader in 1997, Boy George appeared out of nowhere in his office
and started drafting odd bits of material, and before he knew it
a certain Boy George appeared to be writing all of his speeches.
Law Two involved studying your opponent's policies but also getting inside their minds by studying their deepest moral processes.
George's fascination for John Bercow of course has nothing to do
with regard; rather, how he shafted Michael Martin and how that
plot was executed with precision. George also spent a considerable
amount of time getting inside Brown's head, not a job most people
would enjoy, but with George you do know that getting under your
opponent's skin and exposing his style of politics is as important as
undermining his policies. By understanding how Brown operated,
the Tories were able to anticipate his premiership.

Law Three, according to Hague, is if you have to take a risk, make it worthwhile. George is more tactical than strategic but when he makes a big move it tends to really matter.

Law Four: don't forget the first law, just because there are two others!

George responded in typical fashion: he joked that the most important reason for becoming Chancellor was to avoid going down in history as the man who was political strategist to William Hague. Fair point.

Of course, the best line came from Frances, who when told by her husband that he would like to throw a party at Dorneywood to celebrate his birthday said, 'What on earth for? It will be just like you having a wedding to yourself.'

A really good party – small, select (very few politicians there, interestingly).

H and I danced incessantly for the first time in ten years. Loved it.

22 June

Over to Hillsborough for the dreaded garden party. The royal this year is Prince Andrew and as soon as the Patersons find out they appear to receive an urgent recall to the constituency, leaving H and me the honour of hosting him. A dinner with twenty of Northern Ireland's most prominent businessmen and, I have to say, Andrew chairing the discussion round the table is excruciatingly painful to watch: a mixture of blokeyness and royal arrogance. I sit there trying to listen to how brilliant he is and what a good job he is doing as trade envoy when all I am seeing is him in swim-ming shorts, attending topless pool parties at Jeffrey Epstein's mansion, while on his own personal trade mission to get money for his ex-wife. My eyes switch to one of his flunkies and wonder how testing the job must be, dealing with the Prince and all the baggage. Like when he accepted a gift of a $30,000 gold necklace for Beatrice from a convicted Libyan gun smuggler. Actually, that one was easy: the Palace doesn't comment on private gifts to family members.

After dinner we withdraw to the blue room for coffee, and he tells me he received a briefing about me from Laura Hutchings, who works for him, and which he now repeats to me: I am lippy, and dominant but fun, according to Laura. He is very friendly towards me and when coffee is over, he comes over, points to me and says, 'I'll see you upstairs in five!' A rather drunken lady from Business Northern Ireland reels back in laughter and says, 'Her hospitality doesn't extend that far, sir!' She finds her own response so funny I think her already bulging seams might split from the pumping action of her hoots.

Hugo and I go up to Owen's sitting room where Prince Andrew is waiting for us, and the whole sorry saga pours out. He is desperately concerned that his daughters, who have HRH status, are having their royal protection withdrawn. His argument is that they move around in the age of Twitter and Facebook and instant messaging, and that an antagonistic force could be mobilised against them in a matter of minutes, in a restaurant or club etc. I have a good deal of sympathy for him on this. His affection for his daughters is clear. And by all accounts they are both very charming girls. He also says that there is a whole tier of royals currently doing official duties who will soon no longer be there on account of their age and Beatrice and Eugenie are their obvious successors. Below Harry and Wills, there will not be enough of them to carry out royal engagements is his point. I'm puzzled by this and say, 'Are you sure they want to do that? Is that the life they really want?' I am slightly astounded that anyone would even contemplate that role, but I suppose they are not trained to do anything else. He says yes, it is what they want to do. I sit silently but I'm thinking he might consider, in that case, having a quiet word in their shell-likes about taking part in a reality TV series with Fergie and sorrowfully disclosing their troubles on Oprah's sofa, which doesn't exactly chime with their princess status.

He asks H to have a word with DC, to explain to him his

predicament. H suggests that DC is having such a love-in with his mum at the moment maybe he should be the one doing the lobbying.

It is clear there is a serious power struggle taking place between him and Prince Charles, who has made no bones that he'd like the royal family to be streamlined into a smaller, more cost-effective monarchy. Charles, it seems, would prefer that the girls were jettisoned into the 'real' world. A lot of Andrew's embarrassing friendships with oligarchs, and his imploring anyone who will listen to bail out his wife, has clearly strained their brotherly relationship.

To illustrate this, he tells us about a misunderstanding over a grand piano. To lighten the atmosphere Hugo tells him sibling rivalry is also alive and kicking in the Swire family. His father Humphrey on his deathbed left five pieces of wood-wormed mahogany furniture to divvy up and no one is talking to anyone as a result. Quite frankly, I would have used most of it for firewood, given half the chance.

13 August

I have K in Cornwall when the riots break out. The shooting of Mark Duggan by police officers in Tottenham had led, two days later, to local shops being trashed and looted, and the violence was spreading quickly through the capital. DC is about to fly back from holiday in Tuscany, because parliament has been recalled and one Sarah Vine is on the phone late at night. She wants Dave's personal email so she can send him some notes that she and her husband have compiled on the issue. Kate hedges; Sarah rings again, insistent. Kate relents. She then speaks to Michael, who is determined to be part of the action: 'I think, Michael, if you just turn up in Downing Street I'm sure David will be happy to see you.' I think it's the journalist in him: he always has to be there, at the scene of the crash.

In the end, Michael got to wind up the emergency debate in the Commons. Parliamentary orations are his speciality and this one is full of his particular brand of high moral virtue. Good lines about how 'a culture of greed and instant gratification, rootless hedonism and amoral violence' had taken hold. He sings the praises of the police, many of whom were hurt, and those who had defended the community. Then there was some guff about rights without duty and children without parents. It all felt as if he was standing behind a podium on the steps of Downing Street, which is of course where he would most like to be.

24 August

Back from a three-day stay with the Camerons in Polzeath. They are in fine form, if a little manic. Golf at 7.30 a.m. with the gorgeous Giles Andreae, 11 a.m. staged photo shoot at Port Isaac to get the hacks off our backs, boozy barbecue on the beach, pulling tummies in for the paps that are still lurking behind rocks and hiding left-over foie gras canapés, cold-water swim, kip, surfing at 7 p.m., dinner, flop. And that was just the first day.

On that first day we drive down to the beach at Polzeath and are sitting in the car about to get ready for bodysurfing when Saffron shows Siena a BBM picture of a former schoolmate kissing *Made in Chelsea* C-lister Jamie Laing on the cheek. Siena, who has developed an unhealthy obsession, stalking him up and down the King's Road, such is her great love for him, starts a convulsive sobbing fit over this betrayal. The car rocks from side to side with her extremely loud wails. Dave and Sam and their security press their faces against the window to see what's going on.

'He's mine! Mine! How could she? She knows I want to marry him!'

I push a laughing H out the car and it takes about an hour to calm her down. 'All men are double-crossing, adulterous little shits, darling,' I keep telling her. 'You better get used to it now!' What

I'm really thinking is I hope she aims a little higher in life than a two-bit reality TV star, although having met him on one of Siena's stalking sessions, I found him utterly charming and very funny.

Meanwhile H goes bodysurfing with David, and gets infuriated because however hard he tries, David is always faster than him on account of his weight. They are joined in the water by the comedian Harry Enfield, who has a holiday home nearby. When the three of them come out of the water a man comes bouncing up. 'Excuse me, Prime Minister, can we have a photo?' David says fine, but then the man says, 'You,' pointing to Hugo, 'can you step aside, please?' H looks somewhat wounded.

On our first night, DC makes a quick Jag dash up to London to chair a meeting of the National Security Council on the situation in Libya and to issue a statement afterwards about how Tripoli had been liberated. He wasn't going to let Clegg have the podium on this one. He boasts that he does the return trip to Cornwall in three hours and twenty minutes, which is practically supersonic. We wave him off a little fearful that the excitement of it all might bring on another Blairite dose of Liberal evangelism. 'Don't even think about Syria next,' I shout after him. I suspect the humdrum business of domestic politics gets to them all in the end. H quite frankly relieved to have the day off. But then he leaves Downing Street at 4 a.m. the following day to return to Polzeath, arriving 7.30 a.m., H trembling under the white sheets at the thought of another dose of early-morning boot camp.

David is all pumped up and happy; he loves it down here, pointing out all his childhood and teenage snogging haunts to me on a walk. 'What more do I want? A great day on the beach, I'm with my old friends the Swires and I've just won a war.' Conversation is basic and non-political. D talks a lot about sex, as does H – they are typical of a certain type of Englishman who no longer knows how to flirt because they have become terrified of causing offence. What they do instead is become lewd and chauvinistic with each other, which is the safe zone, instead of with us. In fact, if a woman actually came on to them I think their eyes would pop out of their heads, blood would rush to their faces (in DC's case) and they would run for the nearest shelter – probably under their wives' skirts. It's our fault, of course, as women: it's all that vomiting in the street we go in for these days. All those years of cruelly repelling any feeble attempt at gallantry such as giving up bus seats.

The day we leave, we go for a six-mile walk with a whole load of coppers swarming behind. Dave's pace is relentless, there's no time to check out the view at all. At one point, on the coastal path, he asks me not to walk ahead of him. 'Why?' I ask, and he says, 'Because that scent you are wearing is affecting my pheromones. It makes me want to grab you and push you into the bushes and give you one!'

'God, don't do that,' I reply. 'I might get bitten by a tick on my bum and get Lyme's disease.' But he has no idea what Lyme's disease is.

This is not flirting by the Prime Minister. This is probably lewdness. But hell, I'm so starved of masculine interest at my age it made me smile. In fact, it altogether brightened my day. There is still hope, it seems.

I must get more of that Eau d'Italie!

28 September

On the economy, I know it's bad out there, really bad, but it also seems so shambolic. It's the policymakers: they have negligently allowed the eurozone crisis to spread – radical and necessary measures, including debt restructuring, are long overdue. Of course, my Eurosceptic instinct thinks good – collapse, arrivederci, au revoir, auf wiedersehen, pets – but the truth is, the difficulties in the eurozone have so multiplied they are now undermining the strength of the world economy. The eurozone simply can't go on staggering from crisis to crisis like this. Britain and the world need a solution soon, or we will all be going to hell in a handcart.

Though it's nice to know that the 'nutters' have been vindicated after decades of humiliation. The Daniel Hannans of this world, the Bill Cashes, the John Redwoods and the Margaret Thatchers. It seems they were right all along about the euro, about the financial devastation it was going to cause and the social collapse. The pro-Europeans, on the other hand, are keeping a very low profile these days – amongst them the Lib Dems, the *Financial Times*, the CBI, the BBC, that slimeball Tony Blair, Peter Mandelson, Michael Heseltine, Ken Clarke, Danny Alexander. They now look like appeasers in 1940, or communists after the fall of the Berlin Wall.

Those pro-Europeans are still out there, in the rotting woodpile, crawling around. We may need a new treaty very soon, and I'm not sure the likes of the BBC can be trusted not to become part of a new partisan propaganda operation. Quite frankly, it's in their DNA.

29 September

To George Eustice's fortieth drinks party at the Riverside restaurant in St George's Wharf. His girlfriend Katy chatty and smiley as ever. Talk to George Pascoe-Watson, former political editor of the *Sun*, now working for Portland Communications. He uses the word 'we' to mean 'we' in the Conservative Party. No impartiality at all now he has been released from journalism. Mind you, there was not much then either. Discuss Miliband's conference speech and we are of the same mind that it was a suicide note.

We move on to discuss Andy Coulson, and George tells me even Coulson thinks he is going down for perjury. Four years, maybe five. I say the main players in No. 10 are completely naive about Coulson, that they are all blinded by love for him. George adds that he feels sorry for some of his old print colleagues, particularly the ones that were not involved in hacking but are being tarred with the same brush.

'Hey, George, this is England, remember? When one or two go down the rest have to follow. Just look what happened with the

MPs' expenses. The English are never fair when it comes to these matters, it becomes mob rule, you know that.'

David Davis there, looking all pumped up and tanned. 'Why are you not out there earning some money? What about your children's inheritance?' I say.

'Too much on,' he replies. 'Got to exact my revenge on BAE Systems.' (The defence giant has just confirmed that it is cutting almost three thousand jobs, mainly in its military aircraft division, which is based in Davis's constituency.) He says he is going to try to persuade George to set up an enterprise zone there. Will he be able to? Their relationship has always been quite up and down.

Mark Field and Mark Francois are friendly but awkward around Hugo. I think probably a touch of the green-eyed monster there.

I ask the charming Sheryll Murray how she is coping after the death of her husband. She tells me her colleagues have been overwhelmingly kind and she is grateful for her job, but is clearly irked by Geoffrey Cox, who assumed she was to lose her seat in the boundary changes. As it turned out, it is Cox who has ended up sacrificing part of his constituency to the notorious Devon wall reorganisation. Cox is furious. Fuming all over the place. But if anyone deserves to lose their seat it is him, and I tell Sheryll that. The majority of his time is taken up by his QC work rather than his politics.

Have a rant with the brilliant Sheridan Westlake about how useless Central Office is – he has now moved from there to be Eric Pickles's special adviser and all the political researchers, such as me, are suffering as a result. As Ed Llewellyn passes he says, 'Sasha isn't banging on about press releases again, is she, Sheridan?' I am always complaining to anyone who will listen that the staff in Central Office need to be more media trained.

I just smile at Ed, then cup my hand, lower it between his legs, gather up his testicles and squeeze.

Then I leave.

30 September

The only clever thing Labour are on to is identifying working-class women as the new key electoral background. Their new strategy emerged after a leaked memo revealed deep concerns among Dave's team that the government was losing support amongst women. DC and I discussed this on a walk the other day, how women were now at the coalface of the cuts. While men often see the long-term plan, women are waving the electricity bill at them and saying yes, that's all very well, but how the hell are we going to pay this? He is worried about it; I could see it written on his face. I said I didn't know what the answer was; maybe we could do something through the care system, child-care, social housing etc. But I'm never sure you can bribe the electorate financially. They are cleverer than that. The papers are now saying the Tories are ready to rethink big cuts in child benefit. The danger is in treating women as one homogenous mass – what David should probably be doing is engaging them in the policy process. It's all very well having Kate and Gabby (Bertin) around the table, but they are not politicians, they do not hear the worries and concerns of women up and down Britain as MPs do in their surgeries.

I always get worried when a bunch of male politicians think they know what women want. It usually ends up being what they don't want.

Reading latest instalments of Chris Mullins's diaries. He comes across as a fundamentally decent human being, which is true of many diehard Labour supporters. I think the bulk of Labour members are not even necessarily left wing, they just want their views represented. They probably know little about Conservative policy (actually, it often overlaps on immigration, Europe etc.) and will remain unrepentant about state spending, which is also true of their leader. The problem with many of them is that although their views are made in a spirit of deep sincerity and conviction, they just stick to the same old rules.

11 October

Tally ho! They are all out Fox-hunting this week. And I thought Labour had banned it! It's always the same. First the scent of a scandal. A story comes out (in this case, pictures of cocky Foxy and 'mate') and the media pack starts to run. The PM and senior figures express their 'support' or 'confidence' in the Hapless One. H.O. makes a statement in the House, which either clears or damns. Exoneration may be complete if the story is put to bed, but if the hounds continue to run, the story gathers pace . . . Eventually the exhausted quarry either accepts that their position is untenable and resigns, or the PM withdraws his 'confidence'. How far the Fox will be able to run we do not yet know, but Labour are baying for his blood and the Shadow Defence Spokesman, Jim Murphy, is a particularly tenacious hound if ever I saw one. I'm not sure Fantastic Dr Fox can get out of this one. Personally, I think it's all very dodgy.

The Fox hunt starts when we are down in Beaune, so we are a little out of the loop bar texts coming in from David Davis, Greg and Derek Conway, saying Foxy is toast. K responds to my questions by saying it's a case of bad judgement and his chances of surviving are fifty-fifty.

We are the guests of Andrew Mitchell, who is a member of the Confrérie des Chevaliers du Tastevin, a kind of weird order of wine buffs which translates roughly as the Brotherhood of Knights of Wine-Tasting Cups. Andrew, whose father was not only an MP but also a wine merchant, proudly dons a grand yellow and red ribbon. Essentially, it's an exclusive bacchanalian fraternity of Burgundy wine enthusiasts who gather for several banquets a year in the incredibly beautiful twelfth-century Château du Clos de Vougeot. The whole experience is somewhat surreal, however.

The dinner is like a cross between a City livery hall or Masons' banquet, a Gilbert and Sullivan opera and a gathering of small, obscure Eastern European kingdoms, a sort of Noddyland with strange uniforms.

You'd think they take it all very seriously. The evening does indeed start that way, as candidates for membership are approved by the *Grand Pilier* or *Grand Connetable*, and confirmed by the *Grand Conseil*.

It goes on for ages. Finally, we sit down for a huge seven-course meal designed to promote 'viticultural and gastronomic education'. It is continually interrupted by raucous singing, clapping, comic turns and speeches. One of the speeches is given by a rather tipsy young environment minister called Nathalie Kosciusko-Morizet who, swaying somewhat, pulls her speech out from inside her bra. She starts reading it, then looks up and tells the gathering her husband wrote it because he claimed she was ignorant about wine. She rather grandly rips it up before going on to a rambling speech of her own. *Go, sister, go!*

15 October

Fox has gone. Hammond to Defence, then it starts: Greening to Transport and – bloody hell – Chloe Smith to the Treasury. It's that male thing going on: you know, what we know women want. So they promote a twenty-nine-year-old girl with F.A. experience – sorry, one year at Deloitte as a trainee management consultant before joining Central Office. Patronising and delusional vote-seeking driven by focus groups and PR men. Politics at its worst. I have told Hugo he must now put a deadline on his political career. He should fight the next election, and if he is not in the cabinet by then, he should retire to the back benches and try to make some money for our retirement.

DC said to me once, when you start shifting the cards in the pack it's the beginning of the end. He is probably right.

10 December

It feels like David's Falklands moment, that point when something happens to define a political career. Exercising his veto in Europe he has, perhaps even unwittingly, given the nation an idea of who he is and what he stands for. From here on in – however cruel a caricature of his personality, whatever events befall him – that moment becomes exceedingly difficult to change or erase. It was the moment he most certainly needed, and it was opportune: he was looking wishy-washy, merely a manager, even I was beginning to wonder who he is. I tell him this at his Christmas party in the flat at Downing Street and he laughs raucously at my cheek. He says I'm 'such a Tory' and I reply, 'David, I hate to remind you, but before you start thinking you are somehow separate from it all, you are actually the leader of the T-o-r-y Party and, on the whole, they are predominantly Eurosceptic.' He says that no one knows where this thing is going, even he doesn't.

It was all very Notting Hill, but fun. Poor old Sarah Gove, who bends over backwards to please the Camerons, was lumbered with cooking all the food while Samantha was upstairs learning to cut patterns (she wants to set up a fashion business). She then had her hair done! Turning up at her own party feeling perfectly relaxed while Sarah is laden down with dishes of fish pie she has herself cooked.

At the party both DC and Samantha tell me (and Hugo independently) that we are only one of four MP couples at this party, that there are no other politicos. Sam says, 'And the other two are godparents,' Kate being one and Steve Hilton the other. I think we are meant to feel flattered. But looking around at the court of King David it feels as if this is actually the government, here and now. The closeness of this circle is unprecedented. They are all here, the ones that eat, drink, party together, they are all intimately interlocked, some from university days, some from the research unit, some later, such as with us through the selection procedure. We all holiday together, stay in each other's grace-and-favour homes, our

children play together, we text each other bypassing the civil servants. There are old rows, forgiven betrayals and historic rivalries.
This is a very particular, narrow tribe of Britain and their hangers-
on. It's enough to repulse the ordinary man, already angered by
the continuing hold of the British class system. But maybe this is
something else as well; maybe this is more about the reassurance
of tangible relationships, about organic personal bonds. On the
whole, people just don't trust outsiders any more, and even more so
in politics, where the media lurks in the bushes waiting to pounce.
As in politics, the governing class is simply holding up a mirror to a
nation where friendships have replaced all other mediums: church,
family, schools, the idea of social networks is as strong as it has ever
been and in many ways Dave's court reflects this.

30 December

Sir John is on Radio 4 with David Owen, Julia Langdon and
Bernard Ingham to discuss the cabinet papers released under the
thirty-year rule. Sir John on typical impudent form. On Thatcher:
'I think she is a marvellous woman, I love her'. *Er* ...*?!* He tells
us in his uniquely casual way how the French routinely supplied
hookers to the Arabs to smooth arms deals in 1981. How Giscard
d'Estaing was a pompous dauphin. How he nearly completed a
huge arms deal with Saddam Hussein while ensuring that all the
vital parts were faulty. How the leaking from inside No. 10 became
intolerable.
   'Are you accusing me, Sir John, of that?'
   'No, Sir Bernard.'
   Except of course he has already, in his books.
   The programme was fascinating as it showed an uncanny similarity between the state of Britain in 1981 and the ructions of this
year. It revealed the machinations of an unpopular government
trying to reverse a bitter economic inheritance and cope with civil
unrest. The simplicity of the idea that politics is merely cyclical.

Then, as now, Britain was pervaded by a sense of self-doubt. If we are to be encouraged, it is that the government of the day, Thatcher's government, confronted that malaise and recovered. It cut public spending, curbed trade union power and tried to rebuild cities damaged by rioting (ditto, ditto, ditto). Even the bright events had counterparts: Lady Di's wedding and Prince William's. The lesson, clearly, is that the medicine has to be harsh, but if you create the right conditions recovery is sustainable.

2012

Towards the end of 2011, H and I stumbled across a property for sale in the *Western Morning News*. It was outside the constituency, but Hugo suggested we go and take a look anyway. I reluctantly tagged along. We had rented Lincombe Farm, on the Cave estate outside Sidmouth, for nearly a decade, but after the expenses saga, when all the accommodation allowances were reduced, we decided it no longer made sense to rent. It was time to buy a place of our own.

I knew the second I drove up the drive and looked at Chaffcombe's front that it was my dream home in every way. In the words of Robinson Jeffers, 'We had come without knowing it to our inevitable place.' Within a fortnight we had sold our house in Fulham and bought it. Then finding ourselves suddenly homeless in London, where we spent the majority of our time, we moved into the basement flat of my parents' house in Chelsea, renaming it 'the Dungeon'.

Chaffcombe is a Domesday settlement and the site of a medieval manor house that lies in the hilly countryside outside Crediton in central Devon. It is an area of ancient dispersed settlement and disclosure. The house is built of cobb and thatch, which is traditional of the area and surrounded by traditional farm buildings.

5 January

Chaffcombe

Meet the Home Office team, who are obliged to secure premises for high-risk ministers. They don't hide their despair well. The place is built like a stage set: unstable doors, no locks, crumbling window frames, PC Plod as far away as Exeter. I move through the house with the nice head honcho, the amiable Iain. You can see him totting up the costs and wincing as if he has swallowed a whole cactus.

'I think shutters here – much safer.'

I look at Iain, who is looking utterly crestfallen. He looks at his folder again, clutches it to his heart and launches off towards the cider barn, his tide of assistants surging behind him. Occasionally Iain screeches to a halt and reverses a few inches to notice some other glaring security risk, with all his flunkies stacking up behind. He goes into consultation with his team, grunts a few words and writes something down. There are more concertinas of colliding limbs before he is finished, more straightening of bodies, more notes taken, until he thinks he has it.

'I'll be in touch with a programme of works, Mrs Swire.'

H rings and says he hopes I pushed for maximum input.

12 January

H rings up and sheepishly confesses he won't be able to help me move out of Lincombe Farm because a gathering of the Privy Council has been called. I am already doing the London move single-handedly. He then tells me that on my birthday – he is meant to be taking me out to dinner – he has to attend a dinner for Irish tourism at St James's Palace. The combination of the two makes me go ballistic.

Dave was apparently subjected to a trap to make sure he used his veto. It was, they thought, the best way of making future negotiations on a fiscal union to save the euro much simpler if he was out of the picture and would short-circuit the need for lengthy negotiations with Britain on a formal EU treaty. There are also rumours that Dave's veto will be ignored and they will go ahead regardless on things like the transaction tax, which would be entirely illegal. I suggest that when the general public (mostly ours), who are becoming increasingly restless, get wind of this, all hell is going to break loose, that David will be pushed into a corner and have to offer a referendum. George is vehemently against this, but William wants to offer the promise of it in the next manifesto. David sits somewhere in between. Steve wants OUT.

Clegg, meanwhile, is pushing hard for Lords reform and is ignoring all cries that this will be damaging to him. Devo-max is the other concern, with fears that Salmond will get it on the ballot paper after all.

12 February

We have been planting Sir John's Christmas present to us, a large quantity of whips including common alder, silver birch, rowan, hornbeam, aspen and field maple. Such slight things they are too: you could call them twigs. One wonders how they will ever survive, noses just about peeping over their spiral guards to look out at this cold, frozen world.

They are very much my father's choices, and I like to think they say something about him. Nothing too big and brutal like oak and beech, instead silver birch, one of the hardiest broadleaves but dainty with it, feminine with its silvery white bark with grey-green fissures. It is a tree of enchantment. He was always one for the women, my dad.

Then rowan. He has planted a pair at the entrance to the cemetery he has built at Trewinnard: appropriately so, as from the earliest times rowan has been grown on or near to sacred sites. It is said that wherever druidic remains are found, so too is the rowan. It is a small yet incredibly bold tree, its leaves, blossoms and berries making colourful statements on the face of the land, but also something of a loner, as my father is; and yet it likes shading new saplings and is often planted in fresh coppices to protect young trees. My father is, along with my mother, my greatest protector; everything I have or own, including Chaffcombe, is a gift from him.

As for the alder, it mirrors his interests. It is found growing along the banks of streams and rivers, or in low-lying swampy land. My father is and always has been a keen fisherman, as was his grandfather before him, as is his son today. Alders and willows have always stood apart from the others, gazing lovingly into the waters.

The aspen is rarely still, and neither is my father, despite being in his eighties. Its leaves tremble at the slightest movement of air. There is always a project on the go or a country to visit, a book to write, a law to challenge, a plot to take on the taxman; he has never been one to act his age. Margaret Thatcher described him as 'a mixture of gold, dross and mercury'. How right she was. The traditional explanation of the aspen's trembling is that it has the acutest hearing of all trees, and that it moves continuously because of what it hears from afar. My father is selectively deaf, but he can still pick out a political statement buried in a newspaper article or conversation and denounce it for its complete absurdity. His favourite phrase is 'It's ridiculous!', which H says should be engraved on his headstone.

Like him, the hornbeam is strong in character and English in emotion. It is not fine grained – he is unsophisticated and uncultured – and the timber splits easily – he is quick to lose his temper – but it is very strong as a wood and makes good lintels and yokes. The hornbeam has traditionally implied straightforward toil. There are no fast tracks, no flashy solutions for this tree. If something sounds too good to be true it is. Growth, as my parents have taught me, only comes from steady progression. The people you need around you should have sound values too. Do not be tempted by bright lights or tinsel. Stick to the tried and tested, opt for the old raincoat and for God's sake reuse your teabags. I am constantly berated for my extravagances. In the end, the hornbeam represents strength, stubbornness and determination; progression and growth; genuine warmth; moral fibre; passion, ethics and loyalty. All of which my father has in spades.

I don't know how much thought he put in to picking these trees for me, but I know the qualities of each of them are his as well. These are in the mythologies, folklore and superstitions of our culture, many of which were practised by the pagans of the Celtic tribes. And my father is nothing if not a West Country man; he is very much a member of that same tribe.

16 April

George has made a dog's dinner of the latest budget. As a result, he is no longer seen as a brilliant political strategist and Dave's heir apparent. Each day his budget unravels further, which is usually the way of these things. Scrutiny and criticism centring on the 'granny tax', the 'pasty tax' and tax relief for charitable donations. Westminster whispers are that he has his finger in too many pies and should instead stick to cooking the books like most chancellors. This is disputed from inside, but it's clear he took his eye off the detail and as a result the consequences. Although he is surrounded by brilliant people – Rupert Harrison et al. – there is concern that there is no one in his team who questions his policies extensively enough, who sees the dangers and interest groups gathering in the wings. The trouble with George is that he is obsessive about wrong-footing his opponents with tactical announcements. His wheeze to cut the 50p tax rate was economically sound and roused the Tory right, but it totally failed to understand the public mood. This is the problem with a career politician such as he is – he is too clever to be sensible. The nation is more interested in *BGT** than GDP. On the whole, they are emotional rather than intellectual. The government needs to show it has a heart as well as a head, and it hasn't.

H's view is that maybe George exerts too much power, that people don't challenge him enough. Imagine deciding such an important budget between just four of them. There is an inherent arrogance to it all. It's something to do with the power of the executive guarding its position. But H and I move between the two camps (No. 10 and the MPs) and there is a view that everyone outside Dave and George's magic circle is met with condescension – MPs, ministers, journalists all think it. Yes, they invite the MPs to Chequers but it is often interpreted as lording it over them, that the exercise is not about respect or the desire to incorporate different views. It's a 'them' and 'us' mentality but the problem is that when the going gets tough, which it is now, there are few people out there to support them.

20 April

Hugo flies back to Belfast. He is taking part in a seminar organised by the Presbyterian Church to mark the centenary of the signing of the Ulster Covenant. The event is taking place at the City Hall, that wonderful monument to Victorian confidence. Other panel members include H's new best friend Jimmy Deenihan, the culture minister from the Republic, and the Archbishop of York. There is also a Sinn Féin councillor somewhere in the mix. H tells me

---

*   *Britain's Got Talent*, a British television talent show competition created by Simon Cowell.

that the audience mainly comprises of elderly Presbyterians, some of whom come up and thank H profusely for our bailing out the Presbyterian Mutual Society in which many had their savings. Also in the audience, a smattering of former paramilitaries now on the road to redemption. The audience is certainly tested in terms of comprehending anything that is said, what with Deenihan's broad Kerry brogue, Sentamu's at times impenetrable Ugandan English and H's impersonation of Lord Snooty ('It's called Received Pronunciation, Sasha') but they take it all in good humour. At one point, H slips out to go and greet the Taoiseach, who is speaking at the University of Ulster. H arrives in his armoured Land Rover and 'the boys', as he fondly calls them, escort him through the throng. Enda, having been reminded who H is, greets him with a friendly punch on the chest, which had he been wearing a pacemaker would almost certainly have broken it. All he really wanted to know, according to H, was how Owen had got on at the Cheltenham Festival. When H said that he didn't think Owen had picked many winners Enda looked satisfied and moved on to his audience, no doubt punching as he went. Back to wind up the seminar, then a disgusting buffet dinner followed by a not very inspiring speech from the Archbishop, which he read out.

H had asked the Archbishop to stay the night at Hillsborough – he wanted to make friends in case Sentamu gets Canterbury. He is certainly in the running and possibly even the current favourite. In the car on the way to Hillsborough H asks him what his chances of Canterbury are, as he and the boys want to nip down to BJ Eastwood for a quick flutter.

'Is BJ Eastwood a gambling den? I don't like gambling,' he says with a chuckle.

H tells him that we all have mouths to feed and need a bit extra, and that he wants some inside track as to whether he has some illness or other such impediment that would put him out of the running. The Archbishop roars with laughter. The boys can barely believe it, although they must have got used to H's humour by now.

H gives Sentamu a tour of the house then offers him a drink.

Having only drunk lime juice in public, he is now glad to have a glass of something stronger. Brandy, he says. They sit up talking about the Church, gay marriage and the government. He is nice about DC and becomes even nicer when H says what a close friend he is. DC, of course, has a say in who is the next Canterbury. As the brandy takes effect the dog-collarless Archbishop becomes increasingly robust. He thinks DC may lack backbone, is very against gay marriage and longs for a tougher line on most things. He is clearly no fan of the Lib Dems. H says he shall certainly convey his impressions to DC.

A little later, the Archbishop rises from his chair and says he would like another brandy to go and say his prayers with. They bid their farewells and goodnights, and H leaves him happily rolling down the corridor, glass in hand, to make peace with his maker.

23 April

After the budget, I'm afraid the public no longer accepts unreservedly the government's case for a collective effort. The old criticism of being out of touch is back to haunt them. This time it's promoted by Mad Nad Dorries, who accuses DC and GO of being 'arrogant posh boys' (yes, and the news is?) and of being surrounded by a 'tight, narrow clique of a certain group of people' who 'act as a barrier and prevent Cameron and Osborne and others from really understanding and knowing what is happening in the rest of the country'. (Yes, and was it not ever thus?)

Throw into the mix an interview with Osborne Senior (Sir Peter, 17th Baronet) in the *FT* 'How To Spend It' magazine in which he says he is eyeing up a desk that costs £19,000. Oh, and that he is partial to Savile Row tailoring, a particular £39-a-bottle moisturiser and a £35 bath oil, and his fridge is never without an £11-a-pound Manchego cheese. All well and good, but it does undermine his son's 'We're all equally poor and hopeless' message. And as for George's man-of-the-people claim that he wasn't personally affected by the top-rate tax cut (er, just not this year, because the rental income on your huge Notting Hill mansion will only start showing on next year's tax return) – it must make voters question whether we really are all in this together or not.

Dave sees it all unravelling before his eyes. The black dog has descended upon him. He and George are said to be at their lowest ebb since entering government. Dave says it's like watching a version of Angry Birds: all the governments in Europe falling one by one. He's wondering whether his is next. Deep down he apparently is very anxious about winning the next election, certainly outright. He thinks we would have to go into coalition again, and if that happens the party will undoubtedly get rid of him. Others are more optimistic: they say there are still two years to turn the economy around.

24 April

Attend the Josephine Hart Poetry Hour at the Irish embassy. Maurice looking lost and sad without her. Theirs was a great love story, they simply went everywhere together, did everything together. A year on and he is still not himself. Afterwards, a quick dinner in the Commons. Amber (Rudd) comes along, cheerful as ever. She's always a good source for what is going on on the back benches. Conversation comes around to Matt Hancock, who Amber is not sure about. Both she and H think he is way too cocky for someone so young and inexperienced, but then he did train at the knee of one George Osborne before entering parliament.

H says, 'I've always wanted to go up to him and ask him what a man with his hand on his cock is called.'

'Han ... cock?' asks Amber.

'Wanker!' replies H.

1 May

Nice tale from Sir John, who has just returned from a grand weekend stay with the Heseltines. All the former great and goods there, moaning about how young and inexperienced the present lot are. *Plus ça change!* Around the table at lunch are the Salisburys, Douglas Hurd, the Gummers, Tessa and Henry Keswick, Andrew Knight, Marcus Agius.

Suddenly Michael tap-taps his glass with a fork for silence.

'Excuse me, I have an announcement to make.'

Everyone stops talking.

Heseltine continues: 'I have just received a telephone call from Buckingham Palace. David Cameron has resigned, and the Queen has asked me to form a new government.'

They know it's a joke, but Heseltine proceeds to go around the table explaining where and why he will place each one of them in the cabinet, and what he expects them to do. Sir John, as it happens, gets to stay in Defence. Gummer in Environment. So, nothing radical or original or funny. Sir John said it was all a bit odd. I reply, 'Why? He's just never got over not being prime minister. He thinks his whole life is a failure as a result.'

'Yes,' he says, 'you are right. It's extraordinary, isn't it?'

11 May

Michael Gove is down to do a big tour of East Devon schools. He is our first guest at Chaffcombe Manor. H, Gove and I drink three bottles of wine between us and try and put the Conservative Party to rights. Well, at least I do. Hugo is more discreet, more measured. We get on to whether Gove would ever want the leadership. He absolutely denies this; says he could never put his family through it. But the entire conversation is about who supports who, who's in with a chance. He is alarmed/intrigued to hear that Greg Clark and Jeremy Hunt have carved up the Conservative Party between them to try to get the backbenchers on board for any future Hunt bid. (This comes from H, and is the first I have heard of it.) Gove's rivalry with Hunt is well known. We discuss Boris's chances, and George's.

I relay the conversation to K, who says it's all bollocks, he is just spinning. He knows full well how close we are to the 'gang' and he is only conveying what he wants us to hear and pass on. She says he is being particularly obstructive at the moment, not signing off on emails and making unhelpful speeches, the latest of which is about the dominance of the privately educated in public life. Gove calls it 'morally indefensible'. Of course, he is right, but the timing is interesting; could even be considered calculating following Nadine Dorries's comments. She says he is manoeuvring quite blatantly at the moment.

12 June

To Frances Osborne's book launch at Heywood Hill. George is there, all pumped up and pluming like a peacock. He has just got off the stand at the Leveson inquiry and is feeling particularly smug. He's particularly pleased that his enemies, waiting in the wings, will have no dead meat to pick over. 'You enjoyed that too much, George. You were playing with them, weren't you?'

'Yes, I did rather enjoy it,' he replies.

Spiders and legs.

30 June

H slams his red box down on the kitchen table and opens it. It feels like I'm being stopped by a traffic light, one that prohibits any traffic from proceeding. RED. STOP. WAIT. GO. I do go . . . outside. Red, the colour of blood and power. Of kings and cardinals and Roman generals and whores and the devil. The great carrier of government documents.

The sun goes down in a pale fire between the farm buildings. Then everything falls away. The birds, the noise, me. Light changes everything; all the world obsequious and answering to this ball of power. Flowers draw up their petals in a kind of sleep, but not the jasmine, the cool beauty of the night. It actually unbows its head and starts shining, like stars painted on the tombs of pharaohs. I sit under the walkway where the flowers swarm up and over the tiles and I breathe in its scent. Ah yes, the ancient smell of calm. Laboratory tests have found that the smell of jasmine has the power to calm mice. They stop their chaos – running, squealing, fighting; it makes them lie down quietly together in the corner of their cage. The scent molecules apparently transmit messages to the limbic system of the brain, the area involved in controlling emotions. My husband should be sitting here beside me. *Tell me about loneliness, yours, and I will tell you mine.*

Instead, I walk around the house and see H, through the window, in a glare of artificial brightness, still hunched and working on his box. Our marriage is in a difficult place. I barely see him any more; he's always in Ireland or the House or working in the constituency, and when he's home he hardly speaks to me. It is midnight when he finally comes to lie down in the corner of my cage, but it's not from calm, it's from exhaustion. I flare up. It has an effect, because the next day he texts Kate saying if he is not brought back from exile at the next reshuffle his wife is going to divorce him. 'Don't worry,' she replies. 'You are being moved.'

5 July

Last night we had a small party at Walpole Street to celebrate my mother's OBE. Good for her, and well deserved. Very proud. Hague turns up with Arminka (Helić), which is good of them, and Paddy Pantsdown, who M has a love-hate relationship with, stemming back to the Bosnian conflict, in which they were both involved.

I interrupt the financiers Ronald Cohen and Neil Record. 'Are you two commiserating?' Yes, they say, things are really tough out there financially. I tell them it's tough for me too, you know, as a wife in politics. I say I'm either getting a garden or a lover, but I haven't decided which. I'm simply fed up of being left alone by my husband. Ronnie says he might be able to help!

I then corner my husband and say, 'You better call your mistress and tell her you are having dinner with me instead tonight.' That's how desperate I am for company: I am even prepared to go to the House of Commons on a vote night and eat slop.

Poor David, that old devil called Europe is here again. The party keep telling him to have a referendum. He is starting to look vulnerable, just like Major did all those years ago. Worse, Dave, unlike Sir John, hasn't even won an election and he has the Liberal Democrats to deal with in government, not to mention UKIP outside it. And nearly three-quarters of the party members back withdrawal from the EU, as do a growing number of Conservative MPs. And what about outside the cabinet? Boris Johnson, George's potential rival – and the Prime Minister's too – is beating the drum. Who would ever want to be in David's shoes? Europe always tries to bring down Conservative leaders. He's right, though: how on earth can we decide when we have no idea what a new Europe will look like? A referendum commitment now will drag us into a fight with UKIP and the electorate might use it as an opportunity to punish him for other matters. Regarding renegotiation, well, the Germans might just tell him to piss off and not waste their time, which could push him into a corner on an in/out question, and which way would everyone jump then? Nightmare.

3 September

Back from a stay with the Camerons in Polzeath. Always good fun. Lots of booze, high-octane activity and laughs. Sam her usual lefty self. But I'm quite relaxed about it now, even throw her 'let them eat cake' line back at her, which she takes with good humour. But oh my God! Some of her ideas! She literally wants to prise my savings out from under my mattress and dump them in the exchequer with a ribbon on top. The thought that the state is better with my money than I am is quite ludicrous. We agree not to disagree as there could be blood on the floor. Siena asks D the best question: 'Er, Dave, have you ever met Al Qaeda?' And I find his Achilles heel when I ask him: 'Are you actually a Conservative, Dave?' He dives into the surf, furious and flushed, to avoid confronting me, but he turns to H at dinner later: 'How do you cope? With her? Your wife, I mean?' GO rings. He has been having horrendous press lately. Dave comes back to the table. 'I always feel better when I talk to him. There's never any wavering on the confidence or arrogance front, it's quite extraordinary!' D thinks George will never leave politics, it's all he ever thinks about. He does not tip Hugo off about the job he is getting as he is scared things will change and it will raise his hopes. The holiday has lightened Dave's load but then Cornwall is where he is most at peace. He is on good form.

6 September

Reshuffle comes and H gets his new job. He is over the moon. Turns up at the FCO and has the old India office. He appears to have about six members of staff. He rings me up: 'I seem to be running the world.' His new responsibilities: the Far East and South-East Asia; India, Nepal and Bhutan; North America; Latin America (including the Falklands, the Dominican Republic, Haiti and Cuba); Australasia and the Pacific; the Commonwealth as an institution; emerging powers coordination; public diplomacy; the Olympics legacy and the GREAT campaign; economic diplomacy; prosperity work, including the FCO's relations with British business; working in support of Lord Green; drugs and

international crime; Islamic finance; the Chevening Scholarship
programme . . .

'Blimey,' I say, that's quite a menu! K and I agree it's quite
simply the jammiest job to be had in politics. When Dave rings
up to tell him he says: 'I simply need someone with your business
and diplomatic skills. These are all the emerging markets and
I need you to sell GB. I also need you to keep an eye on Warsi,
let me know what she's up to.' Warsi apparently had a bit of a
meltdown when she was demoted. She was originally offered
Commonwealth Minister along with the equalities brief but was
so dismayed by its lack of status that she did a disappearing act.
Negotiations continued over the phone with her writing her own
job description incorporating Pakistan; she was given the new
title Senior Minister of State, thereby putting her above Hugo.
DC has a weak spot when women confront him like this, and
often gives in. K says to me, she will drive Hugo mad, but he
was to stay calm and just ride with it. The FCO will quickly
work out he is the man to deal with, K says. We subsequently
learn that Warsi has already texted Dave asking whether she
can come on the trade mission to South America, which again is
H's area. She also was seen eyeing up Hugo's office until he told
his team to throw their bodies in front of it to protect it from her
grasping clutches and, if necessary, take the bullet. And she is
insisting on having a spad when no other minister is permitted
one despite, it seems, having responsibilities for just two countries, Pakistan and Afghanistan. Of course, to calm her further
David gave her another role as the Faith and Communities
Minister, in Communities and Local Government (CLG) but
this does not seem of much interest to her. She apparently told
Pickles that she would not be attending the morning meeting to
which Pickles allegedly said: 'Well you can just fuck off then.'
I like Warsi, she is clever and has done well for herself, but she
can be difficult.

Mark Simmonds, who like H is like the cat that got the cream,
sidles up to Hugo with his tail up, purring: 'You couldn't give me

South America could you, old chap? You know my wife is from Venezuela.'

'Mark,' H says, 'I'm afraid it's not in my gift to give you whole countries. And I think the fact your wife is from there is not really a good enough reason.' Marks slinks off, mournfully sighing that those extra trips to wifeland might have to wait.

Other tales from the reshuffle abound. They had to call in the SAS to get Andrew Mitchell out of DfID; 'In the end I had to come out with my hands up to avoid collateral bloodshed,' he says to H. It takes them three weeks prior to the reshuffle to persuade him to give it up. He also drives them mad with several demands: he wants David Davis to go into Justice (loyalty a strong theme here) – they say absolutely not; then he wants his spad, Philippa, to be given a job in Downing Street. 'Absolutely not!' says Dave. (The Cameroons have been wary of Andrew since he did the numbers for the David Davis leadership campaign.) Since getting the Chief Whip job Mitchell has become impossibly grand, storming past everyone in Dave's outer office and heading straight for the PM. He feels he needs to have direct contact. K is having none of it, she feels trodden over and firmly plants herself in between the two men to establish her relevance.

We have a sleepless night before the reshuffle because we think Mitch will try to get H in to be his deputy. At 6 a.m. I send a missive off to Downing Street to say this would be unacceptable. 'Don't worry, position safe!' comes the reply, but until it's in the bag H is a nervous wreck; and it's the same day we drop Siena off at boarding school for the first time. Mitch is taking much pleasure in taunting him by saying: 'Pants on, march towards the gunfire, your country needs you. Accept what is offered – I did!' The call came at 3 p.m. and H was finally able to breathe a sigh of relief.

Samantha texts: 'Some of the most awful days of Dave's life but at last over.'

10 September

Reception to greet the vice-president of Brazil with Nick Clegg as host, then on to the Paralympics closing ceremony. All very spectacular, Coldplay in full throttle amid a flotilla of *Mad Max* vehicles, which felt like a metaphor about waste and how the human spirit can make great things out of difficult situations. The presence of Rihanna and Jay-Z mildly irritating, even as singing guests, as it was meant to be a GB display. I look at Dave in the enclosed area, sitting in a Politburo-style row amongst the usual suspects, including Boris. He looks all glum, barely talks to his neighbours (Clegg and Lady Coe) while Boris in his capacity as Mayor of London is lapping it up, getting rounds of applause when he goes down to hand over the flag to the Brazilians.

There seems to be something of a campaign going on at the moment to push Boris back into parliament. Particularly among donors and newspapers (Mail Group), and sources tell me there are around twenty MPs who could well back him for leader. More worryingly, it seems to have captured the public imagination. Boris has been active as well, using the summer to torment David on an hourly basis, his motives both transparent and outrageous. Unfortunately, the Olympics have given him a platform to parade his populist touch without having to worry about anything as trivial as collective responsibility for government policy. The idea of His Blondness with a finger on the nuclear button scares the shit out of me; it also scares the shit out of me that people don't see him as the calculating machine he really is. This is a man who has no obvious political identity or any proven ability to grasp difficult questions and decisions, there is always someone behind the scenes doing it for him, as with all of his election campaigns. He has never shown any loyalty to his party or to his government, only ever to himself. He is also driven by jealousy of Dave. (Partly Dave's fault for not promoting him to the cabinet when he first became leader.)

Inside No. 10 the view is not one of complacency, it is more a sort of *this is where we are at moment in the cycle* kind of attitude. Of course Boris is more popular than Dave, but if it wasn't him it would be someone else. In politics, everyone is always looking over their shoulder for the next king. The view inside No. 10 is the front-runners for any leadership contest at the moment would be Philip Hammond and Michael Gove. But Dave is really pissed off with Gove at the moment because of the way his shifty spad Dominic Cummings appears to be briefing against him.

12 September

Amber made George's PPS. She and about a hundred others are invited down to Dorneywood for a barbecue. When she gets back she tells me how extraordinary it was that Frances did not appear at all, that she later saw her sitting in the kitchen with someone having a chinwag and stayed there for the entire event.

26 September

The grand question of today appears to concern whether or not Mitchell used the word 'pleb' in his excoriation of a Downing Street police officer last week.

Hugo texts Mitch to see if he's OK. 'It's like living in a Kafkaesque nightmare,' comes the reply.

7 October

Shooting weekend at John Lewis's. One of those rare occasions I go out to view the massacre. Jonathan Rothermere there; I tell him he better start supporting Dave, because before he knows it he'll be packing his Louis Vuitton trunks and selling all his lovely mansions if the other lot get in. I think I hear him right, but he says he's doing that anyway. He gets quite threatening about Leveson, they are taking it very personally at the *Mail*. I stiffen my spine and tell him he won't be able to go for Dave if there is cross-party consensus, will he? He looks at bit floored by that.

'You're very feisty this morning, Sasha! What did you have for breakfast?'

John Thurso* is also there, being a former business partner of John's from when they launched Cliveden as a hotel. I sit next to him at dinner. It's fascinating, hearing the views of a Lib Dem. I just sit there and listen. He is scathing about most of his Liberal colleagues in the Commons. He feels his party has given its all and got nothing back from the Conservatives, and that not assisting us with boundary changes is a pure act of revenge in response to House of Lords reform. At the end of the conversation I'm left wondering as to why he is a Liberal Democrat at all, but then politics is tribal and his grandfather Archie Sinclair was the leader of the Liberal Party.

H, watching me, shouts from the bottom end of the table: 'Is she breaking up the coalition? Is she causing trouble with my coalition partner?' Thurso turns to H and says, 'I think I want to marry her.'

Men just love it when you listen to them! It's so damn easy ...

11 October

H looking guilty. 'What?' I ask.

'I've fallen in love!'

'Oh yes, who is it this time?'

'The Panamanian ambassador: she's gorgeous, and just thirty.'

'Thirty! Am I getting old?'

'Yes. Hasta la vista, baby!'

I'm due to meet her at a lunch but Hugo cancels me at the last moment, saying it's inappropriate. That they will be conducting official bilateral talks and I will be bored. Fine, I say, carry on

---

* Viscount Thurso, Liberal Democrat, variously a member of the House of Commons and House of Lords.

flirting. On a drive to Devon, I ask him how a thirty-year-old gets to be ambassador to the UK. 'I guess it can't hurt if your dad is in with the president,' says H.

The Duke of York invites H to Buck Pal. We know what it's about. What part of NO does he not get, says H to me. It's the usual stuff: he feels roleless, that he has decided he is going to act independently. H is pissed off that the Palace keeps throwing him back to the FCO to deal with. Who is actually going to sit him down and tell him, once and for all, that he is not wanted or needed on the diplomatic circuit? Somehow conversation comes around to the Panamanian ambassador.

'Have you met her?' asks the Duke of York.

'Have I!'

'It's very odd,' says the Duke of York. 'When I met her, she said she was pregnant, and the next time I saw her she wasn't pregnant at all.'

'Did you hear correctly? Those South American accents can be lispy. Maybe she said, have you met the president?'

The prince's private secretary is chuckling in the background but his boss's face is expressionless.

2013

5 February

The spectacular downfall of Chris Huhne is an agony to behold. Forget the ghastly exposure of his son's emotional texts about the breakdown of his parents' marriage; forget the revenge of a woman who devoted twenty-eight years to a marriage only to have him run off with a woman who looks like a man; forget a man's glittering political career in tatters: what really hits home is how a life can be brutally destroyed by something so simple as a measly speeding offence, or an altercation at a Downing Street security gate. And with Twitter and blogs and twenty-four-hour news and rolling comment, that pain is exacerbated even further. The electorate want gods above them and are disappointed to find humans who turn out to be just as fallible as themselves. MPs are expected to be faithful to their spouses, bring up their children, be a social worker to their constituents, make decisions on welfare, housing and immigration, be on-call all weekend in the community, fly around the globe for their government only to arrive in a room that could be anywhere in the world for a four-hour meeting then fly all the way back again, as in my husband's case – it's a relentless and often thankless task. It's no surprise that so many of the new intake's marriages have already broken down: the effort of juggling family, parliament and constituency just becomes too much. So why do they do it? Moths, says Matthew Parris: they are simply moths to a burning flame.

6 February

To the 'Icebreakers' Chinese New Year dinner at the Dorchester. That old lion Heseltine the guest speaker. You forget how good he is on a platform. 'I know nothing about you, your business, your markets or indeed the Chinese. However, I can tell you this: the Chinese take a very long-term view. They plan for twenty or twenty-five years. Unlike us in Britain. And if we want to be successful, there is no point saying let's just export goods to China. We have to succeed in our domestic market first. And when I say domestic market I mean Europe. That is where our future lies – Europe!' No change in content, then. He saw H a couple of days later and sounded rather upset. The *Daily Hate* (*Mail*) said everyone had groaned after his speech. Did they? asked Michael. Of course they didn't, said Hugo, reassuring him. But it's amazing he still cares. You can never forget the fault line that runs through this man.

At dinner I sense H is a little agitated as we approach our table but think nothing of it. But when the ambassador, Liu Xiaoming, smooth and good looking, gets up to speak it is clear there is a problem. The speech, for such a neutral event, is overtly antagonistic.

'We don't think it appropriate to impose one's own views and values on others, nor do we believe in "megaphone diplomacy". What we encourage is sincere and equal dialogue on the basis of mutual respect. It's a good way to enhance mutual understanding, strengthen political trust and manage differences. This is the precondition and foundation for healthy and steady growth of China-UK relations.' When I look up the speech later, on the Chinese embassy website, it omits his most audacious criticisms, most notably the difficulty the Chinese are having in getting passports to come here.

I look over at Hugo and he cocks his eyebrow at me, indicating he disapproves of the man's manoeuvring. Later, the head of the Asia desk comes over to Hugo, a man called Wilson, who is equally cross about the speech. This all comes on top of some rather childish behaviour on the part of the Chinese, including the dispatch of diplomats to Edinburgh and Dublin and not to London.

11 February

To Dorneywood for the weekend. Also staying are Catherine and Hugh Powell, Simone Finn, Amber Rudd, with Mark Francois and his new girlfriend coming in for Sunday lunch. George somehow in less confident mood.

At dinner, he goes on a rant about the rebel MPs who opposed gay marriage, how he is most definitely on the right side of history and they are not. He tells me that he had pulled out and re-read all the controversial debates – female emancipation, the abolition of slavery, the introduction of civil partnerships – and they had confirmed to him that they were absolutely right to go forward with it. He also advocates requiring churches to conduct same-sex marriages; when I argue that this is a matter for the churches not the state, he huffs and puffs, clearly annoyed this is, in the end, the collective view. I then say that although both he and David were rightly pro gay marriage, they refused to get their hands dirty in the debate by explaining the detail to the MPs and bringing them around. He just replies in typical George fashion, 'What's the point? They are mostly ridiculous.' George is of course intrinsically urban, he doesn't see England as warm beer, village greens and church on Sunday, unlike David. George has got to that point, that dangerous point in politics when he can no longer be bothered to court favour with those working against him. In that sense he is starting to get tired. He remains, however, totally confident about his approach to everything. He is playing austerity by the book, and he has a submarine attitude to the media: he just stays inside the Treasury, merging the economics with the politics. That is his way. But the trouble is the economy is now flatlining and the man who was considered a Conservative hero, and lauded by the Tory faithful, is now being jeered by the voters. And the more the economy falters the louder and more public the criticism will be.

Later, G says: 'That job Hugo has was absolutely made for him. He's brilliant at it, swanking around the embassies. Charming everyone.'

'It might be made for him, George, but it's going to kill him.'

'Why's it going to kill him?'

'It's not good for him, all that flying around the world. Too much altitude does something bad to your body. It puts too much pressure on it. Look what happened to Hillary Clinton. Nearly dead from a blood clot in her brain.'

'Yeah, Sasha, but look what pressure he has at home!'

George tells me the only time he feels any sense of release from the exhaustions of day-to-day politics is on a long-haul flight.

12 February

H is trying to cope with an extremely pedantic and doctrinaire member of his team. A person probably of the belief that an Oxford education and the FCO on their CV is a suitably stiff anti-toxin to see off all manner of unpleasantness, including the commands of an upstart junior minister. Fortunately for H, this person has announced they will be moving on, 'Unless you would like to keep me for a while longer, Minister.'

'Er no, that's all right, I think I can cope. Maybe you need new challenges.'

H comes home and says he has had a gruelling and tiresome day. His private secretary rang early in the day in a panic. 'The North Koreans have carried out a nuclear test and you are wanted by the media.' H scrambles to get ready, not greatly assisted by me as we have a tug of war with H's red box in the hall, me screeching that he is not to take it on the Tube as it is too much of a security risk. Eventually he gets into the Addison Lee car which was sent after much wrangling earlier in the morning: one of those *there are no cars available, Minister* conversations. H usually walks to work, so he's hardly a burden on the taxpayer. It seems the Foreign Office cars are never available at short notice, even if there is a crisis; they are all too busy ferrying in senior mandarins from their villas in Hampstead Garden Suburb.

He endures an endless round of TV interviews and thanks God that a BBC make-up artist takes pity on him and slaps on some powder as he was beginning to show the thin, yellow, bilious complexion of one who overindulged at dinner with the Guatemalan Foreign Minister the previous night.

Later in the day he tried to call in the North Korean ambassador for the sort of dressing down that is becoming all too regular. Last time he called him in he looked tearful and said that he always thought they could be friends despite everything. This time he was wilier. He informed officials that it was their New Year and he was on holiday, and he couldn't come in at a certain time; they offered other times; none suited. He then added that his wife was unwell and didn't they have any regard or sympathy for her welfare? It was all too much and he wasn't coming in, and that was his final word on the matter. Cunning. H then ordered a letter to be sent to him, wishing his wife a speedy recovery and offering his understanding of his position, but that he had rearranged his diary and expected him in at ten o'clock the following morning. No response. All very cat and mouse. Let's wait and see, says H.

17 February

China is on my mind – and in the papers – again. A totalitarian state with expansionist tendencies; it makes me uncomfortable. When I ask Hugo about this all, he says:

'I can't tell you anything, it's TOP Secret.'

'What? That there are cabinet splits over our relations with China and a new surge in cyberespionage?'

'How do you know that?'

'Just guessed, really. Is that why you went to the National Security Council and came back saying George Osborne was amoral?'

'I can't discuss it, Sasha, I'd have to kill you.'

'You know what I think?'

'No, but I'm sure you are going to tell me.'

'I think David and George are anxious about upsetting the Chinese because they don't want to damage trade relations. George, as usual, has been salivating over the idea of Chinese sovereign wealth building infrastructure projects and wants London to be the leading international centre for trading China's currency.'

'I said I'm not discussing this with you.'

I press on. 'You don't like George's stance. You think, along with Hague and Clegg, that Britain should put principles first, particularly on issues such as Tibet. That as a nation we must not be bullied into changing our values. The Chinese ambassador considers Tibet-related affairs as purely internal affairs of China and doesn't like being told otherwise.'

'Yes: to them, the Dalai Lama is a political exile who hides under the cloak of religion but is in fact actively involved in anti-China, pro-independence activities.'

'Meanwhile at the National Security Council you are all a little bit pissed off that the government is being forced to deal with numerous attempts by the Chinese to spy on our computer networks, including military ones.'

'How do you know this?'

'Don't worry, you didn't tell me anything.'

'Well, who did, then?'

'Isabel Oakeshott, actually. It's on the front page of the *Sunday Times*.'

'Bloody hell, how did they get that?'

H rings up Arminka. It must be the Lib Dems if it's Oakeshott – all her fodder comes from their side. Arminka confirms. Says it's the Eastleigh by-election: they are leaking stuff all over the place. Want the punters to think they are keen on human rights etc.

17–26 February

The biggest-ever trade delegation to leave British shores – about 140 companies – on a PM-led mission to India. Virgin plane chartered. Tremendous jostling for business class seats. No. 10 staff exhausted by peers and captains of industry demanding to either sit on the PM's knee the whole way, or at the very least in the adjacent seat. H is two away from DC, and in considerable comfort – unlike Neil MacGregor, the director of the British Museum, and Peter Simon, founder of the Monsoon chain, both of whom were knee-nibbling at the back of the plane. H says DC in good form. Does his box, slurps back some no doubt much-needed refreshment and goes to bed for the whole journey. While England sleeps! Hectic on arrival. H accompanies Dave to lunch with the Indian PM, Manmohan Singh, and a meeting with the president in the impressive Lutyens-built former Viceroy's Palace.

On the second night Dave, Greg Barker, Kim Darroch (National Security Advisor), Ed Llewellyn, Kate Joseph from No. 10, Craig Oliver the press secretary and Helen James, an old flame of DC's, who they scooped up at the High Commissioner's party for the Queen's birthday, slip away to a much-recommended Indian restaurant. H tells me it is a very convivial evening, with everyone in top form. Of course, the owner, the manager, the waiters, their friends, their children, their children's friends and indeed half of Delhi all have their photo taken with a long-suffering Dave. Then the bill arrives. Ed turns white as a sheet, and holds the bill at arm's length, as if it contains news that North Korea has successfully launched a nuclear attack on Seoul. He then emits a strange noise, a cross between an infant's very first attempt at speech and someone dying from asphyxiation. 'It can't be,' he groans. 'It can't be.' Well, it was. All £4500 of it. It must have been the wine, they all say, looking at Dave accusingly. It had been rather good, apparently. The group make their excuses and exit, leaving Ed to deal with the bill. As he goes, H suggests Ed tries a bit of haggling.

'I can't!' Ed wails. 'That would be a story.'

The group retire to Dave's suite, which is the size of a small Indian state, and continue the party. Much discussion about the bill, and how they are going to have to divvy it up.

The following day they are all up bright and early . . . well, not so bright, but certainly early, for the historic trip to Amritsar. Dave, apparently, is in his element, looking variously moved, inspired, humbled and contrite – sometimes all at once – to the pleasure of the Sikhs and the thirty thousand police on guard to protect him. More than the entire manpower of the Metropolitan Police, as someone ruefully pointed out. In the bus Ed and H talk to Craig Oliver. He starts jotting things down in the notebook he carries everywhere with him. H looks across at Ed. They both raise their eyebrows. 'Did you see?' Ed hisses later. 'He was writing down everything I said. It's a nightmare.' Word is that Oliver is writing a memoir of his time at No. 10. No one trusts him but there doesn't seem to be anything that anyone can do about it.

H spends a couple of days with the Dowager Marchioness and his sister Sophie in Jaipur, then travels on to Park Geun-hye's inauguration as president of South Korea. Arriving in the VIP lounge at Seoul airport, he is told there is to be a formal exchange of presents, so H removes himself to the loo for a quick brush-up, only to be confronted by the most complicated lavatory he has ever seen. Using it quickly, as they are waiting for him outside, he goes to flush it but it is so big and has so many buttons he doesn't know which one to press. Unfortunately, all the instructions are in Korean. He presses the first button. Nothing. Same the second. Losing patience, he then pushes all the buttons at the same time, whereupon a huge jet of water shoots out, drenching his shirt, before even more water appears from nowhere and begins to pour happily over the side of the loo like Niagara Falls. He tries everything to stop this flood but to no avail and runs out screaming for help, only to be confronted by the Korean delegation, who were lined up to greet him. They look on somewhat surprised – but diplomatically expressionless – by this wild and drenched figure gesturing frantically back to the WC. British officials swing into action, and both honour and the ceiling of Seoul airport are saved.

24 February

Sunday night catch-up with K. With the Eastleigh by-election coming up, this Rennard stuff seems like manna from heaven.[*] 'Did you plant it?' I ask.

'God, no! If only we were that clever!'

'Yes, if only!' I sigh.

She thinks it's Clegg's people. They want him gone. Lord Rennard is a powerful though obscure political obsessive operating in the shadows, and a master of political dirty tricks, particularly at by-elections.

3 March

Sunday night train to London, standard class. I usually take the car. It's a pitiful sight to see my husband, knees grazing the seat in front and red box on lap, all 2 or 3 kilograms of slow-grown pine, lined with lead and black satin, attempting to do his homework. Every document I see is 'restricted' or 'classified'. Not for me it isn't, because I can read every line of it. God forbid if he had a stranger next to him or, at rush hour, someone standing overhead. He might as well stand up in the middle of the carriage with a loudhailer and reveal state secrets there and then. It takes freedom of information to new levels, believe me. The man across the aisle is so impressed he can't help saying, 'What are you doing down here with the peasants? I think you have single-handedly restored my faith in politicians.' The *Times* journalist Alice Thomson and her husband Ed Heathcoat Amory, who are on our train, are appalled. Ed says he should snap a picture and hope it goes viral.

The embarrassment continues when Hugo texts to find out

---

[*] Lord Rennard, the Liberal Democrat election guru, was the subject of a report on *Channel 4 News* in February 2013, which alleged a history of sexual harassment during his period as a party official. However, no action was taken against him as it was found there was insufficient evidence to proceed.

where the car is waiting for him at Paddington. There is no car. He is furious. Texts his private secretary. Why is there no car? None are available, he's told. Try the government car service. She comes back: 'None available. Get a taxi, we will reimburse you.'

'I'm not queuing for a taxi on a Sunday night, I'll go on the Tube instead,' he says. We can for the first time feel the panic: ministers are not meant to travel on the Tube with classified documents. At this point she wakes up to the fact that they might be blamed if H is mugged by a member of Al Qaeda and starts apologising profusely. H says it would be interesting to see a log of where all the FCO cars were that night. With the civil servants, he suspects.

4 March

H's private secretary comes into his office: 'Minister, drop everything, an urgent question on Syria has just come in and you are taking it as the Foreign Secretary is away.'

'What? You're bloody joking.'

He has two hours to mug up on a highly sensitive subject which is way outside his brief. He tells me all he sees is a big hole in the ground into which his political career is about to be sucked. He describes his life as being rather like a house of cards: it could collapse at any moment. He is certain that this could be the moment.

The question is tabled about three minutes before the deadline by arch anti-interventionist troublemaker John Baron, who is anxious to caution the government against arming opposition forces in Syria, fearful that weapons could fall into the hands of terrorists. Baron knows full well the Foreign Secretary is in Mali and is presumably taking it to the wire to cause difficulty.

In parliament the MP for Basildon and Billericay – who H calls Baron John on account of his tendency towards self-importance – complained that both sides in the conflict had been accused of committing atrocities, with 'credible reports' of Islamist extremists 'fighting alongside rebels'. H manoeuvres himself well through the difficulty by saying UK aid would involve only 'non-lethal equipment and technical assistance', but deep down he knows that Hague is up for arming the rebels and it could be just a matter of time.

In the lobby he is talking to Richard Benyon when Baron comes into range. 'I'm just going to tell that man that he is a complete cunt—'

'No, you're not,' says Benyon. 'You haven't got the nerve.'

'Just watch me!'

H storms over, but as he starts his onslaught, Baron cuts him short, puts his two hands on Hugo's shoulders and says, 'You did an excellent job in there, well done!'

'Oh, do you think so?' says H, retreating.

'Yes, very well done. Very assured performance.'

'Oh, well, thank you very much, John.'

When he gets back to Benyon, he asks: 'How did it go?'

'Not according to plan. Flattery may have intervened.'

I hear Downing Street has subsequently made an official complaint to John Bercow, who has regularly started to slip these questions in at the last minute, no doubt to cause the government discomfort.

Later that evening a Green Chip dinner, the Commons dining club set up by Cameroons for Cameroons. Lots of laughs. Then Greg (Barker) starts to choke on a lump of meat. When, despite much coughing, the meat refuses to slide down his gullet, Philip Dunne takes him out onto the terrace to perform the Heimlich manoeuvre. H and Rory Stewart go along to see how they are doing. 'Blimey,' says H, 'those Japanese tourists coming down the Thames on that boat must be putting their new Samsung Galaxy cameras into overdrive . . . public schoolboys buggering each other on the Commons terrace. It must be confirming everything they ever thought about the English.'

12 March

There is a nasty nip in the air, and that's outside. Inside the
Commons it is decidedly chillier. Attend the Commonwealth
Day reception. Get Alan Duncan's version of a meeting with the
Ministers of State (Hugo missed it) at 10 Downing Street, and
how marvellous Mark Francois was. I hear a completely different
version from inside No. 10: 'He's a complete idiot!' and 'Useless,
the lot of them. Only one or two will ever make it to cabinet level.'

H has dinner in the Commons, and it seems everyone is in a
corner plotting against Dave and George. He passes a *Newsnight*
journo outside the Strangers' Bar, trying unsuccessfully to get
something out of Eleanor Laing and Liam Fox, who yesterday
made an unhelpful speech calling for radical change in economic
strategy. 'Well, give me the names on that list . . . ' Fox is saying,
clearly calling the journalist's bluff about other plotters.

At dinner, Greg Barker tells the group that the Ministers of State
had told Dave he lacked a narrative. D bounced back with the one
about how we have to keep pace with the global economy and be
on the side of the strivers, but Greg says – and he is one of Dave's
most loyal supporters – it feels as if he never listens to any of them,
and that is their gripe.

H is spoiling for a fight, and when the division bell goes he
catches up with Sarah Wollaston, the MP for Totnes. She has
been splashed over the front page of the *Telegraph*, saying DC is
'running out of time' to rid the party of its 'posh, male and white'
image. In the article she calls on the Prime Minister to reshuffle
his 'inner circle' before May's local elections. Hugo rants at her,
asking her who actually gains from these comments she makes. It
was taken out of context, she complains. Wakey-wakey, says Hugo,
that's what journalists do!

'Women like me will never vote Conservative at the next election,' she says.

'Er, Sarah, but you are a Conservative!' (Or not, as the case
may be.) Then Hugo asks what exactly would she do differently.

'I don't know,' she says, 'I'm not the economist!' – i.e. another one who is minded to say nothing useful at all in the most forthright way possible.

She and H have a history that goes back to the time when she decided to stop supporting Simon Day, a long-standing local politician and family friend who had clocked up thirty years or more of public service. H told her at the time that this was an inappropriate way for someone in her position to behave; that loyalty and hard work should not be dismissed out of hand. They also had a difference of view on who they backed for police commissioner. Hugo's choice won through. She sees all this as H briefing against her.

19 March

Another bad day for my darling. Two Westminster Hall debates, one in the morning on trade then one in the afternoon on Bangladesh, which he knows nothing about. Warsi is away, kissing the feet of the new pope at his inauguration. Then, at five, he is flying out to India for a twenty-four-hour round trip to sign a twenty-year contract to provide liquefied natural gas to Gujarat.

Then, as if it couldn't get worse, Bercow, who loves hauling ministers and prime ministers to the Commons to answer urgent questions by backbenchers at the drop of a hat, puts out another summons. David, who spent two days in Brussels last week in talks with other European leaders, discussing issues including the arms embargo on Syria, decided it wasn't worth his while to make a statement in the Commons so passed the honour on to Hugo, except that this honour should have gone to Lidington as MoS for Europe, who was there, except he wasn't there, he was away, and H had only an hour to prepare. Poor little H was left to explain Dave's absence, and was ridiculed by the usual headbangers such as Bill Cash. He did his best, tried to excuse his friend the absentee and told those gathered there, who were already in a disruptive and unsettled mood, that it was just a talking exercise and that nothing 'exciting' had occurred. This didn't satisfy anyone, of course, including arch-troublemaker Peter Bone, who asked my husband, 'Can you confirm that you were at the meeting?' *Of course he bloody wasn't at the meeting, bonehead.* Still they taunted and teased, like unengaged classroom pupils up against a weak and incompetent teacher. A clearly ironic few words about his performance later came from Simon Hoggart of the *Guardian*: 'I want to praise Mr Swire to the skies for his dazzling exposition of a topic he clearly knew almost nothing about.'

13 April

Chaffcombe

We opened up the hive with Ray (King) who helps us with our bees. It felt like we were entering a church or crematorium for a funeral. One layer after the next, nothing living, nothing operative. A faithful huddle of dead bees around the corpse of their queen. The colony should have been building up at this time of year. The verdict of the post-mortem, which comes from Ray, is that it is the disease nosema; he points at the staining at the top of the brood frames; 'Look at the excreta,' he says. Then he shows us the honey, which proves there was no shortage of food.

What to do? Ray says we will need to take out the frames, clean them up, scrape them out, re-wax with new foundation and make enough room to put a nucleus in. He has a nucleus, he says, which has overwintered; we can have it for £195. Deal, we say.

18 April

Thatcher got a tremendous send-off yesterday. The occasion was traditional and proud and patriotic and intrinsically British. She is now truly a mythical historical figure. I have had low-level depression since she died, as has my mother. She was such an essential part of our lives, and for so long; I barely remember a time she was not in it at some level.

Sir John in hospital having a back operation, which was followed by a prostate operation so he could not make the funeral, but my mother went, sat next to Heseltine, and said it was extraordinarily moving. The overwhelming emotions were also too much for George O, who was very visibly moved to tears. And they weren't any old tears, they were fat, glistening globules of lachrymosity, leaving him red-cheeked, blotched and bare. Cynics said it was put on, of course. But no, George does bleed when pricked, really, he does.

The thing that has really got my goat is the fact that Sir John is not in the Lords. In a week when solemnity and grief have lain alongside her achievements, it suddenly seems totally unjust that my father is the only one of his era not to make it. I ask my father about it over dinner and he laughs; he says he doesn't mind at all, that it's much more distinguished to be a knight and really, life peers are just lobby fodder now, but it still pisses me off.

Unbeknown to me, Hugo is feeling exactly the same way. Furious. He has independently had a word with Kate and also texts George, who replies:

'Is that because your wife wants to become an honourable?'

'Does that mean you consider her dishonourable?'

'NO! NO! NO!' G texts back in a panic.

30 April

H feeling overweight, out of condition and irritable. A beautiful walk through St James's Park, which he does every morning now, lifts his spirits briefly; spring is about to be sprung and the blossoms will be at their very best over the next couple of weeks. His diary, which has back-to-back meetings, induces silent rage. He orders 10 per cent of all meetings to be cut immediately, with more cuts to come. His private secretary responds and offers to remove two superficial meetings over the next ten days, neither of which were remotely important nor relevant in the first place.

Lunch in a restaurant in Buckingham Place, near Swire House; H arrives early. On the Indian High Commissioner's arrival, H leaps to his feet and immediately knocks over his tomato juice, soaking his trousers and shoes. Over lunch he asks what most irritates the High Commissioner about the UK. 'Everything!' comes his shock reply and then he caveats it by adding: 'The family should always be able to disagree.' H says the relationship is and remains a tricky one on account of our imperial past. For the new generation of Indians, this is all ancient history and of little relevance in their rush towards globalisation. For the High Commissioner's generation the wounds are still raw, and resentment is never far below the surface.

Of course, H can't resist white wine at lunch, which makes him acidic and even more grouchy in the afternoon.

12 May

Sunday night, Hugo sitting doing his box. Alexander Hesketh's words are always ringing in his head: 'Remember they are always the enemy, dear boy.' Hugo is looking at papers which apparently quote his words at some meeting, except that he has absolutely no memory of saying any of them. Then there is a piece in his red box stressing how brilliant the civil service is. Ho hum.

I deeply resent that he is lost to me for a good four hours on a Sunday night, and every night if he is home, working on the red box, his new and old mistress. I very much remember the same thing occurring with my father. The first poem I ever wrote as a child was all about the deafening silence in the kitchen as he worked away at his papers. How did I end up with the same life?

17 May

In the president's tent with Kate Hoey at the Devon County Show. 'It's absolutely extraordinary. I haven't seen a single face belonging to the ethnic minorities since coming here,' she says to me. Kate is MP for Vauxhall and has a team of five who deal purely with immigration issues. She is placed next to Francis Fulford, Lord of the Manor of Great Fulford and a well-known mouthy Devon character whose soubriquet is 'Fucker Fulford' on account of his over-use of expletives. He is wearing a filthy tweed suit with gaping moth holes and his hair is greasy and long. Francis's prejudices and outspoken views are somewhere to the right of Genghis Khan, so putting him next to Kate was always going to be high risk. At one point I cast a glance over in their direction, only to have Kate roll her eyeballs back at me in complete exasperation. I don't fare much better, getting a rather elderly gentleman by the name of Williams, who has some estate near Launceston and who bangs on about how David has abandoned his core support.

On Northern Ireland, Kate, who is from the Province, moans about Theresa Villiers: she tells me the Unionists have put in an official complaint. Theresa apparently attended some tea party the other day and spent the entire event sitting down, refusing to talk to anyone. She completely lacks social graces, which are a prerequisite for a secretary of state, and never more so than in Northern Ireland, which is still very old-fashioned in its attitudes.

George Lopes is this year's show president. His son is married to the Duchess of Cornwall's daughter Laura; his wife, Sarah, is an Astor, and was High Sheriff of Devon. One of their daughters works for Kate Hoey, hence her presence here. George gets up to speak, trembling in anticipation of delivering the president's oration; he is clutching a twenty-page document which fills the room with absolute dread. When he starts to speak his voice is a county version of an older Dirk Bogarde; he has a sweeping mane of black hair which his hand regularly irons over to smooth. His speech is all about gourmet food, estate management, eating in posh restaurants in France and family breakdown based on a lack of high quality ingredients finding their way into the households of those in a lower socioeconomic bracket, of which he clearly has very limited knowledge other than from the beating fraternity.

It went something like this: 'Sarah and I like to go to France – French way of life, like going to restaurants, you know the sort, very posh ones. Not long before we run out of things to say to each other and I get out a book, you know, something like *Fast Food Nation* . . . '

His wife, next to Hugo, hisses in his ear: 'Not true! The bastard: I'll get him for that.'

He proceeds to slag off the National Trust, Woodland Trust and RSPB, 'with whom we work very closely on the estate in Scotland, and it's particularly nice to see the chairman of the Game Conservancy Trust here today'. (Clearly with whom he works very closely on his grouse stocks.)

We are then treated to a vignette of life in Britain 2013 as he sees it.

'Mother comes home, puts a fiver on the table. Son comes home, no mother: probably gone out to work. No dinner. Takes the fiver. One quid on a McDonald's hamburger. Four quid on beer. Probably doesn't even bother coming home. Nothing for him there . . . '

He contrasts this with his early life in London: 'Worked in a dungeon in the city for a year. Didn't earn a penny, came home and bought an estate. Dreamt of coming home to . . . ' He stutters, I assume because he can't say mother's cooking: he is remembering a chef was involved.

'Where my brother and father and I always used to have a fight to lick the Devon cream from the silver spoon in the silver jug on the way out of the dining room.'

He touches briefly on politics: 'Taxation, changes to estate cottages, never know when they are going to be needed again, but I bemoan the fact that the countryside we celebrate is being parcelled up into tiny parcels of thirty acres, where people go and build bungalows. I'm reliably informed by a friend –' he looks at Kate '– this has happened already in Ireland, and is happening all around me in South Devon.'

H and I look at each other in amazement. You couldn't make it up even if you tried. But then we are many miles from London after all.

18 May

Texts between Andrew Mitchell and H:

AM (8:33 p.m.): I am sitting listening to David Lidington in your lair (FCO). He is talking about Europe. It may be time to walk the plank.

AM (8:41 p.m.): We have just spent 10 minutes on European integrated transport but now mercifully moved on to environment issues.

H (8:44 p.m.): What on earth are you doing there on a Friday night?

AM (8:46 p.m.): We have now moved on to models of differentiated integration.

AM (8:49 p.m.): He's now welcoming Merkel's comments on European science policy.

AM (8:51 p.m.): We are now listening to European competences and urging a cross-European debate. 25 minutes down and I've a dreadful feeling he's only just getting into his stride.

AM (9:17 p.m.): We are now on the pluses of qualified majority voting.

H (9:28 p.m.): Wait till you get to weighted support on the upland's environmental stewardship . . . he should reach it in the next hour or so . . .

AM (9:30 p.m.): We are currently cruising through Eurobank fiscal neutrality – pros and cons.

AM (10:30 p.m.): We are onto subsidiary and the govt's negotiating position now so I think he's getting into his stride.

AM (11:29 p.m.): On now to Treaty Competences. A lot of arm waving about.

> H (11:34 p.m.): Any mention at all of WTO appointment or OECD agenda? Disappointed he hasn't touched on the EEAS budget yet but am sure he'll get there eventually . . . that is if he isn't orbiting by then from all the aerodynamic arm rotations.

> H (11:39 p.m.): Do you really want to be a commissioner that badly??

AM (11:41 p.m.): We are still on budgetary discipline and the importance of the Maastricht criteria at the moment. One appreciates how Captain Scott must have felt.

AM (12:47 a.m.): Deep into an analysis of the effects of the Lisbon Treaty now but think he could be moving on to Schengen. Could the SAS be sent in to rescue us? Where is DD [David Davis] when one needs him?

AM (9:03 a.m.): As dawn broke – with arms flailing he's passionately defending the social chapter and the right of free movement of people.

> H (9:23 a.m.): When does his speech proper commence?

AM (9:25 a.m.): It commenced at 20:30 last night in the Durbar Court! It peaked during the darkest hour before dawn. Castro eat your heart out!

22 May

Bloody incredible. The private-secretary replacement process is in full flow. Pages and pages of documents from William's private secretary about how Hugo should take one particular candidate – H had asked for a shortlist of five. The PS insists that no one had put in for the job and H would be foolish to allow someone of this grade to slip through the net. In other words, here they are again, manipulating and controlling the ministers by planting their own people.

We have dinner with Sir John, who said when he was in the MOD the same thing happened to him. He insisted that they went for someone from a lower grade. There was a huge fight about it, but he won in the end and said recruit went on to become the top civil servant of his generation. I look through the sole candidate's CV, which is extraordinarily long. It's certainly impressive, but full of the most ridiculous clichéd rhetoric about how she saw the job. H just wants someone who is pleasant to be around, intelligent, does not put hurdles in his way, someone who is not constantly conspiring against him and who laughs at his jokes. Simple. This one just looks like his current PS. The next morning H goes to see Hague's private secretary. 'This is all very Sir Humphrey,' H says. 'Surely you can do better.' The PS looks a little crestfallen, then comes up with another idiotic idea. He says Mark Simmonds is also looking for a PS: why doesn't H interview his candidate too? As the senior minister, he has first choice and Simmons his reject. And, of course, the civil servants will get both their candidates in place. H doesn't believe he is hearing this.

24 May

George's birthday party in the flat at 11 Downing Street last night. All the mateocracy truly there. Catch Dave and H laughing uproariously in a corner so go up to them to find out what is so funny. They are talking about male members; notably Andrew Roberts's. H says he knows someone who, having witnessed it unfurl, was still in recovery. He then goes on to Michael Gove's – apparently his is pretty impressive too.

'Rather like a slinky that comes down the stairs before the rest of the body,' he adds.

Dave thinks this is hilarious. (You must understand our generation have a fond attachment to the slinky.) H goes on to lead another of those male discussions about which women in politics are beddable and which aren't, and I leave him to his laddish moment. And why not? So much of his, and I suspect their, normal humour and male libido is under a regime of political repression.

Thankfully, by the time George comes up to them they have moved on to the Foreign Office, and have a collective moan. Every time H says he has recently visited a country – mostly fly-infested, dictator-led, mineral-rich Graham Greene-type ones – Dave and George in a simultaneous groan say, 'What on earth did you go there for?' H mournfully replies that the civil servants don't like him around much, and prefer him to be orbiting the globe.

'In fact, I could be a tax exile, the number of days I spend out of the country.' He adds he sometimes feels like Carlton-Browne of the FO, the inept diplomat sent to former British colonies that have been abandoned for fifty years; ones that are now attracting the attention of superpowers and mercenaries.

23 June

That perfectly dogged and tiresome Simon Walters of the *Mail on Sunday* has been chasing H all week. The story is that the FCO has leased a very expensive flat for the consul-general on the Peak in Hong Kong from Swire Pacific, and that somehow this has been secured by a family member, one Hugo Swire, who also happens to be the minister for Asia. We agree it writes itself. H tries to point out via the FCO press officer that the Swires do indeed own chunks of Asia, and much of its real estate, so it would be surprising if they did not come into the equation somewhere along the line. The reality, however, is that H descends from a branch of the family born with chips on their shoulders, not ships, as he is fond of saying. He explains to the press office with considerable patience that he has never worked for Swire Pacific, or benefited from their largesse, and that his shares – all three of them – are in a blind trust. Walters then comes back, determined that I have shares in a company I've never heard of, called Opus, which when I google it appears to be a property investment company, again owned by Swire Pacific . . . I wish!

By Saturday night, Walters just can't pin it down, and rings up the head press officer claiming in his frustration that this is an 'FO stitch-up'. The problem is all the MPs and the hacks think H is one of the zillionaire Swires; in this scenario, there would indeed be a huge number of shares lying about, and in most circumstances these shares are usually transferred to the wife to avoid embarrassment.

H is now determined to torment Walters. When H next passes him in a Westminster corridor, he will tap the side of his nose and say, 'You're looking too close to home. Try the Cayman Islands, Simon.' He intends to get David Ruffley and Greg Barker, who talk to him all the time, to send him down some blind alleys. Just for the sport of it, you understand.

14 July

Kate comes down to Chaffcombe. We take the children canoeing on the Tamar. It's the most unbelievably hot day. We have a picnic and even swim in the murky depths.

At dinner, H tells a story of when the whips came in to see Dave with George Young. There was talk about who should move up and down. Who should be sacked. Hugo's name comes up, they tell how he had a bad session at the despatch box and that he has a lofty and arrogant air in the tearoom, that he's not liked. David is apparently extremely agitated, 'I've already sacked him once, I'm not doing it again! NEXT!' he barks back at them. When he comes out, he is fuming, mostly because he knows that, really, it's all about him and the mateocracy and how they want to undermine his supporters and friends. K says this all rings true.

Pillow talk to H that night: 'Are you lofty and arrogant with the backbenchers?'

'Yes,' he says, 'mostly because the bulk of them are a complete bunch of tossers!'

5 September

A good summer all round. Saffron does well in her GCSEs. She is at Reading Festival when the results come through, and she rings us up. The Prime Minister answers the phone (we are staying with them in Polzeath again): 'Well done, Chardonnay, well done.' We are both so proud of her.

The morning we leave I am having breakfast with Sam and Dave, and the whole subject of Syria comes up. There has just been a terrible sarin gas attack on civilians outside Damascus, with many children killed. Sam is overwhelmed with emotion, holding back the tears. She goes on a rant about posh people at dinner parties who call it a civil war, and she says it's not a civil war at all, it's an act of aggression on behalf of Assad and he needs to be stopped.

I ask whether she would send her son there to fight. She goes silent. I say that David is in effect father of the nation, and that is the decision he has to weigh up. He dismisses this immediately by saying we have a professional army and it is their job to fight, that I cannot look at it like that. But I do look at it a little bit like that, because a) I'm a mother and all soldiers have mothers; b) it's how the electorate see it; and c) none of this is in our interest.

I know it's not worth getting into a debate with Samantha

when she is like this; it's best to roll with it and let her expend her energy. I cautiously make some comparisons to Bosnia. Dave says we should have gone into Syria earlier but Obama was too much of a wuss to act. I know something is brewing inside him; he is finding it difficult, standing on the sidelines, letting these atrocities take place. The day after we leave Obama calls him and the rest, they say, is history.

Dave is in a lot of pain: he has a prolapsed disc and has to go back to London via Oxford for an injection. As a result, he is not his usual energetic self on holiday, which comes as something of a relief to Hugo and me.

16 October

Dinner at Crosby Hall with Moran. He tells H and me that he once invited Prince Charles for dinner and the Palace rang up to ask whether the menu would be suitable. 'Well, I've got Michel Roux cooking,' says Moran. The official persists, 'Yes, but what are you feeding him?' Moran does his investigations and comes back: 'Lamb: we are giving him lamb.' The official then goes on to say that the lamb should be sourced from a specific farm in Wales. Moran is exasperated but agrees to ship it in specially. When HRH finally sits down at dinner and peruses the menu, he turns to Moran: 'How interesting! That is the farm I get all my lamb from too. It's so terribly good, don't you think?' I have heard numerous stories along these lines about Charles, and the trivial preparations that need to be made in advance of any visit. It's quite extraordinary that he behaves like that in this day and age.

17 November

H away for ten days in Sri Lanka for the Commonwealth conference, and then on to the Maldives. The Commonwealth has taken an enormous risk in allowing Sri Lanka to host its Heads of Government Meeting, as an endorsement of the host is unavoidable. The current prime minister, Mahinda Rajapaksa, craves this endorsement and does not deserve it. The evidence of crimes against humanity by his troops during and since the climax of the Sri Lankan civil war, collected mainly by British journalists for Channel 4's *Sri Lanka's Killing Fields* documentary, is appalling and authentic beyond doubt. When David and Hugo watch the film, they are equally horrified. In this context, it has been a difficult summit for all in the FCO and the line they take.

As Minister for the Commonwealth Hugo's job is something of a test: the Commonwealth is, after all, a post-war, post-imperial construct of fifty-three countries well capable of ambushing their former colonial manager. Hugo can only attempt strenuous British diplomacy in his attempts to manage expectations, but I imagine he is everything they despise: white, posh, confident, and appearing like a representative of Britain's imperial past. And from what I can see, there is little he can gain; the modern-day Commonwealth can look like a private members' club for corrupt leaders with almost a third of its member states having been accused of serious human rights abuses. Homosexuality is illegal in three-quarters of them, and in most the police run rampant. In the Maldives, for God's sake, a fifteen-year-old rape victim was sentenced to a hundred lashes for fornication. In Gambia, which left the Commonwealth, complaining of 'neo-colonial' standards, police recently rounded up a thousand alleged witches. They were beaten in prison and then forced to drink hallucinogenic potions to drive out the evil spirits. Still, H remains positive; he is convinced that an umbrella of associations that strengthens links between advanced and developing countries is a good thing.

That's not to say these conferences are not testing:

H texts (14 November):

Stuck in very bad-tempered drafting session with 52 other countries and been ganged up against by all of them – and there are a helluvalot of them) The Africans on Zimbabwe in particular. OMG XXX

H (15 November):

Back in conference hall which I left at 2.30 am. Hoping not for a repeat.

Then:

President of Tanzania in next door chair has a cough. That's my latest news.

Prime minister of Singapore just gone to sleep.

(I ask if there is any hot totty to keep him awake.)

H: None. President Zuma now in full flow.

Me: Don't fall asleep yourself you are not important enough!

H: Prime minister of Tonga also now sound asleep

H: And now St Kitts and Nevis . . .

Me: ZZZZZZZZZZZZ WAKE UP!

H: Zuma just got caught out not paying attention . . .

Me: It's all those wives of his! He probably can't handle more than one woman at a time!

H: Know the feeling

Me: Mmmm

H: Final bulletin. Zuma now sound asleep as is his neighbour from the Solomon Islands . . .

H: Sorry . . . and president of Namibia now.

Me: Hilarious. Do you ever get the feeling that all this is pointless?

H: I do get the feeling that my mobile is monitored.

Me: Yes, thought you could be a bit sexier!

1–4 December

Hugo to China with the PM and more than 130 British companies. The second three-day visit to the country. H is sitting up front in the privately chartered Virgin plane, opposite the new Trade Minister, Lord (Ian) Livingston, formerly CEO of BT. H says Ian is cut from a very different cloth to that of his predecessor, Stephen Green, and is a straight-talking Glaswegian. Next door to him is a loquacious woman who started something called the Cambridge Satchel Company. 'To hear her talk, you'd think she'd invented penicillin.'

On arrival in Beijing the PM, plus ministers, head to the Great Hall of the People, where he inspects a guard of honour made up of giants, and then there is a state banquet. H gets to sit next to the Foreign Minister and mercifully, as he is tired, they gobble up course after course at breakneck speed, shake hands, burp and leave. More meetings with the PM and others, then H has a short catch-up with his oldest friend, Michael Cecil, at a hotel. Mike says it is where Tony Blair and Wendi Murdoch supposedly first 'got it on'. Blair has always denied any affair.* A quick walk around Tiananmen Square, then off to the airport and down to Shanghai.

A huge lunchtime banquet in Shanghai the next day, which is well received by the Chinese, not least when one of the horse puppets from *War Horse* prances around the hall. After signing a mutual assistance treaty – though he cannot for the life of him

---

* He has stated that any allegations of an affair with Wendi Murdoch are 'categorically false'.

remember who we have pledged to assist, when or why – H heads off to the campus of the new Wellington College Shanghai, which is a replica of the original school in Berkshire. The purpose of his visit is to unveil the wing that is to be the culture and sports centre, and will also house the cafeteria. It is to be called the Hugo Swire Centre – I jest not. H makes an emotional speech, but rather ruins things by almost throwing himself to the floor when, without warning, the celebratory firecrackers went off and he thought they were under attack. When he stood up he dusted himself down, coughed and carried on, which is what good diplomats do. H was then introduced to the director of sport, the former England football player Carlton Palmer. They were well matched as H had never heard of him and he certainly had never heard of H.

The following morning H, having sat up too late drinking in the hotel with the likes of Karren Brady, has an early flight to Chengdu. His first port of call is an Aids clinic. It's a big success, and then he rushes off to witness the signing of an educational memorandum of understanding, following which he joins the PM at a ceremony to unveil a plaque at WE City, a vast residential project by Hongkong Land, part of Jardine Matheson. On stage are DC, Henry Keswick, Adam Keswick and H. Afterwards Ed Llewellyn says, 'We've just witnessed history in the making. A Swire congratulating Jardines,' to which DC replies, 'Yes, but we had to find the poorest Swire to do it.'

'Damnable cheek,' says H.

2014

6 January

Nice start to 2014 in H's inbox:

> To The Right Honourable Cowardly Low Life C.unt,

> Dear Low Life Cowardly C.unt,

> I am sending this to Members in The Commons.

> I will do it in a couple of sentences.

> You are a morally bankrupt toxic low life c.unt.

Next trip for H: the Falklands. This time he is taking Simon Heffer, who is writing an article for the *Mail* about it. Heffer arrives at Brize Norton fresh from Essex. H describes him as 'all tweeded up, looking like a prosperous bookie on his way to a stalking holiday in Scotland in the 1850s'. H, as previously arranged, has smuggled on board a picnic from Itsu, which they fall upon like hungry vultures during the never-ending flight. Uncomfortable seats which barely recline. H sits one away from Heffer. The seat between them is mercifully empty. He sleeps. Snores. His nose collapses onto his many chins.

First stop is Ascension Island. They are met off the plane by the agent, who is an FCO official and charming to boot. A frightening drive up a hill to his bungalow, which is officially the house of the non-resident governor, who lives on St Helena. A magical place with panoramic views, says H. 'I like this place, as does Simon, who says he could happily spend time here reading, writing and reflecting.'

Back onto the plane a few hours later, and a similar distance on to the Falklands. On their approach Typhoon fighter jets appear on either side of the plane to escort them – or rather H, as the minister – in. They land at Mount Pleasant and are met by the governor, garrison commander and team. H says he immediately gets the point of these islands, marooned as they are in a hostile environment, geographically and politically. Government House is perfect – exactly as it should be. A good position, fluttering Union flag and the scene of Rex Hunt's last stand, with the detritus of war in the kitchen garden, a legacy of the Argie attack in 1982.

Over the coming days they are entertained royally, with endless meetings, receptions and dinners. H says it is exactly like being in a fishing lodge on the west coast of Scotland which is run on rivers of alcohol. They fly over West Falkland, meet some Kelpers, the nickname given to the islanders, some businessmen and the military. They go to a steak night at the local pub, entertain visiting Uruguayan politicians, hold a press conference, tour the school and answer mundane questions from selected students. H also attends the Falkland Islands government meeting and lectures on the importance of changing their judicial processes. Simon apparently loves every minute of it. Officials, particularly the MOD and Philip Hammond, are nervous that Paul Dacre has put him up to write a piece saying this horrid coalition government has abandoned the islands and run down their defences. Heffer sees for himself that nothing could be further from the truth. They visit the cairn to mark where H. Jones* was gunned down, lay a wreath in the pouring rain at the Argentinian cemetery and then in bright sunlight another one at the British Cemetery at San Carlos Bay, which my father inaugurated.

They leave reluctantly, and not before visiting a large colony

---

* Lt-Col Herbert Jones, VC, OBE, killed in action during the Battle of Goose Green, Falkland Islands.

of penguins, from whom Heffer is 'indistinguishable'. On their return they stop off again at Ascension, and this time it is early evening. They are taken to the beach to see some green-backed turtles giving birth – a very moving experience, apparently. 'All in all, a huge success and Hef and I vow to return one day. With you, I hope!'

2 February

The West Hill AGM.

The annual reunion in the Bierkeller, in this case West Hill Village Hall. Hugo greeted by Pamela Marks, who organises all the events. H tries his usual bluff hale and hearty approach but she is quick out of the traps and eyes him warily.

'Well! I'm surprised you deigned to visit us tonight, we thought you had disappeared off the face of the planet.' (He has. Mostly with all his travelling.) 'I don't believe we have seen you for a year.'

He tries a charm offensive, none of which works, so rather irritated retreats saying she clearly hasn't been looking in the right place. The wrong place being the UKIP manifesto. She is followed by one of Hugo's regular correspondents, who is already looking hostile. She says that he has a cheek even turning up at the AGM. When he asks why, she complains volubly about everything, only just stopping short of holding him personally responsible for the flooding and the weather. How long he can tolerate these dragons breathing their fire down his back I just don't know.

The official business is called to order. The chairman, when checking if Hugo is ready to speak, asks if he is 'ready to expose himself'. H repeats this to the audience and adds that although he is a Tory MP, they should not be unduly concerned as he intended to address them fully clothed. And some fell on stony ground.

AGM fine, the same officers elected to the same posts. Average age in their late seventies and early eighties. Money coming in DOWN, membership DOWN, events DOWN, interest in all things to do with immigration and Europe UP! No change there, then. Colonel Peter Morrison, late of the Royal Engineers, reads out the report of the West Hill Conservative Party Forum. CPFs are sent questionnaires by CCHQ, which they then debate and return, in the belief that they have direct input to the party manifesto. We actually suspect they are all placed in a dark corner, to be shredded at the first possible opportunity. West Hill maintains they are one of the most active CPFs, and this year is no different. They hate, in equal measure: foreigners, Europe, defence cuts, gay marriage, Liberals, the BBC, Germans, the Japanese, the coalition and garlic.

H gives them what for in his speech and takes no prisoners. He asks them whether any of them can name a single representative of UKIP other than Nigel Farage. There is silence. He asks them why the Conservative Party (i.e. them) always has to flagellate itself, even when things are going well. They look rather surprised as they always do, and rather hurt.

In the question and answer session a military type tells the audience that he had been in the Falklands, although long before the Argentinian invasion. In response, Hugo says he has visited the islands recently with Simon Heffer, who had been tasked to write that defences were inadequate, and the islanders felt under threat, but he had found the complete opposite.

'Well, that is completely wrong. They *are* exposed,' announces H's interlocutor.

'Er, no, I think you will find they are not.'

'If the Argentinians attack the airport the island will be overrun.'

Hugo is trying to keep calm: 'The Argentinians don't have that capability, and anyway, we have four new Typhoon aircraft which can outgun anything they have. Our defences are very good there.'

'Well, so you say, but this really is not the case.'

By this point H's patience is waning. 'With the greatest of respect, I read the intelligence reports every week and you do not.'

He can't get away soon enough, but not before a woman presses her twelve-point letter into his hand for some light bedtime reading. She focuses on broken promises made by Cameron, that he has not handed power back to the people like he said he would, especially in relation to planning; the EU is equally to blame for this, apparently. She blames the protection of beetle habitats for the flooding of the Somerset Levels; she blames Dave for removing our ancient laws of trespass by allowing fracking; and she says free speech has gone, citing the UKIP man who was pilloried when he said the recent floods were divine retribution for gay marriage.

Hugo screws up the letter, tosses it into the corner of his car and heads home for a large whisky. He is pretty certain that he has to give up politics. He has fallen out of love with these people, and they in turn have fallen out of love with him and his party. When a man has to go . . .

11 February

From: John Nott
Sent: 11 February 2014
To: Nott, Will; SASHA SWIRE
Subject: Floods.

My family has laughed at me for years because I have kept a boat on the top floor of Walpole street. Is it there Sasha? William is at a very low-lying area. What is he doing to prepare his house for a flood? Nothing I am sure. Ha ha Silly old man. Dad

(Sent from my iPad in a luxury hotel in Constantia, South Africa)

Dear Dad
    We are prepared – we have an inflatable dolphin in our cellar.

I bought it for Tabby when she was three. This should get 2 or 3 of the family out of the house safely.

We've also got 3 tins of Hillsdown All Day breakfast dated Dec 1999 which you gave us before the millennium when you were convinced an asteroid was going to hit earth.

What we don't have are any mini anti-radiation suits you were distributing out to certain (male only) grandchildren a few years ago. I'm not entirely sure what your current views on a dirty bomb threat are.

I see that Dawlish is now completely under water –

x

Will

Dad: Very funny. If you think that I intend to come down the Kings Road in my radiation suit to rescue your family, you are mistaken. I shall be selling water at £10 per bottle and further tins of all-day breakfast will cost £100 per tin. Don't come whimpering to me for help. Dad

27 February

All hell has broken loose in Northern Ireland. What's new? Peter Robinson has threatened to resign unless an inquiry is launched into the secret amnesty given to 187 Republican paramilitaries. As the First Minister in a power-sharing government, he was cross at being 'kept in the dark' about such an important issue. Theresa Villiers is holding crisis talks to prevent the coalition between the Democratic Unionist Party and Sinn Féin breaking down.

H is quite relaxed, throws a few unguarded comments to Simon Walters in the lobby (big mistake!) and comes home looking forward to dinner at Ishbilia with his two most favourite women: his wife and his mother, the Dowager. Except when he does get home I tell him that the BBC is reporting that thirty-eight letters granting

amnesty were sent out to 'on the runs' on his and Owen's watch.*
He gulps, sweats, tries to recall such letters ever crossing his desk
and calls Owen. Owen also can't recall much, seems to think this
would have been a devolved issue handled by the PSNI, but he is
ever so slightly nervous too. H puts a call in to Jonathan Caine,
who does not get back to him until the next morning. When he
does ring, they run through it together. Kate then calls from No. 10
and tells him not to tell the press anything. H says it's too late, he
has spoken to Simon Walters, then rings me to say he smells a rat,
given No. 10's interest. Later that day Julian King, the Northern
Ireland Office Director-General, calls. Later, H speaks to Owen,
who is angry. Says the *Telegraph* and Sky News are running stories
that he 'signed thirty-eight letters'. Not true, he maintains. The
thinking is that although ministers were 'told', they did not sign
any of the letters that went out. Owen also says he has received
a press release from No. 10 but was not consulted beforehand by
anyone, including the current Secretary of State. He is cross and
urges H to complain too, which he does, saying he and Owen
should be consulted on every move going forward. The government have set up a judicial inquiry. Owen says it's almost certain
he and H will have to testify. This has some way to run.

19 March

Dave calls Gove from Chequers to give him a bollocking. I'm told
he went ballistic when he read the interview in last week's *FT* in
which Gove attacked the 'preposterous' number of Etonians in
Dave's inner cabinet. Always one of Dave's Achilles heels. I'm
also told that Jo Johnson almost burst into tears when he read it;
the 'Eton thing' overshadowing his modernising credentials and
intellectual ability to do the job. Of course, Gove's aim, helped by

---

* 'On the run' letters guaranteed 187 IRA members, wanted in connection
  with the Troubles between 1969 and 1998, would not be prosecuted for
  any offence.

his wife in another article a fortnight ago, is to dent the chances of Boris Johnson succeeding Dave as party leader after the general election. *Look at me, folks, I'm not from a privileged background like George and Boris, I have a really good back story.* This was promptly followed by Sayeeda Warsi backing Gove when she appeared on a late-night TV show, by producing a mock front page with the headline 'Number 10 takes Eton Mess off the menu'. Trying to make a point about social mobility she said afterwards. Her own career mobility, more like.

Weekly morning meeting for ministers and the Foreign Secretary. Hague tells them to keep it short as it's budget day. Lidington kicks off on Ukraine, with the usual splaying of arms and swivelling eyeballs. H says Lidders is always keen to sit next to Hague, leaving Sayeeda virtually on the floor. H follows. Goes through his list: canvassing support for the motion of human rights in Sri Lanka, similar for North Korea, his trip to Latin America last week, meeting with the Commonwealth Secretary-General etc. When he gets to the end he says gravely, 'And I'm canvassing support for my new campaign.'

'Your new campaign?' asks Hague, intrigued, doing that humming thing of his afterwards.

H spells out the letters slowly: P . . . V . . . V . . . A . . . O . . . E . . . I.

It sounds like a derivative of Hague's PSVI (Preventing Sexual Violence in Conflict Initiative). He immediately perks up: 'What does it stand for, Hugo?' Hague asks in his ee-by-gum tyke way.

'Prevention of Verbal Violence Against Old Etonians Initiative.'

Warsi laughs. 'Ooo, I'll join that!'

'And you, Sayeeda, can be honorary patron.'

4 April

Dave helicoptered into the bee field at Chaffcombe to stay the night. Today, he is to re-open the Dawlish line after the appalling floods decided to bite a chunk out of the headland. He looks tanned, lean and happy.

'That's a very glamorous way to arrive for dinner,' I tell him.

We show him around: 'Sam would be so jealous! She'd love this place.'

I show him a barn. 'Oooo, you could put a snooker table in there!'

'I'm sorry?'

I mutter to H as he walks off, 'So Home Counties.'

'I heard that, Sasha!'

28 April

Because of transport logistics, I join H at this year's East Devon District Scouts' St George's Day parade in Sidmouth.

About four hundred Scouts, Cubs and Beavers are packed into Sidmouth Parish Church for the event, where we sit as local dignitaries next to the mayor and the 'toilet seats' – councillors Graham and Ann Liverton, who have secured this soubriquet as they are always popping up and down in town council meetings. In front of us stood a cross-eyed, happy-clappy, guitar-strumming Scout leader who belted out 'We are marching in the light of God' with alarming regularity, his repertoire obviously limited. This was followed by a rather large Beaver (Scout) encouraging us all to sing 'Our God is a great big God', and to do the actions: we were forced to reach for the ceiling (*he is higher than a skyscraper*, apparently) and then to hold our noses as we dived underwater for the line *he's deeper than a submarine* – which turned out to be good practice for what would occur later.

I meet Sidmouth's new rector, Philip Bourne, as we enter the church. He has decamped from the Green republic of Brighton and Hove, where things are a little more modern, with meat-free Mondays and transgender toilets.

'Yes, I was a little worried about making the switch,' he tells me. 'Mainly because when I was considering it, they told me there were no gays in Sidmouth.'

H pipes up: 'Guess how many votes I lost to UKIP when I supported gay marriage? You can only identify as a Christian around here if you are against homosexuality. Some of the religious right have completely disowned me: for many of them, I am just a bigoted hypocrite.'

'I can just imagine,' sighs the rector. He tells us of a new category, 'Mx', alongside Mr, Ms and Mrs on council forms in Brighton. This apparently prevents an unnecessary sense of exclusion and frustration at being forced to accept a title that doesn't reflect one's gender expression.

'I don't think we will be following suit in Sidmouth any time soon,' says H.

From the church the dignitaries, myself included, made our way through a back door to the seafront to take the salute. The only problem being there have been flash floods while we were in church and Sidmouth's water-carried waste, intended to be removed from the community through sewage pipes, not reintroduced to it, frothed up through the drains, forcing us to walk down the central strip of road to avoid the local residents' turds. Most alarmed was Graham Liverton, who was dressed in a symphony of green, including a brand-new pair of sage-coloured suede loafers. I turned to see him tip-toeing through it, wincing as he went. Think John Inman in *Are You Being Served?* with a bunch of pins in his mouth. By the time the Scouts filed by the smell was so horrendous that instead of raising their arms in salute they were pinching their noses and releasing long groans of agony as they passed.

'We're truly in the shit now with this one,' says Graham.

Meaning the town council, of course.

21 May

Mongolia

An early start for H, to fly up to visit the Rio Tinto Oyu Tolgoi mine in the south Gobi Desert. Arriving at Khanbumbat airport, he is taken to the vast mine and given an extensive briefing and tour. Rio Tinto are delighted by the publicity H's trip is giving them because they are locked in a major dispute with the Mongolian government and the sums involved potentially run to the billions.

Following lunch in the canteen he is taken to a ger, the Mongolian equivalent of a yurt, to meet some tribal elders. This involves huge protocol, in which H is rehearsed in order to avoid giving offence. He sits in the appointed place and it is not long before an elder hands him a snuff bottle with a little spoon. Not unlike a Hollywood dinner party. Greedily, he snorts an amount so large that it could have been the cremated ashes of a favourite camel for all H knows. He passes the bottle to his right, as required, whereupon he is handed a bowl brimming with foul-smelling milk. As he lifts it to his mouth the effects of the snuff come into play and he lets out an Olympic-sized sneeze, followed by another and another, and only just avoids spraying milk over the entire gathering. He leaves, sneezing and eyes streaming, as soon as he can.

Later he is taken to the nearest town, which is in reality a complex of gers and rough shelters a forty-minute drive from the mine in the Gobi Desert. This is all part of the Rio Tinto outreach programme, designed to show what jolly good people they are to those whose copper they are extracting in vast amounts. H is shown the latest example of their munificence, which is to bring over an Australian sheepshearer to show the locals how to shear a camel using electric shears rather than the blunt scissors they are used to. First the camel's head is tied to the bumper of a car, and its legs to another. The herder then pushes the camel over – a surprisingly easy thing to do – and then sets upon it with the shears. H has a go but is scared of cutting the camel, despite his best Vidal Sassoon strokes. This, of course, is really for the press and the Rio Tinto people are delighted to have shots of the British minister so actively engaged in this piece of company-sponsored social outreach. The Mongolians are amazed but not particularly fazed. As soon as their backs are turned, they revert to using their blunt scissors. The Australian sheepshearer is despondent and tells H he will be glad to return home as soon as possible.

7 June

I can only interpret this as a scramble for leadership. Clearly in a panic because Theresa May is romping ahead in the polls (way ahead of Boris, and even further ahead than Michael in a battle for the future leadership of the party), the Education Secretary has taken it on himself to get into a violent and now public argument with our cardboard Home Secretary. Not a good idea! His chosen means of warfare is to express his concerns, by talking to *The Times*, about a 'militant tendency' of extremist Muslims plotting to take over schools, adding he blames 'their influence on reluctance within Whitehall, especially in the Home Office, to confront extremism unless it develops into terrorism'. Ms May has retaliated by saying it's all his fault anyway, as he ignored the warnings. Another illustration of how Michael is a loose cannon; it is also illustrative of his annoying habit of wading into the affairs of other departments and upsetting colleagues. Michael's journalistic background often gets him into trouble (he briefed *The Times*, by the look of it, prompting the leaking of May's letter of complaint). Like many over-excitable journalists, he mistakes headlines for achievements. Dave is now banging their heads together by ordering Michael to apologise and Theresa to sack her closest adviser, Fiona Cunningham.

11 June

Morning meeting on sex trafficking and modern slavery with Theresa May. H says getting into the Home Office is a nightmare now security has been privatised: basically a bunch of clueless receptionists who don't know what they are doing. There is a fast track for departments associated with the Home Office written on the wall. H starts to walk down it, assuming the Foreign Office is associated by virtue of being another government department.

'NO VISITORS DOWN THERE!' someone shouts.

Hugo goes up to the desk. 'But I'm a Foreign Office minister, do I really need to be checked?'

'Yes, you are a visitor, aren't you?'

'But I am having a meeting with the Home Secretary.'

'All visitors have to be checked.'

H throws his hands up in the air and sits on a bench, and Fergus, H's private secretary, takes over. Ten minutes later: 'Is one of you Hugo?'

'Yes, that's me.'

'Put on this badge and follow me.'

The Home Secretary is late because of traffic. Those fat black-cab drivers are moaning about some app that is taking away their business and have blocked the whole of central London. Dumb move on their part, because now everyone knows the name of the app. Theresa arrives flustered. The room is full of ethical, Fair Trade worthies and officials who deal with sex trafficking. Everyone says who they are. When Hugo's turn comes, he turns his badge around. In large letters it says ESCORT REQUIRED.

'I don't want this to be misconstrued, particularly in this meeting.'

Theresa bursts out into spontaneous laughter. There is a stunned silence. No one has ever seen the woman smile before, let alone laugh. It feels historic.

This is followed later by a meeting between H and José Antonio Meade Kuribreña, Mexico's Foreign Minister, and the Prince of Wales to talk over the forthcoming royal/business delegation to Mexico. HRH is running late.

One of the burly policemen in the courtyard outside St James's Palace: 'You are not coming in here until the butler comes!'

H dislikes his aggressive tone but, already agitated by the Home Office debacle, he feels this could rapidly turn into an Andrew

Mitchell moment so pulls back. He is loitering on the pavement across the street, kicking a proverbial can, when he sees a diplomatic car with MEX 1 as its number plate drive up, speak to the policeman and then reverse. This is too much: H goes up to the brick of a copper, who is donning a stab vest.

'Please don't tell me you have turned away the Foreign Minister of Mexico.'

'He's early. I've told him to come back!' he barks.

'He is not early, HRH is late. Is that how we treat visiting dignitaries? It's quite humiliating.'

'Did you hear me, sir? I said he's early.'

Hugo waits on the pavement until he is allowed entry. The same policemen are on the gates. They are rude and aggressive and know they can exploit their power. Heavily unionised, and probably Masons to boot. I don't know anyone in the Westminster village or its vicinity who has not been incensed by their arrogance. There was a time when you could confidently expect some courtesy, but not any more. It is clear that a significant minority of these officers see politicians as their enemy, and as a potential hazard to be dealt with aggressively. They are being told by their union bosses not to be taken advantage of when they are doing precisely that to the politicians. For immediate compliance, they have clearly been instructed to use stern, unambiguous commands that require no interpretation, but this is not the way to handle MPs, visiting diplomats or civil servants. It is a disaster because it only leads to clashes like the one involving Mitchell, and then it becomes a them-and-us situation with junior officers closing ranks and lying about incidents. It is no wonder the police have never been held in lower esteem than they are today.

When the meeting finally takes place, the atmosphere is jovial and friendly. H says Prince Charles has sausage-like fingers, which he can't take his eyes off. They chat about beavers.

'What is your view about beavers on the River Otter? I'm getting a lot of grief from the Goldsmith boys about culling them,' says Hugo.

'In Scotland they are causing absolute devastation in the rivers,' says HRH. He is clearly concerned about the whole rewilding agenda, as are so many of us.

Pepe, the Mexican Foreign Minister, does all the right protocol things: we are so looking forward to having you in Mexico, blah blah blah, we love Hugo, blah blah blah. Then he asks about the business delegation. HRH looks distinctly uncomfortable, as if business is a dirty word; he looks to H to bail him out. Hugo coughs in a timely way. 'His Royal Highness does not really focus on the business side of things; that's left to the government minister.'

The butler arrives with tea and Duchy Originals biscuits, and they all sit down.

HRH to Meade: 'Do you like the biscuits?'

'Oh yes, very nice, Your Royal Highness.'

'I make them, you know.'

'You make them?'

'Yes, we have rows of them in the supermarkets in this country. They are very popular over here, you know, very popular.'

'Yes, they are very tasty.'

The PoW turns to his private secretary: 'We must give him a packet to take home with him.'

12 June

I am increasingly irritated by how David, George and Kate have this monopoly on people's careers in politics, using a completely erroneous set of criteria ('good back story', 'woman', 'ethnic', 'good on TV', 'too posh', 'too mad', 'ghastly'). It's the politics of PR, not the politics of serious government. From one conversation to the next I hear them move their players around the chess board, thinking they are oh so clever by placing him here or her there, often without any knowledge of how they will perform, when half the time they are dismissing a whole generation of MPs, mostly men, who do not tick their cosy boxes and who are often more capable and more experienced.

One minute Von Schnapps* is ghastly and has to go; the next he is not so bad after all, when he delivers a good by-election result. Greening they loathe but must keep in place because she is a woman. Javid gets Culture because they like the fact that he's Muslim and his father was a bus driver in Bristol. Hugo will never go further, because he is male, white, privileged. There is absolutely no reason he could not be Secretary of State for Northern Ireland or Overseas Development Secretary, but they simply won't let it happen.

13 June

The Angelina–Hague roadshow has finally come to an end, and not a moment too soon for H, who was forced to play a B role – or was it a Z role? Certainly a poorly paid extra – for four days. As Rome burnt – Russian tanks crossed the Ukrainian border, Iraq moved closer to a complete break-up, and ISIS forces continued to advance on Baghdad, chopping people's heads off as they went – Dave is seen dining at the Chiltern Firehouse on a date night with Sam, and Hague flanked by Brad Pitt and Angelina Jolie, the light bouncing off the Hollywood couple's stardom onto his sweaty bald patch as they are seen entering the summit at the ExCEL centre. Soon enough, Hague goes off on one, a huge, overwrought eulogy about Angelina's brilliance, power, ability to transform whole countries and their foreign policy. Angelina is a special UN human rights ambassador or some such thing, and in all fairness rushes around the world looking concerned and beautiful at the same time. She and Hague have teamed up on what was PSVI but now seems to be called something completely different. The culmination of all this is a three-day conference, the largest ever of its kind, anywhere at any time, as William keeps on telling H – who has to listen – and anyone else who will listen. William spends the entire

* Grant Shapps.

conference strutting around as if he's just pulled the most beautiful woman in the world, which I suppose he has.

On the first day the ministerial team – Hugo, Warsi, Robertson and Simmonds – are shown to their places. No sign of Lidders, who is no doubt ricocheting around Europe somewhere. Their seats are about six rows from the front, well away from the celebrities and the limelight. A deeply agitated Navid, Sayeeda's special adviser, rushes over to inform the gang that all the senior officials, from the Permanent Under Secretary down, are in the second row. The ministers erupt as one. H is amused, and just thinks *typical*. The others are more enraged. Navid promptly orders the group to rise and follow him like puddle ducks, which H, sensing a drama, does with considerable enthusiasm. They are marched over to the second row to find the PUS on his own, looking preoccupied. Matthew Rycroft, the second most senior official, has apparently already capitulated and yielded his seat despite the anguished protests of the PUS. Navid simply says, 'In two minutes I shall be bringing four ministers to sit here, so sort it out between yourselves who stays and who goes.' Very brave, but yet another illustration of the constant power struggle between the civil servants and the politicians. H says Navid was utterly magnificent and instantly shot up in everyone's estimation. The officials will of course be furious for being confronted like this and will nurse the grudge. A rare one up for the politicians. William will have neither noticed nor cared, although if it was brought to his attention he would simply shy away from personal confrontation – his default position. William is only ever interested in himself; his flunkies, I mean ministers, are mere gnat bites on his ankles, or so he makes them feel.

H spends two days clapping and smiling and in bilateral talks, and begins to wilt at the whole thing. He sits behind Brad and Angelina and is able to inspect them up close. They are both so thin he thinks they must live off half a Ryvita a week; but then he says, 'I suppose they do have a large family to feed. Angelina is rather weird-looking but flawless: tight, glowing skin.' H is also preoccupied by Brad's ears – one doesn't match the other – and that he wears high heels: 'So there! He's not that perfect after all!' The ministers just sit there, getting more and more bored as the mutual masturbation continues, John Kerry giving a rousing speech in which he heaps praise on William and Angelina. But why not Brad while he is at it?

After the big dinner held in Brangelina's honour, Sayeeda is agitating to rush off for a photo op with the Hollywood couple and says: 'Come on, Hugo, are you coming?'

'I couldn't lower myself,' H replies.

The next morning even the man collecting the red box from Walpole Street says, 'Well, there are some perks to your job then ... meeting Angelina and Brad.'

'Yes,' Hugo says, placing a finger to his lips. 'Hush now, she's inside sleeping. We don't want to wake her, do we?'

16 June

Dominic Cummings, Don Michael's (Gove) defenestrated consigliere, has gone tonto again, and has had a serious rant with Alice Thomson in *The Times*. In it, Ed Llewellyn is described as 'a classic third-rate suck-up-kick-down sycophant presiding over a shambolic court'. Craig Oliver, the director of comms, is 'just clueless'. Dave himself is 'a sphinx without a riddle – he bumbles from one shambles to another without the slightest sense of purpose'. 'Everyone is trying to find the secret of David Cameron,' says Mr Cummings *(a consistent criticism)*. 'But he is what he appears to be. He had a picture of Macmillan on his wall – that's all you need to know.' *(Sir John will like that one particularly – he has been saying it for years!)* The discomfort for Kate et al. is that the quotes come from someone who was – and is still – incredibly close to Don Michael.

I have met Cummings a few times; he looks like one of those odd amoebas you find in jars in school science labs, but what always struck me was his over-inflated view of his own importance. Teaming him up with the single most volatile member of the government was always an explosion waiting to happen. It answers the question as to why Andy Coulson originally banned Cummings from government. Except that when Michael got into his department it was so shambolic and he was in such a state of exasperation Dave backed down and allowed Cummings to tag along; a decision they are coming to regret. Cummings still advises Don Michael, unofficially, so will all links have to be broken for Gove to survive? I should think Ed is as bitter and twisted as an empty lemon shell now and will want revenge. And will Dave believe Gove when he says he didn't know what Cummings was up to? I somehow doubt it.

H thinks the whole thing looks so unedifying, the Oxford crew all fighting about each other and with each other.

Last night, H had a drink with Virginia Bottomley, who is now a top headhunter. H is pretty certain he wants to go, but nervous about what will replace it. I am of course encouraging him to make the move. 'Am I employable?' he asks her. 'Outside politics?' She seems to think so, but says 'It's up to God' in terms of what offers he might get. Which is rather odd, but at least she understands the game. He came away a little more encouraged. I'm not a believer, so am not quite so sure!

19 June

Prince Charles was on to something when he referred to Chinese officials as 'appalling old waxworks'. The trouble is, they have evolved from Madame Tussauds into creatures that are vastly more active and arrogant. Apparently, they even know how to smile now.

Yes, the Chinese have been and gone, accompanied by the usual shenanigans. Old 'Swivel Hips', the Chinese ambassador Liu Xiaoming, as we now call him, because of his ability to turn between two opposing systems, has been up to his usual tricks, pushing H and crew to the limits of human endurance with his demands. Apparently not a day had gone by without Charles Powell* having been rung. Charles then calls No. 10 and so on, leaving Ed tearing his hair out and screaming at the walls. The only person seemingly indifferent to all this appears to be William Hague. Swivel Hips had been pushing the line that the Premier must see the Queen, otherwise the visit will be pulled. H and crew pointed out it was not a state visit but of course everyone capitulated as H knew they would.

Swivel Hips then insists Premier Li must have a guard of honour. More capitulation. More agreement.

H is despatched, along with the newly knighted ambassador to Beijing, Sebastian Wood, to Heathrow to officially welcome the Premier. Oh, the lot of a junior minister! There has already been trouble brewing at site as Swivel Hips has spotted the red carpet, which is in all fairness apparently more like a bathmat, and Swivel Hips is now demanding an Oscar-night carpet stretching all the way up to the aircraft, as befits the standing of a powerbroker who holds the key to billions of pounds in trade deals.

H is sent to deal with this diplomatic incident, and on making enquiries is first told there is a health and safety issue, before this excuse is withdrawn and replaced with 'We only use the long carpet for state visits.' Panic swamps him. He begs the boss of Heathrow not to tell the ambassador, but it is too late. Luckily, Swivel Hips is now even more distracted by another issue: that of where the Queen sits during the meeting with the Premier. Apparently, if they stand it will look perfunctory to the Chinese. H tells Swivel Hips it would take a braver man than him to tell Her Majesty what to do in her own house, in her own meeting, but he is not interested, and becomes even more agitated by this minion's refusal to kowtow to him. H scores another point by saying that as it is Royal Ascot week, she will anyway have Windsor filling up with guests and her mind will be on the racing. Swivel Hips looks daggers at H and storms off to irritate someone else.

---

* Baron Powell of Bayswater, KCMG, British diplomat, politician and businessman.

Both H and I complained to Ed at Downing Street the night before about how Swivel Hips needed taking down a peg or two; could they not speak to the Premier? 'Yes,' he told us, 'we intend to do that, we can't take much more of him either.' (Later, when I asked K whether this had happened, she told me it had, but added that the Premier didn't seem to be listening. Surprise surprise.)

All is carefully choreographed and rehearsed, so of course all goes wrong. The plane parks at an odd angle, forcing Li Keqiang and his wife to descend onto wet grass. H has a horrible thought that they might sink and fall over, then climb back onto the plane in a huff, but all is OK. They are all then meant to proceed to the VIP room while papers etc. are sorted out. But Swivel Hips typically has other plans and leads them straight to their car. No one knows what to do because the convoy is not ready to leave. H asks how long it will take to process the rest of the entourage and is told twenty minutes. He explodes, saying that they cannot have Li and his wife sitting in the car, stationary, for twenty minutes, and tells the convoy to speed off to the big smoke, pronto.

The day continues with H presiding over the signing of twenty-four memoranda of understanding, worth about £18 billion, in an ornately decorated state room full of bankers, businessmen, politicians. *Ker-ching, ker-ching* went the cash registers, *roll up, boys, let's sell our souls to the devil while we're about it.* Transport Secretary Patrick McLoughlin, who is about to receive an injection of Chinese cash for HS2, can't believe his luck. Two Brains Willetts was there with open arms: *Come on over to our universities, all 1.3 billion of you!* Even Dave looked as if he had won the lottery. And Li was hinting at yet more moolah to come. H does his bit; he has been well prepped in pronunciation, but struggles at times. DC, standing with Li in front of the respective national flags, catches H's eye with that look that he throws out at his friends, encouraging them to struggle on manfully despite the hardships.

At the formal bilateral with William Hague and their Foreign Minister, Wang, commercial deals are positioned like drips in the veins of the FCO, drips that can be pulled at any time if conditions are not met – which means you don't go and have a cuppa with the Dalai Lama any time soon, all right?

The Ambassador has written a positive article in *The Times* on the advent of his trip, but Swivel Hips in an interview claimed that the UK was now only the third most important country in Europe as far as the Chinese were concerned. H and crew mention this at every opportunity, saying how sad they think this is. That's how you do things on this circuit. Anyway, it works because the Chinese look wounded and embarrassed; this is clearly not their line – or not officially, anyway.

At the banquet that night at the Natural History Museum. H and the other ministers arrive late as they have been voting in the Commons. This is clearly regarded as *lèse-majesté* by the Duke of York, who is frosty. At one point, to H's amazement, he leans over the table to Wang and, waving his finger at the MPs, says that whereas ministers come and go, the important and enduring relationship is between them – the Chinese – and the royal family.

All the great and the good are there, including George, who is sitting next to Premier Li. H opposite. GO in a pseudo-erotic bitchy way starts to tease H about how his good and dear friend is sadly one of the poor Swires; that the poor chap missed out on the billions made after the Opium Wars, in which the Swires, unlike Jardines, played no part. Mr Li's teeth gleam; he is much enjoying the spat. H retaliates by telling Li that if George is making a speech he would do well to drink as much rice wine as possible beforehand. GO looks faintly surprised at this disrespect: *I am the bloody Chancellor, Hugo!*

After dinner, H sees Jacob Rothschild, who says he has made a gaffe by asking Merlin Swire if he is Hugo's son. Merlin, who is only fourteen years younger than H, is of course delighted. Henry Keswick tells H he is starting a new fund and will be asking my husband to contribute. It is, he says, to fund the repatriation of Swivel Hips. He beams with delight at his own joke and wobbles off happily into the night.

As Leo Lewis put it in *The Times*, this is the culmination of a two-year experiment – at which my husband has been at the coalface – of 'a ruthlessly scientific probe of the mental and physical strengths and weaknesses of the old-world order and Britain has been chosen as the lab rat'. China's experiment with the UK is to make us learn the new reality and that is that it soon will be in control, if it is not already. GO has not only put out the red carpet, he is lying on it and they are trampling all over him.

H comes home that night and says he spent the whole day worrying that he'd mixed up the two men, President Xi Jinping and Premier Li Keqiang, and kept humming Lou Reed's 'Walk on the Wild Side' to himself, '... *shaved her legs and then Li was a Xi ...*', which probably only confused things further.

4 July

H has been asked to conduct the auction at the annual Conservative Summer Ball. He decides to include a personal item among the lots. The incredibly straight American wife of one of the hedgies on our table asks H disapprovingly what is in his Waitrose plastic bag. 'Oh, that,' he says, 'is a pot of honey. I intend to auction it off to the highest bidder. In fact, I intend to get a world record for it.'

'Gee,' she says, 'that's what I just love about you English. If this was a gala ball in the States the bag would be gold plated and wrapped in silk,' balls in America being the main social networking hubs of the elite. H whispers to me, 'At least it's a Waitrose carrier – I nearly put it in a Morrisons one.'

I have the pleasure of her husband, who is affable enough. We get chatting about properties and I ask him where his country residence is. 'The Cotswolds,' he replies.

'Ah,' I say, 'you must be a member of the Chipping Norton set, then.'

'No,' he replies, 'we can't break into that set – it's a closed shop – so we have decided to sell up.' Someone needs to explain to this man that mucking around with the Freuds, Rebekah Brooks, Jeremy Clarkson et al. is not quite as cool as he thinks.

Anyway, the auction goes splendidly. H, on the podium, tells the audience, 'I have something here that none of you can buy!' This immediately silences the assorted deep-pocketed lobbyists, hedge-fund grandees and Russian oligarchs, because for many in the room there is nothing, absolutely nothing, they can't buy.

'The Prime Minister has one, the Chancellor has one, and now you too can buy one.' He pulls a single jar of Chaffcombe honey out of his Waitrose bag.

'A jar of my very own honey!'

There are twitters, and the bidding starts. Soon enough it becomes furious, competitive. The room is in uproar. H has got the price up to £15,000, almost nine thousand times what it would retail for. Everyone is blown away by the excess. H, of course, is pleased, but thinks Miliband will make political hay with this, even though the identity of the five-figure bidder remains unknown.

It's as though the downturn never happened.

8 July

A Cabinet Office recruitment guide has been leaked to the papers. It advises top officials that they should have the whip hand, and be alert to ministers' 'irrational' demands. Apparently, top-performing permanent secretaries should have 'resilience – mental, emotional and personal toughness' – but then aren't these the self-same attributes required by any minister dealing with them? Of course, this is like a red rag to a bull for Francis Maude and Simone Finn, who work together in the Cabinet Office and who feel it is their duty to take on the arrogance and complacency of the entire civil service. Francis, who only saw the guidance in the past two weeks, is said to be outraged at suggestions that permanent secretaries could decide when they wanted to back ministers.

He now intends to update the guidelines, which will cause even more friction.

Today, H was leaving the Foreign Office in a government car when he was unexpectedly joined by James, one of his assistant private secretaries, and Fergus. Before you know it, H is the jam in their sandwich on the back seat of the car.

'Minister, just one more thing.' (Dread phrase. Means more on-the-spot decisions.)

'Yes?'

'We think that when you said you weren't sure about appointing a permanent official to the Commonwealth, what you really meant was that you wanted to.'

'Did I?'

'Well, certainly that would seem to chime with the Foreign Secretary's view.'

'But I thought I said I wasn't convinced.'

'Ah, but the merits, Minister, the merits. You are quite correct in thinking it's the right thing to do.'

'I am?'

'Yes, most definitely, Minister, you are.'

H retreats. Gives up. Waves them out of the car as he is already late.

'Oh well, do it, then. And well done, you budding Sir Humphreys, I've never been victim of such a well-coordinated pincer movement before. I expect many more.'

Fergus and James protest. 'No, Minister, it's not like that at all. It's what *you* wanted.'

'Could have fooled me!'

Benyon in the lobby: 'Well done on the honey.'

'Yes, I'd have trouble if a journalist asked me how much a pint of milk was, but I could now tell him how much a jar of honey costs,' replies H.

*

Reshuffle speculation ranging from 'fevered' to 'panicked'. Delay apparently is what to do about a problem called 'Michael'. He has become so unpopular in the Education Department and David is starting to see him as a block to his reform agenda. David wants to make him Chief Whip but, having said yes, he has now changed his mind. Also, William Hague wants to go but they need to keep him hanging on until the election. But we know it will be ladies' night – that is confirmed – and quite wide sweeping in second rank. Hugo to stay where he is.

Annual summer dinner at Jane Rayne's* in St John's Wood. The Cartier dinner at the Chelsea Flower Show crowd, but in reduced numbers. I sit next to Evelyn Rothschild, who has that marvellous flirt Princess Michael of Kent on his other side. I watch her with utter fascination, fawning over Rothschild, flattering him: 'Oh darling, I'm so glad you are next to me.' Her head butts around him like a cat, her tail held high with a little hook on the end, and she is purring with satisfaction. You must really like men to do that and she clearly does – especially rich ones.

I am less enamoured when he turns my way. A lot of I did this, I sat on this board, I'm into youth promotion, I gave that ballet dancer his big break, I ran the Derby, I was the *Telegraph*, *The Economist*, I'm doing trade in India, I've done China, the government should send money to the regions, I'm brilliant, I'm bored, I can learn more, I do not align myself with any party, my wife's brilliant, I always go for younger women, I was the executor of Max Rayne's estate, I live in Buckinghamshire in a National Trust house, Theresa May is useless, I rang up Michael Gove to tell him he should license imams, I am a chocolatier, I'm not a banker *(yes you are!)*, I gave up before they did all those bad things so don't accuse me, I'm not a banker.

I try to shift the conversation off his achievements, and say how nervous I am of Israel's Operation Protective Edge into Gaza;

---

* Lady Jane Rayne, daughter of 8th Marquess of Londonderry, widow of Lord (Max) Rayne.

Israeli Air Force jets and Navy ships are busy bombarding Hamas and Islamic Jihad targets there. It stops him in his tracks: why on earth am I worried about that? Because my seventeen-year-old daughter is doing work experience in the West Bank and Tel Aviv with the Portland Trust, I say, but somehow the conversation veers back to him and how he was involved in inter-faith dialogue with the Duke of Edinburgh and King Hussein, who he was at school with, and did I know that he went with the Duke to a small crypt on the Mount of Olives, where Princess Alice, the Duke's mother, who also happened to be a Greek orthodox nun who saved the lives of many Jews in Nazi-occupied Athens, was laid to rest. He went on to say how controversial the visit had been because it broke the ban that had been in place since 1948, that members of the royal family were not allowed to visit Israel.

Yes, but what about the Palestinians?

'They should bung the whole lot over into Jordan, get rid of them once and for all.'

'Well, you would say that, wouldn't you?' I huff. 'Anyway, Jordan's refugee camps are already bursting at the seams. They can't take much more.'

'You don't really believe in a two-state solution?' he asks.

'Yes, actually I do.'

He tells me he is tired and needs to leave, rather like a petulant child, and I say he can't do that because he has a Princess on the other side of him, and it would also not be good for my self-esteem to have an empty chair beside me. I tell him if he sits tight a little bit longer I will give him a lift home, but he must behave until then, and show some manners.

H is also having a terrible time. 'The trouble is, Hugo, this is a room full of me, me, ME,' I whisper. 'Come on, let's go . . . ' We are accosted by Prince Michael of Kent, who kindly thanks H for hosting him at Hillsborough. 'Are you still there?' he asks.

'No, I'm Minister of State at the Foreign Office.'

'Minister of State at the Foreign Office – what does that mean?'

We both sigh, then scoop up Evelyn and head for the car, which he can hardly get into. As we drop him off, he tries to give me his card. I joke, 'Yes, but you have nothing that I want!'

  H grabs it instead.

16 July

Reshuffle over, with some heart-stopping moments. How I hate them. Mostly dominated by Dave's demotion of Michael. For all his success at Education, and his closeness to the Chancellor, his tendency to pick fights and his toxic personal ratings have done for him. They just couldn't take it any more; in particular, David couldn't take it any more, especially after his Etonian rant. Which goes to show that all political careers end in tears – although I suspect this is not the last we will see of him. Dave looked tired on screen yesterday and he hates picking fights. Of course, he spun it as a sideways move, and the talk was that Michael will have an expanded role in the party's broadcast strategy, but it won't be any more than he does now. Besides, why would you put someone on TV when his personal poll ratings are so dire, especially in the run-up to an election? I watch Michael lying through his teeth, saying how honoured and flattered he is and what an important role he has been given, but we all know it's a demotion and so does he, and it shows. Mind you, all that scheming etc.: he must be in the right job.

  The real saga started a week before the reshuffle when Dave put it to Michael he wanted to move him to Chief Whip. It was, after all, the job he had told Dave he wanted; clearly in those heady days before his numerous implosions and when he still looked like a leadership prospect. A perfect job to get the MPs on side. The morning after he was told, and having mulled over the conse-quences with Sarah, he wrote a long email to Dave saying why he didn't want the job and was not going to take it, which of course threw the whole reshuffle out. Dave went ballistic when anyone tried to suggest keeping him at D of E.

'I'm the PM, this is what is happening and no one is overruling me. It's all decided.'

'You try,' K later says to George. 'But I warn you, he is in a belligerent mood.' G rings him. Dave still not having it. Goes on another rant about how he will not be overruled, and this is what he wants, and how he is never having Michael or Sarah or his children in his house ever again.

G to K: 'You're right: he's furious. He's not budging. I got an earful as well.'

Gove is told. K then becomes the sitting duck. A tirade of emails is fired off from Sarah. She even tweets that David will live to regret the decision. As K tells me mournfully, no one else gets this tirade except her. And then they'll all probably be besties again afterwards.

Further negotiations. The Goves are sweetened with an offer of a flat in Admiralty House – as it happens, my family's old flat, where I lived when I was eighteen and my father was Defence Secretary. They are also given a car. Michael takes the job but insists he is now in on all reshuffle meetings, since he is going to be Chief Whip. OK, come on in, they stupidly say, indulging him.

The heart-stopping moment comes when I read on the Conservative Home running blog – Hugo in Washington, asleep as this all unfolds – that H's job had been offered to Liam Fox, who turned it down, which must mean H was going to be sacked. I fire off a text to K, who stiffly replies: 'What do you mean? Hugo was staying as MoS in FO but possibly switched to Middle East portfolio, but I was not involved with internal jobs. There is a difference between a job and a portfolio, Sasha.' Still, H and I a little peeved we were not aware that this had been put on the table – but realistically, why should we be? The Fox offer was bumbling; he even had the indignity of seven-year-old Gavin Williamson (Dave's current PPS and Hugo's former PPS) being dispatched to sound him out. Dave had thought of giving him Northern Ireland, but was concerned that if Theresa Villiers was moved to Attorney General she would see it as a demotion. They opted for the Foreign Office instead and, being a neocon, thought they could not give Fox the Middle East brief, so they went for Hugo's position.

Amber is elated she has got a PUS job – perhaps a little prematurely, but then she is a woman. She tells me of enmity against H in the Whips' Office, particularly from Desmond Swayne and George Young. They apparently despise the way H refuses to suck up to them, and how he has a direct line to Dave. At the last reshuffle meeting, even before they sat down, DC said: 'I'm not sacking Hugo, so don't even raise it! You just want to get rid of him because he is my friend and I'm not going to.' There was apparently a steely silence before they got down to business.

19 July

From the *Mail on Sunday*:

> David Cameron has some bridge-building to do with fellow Old Etonian Hugo Swire. Away on a far-flung mission last week, Foreign Office Minister Mr Swire called London to check all was OK.
>
> 'Not exactly, Minister,' said an FCO flunkey. 'They've offered your job to Liam Fox in the reshuffle.'
>
> Cue splutters of long-distance indignation from Swire.
>
> To add insult to injury, he later discovered Fox turned it down ... as not worth having.

DC rings, having read the piece. Hugo is on the train from Devon to London.

'Oh God, you don't believe any of it, do you?'

'Yeah, thanks a bunch for putting my job on eBay, Dave.'

'I wasn't going to move you, I promise, I was going to put you in the Middle East brief. Oh God, does Mrs Swire hate me again?'

'It's fine. She's fine.'

'I didn't want Fox back anyway. Although he's been loyal, I'm glad he turned it down.'

'It's OK, Dave, really.'

'Not many Cameroons left. In fact they've all gone, the old gang. You're still here, at least.'

'Yes, you could put me in a glass case in a museum, I'm that much of a curiosity. I probably *am* the last one left.'

'Yes, I'm glad you decided to stay till the bitter end.'

'We fight on and we fight to win.'

They switch to small talk.

'Look,' says H, 'I'll see you in Scotland for the opening ceremony of the Commonwealth Games.'

'Why are you going be there?'

'Because, David, I am Commonwealth Minister . . . or should I say, I'm *still* Commonwealth Minister.'

22–25 July

Glasgow

The Commonwealth Games. H's first duty is to meet and greet some of the visiting dignitaries. Bilaterals with the president of Mauritius, then the rather imposing prime minister of Fiji, Frank Bainimarama, and finally the president of Trinidad and Tobago. A uniformed functionary appears, rehearses H's name and position and then announces him to the president as if they were in a large crowd at the presidential palace. In fact, it is just the two of them plus his assistant private secretary in rather a manky basement room of a hotel. Within minutes the president is complaining about the size of his room, the lack of air conditioning etc. H attempts to humour him by saying that heating is usually more important than air conditioning in Glasgow, but he is not convinced. He repeatedly reassures H that he is not fixated by protocol, but you know, you know . . . Later that evening, H learns that the president has packed up and left for London, missing the opening ceremony. All this because he feels that his tremendous importance hasn't been properly recognised. But then, he's not fixated by protocol.

H tells me on the phone that the opening ceremony was pretty terrible until Susan Boyle forgot the opening line of 'Mull of Kintyre', which is all but impossible, and the great veteran rocker Rod (he really should be Sir Rod by now) Stewart appeared screeching on the stage. Before this, H had been at a reception behind the royal box. He introduces Peter Robinson to lots of dignitaries, including President Tan of Singapore, who agrees to visit Northern Ireland, which H says could be good news for the economy there. All talk is of how the teams will perform. Peter tells one and all in his Belfast drawl that Northern Ireland's two best disciplines are shooting and boxing, which is not only funny but apparently true. H spots Ed Miliband and wife sitting on their own in a corner, looking glum and disconnected, so goes over and introduces him to a couple of presidents. 'It transpires that he has no small talk and simply cannot connect on a human social level. Quite extraordinary.' In desperation, H asks Nick Clegg to come and say hello, telling him about Miliband's handicap. 'Oh yes, I'm happy to do that,' he says cheerily. 'After all, I'm known as Chit-Chat Clegg.' If that is really the only thing he thinks people call him, he is living in a state of total self-delusion.

The Duchess of Cornwall is incredibly friendly: she and H chat about their forthcoming trip to Mexico. The PM is there, smiling and saying that Camilla is 'eminently deployable', chuckling at his own joke; she generously shares it, laughing. The innuendo is clear. There is certainly chemistry between the two, but Camilla is of course a 'pro' when it comes to men. Later, Dave tells H that he finds it increasingly difficult to understand what she says as she leans over and mutters at him; he says it's as if she's always got the end of a fag sticking out of the corner of her mouth and a gin and tonic clinking in her hand. She famously hates these public events and DC says he always goads her by saying, 'Don't worry, only another two hours to go,' at which she groans.

H breakfasts with Dave the following morning. He is on robust form, having been swimming in the icy sea off Shetland the previous day. The indomitable Liz Sugg* briefs Dave for an interview he is to give to the Scottish press later that morning. She runs him through some likely questions, such as 'What is your favourite sport?', it being the Commonwealth Games. H tells me he makes the sign of antlers on his head and D roars with laughter and groans at the same time. 'I think not,' he says. 'I think not.' H advises him to emphasise the point that his name is actually Cameron, a point that seems to have completely escaped him.

Later that day ...

H travels down to Dumfries House for a roundtable discussion on Commonwealth small-island states. The Prince of Wales is immaculate in a cream suit with highly polished brogues, and justifiably pleased as punch with what he has done with the house and grounds. H says Fawcett the Fence,† who runs it all, hovers in the background in a bright blue suit and polished brogues, seeking to emulate his boss, who he has dressed all these years. Apparently, he is lethal, has the ear of the PoW and does anyone down if they look like undermining him. 'An interesting character that Fawcett,' says H.

'I like the Prince more and more, but I continue to be fascinated by his thick Hanoverian hands. They are not the hands or fingers of a prince. Perhaps Fawcett could put them on eBay and get him some new ones,' H jokes.

---

* David Cameron's head of operations at No. 10; created Baroness Sugg in the 2015 Dissolution Honours.
† Michael Fawcett, former long-term valet and assistant to the Prince of Wales. His nickname results from a scandal involving the sale of unwanted royal gifts in 2003.

5 August

Fergus comes into H's office. 'Baroness Warsi has just resigned,' he says breathlessly. She's finally gone. Last night she was at the First World War service in Westminster Abbey, where she extinguished a candle. This morning she's gone. It later transpires that she'd rung Philip Hammond this morning but hadn't said she was about to go. Likewise, DC. She rang him just before tweeting she was resigning. Not the way it's normally done and the exchange of letters between her and the PM was couched in angry and resentful terms – on both sides.

H rings her on her mobile. She sounds genuinely sad and says this is the only call she's answered. She says she couldn't defend the FCO line on Gaza any more, and went on to say how much she admired and respected H. Flattering, but goodness knows why. H said she would always be remembered for a principled resignation. Of course, she was gagging to go in the recent reshuffle, but was persuaded to stay by DC.

Later on, H sees the Foreign Secretary Philip Hammond in a meeting. He says he was amazed that so much policy prior to him arriving at the FCO was instigated by the spads.

Hammond also says he wants to bring ministers in line. There will be less LGBT human rights (a dig at Hague, clearly) and more on Britain's economic priorities. He is not going to live in Carlton Gardens and probably not at Chevening, as he has his own house in Surrey, which his PS says is not insubstantial. It's Philip and H's first meeting. He is a poor timekeeper, unlike WH, who was particular on this matter. They talk about China and Russia. An interesting conversation, but H steers him back on course to discuss his list of things. Philip says Tobias Ellwood has joint American citizenship and is too close to the States. He wants to give the brief to H, who says fine, but he doesn't want to lose any territory in exchange. Philip agrees.

Hammond says he can't see why Sayeeda has chosen to go today, when there are the first signs of a genuine resolution on this difficult issue. He says Sayeeda had said H was unhappy about it as well. H confirmed he was, and they discuss the whole question. H says to me afterwards he is very dry but quite thoughtful and actually says he has always rather liked him. A potential PM, he thinks.

14 October

The fallout from the Scottish independence referendum rolls on. David was apparently on the floor with worry during that last week, and on the night muddled through with plenty of gallows humour. There were times when he thought he was a goner. My husband was equally all over the place, could hardly sleep, such were his nerves it could go the wrong way. He has always been a great believer in the Union. But I think what really tilted him over the edge was the thought that the Scots might reclaim their forests and moors as their own playgrounds. H doesn't seem to understand that, despite his lineage being overwhelmingly Scottish, he is also a member of a political tribe that, according to the Scots, bled their country dry, particularly the ship-building and mining industries.

Anyway, he needs to calm down, which I imagine he will; as I imagine the nation will. The only one who won't is Ed Miliband, who listened to the PM's victory-speech pivot to 'English Votes for English Laws' with utter dismay. Labour wants to delay any fundamental decisions like this until after 2015 election as part of a wide-ranging constitutional review. They want Scottish MPs to sit in the UK parliament on equal terms. His problem is that his position looks exactly like what it is: a partisan attempt to keep Labour's Scottish advantage intact. He knows, like us, that many of those Labour seats in Scotland will turn SNP at the election, such is the force of the wind up their arses.

15 October

State Dinner at Buckingham Palace for Dr Tony Tan, the president of Singapore. A lot of small talk beforehand. H is chatting to two ladies-in-waiting whom he knows. They are tittering because one of them has been placed next door to someone she claims is called 'Fat Cock' – or at least that's how it's pronounced – and they are trying to identify which of the guests it might be. Boy George appears, looking like a caddish extra on *Downton Abbey*. 'Ah, Chancellor,' H says, introducing him to the giggling tiaraed ladies and explaining their quest. 'Well, ladies, there's only one way of finding out,' he says to their delight, before moving off, chuckling.

11 November

H takes Toby, his Commons researcher, down to Rochester and Strood in Kent for a spot of canvassing for the upcoming by-election. This is his second visit. All MPs are obliged to do three. Within seconds of heading down the high street someone brushes past them muttering, 'How many disabled people have you murdered today, scum?' H tells Toby not to be alarmed; this is a traditional greeting in this part of the world. He is not convinced. They run into Nick Hurd, who tells them that he has just seen another colleague in a state of considerable shock: he had rung a doorbell, only to be greeted by an elderly and rather large Jamaican lady, who said, 'Hello darlin', don't worry, I haven't seen cock for two weeks and my vagina is too tight for you.' Toby asks H, 'Was that another traditional form of welcome in these parts?' Toby informs both that only last week the office had received a letter from a constituent complaining about the NHS's treatment of her mother's condition, which was a 'packed vagina'. Nick and H look at each other quizzically and immediately pull out their mobiles to google it.

Later, chaos in the House over the EU arrest warrant. Rebels take Cameron to the brink. Most MPs had no idea what was going on or what it was they were being asked to vote on. Brooks Newmark appears at the vote and is treated like a returning hero – not least by the women, which was somewhat surprising, says H. Crispin Blunt comes over, grinning, and tells Brooks that he is now free to come with him to Jordan. H chips in, 'Really, Crispin, I don't think you should be tempting Brooks with Jordan at this stage in his recovery,' at which Brooks becomes all excited and says, 'But I don't fancy Jordan. Her tits are too big. I like girls with small tits.' H replies, 'Oh dear, Brooks, I see we're in the early stages of recovery. I think they'd better double up on your dose.'

23 November

H's brilliant idea to suck up to the Queen of Bhutan is taking up more time than he envisaged. When he visited the Dragon Kingdom, the first serving British minister ever to do so, he was rewarded with an audience by the King and Queen. Both charming, H says, and she rather beautiful. They took great pride in showing H their modest English cottage garden, which they tend themselves. On his return, H has the idea of getting a rose named after the Queen and instructs his office to contact David Austin Roses.

It transpires that Mr David Austin actually exists, and very precious he has proved to be. He is apparently suspicious of naming roses after royals who have no interest in gardening matters, and has sent someone out to speak to the head botanist in Bhutan. It would probably be easier to get a rose named after Elton John or Beyoncé – certainly Cliff Richard – but still H persists. The young Bhutan royals are aching to meet the Queen – our Queen, that is – and it's H's idea that they come to the Chelsea Flower Show to see the rose and meet the Queen. Simple. 'Only Mr David Austin remains in the way of my cunning plan.'

H attends Mary Soames's service of thanksgiving, which

is a very grand affair in Westminster Abbey. Trumpeters and buglers from the Household Cavalry, John Major reading the lesson. Charles and Camilla, of course, and an excellent eulogy by William Shawcross. H is struck by how grey and old everyone looked. On the way out he stupidly mentions the Scottish referendum to Archie Stirling, who loses no time in telling him how 'you lot completely fucked it up' and how angry it made him. H teases him, pointing out that he had started his own party in Scotland, and Archie concedes that it had not generated much support. 'Not even on the estate?' H asks innocently. Archie claims he is thinking of restarting it, which we are sure will be the answer to something, but are at a loss to think what.

28 November

Andrew Mitchell lost his libel cases against the *Sun* and PC Toby Rowland yesterday, with Mr Justice Mitting ruling that 'on the balance of probabilities' he 'did speak the words alleged or something so close to them as to amount to the same, including the politically toxic word pleb'. Hugo and I think he might actually have used the word 'Plod'. In the pictures of Andrew coming out of court, he looked utterly shattered, Sharon and their daughter holding on to him with scaffolding arms for support.

The talk at Westminster is generally why? Why did he bring these cases to court? He is facing a three-million-pound legal bill, embarrassment, and no hope of returning to the cabinet. The undeniable truth is that he did swear at the officers at the gate – he admits as much – and even though these police officers can be aggressive, you cannot lose your dignity. If you do, the public can only be forgiven for thinking that politicians believe the trappings of power somehow elevate them above the people they govern. It just further disconnects people from their political representatives.

2 December

The dreaded Bercow grants an emergency debate about China's decision to bar the Foreign Affairs Committee from visiting Hong Kong, which has seen months of pro-democracy protests. Requesting a debate, the committee's chairman, Sir Richard Ottaway, said the refusal was an 'affront to this House and to men and women of the free world'. Hammond told Hugo he was doing a runner to a NATO summit and he would have to take it. H gulped. Emergency debates are rare in the House of Commons and take precedence over all other business, and can be up to three hours long. If people start to grandstand, which H suspected they would, it was going to be a long and hard call.

H has been dealing with the pressure of this issue for a while. China is upset about the inquiry, which will look into the UK's relations with Hong Kong some thirty years after the signing of the Joint Declaration. He could see it coming and had briefed Hammond, who decided to take a much tougher stance than his predecessor. The fly in the ointment has always been one Mr Osborne, who is desperate not to rock the slow trade boat to China, but even now No. 10 is getting tired of the shenanigans. Finally, out comes the statement that China is 'mistaken' to bar the committee as it was 'counter-productive'. No. 10 says the move just 'amplified' concerns about the situation there. Beijing in turn has accused the committee of 'interfering' in China's internal affairs. The debate goes OK, with the usual suspects saying that the government is being supine etc. Meanwhile Swivel Hips who H had wanted to call in to the FCO, has swivelled off to Beijing. Hugo is meant to be going to Hong Kong in the new year, but is yet to be granted a visa. They have, however, deemed it safe to issue one to Fergus, maybe in the belief that he can go instead of the minister. They really do get it wrong, these Chinese.

11 December

Following a fantastic weekend in Ireland with our dear friends Ken
and Brenda Rohan, we are brimming with ideas to be rid of the
deer that are particularly partial to nibbling our new ornamental
trees. Ken gets hair off hairdressers' floors, puts a handful of it in a
nylon stocking pouch and lets it dangle from a tree. But he tells us
the best deterrent is lion dung, that some primeval instinct tells the
deer to scarper as quickly as their elegant little legs will carry them.
H puts his thinking cap on – he is very good at sourcing people
and things – and approaches Fergus, asking whether Uncle Reggie
(Heyworth, he who owns the Cotswold Wildlife Park) could possibly spare a sack. Said sack is due to arrive at the Foreign Office
any day, driven up by Fergus's mother. She does warn H that it is
the most potent and foul-smelling of all dungs known to man, so we
will be expecting a dressing down from the Permanent Secretary,
who has already had the indignity of our new and over-excitable
cockapoo puppy Rocco depositing something malodorous and
brown outside his office the other day.

Theresa Villiers is away and Anne Milton, Deputy Whip, asks
Hugo to sit on the front bench to support Andrew Murrison, PUS
Northern Ireland, and he duly obliges. There is a lot of ribbing and
jeering from the Irish brigade, as there is much speculation that
he will replace Theresa. (Not speculation from H, I might add.) It
is just before PMQs and the head honchos start filing in, looking
for a place. First George boots him out. H shuffles down, then
Hammond comes in. 'Do you want my seat?' H asks. He shuffles
down again and finds himself sitting next to Liz Truss, who says:
'Oh, that's a good idea. Next time I'll get George Eustice [being
a junior minister in her department] in early to save me a place
as well!' It's the closest H has ever got to telling a woman, apart
from me, to fuck off.

2015

11 February

An independent calling herself Claire Wright is causing us no end of trouble down on the local patch. Unfortunately, she has a background in PR and is quite a good operator, but she is starting to attack Hugo on a personal level which infuriates me.

3 March

Mexican state visit. All the usual pomp and ceremony, with the Queen welcoming Enrique Peña Nieto and his soap-star wife, Angelica Rivera, for a three-day visit amid growing pressure against the president over the abduction and apparent murder of forty-three students. The Mexicans love H, particularly the Foreign Minister José Antonio Meade, who is so enamoured he wants to give him some gong. And, he stresses, they are only giving three of them out!

En route to the dining room at Buckingham Palace, I notice all the Mexicans are bedecked with medals the Queen has given to them. I say to Dave as we walk in, 'How come their ministers get all the dingle-dangles and ours don't?' He says, not now Sasha, or something along those lines, but he is smiling. I am wary on this score. My father was offered a medal, but the Foreign Office said he was not allowed to accept it – apparently Elizabeth I's comment, 'my dogs wear *my* collars', still applied. Next thing he noticed was that Margaret Thatcher was wearing it on her collar.

The thing about these dinners is that they are quick. Everything racing towards the tribute at the end, where the warm ties between the two countries are stressed. Food disgusting as usual, lamb overcooked, chairs taken away before you have finished your pudding, then the toasts, then the bagpipes. I steal a glimpse at Prince Charles, who is sitting next to the First Lady and does not appear to be saying a single word to her. The Duke of Edinburgh, Camilla and Princess Anne there among the 170 guests, along with a lost Prince Andrew, who is currently denying suggestions of impropriety with minors through his friendship with sex offender Jeffrey Epstein.

After dinner, H and I get talking to the Mexican-American actress Salma Hayek, who is married to François-Henri Pinault, the mega rich CEO of the Kering luxury goods group that owns Gucci, Saint Laurent, Stella McCartney, Alexander McQueen and Bottega Veneta among others. Good move if you are into designer labels. She is perfectly charming, does not give off a boss's wife or I'm a famous film star vibe. She tells us how much she loved the bagpipes. H suggests she gets a piper and has him play outside her bedroom window every morning, like the Queen. She likes this idea, and giggles flirtatiously. I tell her I don't need bagpipes as I'm already married to an old windbag.

I'm then left stranded with some smoothie. He asks me why I'm here, i.e. am I a person of consequence? I explain I'm merely an MP's wife, and a very fed up one at that. Oh, he asks, why is that? I tell him I have just had a series of tests done and that I was found to be deficient in vitamin D. This is on account of my husband being so busy I never get to go on holiday and bathe in luxurious sunshine. I say I am either getting a lover to take me, but that is probably not an option as I am too old, or I am going to Lastminute.com before it is too late, and I become as shrivelled-up and milky-white as an old maid with osteoporosis. So, he says to me:

'Where do you want to go? I'll take you. South of France?'

'Definitely not! The South of France is so yesterday.'

'How about Ibiza?'

'Too hedonistic.'

'I know,' he says, 'Corsica: I'll take you to the lovely island of Corsica.'

'Yes, I like the sound of that. How will I get there?'

'I will fly you there in my private plane.'

'That's no good, I hate flying.'

'All right, I'll send you my super yacht.'

'OK, it's a deal.'

It was all going so well, but suddenly he is crowded by a load of men who want to talk to him about oil in Mexico and I am reunited with my husband. Hugo asks me what I was talking to 'that man' about.

'He's taking me to Corsica and I've no idea who he is, and before you say anything I have to tell you that I don't care if he is a drug-smuggling, coke-snorting, thrice-married lunatic who wants to bang me up in his harem, I'm going. I need a holiday and some attention, neither of which you are providing for me.'

'He's big, very big,' he says. 'One of the biggest in the country – oil it seems, and a Conservative donor. Middle Eastern. Dave loves him.'

I see him the next night as I'm marched in for the Guildhall dinner. He points at me and shouts 'Corsica!' Hugo thinks it's a bit much, him trying to whisk me off in his super yacht. I think he just felt sorry for me. Besides, those big boys can buy anything they want and someone of my great maturity would not be top of their shopping list. Nice my husband thinks I can still pull, though.

13 March

The first pre-election hustings. It's in Sidmouth and organised by the Federation of Small Businesses, with guests invited by them. It's suggested in some parts that it's an open meeting, I assume to swell attendance by our opponent's acolytes. We discover and Hugo threatens to empty-chair it, and if anyone is not asked by direct invitation, not to be allowed in. It is at Kennaway House, of which H is the patron and he holds a surgery beforehand. Toby, H's excellent researcher, puts up posters everywhere on the building, advertising his surgery with a picture of him grinning in an Alan B'stard sort of way. Two men try and take them down but are seen off by the manager. H says hello to everyone except Ms Wright who he has started to loathe.

The UKIP candidate has been in correspondence with H for months about an obscure row he is having with HMRC. He is extremely polite to H. HMRC is his defining theme. He sleeps and eats the injustice inflicted on him by that organisation, and sure enough he manages to turn every question back to it. That, and blaming the EU for everything including the potholes on Devon's roads, which is quite a remarkable achievement. *Question Time* à la Dimbleby it was not. Thirty people only.

27 March

H did the auction at the Black and White Ball in early February, the whole room eating out of his hand and laughing. 'Bet Nicky bloody Morgan or Liz bloody Truss couldn't do that,' he said smugly as he sat down. As it turns out, Nicky bloody Morgan or Liz bloody Truss would be very pleased they didn't have that particular pleasure, now that the shit has hit the fan.

On the night, we are on the top table with Dave and Sam, hosted by Andrew and Zoe Law. She is charming but he refuses to acknowledge me, to say hello to me, goodbye to me. Before dinner H tells Michael Spencer how I dared to suggest he was after a seat in the House of Lords: 'No, he wouldn't get that. He wouldn't like it at all,' Michael says.

When the time comes for the auction, H walks to the lectern to sell his luxury wares. He eyes the north face of the problem to be scaled; the room is excitable and talking over him, and he needs to up the bidding. He usually does this by throwing in some jokes, as if throwing red meat to lions to rouse them. At least there are no Fleet Street seamstresses in the room. Andrew Feldman had vouched for that, telling H that the vetting process had been much stricter this year. Across the room, he spots IDS and a switch goes on: Secretary of State for Work and Pensions making changes to the welfare state, benefits reform etc. – that is the pool from which he must fish some jokes. A man next to Duncan Smith keeps raising his hand to bid. This is good, this is good: the man is rich – he is going up in £10,000 increments.

'£60,000?' H teases. 'Iain, persuade him. He's not on benefits, is he? Well, if he is, then he can afford it.' I silently roll my eyes to the ceiling as everyone around me laughs.

The auction goes on. H comments on the expensive cars the guests drive as he desperately tries to sell a hybrid vehicle, without much success. 'It's quite naff to have Bentleys and Rolls-Royces and Ferraris, because anybody could have them,' he says, trying to appeal to their green credentials. And then, 'In the good old days of MPs' expenses we could have them too – but we don't any more.' The crowd laugh and boo in equal measure.

In the taxi home I say, 'What were you thinking? An Old Etonian going on about benefits? Christ, Hugo!'

'Sasha, it was a joke. A J-O-K-E! I might not know the price of a pint of milk, but I do know that you don't get sixty grand on benefits. I'm not going to start self-flagellating about this.'

'I can tell you, if that gets out it sure as hell ain't going to benefit you.'

As sure as night follows day, it turns out H was secretly filmed by *Dispatches*, one of those undercover-type TV programmes. Not helpful before an election, not helpful at all. And guess who are going to have to cling to the life raft as the waters rise over our heads? Me and Toby, that's who.

Claire Wright is like a rat up a drainpipe. She puts out a press release: 'What is funny about people who face a daily battle trying to survive on benefits? It is not funny for those who struggle to scrape together the funds in an attempt to make ends meet. It is not funny for the many thousands who have to use food banks.' She bangs on about H having no sympathy and empathy, that it reveals him in a callous light and scoffs at the suggestion that 'we are all in it together'.

Local and national newspapers are full of it, and the comments below the stories keep coming, more and more and more of them.

Eric the Cat: We never had a Hugo at our comprehensive!

now proven to be an utter arrogant prat

Hugo Swire. Sounds like a name made up by writers of a 'Carry On' movie for the part of a shifty, patronising, upper class, toff.

The Tories, and their cronies, really are on another planet. Let us hope, come May, this vile little oik has experience of life on the dole, so he can see how much you can buy on £71 per week.......

Ham shanker!!!!!!

Ham shanker? That's a new one.

A few days after the media bogwashing, Dave sees H and comments how unfair it was on him, being the centrepiece of the scandal about party funding and high-end donors when he was only raising money for the party. H says: 'That's it, I'm never bloody doing one again. Ever! However much you beg me.' Dave replies: 'That's OK, Samantha says she is never going to do the Black and White Ball again either.' But it's a sorry state of affairs, because Hugo is quite simply the best auctioneer in town and has raised many millions for charities. They will be the real losers in all of this.

30 March

David meets the Queen today, to mark the formal start of the general election campaign. It will be based on the usual fear tactics: families facing a £3000 tax bombshell if Ed Miliband gets into office, blah, blah, blah. Meanwhile, Miliband is pushing the message that the biggest threat to British business is the prospect of exit from the EU. Blah! Blah! Blah!

12 April

I speak to Kate, who is accompanying David everywhere on his tours. She rises at 5.30 a.m. and gets back at 10 p.m. She is completely exhausted. She sounded worried, saying it's very tense out there, and tight. Problem areas are the marginals, where the Lib Dems are moving to Labour, not us. She says, thank God for Nicola Sturgeon, otherwise we would be heading for a Labour majority.

My gut feeling is that we are not going to make it. And if we do, it will be impossible to govern. Dave lacks passion. He is a victim of a new media age. He starts his day at 5.45, learning what the threats are and how to dodge them. The news now moves like an Exocet through the day, it can race all around the world exploding its clusters before the truth has even got up and it makes him bland, or should I say blander. He is determined to play safe. Meanwhile Miliband is on to something. His pledge to abolish non-dom status is clever, it's the 'people versus the powerful' tactic, he is also fearless in proposing policies that break with the consensus. He might slip up with this down the road, but at the moment he makes us look like defenders of the status quo.

If I was tempted to vote Labour, it would be for one reason, and one reason alone. It would be because of social division, the terrible gap between rich and poor. The Labour Party still has a modicum of instinct to deal with this, whereas we as a party are too harsh in distributing help to the poor, we are unforgiving of personal circumstances, relentless in telling people to stop whingeing and make a go of it. I have been so blessed: how do I know what suffering is under such circumstances? Would I have the strength to pull myself up and dust myself down? I don't know.

You can see the view if you look hard enough. We live in two countries: one, an affluent city-state run by the media and politicians, and the other a hinterland full of the 'others'. But then I also think, how can anyone be so bloody stupid as to vote for them?

I call Amber in Hastings, a noted marginal. She says that some days she thinks she can do it and some days not. Realistically, she will need a swing of 3 per cent to hold it. Apparently central command keep asking her what ministers she wants down there and she keeps telling them to stay away. We talk about how it's a very sexist, traditional campaign with old ideas. The right to buy housing association properties is mad; Amber says no one in her constituency's housing associations properties want to buy their homes. It's all the George and Dave show, but my daughter's generation are looking at Nicola Sturgeon and deeply admiring her as a feminist icon, and find her politics appealing. Where are the Conservative women? At which Amber laughs and says, 'They asked me if I wanted Samantha down here.'

The hustings in East Devon can be quite tiresome and the level of debate hovers somewhere near the bottom end of sixth form. H spends the entire time trying not to be riled by Claire Wright. The poor old UKIP candidate looks wobblier every day; our nightmare is that he croaks, in which case we fear we would have to re-run the entire election locally. At the last hustings he was rabbiting on about the national debt and, forgetting its size, asked H how much it was. Of course, H couldn't remember either, so he apologised and said he hadn't been listening, which elicited a good laugh from the student audience.

25 April

H goes up to London for Anzac Day. They all rehearse at the FCO, but Cleggers nowhere to be seen, so someone stands in for him. At one point Ed Miliband says, 'So Nick turns to the left first?' At which H quips, 'Ah yes, but then to the right. He might still muck everything up for all of us.' Ed Miliband laughs. H finds him, on this occasion, rather charming. The campaign has certainly not diminished him; it's enhanced him, if anything. But then politicians are at their most deluded at election time; he probably thinks Labour is on the verge of snatching back power.

The ceremony goes off OK, although H's wreath for the Overseas Territories is impossibly heavy and his arms ache as he has to hold it in front of him for what seems an age. Afterwards they are meant to let the 'protected people', predominantly royals, leave and the poor 'unprotected' also-rans stay behind for the march past. Of course, they all do it wrong and leave together, only to discover the service at Westminster Abbey doesn't start for an hour. H takes everyone to the Westminster Arms for a stomach-settler including a rather nice former Royal Marine from the SNP who is their minister for something or other; Andrew Murrison, who was meant to be organising them; and Jeffrey Donaldson, the DUP MP, who tells H he will ensure all the DUP do a deal with us not Labour. Let's wait and see.

4 May

Lizzie Pitman, another member of the Gove clique, has been inserted at Campaign HQ, much to the irritation of Lynton Crosby. Gove, rather like Thomas Cromwell, likes to have his people placed everywhere. Curiously Michael has no official role in the running of the campaign, which he must regard as a clear oversight. Lizzie has been leaning on H to lead the Conservative battle bus in the South-West. Eventually H agrees and a date is set.

H meets the bus in Carbis Bay, outside St Ives. Everyone is dreading it as these volunteers have firm rules. They have to stop regularly for long breaks and refuse to deliver leaflets. 'They are here to persuade,' according to Ellie, a CCHQ lovely who emerges from the bus not looking a day over thirteen. What follows her is almost beyond description. Like Noah's Ark they emerge two by two, each pair more extraordinary than the next. In fact, H says he has never met a weirder bunch in his life. He tells everyone who will listen that he is reminded of the film *Night of the Living Dead*, when zombies take over the world. Off they go around St Ives. Sam Swire, H's cousin who has been working valiantly for the Tory candidate Derek Thomas, texts H later, 'How's it going?', to which H texts back, 'Van full of men with white coats just pulled up and took them all away ... if only!'

They lunch at the Premier Inn and afterwards attempt a full-frontal assault on Hayle with George and Katy Eustice, Nick Herbert and his husband Jason, and George's team, who view the whole thing with exasperation and trepidation as they fear this lot will actually lose them votes. They are meant to go on to Camborne but the Eustices have a furious row in the car park, and George says meekly that on account of the weather he is calling it a day, although he was really most grateful to them all for coming. But not before they all have to go and have the ice cream they've been promised at Hell's Mouth. H goes on ahead in his car, to catch up endless emails and phone calls. Still no bus. He rings George. Apparently, in the three-odd miles it had to travel – on a single-track road – they had got lost. They arrive an hour later, having nearly driven off a precipice, *Italian Job*-style, down an unmarked coastal path. Some of them are shaking and in tears. George and H make their excuses and leave. The consensus later is this must have been one of the great Von Schnapps's ideas taken from some American self-help book on communicating. It didn't work in practice. This was not rent-a-crowd, it was rent-a-canvasser. Oh God. Is this wretched campaign ever going to end?

5 May

Claire Wright's people think we are living under a tinpot dictatorship (the Conservative-led East Devon District Council), and that the Conservatives are somehow going to fiddle the votes. They have now started intimidating officers so that when the postal votes come in, they stick stickers on the box to indicate they have overseen the proceedings. Mark Williams, the returning officer, and his staff are feeling increasingly irritated by their high-handed actions. The indomitable Jill Elson, Hugo's stalwart campaign manager, is asking us to be extra vigilant on polling day, which is in two days' time, as she feels the East Devon Alliance (Claire's people) are causing no end of trouble. This lack of trust is absolutely awful for the staff, she says, many of whom are regularly employed at election time. She asks our campaign team to go in to the polling stations to introduce themselves to the polling clerks and thank them for what they are doing, and at the same time note if the EDA have a polling clerk inside the polling station; telling is meant to be done outside. H will also be visiting every polling station and committee room, which he has done every election day since becoming the MP here.

7 May

Polling Day

Speak to K in the morning. She is utterly shattered. 'Where are you?' I ask. 'At the Feathers in Woodstock,' she replies. How nice. 'Not really,' comes the reply. In fact, she was dumped in a field at 10 p.m. last night by helicopter, and had to crawl to the nearest pub/hotel with the team. Dave went back home to Dean. Sam is anxious about everyone piling in there. I would be the same. You just want to be near family in times like these. K also wants to be around loved ones; she is fed up with the entire circus, lots of people she says she doesn't even like. She tells me David is being marvellous but George is much jumpier. I think he, unlike David, will find it much more difficult to adjust if it all ends.

8 May

It's a long night but when the exit polls come out, we are astonished: they do not match the opinion polls at all. Can they be right? Even Dave is flabbergasted, having been rung earlier in the day by Andrew Cooper, his former No. 10 pollster, who said it was all over for him. (Well that was a well-deserved peerage!) We get to the count at 1 a.m. and the result does not come through until six hours later. We are pretty sure we have won by the time we arrive. As it turns out, H increases his majority by 3147, winning 25,401 of the votes (46.4 per cent). Still, Claire took the runner-up position with 13,140 votes. The story of the night, the complete collapse of the Lib Dems, was reflected locally: here, they trailed in second last.

The national picture is much more extraordinary. Through the night I'm texting K, asking if this really is happening and she is texting back that it is 'unbelievable', 'mind-blowing'. When I ask her if we are going to get a majority, she says, 'I think we might.' DC could not have hoped for a better election night. The exit poll indicated he would hold on to power, while big Labour and Liberal Democrat names like Ed Balls and Vince Cable would lose their seats, but no one believed it until it actually happened. Before the results, expectation had been rife that Britain would be getting another hung parliament. In the end, it was Nicola Sturgeon who won it for us; her, and the fact that we were the incumbent government and had started to turn things around. The idea that Lynton Crosby had anything to do with it is debatable: in fact, our campaign was appalling. K defends it, saying I can't overestimate how much shit was thrown at them, from people saying do this, do that, change direction, but it was pretty clear to anyone out canvassing that what was really freaking out the electorate was a possible Labour-SNP tie-up.

13 May

Hugo and I on tenterhooks during the reshuffle. H is pleased to be back in the FCO but has decided to do it for a year only. There is no point waiting for Dave to promote him to the cabinet; he never will. He is getting on and there will be no time to build a second career if he doesn't start soon. We need to take back control. But overall, the reshuffle was skilful: at first sight it seemed less like a reshuffle and more like a re-appoint, with more than half of the old cabinet – and almost all those in the top jobs – keeping their posts. It reflects Dave's long-held belief that ministers need time to master their briefs and moving them merely strengthens the hands of those inside and outside departments who are resisting their agenda.

We are both very flat and very tired from the election, and reshuffles always disappoint. H generously concedes the cabinet looks like modern Britain; his face simply doesn't fit and he has to learn to accept that.

21 May

Back to school. H sees Andrea Leadsom in the lobby. She calls herself and Amber the 'Dream Team' in Climate and Energy. 'Are you going to Paris?' he asks. 'No,' she says, 'I'll leave that to Amber. I'm not a great believer in all this climate change stuff.'

It beggars belief! George apparently hates her. H and I can only conclude that she was put there to fall on her sword.

The No. 10 crew are busy attending Steve Hilton's book launch, no doubt. He attacks the big corporations for not being human – a bit odd, that, when his wife Rachel Whetstone is the ultimate corporate employee. I mean, didn't Google start out as disruptive but became a corporate hierarchy which didn't exactly welcome other new entrants into its sphere of business?

We were discussing, H and I, how we haven't seen or spoken

to G for quite a while now. We just watch him from outside the arena. Someone has clearly told him to say 'working people' in all his soundbites, which is ridiculous, since most people work in some form or another. On TV he looks even smugger than usual, and seems to be up to his megalomaniac tricks again, forever distracted by great and not-so-great causes. Now he's overseeing the Northern Powerhouse project, next he will be re-negotiating Britain's relationship with the EU; he might even be plotting to succeed Dave. Trouble is, we don't need a part-time chancellor: there is still much to do. He is like Gove; he has to be at the scene of the car crash, because only then can he receive the medal for cutting the victim from the wreckage. Everything is planned, timed, manipulated to his own ends.

6 June

Back from Marrakesh after an orgy of opulence and bacchanalian revelry in honour of Michael Spencer's sixtieth. Michael had generously chartered a jet for hundreds of his besties from the worlds of finance, buffalo-hunting and politics. Dinner in a riad, with burning flares and belly dancers, switched next day to an Ibiza-style techno pool party, the hired help in red *Baywatch*-babe swimming costumes, and culminated in an evening of dinner and dancing at the Palais Namaskar. That was the long-dress event. In fact, it cost me more in grooming than it would have done to buy my flight there. Mingling with the rich takes stamina and cash. I knew it was going to be big when on the Gatwick Express we saw the first of the many guests: Andrew Roberts. Andrew does not go anywhere outside name-dropping territory. I'd barely sat down before he said, 'My wife is CEO of Brunswick Global.' *Yes, I know, Andrew. You tell me that every time I see you.* According to my sources, she rakes in about a million a year, enabling Andrew to write full time. I'd love her as well if she did that for me. He turns to Hugo and says he has been trying to get him along to some dinner with

Henry Kissinger, but that H's office never seems to reply. Then he has the temerity to say: 'I want to find out what's happened in the system, because if it's happened to you, it might have happened to someone more important I have tried to invite.' He very pointedly says I am not invited. I reply, pointedly, that I'm not particularly interested in coming anyway, but secretly I'm rather annoyed and feel dismissed and unimportant. But then I'm only the wife.

Poolside, I meet someone called Jez. Jez is in the money game and, judging from my conversation with him, he does not have much of a hinterland, except for the slaughter of birds on his two grouse moors. 'You don't know me,' he says, 'but I have attention deficit hyperactivity disorder.'

'Oh really? Poor you! What does that involve?'

'I have a short attention span, I'm restless and fidgety.' And before I know it he's gone; he has jumped into the swimming pool and most of the water has jumped out. Yes, he was large and blubbery; lucky he's rich, as that doesn't seem to be an impediment above a certain level of wealth. David Ross, who made a fortune from Carphone Warehouse, is sitting talking to Hugo. He also has a grouse moor. I talk to the politicos – Francis Maude, Alan Duncan, Andrew Mitchell, Nicholas Soames – then go for a wander around the pool with H.

The wind is getting up and suddenly I am felled by about three poolside lilos, and do a triple somersault in the air, which the politicos find hysterical. Anyway, I pick myself up and move on, determined not to be beaten. On my travels I come across Michael for the first time. He looks exhausted, unshaven, sitting cross-legged under a tree with a friend sprawled out on the grass next to him. I say something along the lines of 'cracking party', and that I'm having a massage later. 'Enjoy!' he winks at me.

At dinner, I sit next to someone called Fat Mike Sherwood, who is a bit of a pill. He is very big in the Eurobond game; broad in beam, very short, and very, very uncommunicative. Fat Mike works/runs/sells his soul to that residence of Satan, Goldman Sachs. He does something called syndication, which apparently is

a posh word for parcelling up a deal and selling it to other inves-
tors. Boring. When we attempted to connect, he told me he hates
England in the summer; I know at this point we have absolutely
nada in common. I try to say, come to my wildflower meadow in
June, and he practically spits the word 'flower' into my lobster
risotto – and that's before I even get to meadow! 'Boats,' he says.
'The summer should be all about boats.' By which I presume he
means gin palaces.

The evening is peppered with speeches from those who know
and love and have made a lot of money from Michael. Hell, I'd
eulogise too if I fell into that category! Then a smooth old crooner
starts dishing out Dean Martin songs. We are forced to stand on
our chairs, clamp our hands into the moist palms of our neighbours, hoist our arms in the air and swing them to the words
'That's amore'. It's at this point Fat Mike gets a little competitive: not
for him a gentle singalong, oh no. Fat Mike is shouting, whooping,
hollering the words, it's as if he is back on the trading floor – all
very *Wolf of Wall Street*. Meanwhile, his arm-swings are getting
broader and more tidal; he shouts over to wife, asking whether it's
too late to add 'That's Amore' to his own shindig in Sardinia the
following weekend, and I take another huge wave, which is tough
when you are only just about balancing on six-inch stilettos on a
creaky chair, then another one and that's it, I'm getting pissed off.
I send a tsunami back his way, literally shoving him back, and he
tumbles down onto the floor. Mike knows what a fall is all about,
it's his area of expertise, so he mounts once more and we are
swinging together with quite extraordinary violence, trying to kill
each other. He says to Hugo afterwards: 'That wife of yours – she's
quite sparky, mate! Can you cope?'

10 June

The honeymoon seems to be over for DC. He tried to shut down
the debate earlier this week on whether ministers could vote in a

referendum without losing their jobs. Not a good move. He needs to understand that refusing to entertain the 'hypothetical' question will not be acceptable to his party. It should of course be a matter of conscience for front and backbenchers alike, and it is clearly the mature and rational thing to do. Boris Johnson has barrelled in too, arguing that it would be 'safer and more harmonious' to give ministers their freedom. Hammond is already under pressure from Owen Paterson and Dominic Grieve, who are accusing him of rigging the referendum and of spending taxpayers' money to do so. This EU hokey-cokey is just going to run and run, with the headbangers leading the charge.

11 June

Hugo stays with DC at the residence in Brussels. 'How was he?' I ask. 'Very pumped up,' comes the reply.

'Funny?'

'On his terms.' Which translates as everyone was fawning around him, laughing at his jokes not H's. I watched him on PMQs before he flew out: smug beyond belief, even po-faced Harriet Harman had to slap him down: 'On the Right Honourable Gentleman's initial response to my question, may I just say that the Right Honourable Gentleman won the election and he is the Prime Minister, so he does not need to do ranting and sneering and gloating. He can just answer the question. Frankly, he should show a bit more class.' How they laughed, George especially, hooting and rolling. K tells me they are impossible at the moment; best avoided for at least three months, though that's not a luxury she can aspire to. She says she bumped into Sarah Gove at some party, who said what an utter nightmare it was living with her husband, implying that his head was so swelled he looked like the elephant man. But then, as Lord Chancellor he is grander than Dave these days!

According to K, on the last day of campaigning, when they

suspected it was all over, the four of them – G, Dave, K and Sam – went for a walk. Let's do up our cabinet, just for fun, G and D said. They thought Gove should stay as Chief Whip. K stops them: 'Are you barking mad? He's crap as Chief Whip and absolutely hates doing it.' So Gove clearly has Kate to thank; it hadn't even occurred to them to move him.

24 June

Amal Clooney comes in to see H, but he's annoyed that Dave has snitched her first. Not least because he fears the PM won't be properly briefed and will say the wrong thing.

26 June

The newly elevated Amber texts asking whether we are going down to Dorneywood, and can she catch a lift. My reply is sharp and to the point: no. We are not of any use to GO any more and not interested in his plotting for PM. Have fun being manipulated.

Jacky Lambert, head of fundraising activities for her old Oxford college and who collects important people like others collect stamps or seashells, puts in numerous requests for an audience with Hugo; she has clearly cottoned on to the fact he might well be useful to her.

H preps his staff before the visit: 'Lay it on thick, folks, I want it to be like walking into Mussolini's office in 1941. I want – no, I demand – formal double-door openings, "The minister will see you now." I want lots of "Yes, Minister, No, Minister." I want you all to be very polite but very formal. Tight smiles, straight backs. Bloody walk backwards if you have to. Understand?'

'Leave it with me, Minister,' says the ever-reliable Fergus. 'We will not disappoint.'

It is apparently a performance that would warrant a standing ovation. As Jacky turns to go, she says, 'Gosh, Hugo, it's easier to get into No. 10 than into here!'

Saffron, newly crowned an adult, steps out of the National Portrait Gallery into Trafalgar Square, only to be confronted by the usual demo. This time it's on behalf of the Falun Gong practitioners, they of an advanced system for improving mind and body, through the teachings of one Falun Gong. The snag is it's rooted in years of traditional Chinese culture and the Chinese government don't like it. In fact they don't like much that they perceive as being popular with the 'little' people which is ironic really since the party was founded for and by the 'little' people. According to the literature, now in Saffron's hands, some sixty thousand of their people have been wiped out. She dutifully signs the petition, giving her name and address. Her name is flashed up on the screen above her as a new recruit. Seconds later so is her father's, informing the gathered masses that he will be the recipient of all the signatures.

16 August

The deadline for bringing sexual assault charges against Julian Assange has expired, so the Swedes have dropped their investigation, though they do still want to interview him about allegations of rape. Before he leaves for our family summer holiday, H calls in the Ecuadorian ambassador, who is housing Assange, and gives him a seriously hard time. The ambassador tries to change the subject.

'Would you like to come to Ecuador, Minister? I can arrange it for you, Minister.'

'No, thank you very much, not at the moment. I don't feel relations between our two countries justify a visit at present. Although I will come one day, because I need a new panama hat and would quite like a trip to the Galapagos.'

*

Nicola Sturgeon wants to talk to Hugo about the impending visit of President Xi to England. Hugo wants to talk to Nicola about not inviting him to Scotland. The officials come in: 'We have arranged the call.'

'It won't happen.'

'No, Minister, it will. It's happening.'

'It won't happen.'

The No. 10 switchboard comes on the line: 'We have the First Minister of Scotland on the line for you, Minister. Will you take the call?'

'See,' says Fergus. 'Here she comes.'

Hugo shakes his head.

'Sorry, Minister, can you hold? There is a delay.'

A minute later: 'We have been told the First Minister now has to attend a meeting. Shall we book another call with her?'

'No, don't bother.'

'Are you sure, Minister?'

'I'm sure.'

There was no way Nicola Sturgeon was going to be told by a British minister who she could and couldn't have to Scotland.

17 August

Trewinnard

H and I draw up a contract for our client:

A CONTRACT TO BE SIGNED BETWEEN THE RT. HONOURABLE SIR JOHN NOTT, KCB AND ROCCO (THE SWIRES' COCKAPOO)

You shall refer to me at all times by my given name and not 'you bloody dog'.

I am not to be kicked or shouted at.

I am allowed to sleep in your chair (on a towel) but you have precedence.

If I bark it is because I am trying to tell you something but cannot speak your language. I am not trying to annoy you.

I want you to play with me because I love and respect you, and I would like to be like you if I was human.

Please do not run me over. I am only one year old and not very car aware.

Why not take me for a walk and we can get to know each other better?

My father's reply:

SASHA. Actually, I rather like your dog. As dogs go he is friendly and amenable. NO, I do not love your dog but it is difficult to love someone else's dog. He is more poodle than spaniel. In fact, if he had a pink ribbon and a diamond necklace around his neck he would be a champion Tart's dog. Yes, he is a Tart's dog and would be accepted in High Society or in places like the FCO, much the same thing.

I am reminded that the Permanent Secretary in Trade spoke to me about Sally now Baroness Oppenheim's dog. He told me that she arrived in the office very late after her morning hair appointment. Her officials found this surprising for a Minister of State but they were upset about her dog which got under her Private Secretary's feet. He reminded me that Trade, unlike the FCO, was a working department. I expressed my complete satisfaction with Sally's work ethic.

To return to your dog I am remorseful that I did breach the Contract on more than one occasion by addressing him as 'bloody dog' but I was provoked by his inability to keep to his side of the bargain. When he was not under my feet he slept all day on my chair. He made no effort to give me precedence on my own chair and out of the kindness of my heart I did not remove him roughly from my chair. If I compare your Tart's poodle with Philippa's [Hugo's mother's] dog [a whippet], your dog does not fare well. Philippa's dog is built for speed and would perform well against a bolting rabbit if he was ever allowed his freedom. I have not discovered whether your dog can perform any useful function. He can chase a ball but does not know how to retrieve it: i.e. he is a consummate Tart's dog giving satisfaction without effort. Given his untrained state I hope he is covered by third party insurance as his passion for getting under car wheels will surely cause a serious accident, possibly loss of life. So, I come to the nub of the problem. I confess that I have demonstrated a sliver of jealousy. After 54 years with Miloska I was never once allowed to bring my working spaniels into the kitchen. They were banished to the kennels where your sister-in-law's dogs lived comfortably enough. Why should your poodle be allowed to live in my kitchen and on my chair when my spaniels were not allowed to do so? What is so special about your poodle and my daughter that they are permitted to breach the long-standing rules of the house. It is hugely unfair.

I am asking my secretary to scan the contract. Penny will forward it to you on Minorca, so that it is in the Archive. When you are bored with your holiday island in a few days' time you can amend it to align it with reality. Love. Dad

20 August

Minorca

No Wi-Fi. No news. Bliss. In 1963, Harold Macmillan wrote: 'One feels better mentally and morally, not to be absorbing unconsciously all that steady stream of falsehood, innuendo, poison which makes up the press today, apart from the purely informative sections. "Gossip" in one form or another, is the main theme and mainstay of modern journalism. Altho' there are nowadays no servants, we are all regarded as making up a vast "servants" hall.'

The only comfort is that the press is now completely discredited, following Leveson, then the completely miscalled election result and now a complete failure to foresee Jeremy Corbyn's romp to the finishing line. How did they fail to notice a resurgent quasi-lurch to the left? I mean, think Greece, think Scotland. You don't have to be Andrew Marr to tell the difference between a Miliband left and a Corbyn left. Andrew Marr and his Guardianista commentariat chums (and wife) are Miliband left, so is most of the current Parliamentary Labour Party, but the membership is nowhere near them; they like the beard, the honesty, the fact he shakes hands with Palestinian freedom fighters (that's the only bit of him I like too). They ignore the fact that he is clearly unelectable because he speaks to their lost socialist souls, unlike Tony Blair, Peter Mandelson, Yvette Cooper. Blair, who is making ridiculous damaging interventions, thinks he should be credited for saving the Labour Party when really he destroyed it. The party is now completely divided. 2020 may be a dim, far-off date in the diary, but whichever side will win there's going to be plenty of internecine warfare in the meantime. In fact, any manner of things could happen (watch Keir Starmer rise and rise).

1 September

Not sure the Chancellor will be quite so smug when he returns to Westminster next week. Boris is rumoured to start his onslaught this autumn. And he only plays the fool, remember – though whether he is one is debatable. The stock markets are pretty wobbly, China's mostly, so it's interesting George is putting out statements from his sun lounger (or dude ranch saddle) that 'we are not immune to what goes on in the world'. The snag is, if there is a wobble we are not remotely prepared for it. In 2008, the national debt was 37 per cent of GDP – fairly low, and it enabled Labour to borrow out of the crisis – but now it stands at a whopping 80 per cent of GDP. There is simply no wiggle room. When Corbyn becomes leader (which is looking like a dead cert) you can bet he will start banging on about austerity big time – George is going to look very tarnished countering this at the best of times, and particularly when people wise up to the fact that he has swollen the national debt to £1.5 trillion and now wants even more of their money – about £56,000 per household, to be precise.

Yes, he inherited a bag of debt, but he has not been in any rush to correct it. Way too unpopular. First, he said he would get the maths right in five years; now he is saying ten. If ever there was an illustration of how perceptions twist politics, this is it: for five years he has banged on about restraint and fiscal prudence – it suited the narrative – but all the while he was continuing to borrow £190 million a day. For years he has been criticising Greece while our debt is six times larger. There are few certainties in life but birth, death and financial crashes. Our borrowing is completely out of control and he has raided pensions, which is not a good motivator for saving. He might be lucky – they (D and G) are, after all, the luckiest duo on the planet – but he is and always has been a gamblin' man. Maybe he should start praying instead: a new bubble and a wider correction, and he's toast.

14 September

After 'Jez We Can' became 'Jez He Bloody Did It!' over the weekend, all bets are off. It was expected, but the bucket of shit being deposited on the man quite frankly stinks. Particularly with his Middle East quotes: clearly, the majority of them have been taken out of context. My God, the Jewish lobby will be throwing the kitchen sink at this one! The *Sun* reports Corbyn feels so guilty about his politics that he will appoint a Minister for Jews in a bid to draw a line under criticism of his links to anti-Semites.

Yes, yes, the guy is a rabid left-wing loony, but he's gonna get shafted before he gets elected. We hope. We very much hope. Of course, the interesting thing is the timeline: do the backbenchers stew for a while in the knowledge that most of their seats are union-backed? Or will there be a purge? Will the party split? Will they dare to rebel? Will Corbyn pull back from his extreme socialist views? If he doesn't, there is going to be the most almighty clash in the Labour Party, creating a chink for the Lib Dems to slip back into being a party of consequence.

In other news, European politicians have been panicked by the dramatic increase in the number of migrants heading their way and have urgently convened a meeting to try and work out what to do. Germany, who at first welcomed them with open arms is now conceding that it will have to close its own border with Austria due to the overwhelming numbers coming into the country. Merkel, normally such an astute politician, has completely cocked up. DC got it right: take the refugees from the camps. If you give them asylum after they travel it encourages them to risk their lives to come.

20 September

George is in Beijing at the moment, making pronouncements about new dawns. He has declared no economy in the West is as open to Chinese investment as that of the UK. Now he wants to get the Chinese involved in our nuclear industry. Ministers are saying there should be no obstacle to China designing and building a plant at Bradwell in Essex. In my book, it's just short-term gain for long-term pain. Why can't we use Brit money instead? In most other countries – the US, Canada, Australia – foreign companies are banned from owning critical infrastructure. And it's not as if the Chinese aren't already involved in some of our key industries, like telecommunications – which, given the range of offensive Chinese hacking, you would have thought we'd have been more cautious about. I am a hawk when it comes to these matters: Beijing's industrial strategy, its approach to technology and its foreign dealings has always made me shit scared. It's times like these when I wish we had a more effective opposition.

21 September

Did Dave really stick his dick in a dead pig's mouth, as Isabel Oakeshott and Michael Ashcroft allege in their book? And who has told them these porkies? I must find out . . .

The press have Mark Field as number-one suspect. But Vaizey and even Gove are being mooted. But no one knows.

15 October

At the Hong Kong Association dinner, Swivel Hips sidles up to Hugo with that menacing grin of his. The Chinese state visit is imminent, and Swivel Hips is edgy, very edgy. He tells H that Minister Wang – H's opposite number – wants to see him to discuss outstanding matters. 'Oh, what are they?' asks Hugo. Seating, apparently, and the joint communiqué and security for the visit. H sighs, this has all been sorted, but plays dumb: 'Oh really, Ambassador? I wasn't aware he was coming in to see me. It's not in the diary, and besides, I'm off to the constituency.'

'Ah, so you delay trip to constituency. How far?'

'Four hours, Ambassador. I suppose I could squeeze him in in the morning, before I leave.'

'No, he get in afternoon. You rearrange?'

'No, not possible.'

'What about Sir Julian King? Does he have constituency?'

'No, Ambassador, he is an official not a politician.'

'Good! You order him, then.'

'Ambassador, there is no need: your people have been talking to our people for months now.'

Hugo puts his arm around his shoulders: 'Just relax, it's going to be all right. It's going to be a great visit and you will get a nice big fat job back in Beijing as a result.'

He smiles. 'You think so?'

'I know so!'

Negotiations are following their predictable course. The Chinese had insisted their security people should be allowed to run alongside the carriage conveying the Queen and the president down the Mall, to which the Met responded that if they tried it they would be treated as terrorists and shot on sight.

Hugo nips into the Whips' Office. These are shark-infested waters for him, so he's a brave man. Whips don't like their MPs to have direct access to the top, as it undermines their power. Nicky Morgan and Anna Soubry are there. Somehow the subject of the state dinner comes up.

'Are you going to the state dinner, Nicky?' asks Anna.

'No,' she replies, rather disappointedly.

'No, nor am I. Not invited.'

'I am,' H butts in cheerily.

'You!' exclaims Anna. 'Why the hell have you been invited?'

'Er, probably because I am the Minister for China.'

'Yes, and Hugo is very royal, after all, isn't he, Anna?' says Nicky, turning the knife.

Perceptions, perceptions.

21 October

Trumpets, red carpets, a carriage trip down the Mall with Chinese officials in blue tracksuits conducting obedient Chinese expats waving flags excitedly. The official address before parliament is a circus. The Chinese arrive at Westminster in great numbers, with busloads of apparatchiks – so many were there they miscalculated the seating. The little weasel Bercow walked in with the Chinese president and then, losing no opportunity to grandstand, pompously declaimed how many Asian leaders he had welcomed to Parliament and what excellent champions of democracy they were, the latest of whom being Aung San Suu Kyi of Burma. Dave looked furious as Bercow lectured the president that the world was watching him and China. In fairness to the little creep, he has been a long-standing supporter of the Dalai Lama. But none of this is helpful at a time when Dave's government is so desperate for Chinese investment and cash.

H comes home to change for the state dinner at Buck Pal. He's exasperated. Exhausted. He says a Chinese official, posing as an interpreter, tried to wrench open the door of the carriage and jump inside today. He was intercepted by members of the diplomatic protection squad. 'You couldn't make it up!' H thinks the Metropolitan Police have been bullied into doing much of China's bidding. Nothing has been off limits; an absolute clash of civilisations and protocols.

The dinner is a Trojan horse if I ever saw one. We have to drive through the rent-a-crowd who have been bussed in by the Chinese embassy to drown out the voices raging about Tibet. Students mostly, who must want their visas renewed. Dissent is about the dirtiest word in the Chinese dictionary and they were having none of it, not even on foreign soil.

Once inside, the rumour swirling around the room is that many more Chinese have turned up than are on the guest list. All are bearing passable invitations, but they are not authentic enough to fool hawk-eyed Palace officials. I cannot believe that they would really try to gatecrash a state banquet, but who knows?

Drinks before the dinner proper. George, looking nervous, is skulking in a corner, hoping that the cementing of economic ties between the two countries is going to save his bacon. Mr Xi Sho-pping (that's what I call him now, as his country wants to buy up everything British) arrives with his attractive wife, their smiles tightly stretched like rubber bands. Of course, we know what lies behind them: *fuck you all, we are the masters now.*

I gently tease the Queen's Private Secretary, Sir Christopher Geidt, KCB, KCVO, OBE, lifting each of his medals up in turn.

'So, what's that one for? Ironing the Queen's pyjamas? And that one – is that for polishing her shoes? And what's that one?'

'Order of the Bath,' he says with good humour.

'What? Running it?'

On a similar theme, Hugo closes in on William Astor, Dave's stepfather-in-law. Hugo lifts a rather sad, small medal off his chest. 'What's that one for, William?'

'It's for many years of financial support to the Islay auxiliary coastguard. The only other recipient was Bruno Schroder,' he says proudly.

'You can't possibly wear that here!'

William very defiantly replies, 'Why not? It's all I've got.' He dismissively sweeps H's hand away from his chest and walks off to find his wife.

Then the line-up. The Duke of Edinburgh asks Hugo if he is a Hong Kong Swire. 'Genetically, but not financially.' (Old line, chip-versus-ship line, overused line, but always the best line in situations like these.) He laughs so hard H thinks it might fell him.

We go into the dining room; Dave sidles up to Hugo when he is not looking and spanks his bottom with a programme. This is caught on camera, and quickly goes viral on Twitter. *(D subsequently sends him a text, saying he hopes he has not ruined H's career, but now every time he sees Hugo he greets him with a pat on the bum. H says not to worry, his bum is now more famous than Kim Kardashian's.)*

I'm becoming quite a regular at these events and the format doesn't change. Always the same school food: poached fish with a watery cream sauce – poached fish is already watery, folks – for the starter, then Balmoral venison fillet, which should be kissed by the heat not bludgeoned with it until its blood vessels have all closed up. The usual herding of guests to get moving, eat up, leave. *The Queen and the Duke of Edinburgh are very old, they need to go to bed early, which absolutely is fair enough.*

H sits next to China's main finance man. He had been prepped by officials to discuss the cheap Chinese steel flooding the market, but the man looks bored rigid as the Duke of Gloucester drones on and on and on; it takes all of H's diplomatic skills to bring him back to the issue at hand. The evening finishes with pipe music from 4th Battalion The Royal Regiment of Scotland and the Army School of Bagpipe Music and Highland Drumming. 'Ouch!' says my neighbour, the High Commissioner of Australia.

Oh God, I hate myself for being so blasé about it all. So cynical. But wait – there's more!

All eyes are not on the Duchess of Cambridge, who takes pride of place due to her good looks, but Jezza. Would he wear white tie? Wouldn't he? Yes, he was in the appropriate attire, although as David Tang* pointed out to me, two buttons were missing from his shirt and instead of a white handkerchief he had a red biro sticking out of his top pocket. Corbyn subsequently said it was the most boring night of his life.

They are extraordinary, these events. Full of flunkies and civil servants, bent double from the weight of all the gongs and titles they have awarded themselves. Only a tiny number of outsiders are invited, and those who are there are the pushy ones. David Tang boasts, 'I bullied the Prime Minister into inviting me when we were holidaying with them this summer', which strikes me as unlikely.

After dinner we have coffee and brandy in another room. Hugo goes off with Ed Llewellyn into a corner. I approach them: 'Chinese whispers?' H is moaning about Priti Patel screwing up the upcoming Modi visit and says he is so fed up he is going to sharpen his elbows, so he gets further up the greasy pole. 'Oh no, don't!' pleads Ed. 'We have too many of those. 'Yes, yes,' says Hugo, 'I'm too nice, everyone walks all over me. I'm changing tactics.' When he moves off, I ask Ed what the gossip is in No. 10.

'Well, the EU negotiations are—'

'No, no, I mean who's shagging who?'

---

* Sir David Wing-cheung Tang, KBE, businessman and socialite.

'I reckon you know more about that than I do!'

'Yes, I probably do.'

'I know you do.'

'Anyway, I'm not really interested in you lot any more.'

'Oh, why?'

'I've decided you have developed a bunker mentality, and have been in power too long.'

'Oh, don't say that, don't stop loving us. We all love you, Sasha.'

'That's because I am vastly superior to the lot of you. Now, when is this referendum?'

'2017.'

'Right, well, I was in, but now I'm out.'

'You can't be serious?'

'You're just a bloody Europhile, Ed. And you need to work harder, because there are a lot like me out there, wavering on the sidelines.'

'Yes, I know.'

And off goes the pint-sized Welshman to look for his boss.

23 October

H was in No. 10 for a meeting when he was told that Bercow has agreed to an urgent question on human rights in China. Not helpful when we are in the middle of a full-blown state visit. Bercow looked very smug as H sat there uncomfortably while all the vitriol against the Chinese from MPs spilt out. H said what he always says, better to have a dialogue than not, better to have a quiet word in their shell-like rather than grandstanding, but the MPs were having none of it. I'm watching H at home at the dispatch box. At one point, to my horror, he says pompously: 'In my travels around the globe – looking after two-thirds of the world, as I am obliged to do – I have observed that our own human rights are way better than those in the majority of countries.' Some time later, Mr Bone, who clearly had been brewing a reply to H's arrogance, dished up:

'I will sleep better in my beds tonight.' *(Does Mrs Bone know he sleeps in beds other than her own?)* Mr Bone clarified quickly for Mrs Bone: 'In *my* bed tonight, knowing that the minister is looking after two-thirds of the world. I would sleep even tighter if I knew who was looking after the other third.'

30 October

Emotionally exhausted now that the 2015 Westminster Dog of the Year competition has reached its climax. Hugo and Sue Townsend, Hugo's long-suffering secretary, have been talking about nothing else all year. Rocco himself did three deposits in the house the night before. H has surprised me with his blatant attempts to recruit as many voters as he could. Thankfully, he wasn't caught red handed (or pawed) sending out pleading emails. The whole of Cheltenham Ladies' College (except one matron, who said she wouldn't do it because she was not a Conservative) and the University of Edinburgh, and Hugo's sister Sophie's Facebook friends (all six billion), meant the 'paw-blic vote' category was in the bag. H takes Rocco on the *Daily Politics* show. Andrew Neil asks him why he didn't win the overall title; that honour went to Lady, an opera-warbling schnauzer cross, and Godiva, a miniature schnauzer, who belong to Andrea Jenkyns, the new MP who snipped Ed Balls off at the election. 'We won the democratic people's vote,' H says. Yes, and that's the vote that counts.

'Well, until it's overturned by the Lords,' he adds.

12 November

Modi comes to town. Priti Patel has been inserting herself into this trip at every turn. As the PM's Indian Diaspora Champion she does have a role, but she is behaving like the Minister for India, which is actually what Hugo is. Sure enough, she turns up at the

VIP suite to greet Modi. She has also done all the press that morning, at Craig Oliver's insistence, and got herself invited to a small lunch with the Queen when we were told no ministers were invited. H has thrown a wobbly and accused No. 10 of being run as it was in the Blair/Campbell days, which has had a startling effect, with everyone from the PM down contacting H and reassuring him what a wonderful job he is doing. Just goes to show a little complaining now and then doesn't do any harm. I wish H was more assertive sometimes, although his particular charm is that he isn't.

Modi descends from the Air India plane and greets H warmly with a man hug. 'I am now presumably Sikh target number one, as this image was beamed around the world.' They head off after the formal greetings to the VIP suite, where in the small talk that ensues Modi tells H he has less hair than when they last met in Gujarat.

16 November

Weekend at Chequers, although a seriously disrupted one. Quiet supper on the Friday night after the Modi rally at Wembley; just us, them, and the delightful Theo and Flora Rycroft, Sam Cameron's half-sister and her husband. Then, as we are having coffee, the news comes in about the bombing in Paris. This is bad, really bad, sighs David. H, who is duty minister, rushes up to London with David for a Cobra meeting and doesn't come back until late afternoon as he has to see Modi off at Heathrow. Randal Dunluce and Aurora, Evgeny Lebedev and the Vaizeys arrive for Saturday lunch.

Dave wanders around, looking bored by this invasion of guests. He often goes off to hide in his study. Or play ping-pong with Elwyn, with whom he is extremely loving, tactile and attentive. He does not show much interest in any of the wives apart from his own, nor in the Russian billionaire. He likes me because I am not remotely nervous around him; I'm cheeky, occasionally lewd and sometimes a little bit too challenging. At dinner, we cover such diverse topics as bombing Syria, STDs at Oxford and my menopausal symptoms and libido. Ed Vaizey, across the table, cranes his neck to listen in on this one; it's like they both want to know what is coming their way with their wives. When I announce that I enjoy sex much more in my fifties than in my forties, they express surprise but lean back and release huge sighs of relief with faces that read *Oh good, it's going to be all right, then*. 'But only if you slap patches on their backsides,' and they sit up again, ramrod straight, and ask questions about that too. It feels like they are young boys learning how to use a condom.

Regarding Syria, I shout at Dave, saying all his plans are flawed, that he won't get a vote through parliament anyway and all he'll do is create just another vacuum for subsets to take over while even more jihadists are recruited on home turf. He is stuck in this groove of not doing something when we had the chance and the dangers of not doing anything now. But it is so much more complex than that. For example, what the hell comes after, I ask. He mumbles something about unity governments and the Kurds being involved. But that's if any are left after Putin has annihilated them, I say. I repeat: his plan is too vague. Look at Egypt, Libya, Iraq – unity governments have all failed, the Arab Spring has failed. He thinks, and I agree with him on this, the main thing is to bring Putin on board, and is hoping he can persuade him – during his meeting at the G20 – to stop killing Assad's opposition and target ISIS instead.

We talk briefly about Palestine and Israel, and he follows the Osborne line on this: nothing will ever change, this will go on for years and there will be no two-state solution. I just think he is so wrong on all of it. I tell him he needs to be more interested; that the disappointment in not finding a solution has a knock-on effect on shaping our own homegrown terrorists.

We touch briefly on Hugo and he tells me he would definitely have been in the cabinet if it were not for his women quotas. He admits that men in the party have suffered as a result, Hugo and Ed amongst them, and he's not very flattering about most of the women, except Pushy Patel and Theresa May. Overall, I found him rather contemplative, troubled by Paris, but also by the prospect of his own demise. I don't think he likes to be reminded that the clock is ticking. But then, why would you? He is probably rather nervous, as Hugo is, as to what comes next. When we talk about Boris and George, and who takes over, he is polite but wants to move swiftly on.

I come home thinking we are coming to the end of an era. That we had had a great fairground ride, full of ups and downs, but the future is going to be very different and probably not as exciting.

Back to the weekend. I confess I was a little intrigued to meet Lebedev. According to Piers Morgan, he is 'one of the most charming, well-connected, exotically attired and fascinating figures in English society right now'. Of course, the flattery of media moguls by jobbing journos needs to be taken with a degree of caution – especially from him. The man, not the myth, is visibly very nervy when he arrives and it's not until Dave has gone that he relaxes, but only by degrees. Maybe it's so completely out of his comfort zone (*Hello!* magazine, Elton John, Liz Hurley et al.). He's something of a charisma-free zone but again, it was difficult to tell: he gives nothing away. H reckons his mysteriousness is all about his loneliness and he does strike you as a Gatsby figure. He's rumoured to have odd fads and this comes over when he shows an extraordinary interest in the Chaffcombe honey I brought as a gift. We are having breakfast in the dining room and I am talking about it, saying it's an elixir that can cure all known bacterial infections in one fell swoop. I explain that most shop-bought honey is dead, and without beneficial nutrients, because it has been over processed – it's why it is aroma-free – and he immediately stops his conversation with his neighbour, reaches across the table, grabs it and tries it.

Soon after, on a walk, he expresses his dislike of the vulgar Russians flooding London. 'I don't know any of them,' he tells me. He's a fastidious bachelor, taking great care with his personal appearance, but says he dates English women – usually ones to be found in the pages of *Tatler* or *Hello!*

What I do find extraordinary, and have to pinch myself slightly, is how he has managed to penetrate the very core of the English political establishment by buying a newspaper. Bearing in mind that Lebedev's father was a graduate of the KGB's Red Banner Institute and an operative who worked at the Soviet embassy in London in the late eighties. Alexander these days is still pally with Putin.

On Sunday we walk to the Plough pub. Flora and I tease him about how we are the impoverished wives of men in public service and have concocted a plan to kidnap him. We will be gentle with him, and feed him borscht and possibly rhubarb crumble, and he will fall in love with us, his captors, because that's always what happens in kidnapping situations. I tell him I'm a little troubled by his bodyguards, who are sitting in his Rolls-Royce in the car park, but my plan is to grab a Kalashnikov off the police at the Chequers entrance and overcome him while he is sleeping.

'You have got it all worked out then,' he says.

'Yes, and then you will give us the twenty-million-pound ransom anyway because you love us. You *have* got twenty million, haven't you? Cause I'm not going through all this effort if you haven't.' He doesn't answer. Probably one of the reasons why the *Independent* is going digital.

Kate says of the times he has come to No. 10, she is none the wiser about what he wants by the time he leaves. But she still likes talking to him about Russian ballet.

Samantha has blossomed into her role. She has become the perfect hostess, smoothing over all the nerves of her guests and making them feel welcome. Before everyone arrives on Saturday, she takes me into her bedroom to try on all her samples for her burgeoning fashion business. She has real talent as a designer and has produced a collection that even I would buy. She intends to launch it next year. They will throw the book at her, of course, for exploiting her position, but she dismisses the threat of this by saying all publicity is good publicity. There is a lot of her mother in her.

18 November

H is chatting to Amber on the front bench. She tells him she has
finally broken up with Kwasi (Kwarteng) after a long on-off relationship. 'It was increasingly difficult, being around a rising star.'

'Gosh, is that really how you felt?'

The joke is lost on her: 'No, Hugo, mc: I'm the rising
star, not him!'

'Oh, right. You – you are the star. Of course you are, Amber.'

2 December

The whole thing is a sham, MPs approving UK action including
airstrikes against ISIS. I also doubt ISIS will be quaking in their
boots at the prospect of being bombed. Apparently, they have
already moved operations to the coast of Libya. Another one of
Dave's overseas triumphs. And where is his phantom army of seventy thousand coming from, exactly? It feels like dodgy dossiers
are being replaced by bogus battalions. Truth is, it's all about Dave
and George and Ed's obsession with the country retaking its place
at the top table and working with its allies to eradicate the Islamic
State menace. Even they admit bombing is only likely to make a
limited contribution to the broader coalition objective of destroy-
ing ISIS. The general consensus among politicians and military
folk is that ground forces will still be required.

3 December

Hilary Benn's speech really was the clincher. It persuaded many
Labour MPs to back airstrikes. They then found themselves on the
receiving end of vile abuse online. 'Enjoying sleeping when the first
child dies,' was one of the messages to Stella Creasy, while Benn
attracted disgust and threats from anti-war activists, who said he

had brought shame on his family. Jeremy Corbyn has been called to expel party members who abuse and threaten parliamentarians. When did politics start getting so nasty? Does it coincide with Corbyn as leader? In the run-up to the vote, he was decidedly menacing, telling MPs considering voting for action that they would have no 'hiding place'. Of course, Corbyn has no respect for Britain's security, but he should at least acknowledge democracy.

2016

17 January

Over to Kate's for a gossip. We laugh over an article that appeared in the *Mail* two weeks ago, which was sourced from an Oxford student newspaper and churned up her Oxford days. The article has a complicated 'family tree' showing 'Who's Had Who', with 'Lazy' Vaizey scoring the most. Not so lazy after all, it seems. K says none of the men listed – fund manager Bruno Paulson, George Osborne, PR bod Hugh Cameron, Anthony Frieze and Ed Vaizey – ever had the privilege. Vaizey implies otherwise, which drives K nuts: 'Well, I've not "had" Antoine Palmer and it would be ungallant to comment on the rest' is his quote. The morning it came out, she arrived at No. 10 fuming.

'Are you sure?' asks Dave.

'Women always remember who they sleep with, Dave,' she huffs. She fires off an email asking Eddy, as she calls him, to put out a statement that they did not have carnal relations. Vaizey texts back:

'I can confirm, you were not on my lay line.'

'Eddy' then emails No. 10, cc-ing the PM, the Director of Communications, the new Baroness herself, the Permanent Secretary and the Culture spad, and saying that he is prepared to issue a statement that Kate never put out, but only if they meet five demands to do with his brief. K says to me, 'He's nothing if not original.'

18 January

H back from a trip to Sri Lanka and the Maldives. In Colombo he stayed in the newly refurbished High Commission, which has recently been rebuilt at a cost of £5 million, after the original building was eaten by some very grateful serrated-jawed termites. Of course, the contract to build the original building had gone to a Brighton-based builder who they couldn't afterwards find as he was a one-man band. 'Ah, the joys of government procurement,' H tells me. He has now asked for a full report of what happened. Everyone will no doubt be covering their tracks which is the way of these things, 'The problem was the man should have sprayed the ground with pesticide before building the damn thing!'

The trip is dominated by the plight of Mohamed Nasheed, the first democratically elected president of the Maldives, who has been sentenced to thirteen years in prison by his political opponents. The FCO were very keen to get him out of this undesirable location. While there, H had been rung by Peter Mandelson, who also appears to have a dog in this fight. He is long-winded and pompous and almost trying to claim success for having got this far.

Having landed in the country, H tells me he was involved in the most intensive negotiations of his life so far, racing between the President, the Foreign Minister and others in a bout of diplomatic gymnastics to secure Nasheed's release. H almost combusts with kerosene-fuelled rage at being misled, blasts off in a mad craze back to the Maldives Foreign Office, all of which is filmed and on TV, unbeknownst to him. Frantic calls from Amal Clooney in Washington, who is also lobbying heavily on Nasheed's behalf, and John Kerry – both try desperately to get through to H.

Of course, the Maldives government didn't want to let Nasheed out of the country as they knew he would run an effective campaign against them from overseas. H, on sparky form, threatened them, mentioning travel bans and sanctions. He would have sent in the fleet if he had one at his disposal. Of course, as anticipated, they ratcheted up the conditions on Nasheed being allowed to travel abroad for 'medical treatment', at one point demanding he nominated a family member as a hostage. Eventually, H leaves the Maldives, having made the position clear. On landing in London, he is informed Nasheed has finally been released and was in Colombo, en route for the UK. Mission accomplished.

24 January

H discovered, from bumping into Jonny Hall, No. 10 foreign affairs adviser, that Nasheed, Amal and the caravan are coming in to see DC on Saturday morning. No thought of inviting H, who actually sprung Nasheed from jail, so he invites himself.

Thinking David would be in his usual weekend chillout wear of jeans and a dark shirt, which he believes disguises his middle-aged spread, H opts for a casual tweed jacket and brown shoes. On arrival, D immediately spots this and says, 'Brown in town?' to which H replies, 'I am not normally in "town" on a Saturday, David.' Everyone else is in suits, so H borrows a club tie from Ed Llewellyn, puts it on, and then says to everyone how he now looks like a paedophile maths teacher at a prep school. They all agree, laughing.

As they wait for the visitors, David says he wishes H would stop making trouble over Tony Blair staying in embassies around the world, as he too will be an ex-PM one day and will want to do the same. Hugo tells him to talk to Potato Head, Andrew Bridgen, as he is the one who has been submitting all the FOIs.

The Nasheed gang arrive. Formal exchanges in front of the press in the white drawing room. Amal, quick as lightning and as direct, occupies the chair next door to the PM, in which H would normally sit, thus ensuring she gets in all the close-up photos. Savvy, that one! H is perfectly content with this, as he is rather embarrassed by his appearance and doesn't want it to go 'live' with it. Nasheed is graciously full of praise for H's role in getting him out of his Maldivian cell. Others join in to laud the part H played. Ed says later he had no idea. Of course, no one at No. 10 has any idea about anything other than what they deem to be the problem of the hour. And of course that's Europe, Europe and

Europe currently. On the way out, David asks Ed if he has spoken to Juncker, and tells him to tell Juncker that he wants to do a deal.

H slips out of the front door of No. 10 to see Amal and the Nasheed gang still speaking to the assembled press as they climb into their hired-for-the-occasion fleet of black presidential-looking limos. They are pros, these people. One of the journalists comes running over, camera in hand, asking if H was involved in 'any of this'. H shrugs enigmatically and smiles, and wanders back to the Foreign Office to pick up some papers.

4 February

David's renegotiations with the EU are a failure. Show me where anything has changed. The EU still has the upper hand in our relationship with them. We have been love-bombed by the Ed and Dave Show (GO staying out of the picture, obviously, because he has leadership concerns with the right of the party) all because they, and particularly Ed, can't say boo to Brussels. Oh, they think they are so much cleverer than the rest of us, that we could all be squashed under the bulldozer of their campaign. I know it's tough over there, those Euros aren't at all like us, and I don't want to undervalue Dave's sturdy personal resolve to find a solution in his renegotiation and referendum strategy, but he should have started from a much higher mountain and climbed down from its peak. Not start halfway down and slide to the bottom. Trouble is, political leaders always go native. It's because they have direct and familiar contact with the players; they quickly become misty-eyed in their dealings with them.

9 February

Black and White Ball. We are last-minute invitees. The table is hosted by Alisa Swidler and her husband Joshua. Also on the table are Benjamin Tansey, Jacob and Gaby Lyons, Eitan Na'eh (deputy ambassador of Israel) and his wife Cheryl, and Sarah and Tony Pidgley, the founder and group chairman of Berkeley Group Holdings. Alisa picks the best two men, my husband being one of them, and then shoves all of the women to the other side of the table, so we can natter, no doubt about cake-making and children. Dave comes up and kisses me.

'Look, they have put all us women together,' I say. 'And look at that table behind: all the Indian women on one side and all the men on the other; it looks like a Labour selection meeting in Bradford. What is going on in the Conservative Party? All this stuff you are doing to project a modern and diverse face of the Tory Party is completely fake.'

'Yes, it is a bit odd, I agree.'

When I complain to Amber, bearing in mind that she is a committed, if adaptable, feminist she just says, 'What's wrong with sitting next to women, Sasha?'

'I can't flirt with them, that what's wrong with them.'

'Yeah, fair point ... ' And she's gone, hotly pursued by some donor who is keen on renewables, for which she has cut off his subsidies. She tells me she has had too much drink to handle him.

10 February

Book H in for a colonoscopy and endoscopy at a private clinic. The consultant's name is spoken with reverence by the bottom and abdomen brigade. He is a tall man with a well-lunched tummy, and he comes across as gloomy, which is to be expected, I suppose, when you spend your entire life looking up people's anal passages, hoping the wind doesn't blow your way. I suspect he has sold a portion of his soul to the worried well and longs to stumble across more juicy tumours, but hell, there are school fees to pay.

Afterwards, H and I go for a follow-up appointment at the clinic. The consultant can barely summon the interest to look up from his scribbling as he asks the usual questions: do you smoke? How much do you drink? Do you have acid reflux when you lie down? Do you have a history of gallstones in your family? Blah, blah, blah. H outlines his symptoms, including one embarrassing episode of being caught short two years earlier.

'Yeah,' I interrupt. 'And it was in my car!'

The consultant looks up, assessing the comment seriously. I continue: 'But then, when you have children, dogs etc. you are used to picking up poo.'

He puts down his pen and sighs. 'I know, I have budgerigars and they are a nightmare. They shit everywhere.'

'Really?'

'I had one and that was all right, but when the second came along they couldn't stop.'

'Noisy too, I suspect.'

'Never stopped.'

'The best thing to do with budgies is open the window and let them fly away.'

'Didn't need to: the dog got one.'

I gasp, then let out a chuckle. 'What kind of dog?'

'A pointer.

'He spent two whole years with his head rotating in a circle, watching them fly around the kitchen ceiling making him dizzy, and then one day one of them stupidly dropped to his level and *GULP!*

'My wife was in tears, of course. Wrestled what was left of it out of its mouth and presented it to me in her hands like an offering.'

He goes on to say he took said dog to the vet because of a blockage. No doubt caused by all the budgie-swallowing. He told the vet he wanted a scan: bearing in mind the insides of dogs are not too dissimilar to the insides of humans, he had already diagnosed the problem. But the vet was less than forthcoming, clearly seeing the economic potential of coming up with his own diagnosis. He started listing all the things that might have caused the upset, including, last but not least, sword-swallowing!

'So, I say to the vet, "Are you seriously saying that my pointer's problem has been caused by plunging a sword down his throat?"

'"I'm only doing my job. I'm just ruling out possible causes."'

The consultant then goes off on a violent diatribe. He tells us all vets are morons and compares them to the pig-ignorant registrars he deals with on a daily basis. As for their fees, simply extortionate. He has a point. I say, 'It's a racket – not unlike your game.'

And so, our session ends, several hundred pounds later, having spent the bulk of the time talking about his dog's gastric problems rather than my dog's gastric problems. *C'est la vie. C'est Harley Street.*

21 February

This is real Conservative drama. Boris unexpectedly comes out for the EU referendum. One can't help wondering why he is suddenly taking an epic political risk after years of playing it safe, but maybe he has weighed up where the votes for leadership lie. No. 10 are starting to get really neurotic. Dave feels he is being stabbed in the back by Gove et al., but that's ridiculous: it's an issue that is bigger than even him. The No. 10 master plan was for Michael Gove's loyalty to Cameron to trump his convictions; Priti Patel to be daunted by the prospect of dashing her career prospects; and for Boris to do what he was expected to do, but when has he ever done that? The plan was to leave Eurosceptic old guard nutters led by Iain Duncan Smith, of fifty or so backbenchers and some disaffected spads to lead the out campaign. Now Graham Brady is predicting half the parliamentary party will be joining the leave campaign.

I don't think they will win, but it's going to run close.

I go over to Kate's to unload. I say we mustn't fall out over this, but there is a point when she gets a little menacing about Hugo. H is in Canada on an FCO trip and is missing the drama. I tell her he is genuinely torn, but if he goes for leave David must not hold it against him; the issue is big, and about the country and not just David's career. K says he is taking it very personally and that he will be destroyed if he loses the campaign.

'But Kate, Dave has already said he is not serving a third term. He is leaving anyway.'

'He will be furious if Hugo does not show him loyalty.'

I say this is ridiculous. H's political career is coming to an end and he does not expect any promotion; he can do what he wants. I don't say it, but I think fuck the lot of them. Loyalty is always a one-way street. H has been there from the start, has been sacked from Culture, had his job offered to a political enemy, had two-bit inexperienced MPs leapfrog over him for PR reasons and been sent into permanent exile. Good old Hugo.

She tells me that Dave and George are pumping out purple exhortations at the betrayals but seem angrier at the treachery of Michael's departure than at Boris's. Gove apparently picked the worst moment to tell the PM of his decision: right when Dave was slogging it out at the negotiations in Brussels. Boris played them until the end, only texting Dave twelve minutes before he came out and announced. And as for that Priti . . . pathetic! George wants to get nasty but is being reined in – though for how long? He will work out that Boris is his main leadership rival and want to do him in early.

24 February

Dave chases H by voicemail, suspicious he might be turning. They agree to meet in his Commons office after PMQs. David has just finished bashing Corbyn, telling him if his mother were present she would tell him to stand up straight, do his tie up and sing the national anthem. Which the backbenchers deeply enjoyed. On H's arrival, DC is busy trying to ring his mother to warn her about the likely press maelstrom.

He is in a warm and friendly mood. H sometimes forgets that they are by now old friends; it's been over sixteen years, and there is nothing of the PM to his minister in their relationship. H confesses to being torn over the EU. Dave agrees on the ghastliness of much of it, the overpowering arrogance of some commissioners. '*You* think they're awful?' he says at one point. 'I have to deal with them!' H says that what irks him is that when it's all over, and assuming Dave wins, he will be told he has to re-form the cabinet to heal the party, bringing in the likes of Brady and Fox, who have done nothing but stab him in the back. He groans, 'I know, I know.' He tells H that they are both practical sensible Tories who think identically on the majority of issues. Pragmatism trumping ideology. Of course, he is right. H tells me Dave was almost tearful about Michael Gove, who he claims had never even hinted that he would campaign to exit the EU. Interesting to see if that wound heals in the future. H leaves, telling DC that he has never let him down yet, and won't now.

29 February

Andrew Feldman, in a spot of bother with the Clarke* scandal, reduces his fiftieth birthday celebrations to a dinner for forty somewhere in the City of London. The Goves ring up and say, 'Do you still want us?' Feldman is thinking he can't disinvite them now. It all goes wrong when Sarah and Sam, fur flying, have a set-to at the party, with everyone watching and listening in. When the wives get nasty, you know the men have a problem.

It's an interesting one, the wives. Last week Sarah wrote a column about the 'torture' she and her husband faced over his decision to back the campaign to leave. K is disgusted: 'She should keep her personal reflections to herself.' Personally, I rather enjoyed

---

* Mark Clarke, former chairman of Conservative Future, was accused of bullying younger activists. Clarke strongly refuted any suggestion of wrongdoing.

it and thought it well written. Political wives are deeply involved but have no official status. Do we play submissive? Do we play supportive? Do we get lippy? It's a difficult call, one we all have to weigh up individually. At least the days where we are wheeled out as an echo are over. Miriam Gonzalez Durantez, Marina Wheeler, Sarah Vine – they are all intelligent, active players and there is no question that they have helped mould the debate. The trouble is, women like Sarah want the credit for it themselves. Of course, they should try to stand as MPs in their own right, but they don't because they get all the benefits of being close to power without having to do the work.

G tells a good story about how Miriam was asked to edit the *Today* programme over Christmas, and wrote to Paul Dacre to ask whether she could interview him. In her letter, she said that he had only ever referred to her as Mrs Clegg, but that she would be doing the programme as Miriam Gonzalez Durantez. Dacre wrote a curt letter back, refusing. And then the PS: 'You have only been asked to do the programme because you *are* Mrs Clegg.'

Meanwhile, down at Chaffcombe we are having difficult conversations about why we are backing remain when our instincts are to leave. I have to somehow justify it to myself as well as convincing H. I spend the whole weekend drafting an article for Hugo for the local press on why he is supporting in, and we finally decide to do it from a foreign-affairs perspective. I write that membership of the EU, like our membership of NATO and the UN, amplifies the UK's power and influence on the world stage at this dangerous time. But mostly the article stresses the importance of the Western alliance, which has done so much to keep peace in a post-war Europe, and how a rift will separate nations and create vacuums.

1 March

H to dinner at 5 Hertford Street to celebrate Lord Barker of Battle's fiftieth. Greg, rather like the Queen, seems to be having at least three birthdays to celebrate this great milestone. The other guests are David and George. Naturally. H walks there from the Foreign Office and arrives to find Greg perched opposite the front door, looking excited. He is relaxed, having just flown in from Nairobi. They dine in the private room upstairs; delicious food and away from staring eyes and cupped ears. Of course, the coming referendum and the leadership question (more when Dave left) dominates. They spend a lot of time discussing tactics after 23 June. D is very fired up about Boris and determined to finish him off. He shows the group a text from Boris saying, basically, 'don't worry, you'll win', which he is going to use at a critical time. Talk of Michael Gove and betrayal. The general consensus is that Sarah has persuaded Michael that he could become the next leader.

After D leaves, George says he will have to go – he will want to go – if they lose, and H echoes this. G at one point says, 'Don't worry, you'll join Greg,' meaning the Lords. Let's see. George also says D is head and shoulders above anyone at the moment, as was Blair; his loyalty knows no bounds. H asks him if he sees Blair, and he confirms he does, a couple of times a year, but adds that Blair is much reduced, haunted even, and basically travels the world like a war criminal – albeit a very rich one on the make. They talk about G's prospects of succeeding D and agree it all depends on the economy and timing. Clearly the plan is not to let Boris through to the membership. Priti Patel would be better. H asks about Sajid Javid, at which G laughs dismissively, saying, 'I don't think he's ever quite lifted off past the control tower. Do you?' They decide there is no point doing anything until after 23 June. G says he has asked Amber to Dorneywood, and would we mind? H said she was a very old friend and Siena's godmother, and suggested he ask her to bring Kwasi Kwarteng, as that seems to be on again. G likes the idea, so H texts Amber. It is agreed. Should be good, as Kwasi is pro-leave.

Norman Lamont had sent Dave a text, saying he was out. Dave sends a text back from his flat in No. 11: 'I am standing in exactly the same place you were when everything was falling apart [Black Wednesday] but I stood by you.'

6 March

Return from an overnight stay at Dorneywood, H and I mildly depressed by the frosty atmosphere between Frances and George. They barely talk to each other these days. He, as usual, holds court. In fact, between H, Kwasi and G, we women felt almost superfluous. Kwasi is essentially an academic; he is enthusiastic and bombastic, and barely draws breath. H can be just as bad. I have a quiet word with G before dinner and find him consumed by leadership tactics. I tell him he needs to do some soft stuff, that his main problem is image, but it worries me when I see him and Frances together as a couple, as I know it won't work. There is already much speculation about the state of their marriage behind bent hands at Westminster. He reckons he can get the MPs' nomination but is not so sure about the party's. He thinks it's Boris's to lose at the moment. He tells me that, historically, no outsider has beaten a chancellor to the leadership. He is always one for context and historical precedent; it gives him a sense of security, even arrogance. The referendum is not really talked about but when he says they are renovating Dorneywood I say, 'What's the point? You'll be out of here in two months.'

'Well, then I'll have done it up for Andrea Leadsom. So lucky her.'

We leave after breakfast, but not before G watches Boris on *Andrew Marr*. At one point I turn to look at G; it was like looking at a child who is about to commit some terrible torture on one of God's weaker creatures.

I often think about Boy George. He is such a curious political specimen in so many ways. Yes, he is highly privileged, but he has suffered much mockery as well. I guess that's what happens. Yes, he has a heart, a hinterland, dimensions, passions, and he bleeds when he is cut, but you rarely see that side of him. He is excellent company in private and can be hilariously funny, but he doesn't mind how he gets his way.

7 March

Proposals for asylum claims to all be channelled through the European Asylum Support Office is tormenting the Eurosceptics, who just see it as another unsubtle power grab via another treaty change. The 'in' lot just say by return, calm down, it's all OK, we won't have to do anything we don't want to do, but what they are failing to mention is that we might be deprived of existing powers such as the one permitting us to transfer thousands of asylum seekers to other countries on the European continent. Such proposals are already a huge help to the leave side, with Boris writing in the *Telegraph* this morning about the EU's mission creep: 'It's time we learnt the lesson. The federalists do mean it when they sketch out these programmes. The ratchet is clicking forwards. When you come to vote, the status quo is not on offer.'

9 March

Date: 8 March 2016 11:49:50 GMT
To: Hugo Swire
Subject: Honey! [OFFICIAL]

Dear Hugo,
   I hope you are well.
   I have just had a rather unique call from a lady in Evgeny Lebedev's office. He loved the honey that you gave the PM at Chequers in November, and has tasked his assistant to find out where it was from. I have explained to her that you have your

own bees and that I suspect the mystery honey was from your
own hives. If that is the case, I don't suppose you would have
a spare jar for him?

    Sorry to bother you with quite such a random little enquiry!

    Best wishes,

    Rosie

Hugo replies that if Mr Lebedev wishes to have some of his
honey, he should call him himself and he would willingly give him
a couple of jars.

22 March

The resignation of IDS feels like the present regime is now in its final
throes. It will be very difficult for George to pull back from this.

David is trying to hold it together, and has put Stephen Crabb
into the DWP. He got up in the Commons and announced he was
formally pulling the plug on the PIP proposals that had driven his
predecessor over the edge. Where the £4 billion is going to come
from is anyone's guess.

Dave seems to be spending a lot of his time these days talking to
EU ministers about the migrant crisis. Dead children on beaches,
people climbing ashore from dinghies, Belgian jihadists blowing up
airport terminals. It is the biggest, most tragic story of our times. I
vacillate between two positions. My gut instinct, rather like Boris's,
is that immigration is good for this country but that we must make
a distinction between economic migrants and refugees. Then there
is the brutal truth that success and development drive immigration
rather than deter it and we continue to be a successful economy.
Sure, we can fight it on a superficial level but short of a meteor hitting our country, our future is one of worlds banging at our door.
People will come. People always come. Their hearts are stronger
than our heads or our will to stop them. Not even a referendum
can do that.

10 May

H sits next to Theresa May on the front bench. 'How are you, Theresa?'

'All the better for seeing you, Hugo,' she replies. H, for a brief moment, is flattered, and then pinches himself to make sure he's awake. The leadership campaign is clearly on.

Elsewhere Dave continues with Project Fear, giving a big speech on how we are all going to war – how stupid does he think we are? Brexiteers have sought to laugh off his suggestion, with Michael Fabricant mischievously asking in the Commons yesterday whether parliament had 'made provision for fire service or . . . missiles of defence, should war imminently break out upon our leaving the EU?' Creepy Bercow confirmed that no such preparations had been made.*

Dave's speech coincided with five former NATO secretaries-general writing to the *Telegraph* to warn that Brexit would 'give succour to the West's enemies'. 'At a time of such global instability, and when NATO is trying to reinforce its role in Eastern Europe, it would be very troubling if the UK ended its membership of the EU,' they write. I suppose they have a point, and it is one that H shares.

This intervention may not change many voters' minds by itself. But it will serve a more useful purpose: countering argument that leaving the EU will be fine as NATO can keep order. Boris said as much yesterday, when he argued that the EU's 'anti-democratic tendencies' had become 'a force for instability and alienation', while it's 'the Nato guarantee that has really underpinned peace in Europe'. Then William Hague in his *Telegraph* column: 'The EU nevertheless provides a structure that restrains the centuries-old rivalries of continental Europe. Everything I saw as Foreign Secretary corroborates what David Cameron and recently retired

---

* Fabricant later quipped to the gossip columns: 'I see myself in a tin hat manning the stirrup pumps on the roof of Westminster Hall as a fire watcher'. Yes, that about sums up his talent.

intelligence chiefs have said in recent days.' Thirteen former US secretaries of state and national security advisers have come out in *The Times* to ram this point home, warning that Brexit would leave Britain's place in the world 'diminished'. To be honest, I changed my mind purely for these reasons.

Meanwhile, IDS is on the warpath, slagging off Dave's pathetic negotiations in Europe. He is claiming that Dave dropped the demand for an emergency brake on immigration at Germany's request, saying: 'It's like they were sitting in a room, even when they were not there. There was a spare chair for them – called the German chair. They have a de facto veto over everything.' No. 10 won't like that, as the Prime Minister has been made to look like Angela Merkel's puppet.

More worrying is that the latest average in the polls suggests that both sides are level-pegging. Remain will need to try harder to break out into a clear lead.

7 June

DC still taking it all very badly. Particularly as regards Michael and now Steve Hilton. He is irritated by Gove and Cummings's political relationship, which is very intense and exclusive. Unnaturally close. It's the paranoia of a government under threat. And the paranoia of a man who is on the verge of losing power. He sends H a rather sad text: 'You are my only friend left.'

Kate asks about my father. He is prominent on the leave side and it's filtering back to them in No. 10. Dave never once included Sir John in anything, unlike all his generation of politicians. I tell her my father has always loathed the PR side of the Cameron government and the fact that David is not an ideologue. He has never been a fan. Really, it's just an analogue versus digital contest, but if David had been clever, he would have recruited him at the start and he would have benefited from his political nous as he did with Heseltine, brought him into the big tent. This is the payback.

9 June

Rows at home in Walpole Street. H is furious that Sir John is about to do an interview with the *Telegraph*, slagging off David. Then Mum has a go at him. Dad storms upstairs in a huff. He has been increasingly annoyed by the gusto with which David and George have been campaigning for a remain vote and tells the journalist that he has taken the step of suspending his party membership, 'until we have a change of leadership'. It's not helpful. K texts to say 'her heart sank' when she read it. The Dowager commented that 'he looked very handsome in his photograph'.

10 June

Amber did the ITV debate last night. Five women and Boris. It's a tactic from No. 10. They think it will be difficult for Boris to take on the women with his lothario reputation. It all started off normally, the remainers implying that quitting the EU would be a leap in the dark. Leavers were upbeat about Britain and that it had a great future if it went it alone. Amber was good, but Boris was the best I've seen him. It was the first time that I thought he could be leader.

Amber made what many have interpreted as a huge error, though: she turned personal against Boris. Watching it felt as if George O, rival candidate, was feeding her positions into her earpiece from the control tower. On immigration, the hot topic of the day, she was brought into land with a line that it is 'a complex problem . . . you need to look at the numbers. But the only number Boris is interested in is Number 10!' And then the crash-landing, the killer line: 'Boris is the life and soul of the party. But he isn't the man you want driving you home at the end of the evening.'

I text her and ask her if there has been a backlash. She calls straight away, laughing. 'Yes,' she tells me, 'from the Irish Society, who say I have been racist after pressing Boris about the claim on the leave campaign bus that it costs £350 million a week to be a

member of the EU.' Amber had got snarky, and told the debate:
'We're going to repaint that bus and put a leprechaun on one end,
and a great big rainbow on one side and a pot of gold at the end.'
She says the response has generally been mixed, depending which
side you are on. But adds, 'I believed in what I was saying, I'm
cross about all these lies they are peddling: I wanted to do it, no
one forced me, Sasha. Boris is doing this all for the wrong reasons
and I don't mind saying so, even though I know if he wins I have
burnt my bridges.'

She had a list of lines on her lectern, that she had prepared; 'I
got half of them in, so I'm quite pleased.'

It might well be Amber's breakthrough moment.

14 June

Dinner in Kensington, hosted by Roland Rudd. In attendance:
Chief of the General Staff General Sir Nick Carter and Lady
Carter; Steven and Annie Murphy (founder, Murphy and
Partners parenting counsellors); John Pienaar (chief political
correspondent at the BBC) and his wife Penny Davies; Wafic
Saïd; Anna and Joseph Schull (chairman of Warburg Pincus);
Sir Anthony Seldon, vice-chancellor of the University of
Buckingham; Radek Sikorski, ex Foreign Minister of Poland and
now senior fellow at the Center for European Studies, Harvard;
the journalist Anne Applebaum; Ambassador Pasquale and
Karen Terracciano; and a very irritating Hugo Dixon.[*]

There is a roundtable discussion, with H, Roland and
Hugo Dixon dominating, alongside Radek Sikorski and Anne
Applebaum. On the whole, this lot are mostly tired, deluded
Blairites at the champagne end of the spectrum. There is a lot
of slagging off of Cameron, looking for a new saviour to turn
the campaign around in the last few days and a general air of

---

[*] Journalist and campaigner. Deputy chair of the People's Vote campaign. A
    great-grandson of Winston Churchill.

hopelessness. They come up with Gordon Brown. 'Please!' I whine, but they turn their guns on me, barely able to contain their admiration for the man. I find Sir Anthony Seldon tiresome and arrogant (though he subsequently sent a nice note to H). Dixon worse. For this elite, it's all about the intellectual detail. I try to interject, that this campaign is hitting the heart, not the head, but I don't think that any of them have had any contact with or understanding of the leave voter. The nice John Pienaar backs me up: 'No, Sasha is right, listen to her. I'm getting this on the streets as well.'

Anne, John Pienaar and I all are sure we are going to lose the referendum, but a show of hands around the table thinks not.

During the roundtable discussion, each guest is given a chance to do a turn. In the middle of Wafic Saïd's contribution my phone goes off, it's Siena, but I can't find my bag. I had put it on the floor, and someone has kicked it down the opposite end of the table. I start crawling on my hands and knees, looking for it between everyone's legs. The Chief of the General Staff turns to H and says in a pompous way, 'Very embarrassing.'

'Yes,' replies H, 'but I'm afraid that's my wife.' Then he quips, 'If you put a tenner in the bowl she might come down our end like the old days.'

The Chief of the General Staff looks appalled.

15 June

GO makes an astonishing series of threats about a spending-cuts-and-tax-rises emergency budget he promises to deliver if Britain votes to leave the EU next Thursday.

I send Kate a text. Why, why, why, has he done this? 'It just smacks of panic,' she says curtly, 'it's not meant for you.' What she means is that it is for the undecided, and there are a lot out there, or they think there are, and it's been done to scare them. We speak later and she tells me that the private polling tells them consistently that people fear the economic consequences of leaving and that is why they are pushing this line as hard as they can. She concedes that G woke up the next morning utterly depressed, asking himself what had he done. His view was that he had to take the hit and damn the consequences, but he was hating the response and headlines.

It might work, all this scaremongering, but I'm not sure. I'm also not sure George hasn't written his longest suicide note to date.

16 June

The murder of Jo Cox has devastated everyone. What it has high-lighted – and I have written a blog post to this effect for Hugo's website – is that our politics and public discourse have become so intolerant and vicious that respect is in short supply. We see it locally since Claire Wright became Hugo's opponent, vying for the seat of East Devon. Her followers are totally unrestrained in their personal attacks: there is even a whole website, called East Devon Watch, that perpetuates a completely new type of politics, one that encourages paranoia and hate. We need to expel this extremism and promote a new respect for public institutions and democracy, the rule of law and other cultures, but I fear so much hatred has already been injected into the political bloodstream, mostly via the internet, that it will be difficult to pull back from it. The referendum campaign has not helped: all the normal rules of political engagement have been suspended, traditional party lines washed away as MPs trade insults and foster contempt. The whole world of politics is at a terrible low.

We can only hope that if anything comes from the death of Jo Cox, it is a new respect for MPs, most of whom are genuinely honourable, work hard and try to do the right things.

23 June

Texts between D and H, 4–23 June:

> H: Are you OK? I am just back from my travels. I fear you
> are going to have to hold your nose after we win with
> some of our dear colleagues.

D: Good to hear from one of my remaining few friends!!

> H: Dinner on me when victory is ours!

D: We can do the 'bonkers' list with some new additions.

> H: Feel in my bones we are going to be OK

D: Thanks. Butterflies . . .

> H: Hopefully not. The average life of a butterfly is 5
> to 14 days!

27 June

The longest weekend in our political life. It starts Thursday night,
referendum night. H and I, foolishly deceived by the polls, decide
to accept Rupert Soames's invitation to spend the next three days
in the wilds of west Scotland. The campaign has been so long
and venomous, we feel we deserve some rest and restoration.
We board the dated and grubby night sleeper run by Serco,
of which Rupert is chairman, and get through masses of gut-
rotting cheapo vino and crisps in the dining car while awaiting
the result. The Orient Express it ain't, but a full refurbishment
is on its way. I go to bed at around eleven and wake at two. I'm
stunned by the early results and text Kate immediately: 'I'm
worried. Are you?'

'Yes' comes the reply. I decide to wake H because if she's saying
that from inside the No. 10 bunker, I know we are going to lose.

I go to H's compartment but he is sleeping so deeply I can't rouse him, so go back to bed. By five, it's all over and I wake him, this time successfully, to tell him we have lost, and that we need to get back to London to prop up Dave. Rupert agrees to stop the train at Blair Atholl; it is 6 a.m. and we get off the train in the middle of bloody nowhere. The tiny station is hugged by bruised Scottish hills and has a traditional signal box and a Victorian ticket office and waiting room. It feels as if we are in a Hitchcock thriller. All very *39 Steps*. We eventually take a chug-chug back down to Edinburgh.

The train to London is interminable and full of Scots tanked up on football and lager. Saffron rings, crying, she is furious that old people and white van man have stolen her future. I tell her she should have made more of her friends get out of bed and vote.

While we are on the train Dave comes out of Downing Street to give his resignation speech. Sam is in tears (later she tells me that, having been up all night, she didn't think she could go out there without drinking a large Negroni. When they walked back inside, Dave apparently recoiled from her gin-sodden breath.)

We are both stunned and sad. Really sad. Boris and Gove come out into the blinking Brexit dawn a bit later, looking, as Alastair Campbell commented, like two people who have watched their spaniel being hit by a freight train. A sleep-deprived Boris tries to look upbeat but fails miserably. Gove, standing by his side, looks as if reality has just slapped him in the face with a cold kipper. Of course, neither were expecting this result. It just felt so monumental. Everyone walking about like the living dead not quite knowing what they had done. The victors trying to stay calm, the losers seeking to lay blame.

We get to London by four – it feels as if we have been on the train for twenty-four hours – and crawl back home. The bad news keeps coming. Jonathan Hill, our EU commissioner and a close ally of Dave, resigns without telling anyone in Downing Street. Now there is no insider. We decide to go for a curry. Not only is our political world being whacked by tidal waves, we are also physically rocking from side to side, an affliction commonly experienced after a long journey. In fact, we feel so nauseous we can't each eat much and go home shattered and shaking.

H texts Dave on the bus home and says we are around if he wants cheering up. He texts straight back and asks us to get down to Dean with two fat Cohibas and plenty of booze the next day. In the morning we are still in this dreamlike situation. K rings me in tears. She wants to come over. She is obviously worried about her future. She comes with me to the hairdresser, reliving the night before; they are all finding it bizarre, being on the losing side for the first time. K tells us that Andrew Feldman wants to send Graham Brady a date for calling a leadership election, for 22 September. No, says George O, it has to be 25 September. That date would make him the longest-serving Tory Chancellor. We all laugh: even at the end he is thinking about his place in history.

We get down to Dean by 5 p.m. Dave is not there when we arrive, but Sam is. She is naturally devastated – not by Dave's departure, but by the decision, the 'stupid, ill thought through' decision the country has made. She tells me she tries to hide her emotions and fears from Dave, but is sick with worry about what will happen to the country in terms of inward investment and businesses, and doesn't know whether to carry on with her fashion business. I scoop her up in my arms – which is unlike me – and tell her it's going to be OK, that politics finds its level and so does trade, and that businesspeople like her won't stop doing business with each other. Secretly, I'm mildly excited about Brexit, but don't dare show that down here.

When Dave arrives, he makes a lethal Negroni before we all progress to endless bottles of wine, rounding it off with whisky and brandy. Over a dinner of mushrooms on toast followed by juicy pork chops, David is incandescent with anger, which is almost wholly directed against Michael. He tells us that if he had any idea Michael would have done this he probably wouldn't have called a referendum, but that there was never any indication he held such strong views. Which is slightly odd, as Michael has always been known as a Eurosceptic. He tells us that even Sarah had said Michael would back him. As for Boris, he says the whole thing is mad; that he had always been a supporter of Europe and free movement and migration, that this whole episode was to do with his leadership ambitions, nothing else, and that he despised his lack of ideology, which is a tad ironic really. David tells us Boris had consistently shown he was wobbly, even 'depressed', at trying to work out which way to go, leading D to believe he was, like many of us, a reluctant remainer. Then, when he switched sides, Boris was telling him via texts that Brexit would be trodden on *(the actual text said it 'would be crushed like the toad beneath the harrow')* and that he (David) would survive, the last one coming about ten minutes before he was appointing himself as head of the leave campaign . . . Clearly covering all bases. Of course, the assumption then was that D would win.

Dave goes on a rant about Theresa May, and how difficult she was throughout his premiership. That Hammond and she advised him not to go hard on an emergency brake for immigration when he went off to negotiate with Merkel. He also expresses his utter frustration that she refused to back him during the referendum, clearly because of her own leadership ambitions, and that whenever he put a call in to get her on a platform somewhere she made some lousy excuse, like she was going on holiday with her husband.

He hisses at the mere mention of Theresa Villiers and Priti Patel, women who he perceives he has given a leg-up to. But he concedes, when pushed by us, that he would go for Boris over Michael any day. Michael, he says, is a radical, an iconoclast, that all his ideas are subversive, that he would make a terrible leader, he is too extreme; that Michael, as he once said, 'believes the world makes progress through a process of creative destruction'. The general consensus is, deep down, Michael even knows this himself, but Sarah's ambitions will be pushing him to the front. We also agree that Michael has always been disingenuous: you never really know what he is thinking, but it's usually not what he is saying. Dave really wants someone normal to be the stop-Boris

candidate and keeps saying Amber is 'normal'; she's someone the
Cameroons can coalesce around. I look surprised by this and say
I doubt she will be interested (I ring her later and she says exactly
that) but Dave asks me to ask her discreetly. He likes Jeremy Hunt
but thinks Amber would be better.

After dinner, we go through to the sitting room. Sam conks
out on the sofa; a whole set of children sit on her, but she does not
wake up. Dave and H are now chomping on cigars. D tells H about
the cabinet reshuffle he was planning in September: Priti out,
Hammond out, Hugo in as Secretary of State for Culture. Hugo
starts drinking to new levels now; he has waited all his political
career to be in the cabinet and now the opportunity is gone.

I ask what Dave would have done with Boris, and he replies
'Minister for Housing'. He could dump the whole problem on him
and see if he swims. That would have gone down like a lead balloon. Of course, if Boris had stayed on side, he probably could have
had his pick of jobs. And George, what about George? He does not
have a bad word to say about him. He admires him enormously.
And yet I don't think this is the view of many remainers, who saw
his input as a hindrance, particularly with his specific and dire
warnings about the economy, which ultimately were not believed.
We all laugh raucously when Dave tells us that when Ruth
Davidson was asked whether she would appear on a remain panel
(the one she subsequently did so well in) along with Angela Eagle,
she said, 'You can't have two shovel-faced lesbians on together!'

David, unsurprisingly, has not been sleeping well, but tonight,
having vented, he sleeps soundly.

On Sunday evening, the news is still coming in thick and fast. I
speak to K; she says Gove is ringing up Jeremy Heywood, saying
he wants full access to any negotiations that go on in Downing
Street from now on. GO, meanwhile, is weighing up whether to
back Boris, because Gove is putting pressure on him to declare.
He obviously wants that threat out of the way. I tell K that George
must pace himself, there might be a big backlash with the collaps-
ing markets and he is in with a second chance, but really, how

could he deliver on something he didn't believe in? Amber is being called up by everyone. Gove, she says, is charming: *we do hope you will consider supporting us, I thought your attacks on Boris were hilarious* etc. She says he strongly implied she will stay in her job. Amber says Theresa gets someone from her campaign team to ring her, that she has no contact with the MPs and never has done.

My main fear is Boris, who now looks like a shoo-in. Will his gift for winning votes translate into a focused and successful prime minister who leads his nation out of Europe? I just don't know.

If only Theresa May were more human. The choice is quite frankly dire.

30 June

A minute is a long time in politics these days. It's only 11.07 a.m. and Gove has just entered the leadership race, saying Boris doesn't have what it takes and he does – have what it takes, that is. The first sign of trouble in the camp was when Sarah Gove apparently sent an email to her husband – but oops, it went to someone else entirely – asking just how popular Boris was with the rank-and-file and telling Michael to hedge his bets till he got a firm job. H says it was a very cheap glue that stuck Gove and Boris together; that it was bound to come apart. Dave and K said as much too. They are enjoying the spectacle. My assessment is that Gove wanted to pin down a George Osborne-type role for himself and Boris was not giving it to him. Gove would also have been pushing for Osborne to get Foreign Secretary but Boris didn't want all the Cameroons in his nest, doing a cuckoo on him. But he clocked this a little too late. Looks like Theresa is the front-runner now.

11.52 a.m. Boris is not standing. Bloody hell! All the build-up and then the punchline. His supporters look shell-shocked. Nadine Dorries is seen crying. Gove versus May for a showdown? Or will Gove and May do a deal now, with no leadership election?

He's something else, that man Gove. Or was it all a carefully constructed plot in which Sarah, Cummings, Boles and the advisers, and possibly Osborne, helped him move across the chess board? Who knows. I wouldn't put anything past him.

To the American Embassy for their huge Independence Day party.

Roland Rudd is there; he's devastated by the referendum result.

Theresa arrives, and suddenly everyone wants to take selfies with her. We are all laughing with her, 'Roll up, five pounds a snap – we've got a campaign to fund.'

When we come home, H calls up Gav (Williamson), Theresa's campaign supremo. 'We're in!' H says. Because we just think she is the best of a bad, mad bunch.

Later, Dave texts H:

Sam will kill you if you back Gove. As Nancy would say 'just saying'. Loved the weekend.

H: I had not thought otherwise.

D: Good man. What a day!

1 July

Michael launches his leadership campaign with a five-thousand-word composition at the Policy Exchange. So far and so far-reaching, across so many departments, we all thought it was a bit too well prepared, as if it had been lurking in a drawer waiting to be summoned. But all the hacks really wanted to know was which *Game of Thrones* character he identified with and why, but he refused to answer.

3 July

We stay with John and Suzy Lewis. Gove has nailed down all of the Donhead St Mary donors, and was coming to lunch but pulled out when he decided to stand. John has secretly been raising money for him. Treacherous bastard, I say. 'No, he's a man of principle; you've got it wrong,' he tells me. Dominic Lawson is also there. Gove rings three or four times, asking for him. Lawson is clearly in his camp. Michael starts to chase H. Probably because Gavin has not yet released H's name for Theresa. When they speak, he says, 'If you don't support me publicly, can you do it privately?'

'No, Michael, I'm not like that,' says H.

6 July

In the lobbies Andrew Mitchell comes up to H to talk about the email leaked to today's *Times* from someone at Invesco, where Andrea Leadsom, who is in the race, worked. They are utterly incredulous about the claims she has made about her role there. She was in fact just the assistant to the chief investment officer and had no executive position at all. Clearly, she is bigging up her economic competence, which has become one of her main selling points. H tells Gav, saying we can't possibly have a PM who has falsified her CV.

Andrew says, 'Vote Gove, stop Leadsom.'

'No, Andrew,' H replies. 'Vote Gove, get Gove.'

*

Greg's rooftop birthday party in Soho.

Andrew tells me he has been secretly working on Boris's behalf for a year and that he promised him Defence Secretary. He also told H that David had promised him a senior job in the FCO. H then tells Andrew that Dave had promised to put him in the cabinet.

'In what position?'

'Sorry, can't say because you're so indiscreet.'

'You mean you would be senior to me?'

'Yes, afraid so,' H says with some satisfaction.

Francis Maude is there. All chipper. He's in Gove's camp. 'I've finally discovered I'm an anarchist,' he says, which was already evident to most of us from his pulling down of UKTI and the civil service. He asks who we are going for. Theresa. 'Urgh, how could you? She is so boring and grey.'

'Pot calling kettle black, Francis, you were the most boring politician of the century until Simone [Finn] came along and gave you some colour,' I say.

Later on, I am speaking to former MP David Ruffley: 'Oh, Sasha, you are so Hollywood, so glamorous in those dark glasses.'

'Darlink, maybe I have a black eye, maybe I don't want anyone to know I'm stoned, or maybe I'm fifty-three and I look better with them on than off.'

He tells me that Petronella (Wyatt) is in tears the whole time about Boris. Odd that, considering how he treated her, and how Ruffley is her current squeeze.

H talking to GO. They both look around suddenly. The sun is shining. The Mariachi band is playing. The cocktails are kicking in. 'Aah,' says George, 'this is what freedom looks like!'

H replies, 'You mean we will be able to give a party like this for our friends?'

'Yes, and more.'

Hugo moves on and I talk to George. I tell him he fucked up, that he and Gove got too obsessed with the handing out of jobs. 'Gove just wanted to be you,' I say. He smirks. 'Does Dave know you have been backing Michael?' George gives me his most snide smile. Best he keeps that one to himself, I warn. I tell him he needs to get out of politics now. I also ask what Andrea was like in the Treasury; he says he wasn't happy with her.

Frances says George has had lots of offers, and could I possibly tell him to leave politics because he won't listen to her? She says that in a couple of years' time the offers will all have dried up. On the same subject, K tells me she has had an offer from Matthew Freud to run Comic Relief, which she promptly turned down. 'I don't do celebrities,' she told him. So, it's starting to happen for them all.

Finally, I tell Dave that H is bringing in the Dowager, with Chardonnay (aka Saffron), to No. 10 tomorrow, and that he needs to put out the red carpet in Downing Street. Use his full diplomatic charm. 'Sorry, no can do. I'll be in the House with the Chilcott report,' he says.

8 July

H to Dave: you all ok?

D: Fine. Stuck in dull NATO dinner. Makes me almost miss the EU council meetings.

10 July

To Cheltenham for the weekend, as it's Siena's school speech day on the Saturday. Amber is the guest speaker. We shack up in a hotel room together on Friday night, to save money. If the red tops were following her, they'd have quite the scoop: MINISTER IN BED WITH MP's WIFE. We get legless with her gloriously young-looking (but sixty-year-old) sister Mandy over dinner. Amber's speech the next day is full of confidence. I have known Amber since we were eighteen, and she really has had the most extraordinary transformation; her early working life was not peppered with much success at all. In her bed curlers and big pants, she tells me that her CV would not have remotely stood up to the kind of scrutiny Andrea's has received. I ask about her. She tells me she is kind, clever even, but bangs on about her children ad nauseam – which is interesting, since her husband stays at home to look after them, apparently.

The *Sunday Times* interview is in by midnight on Saturday. Leadsom says she didn't mean to cause offence in any way, and that she hated the very thought of motherhood becoming a factor in the campaign – which, of course, is why she referenced the tangible stake in the country's future that having kids has given her. All intended to give her a political advantage and steer attention to May's unsuccessful attempt to become a mother herself. Can you imagine this conversation happening if the leadership race were all-male?

Amber is disgusted by her words. For me, they just reflect her complete and utter inexperience and incompetence. Not sure that friendship will survive despite a truce lunch in which Andrea spelt out her ambition to be chancellor and told Amber she was playing her cards accordingly.

11 July

Another crazy, crazy day. All our fears about Andrea have been quelled, as today she committed hara-kiri and pulled out, in the 'best interests of the country', which, of course, has absolutely nothing to do with the calamitous error of judgement made when she went into that interview and talked about motherhood.

Theresa will now be crowned queen without going before the rabid right-wing loonies that we count among our members.

Almost immediately, her new bezzies were squirming around her like snakes in a bucket. And Conservative MPs are good at shedding their skin when they sense power might be drawn away from them – and they are even more slimy if they think they are in with a chance of some of that power. As for Theresa, she was her usual expressionless self, even for such a historic day, but she did smile, and she did kiss Denis, or whatever he's called.

But the drama didn't end there: the confirmation of a new

leader, and ejector-button time for my friend Dave. Gosh, isn't it brutal! Out of Downing Street weeks earlier than expected, but that's the ruthless Tory way. He is suddenly very yesterday.

After speaking to the 1922 Committee, May was escorted by her hopeful heavies to St Stephen's Entrance, where Tory MPs had gathered, grins zipped to lips, adoration blazing in their eyes. *Where's H?* I ring him. 'She's been and gone,' I tell him. He is not remotely interested. I relay how Amber's elbows were the pointiest, standing right next to her; that Alan Duncan looked fit to burst, thinking he was back in the game; that, behind her, straining to get into the picture, were a bouncing Liam Fox and David Davis grinning ear to ear. No Andrew (Mitchell): he clearly miscalculated this one.

I'm fearful that the dreadful generation Dave leapfrogged over to modernise the party will all be given places again. Groundhog Day. I hope not. But as Dave said to Kate, it looks as if Theresa is turning to the left when her party is now turning to the right.

H has a chat with Hammond back at the FCO, where he is still a minister. He is not, as H first thought, that close to May. Some even say he still nurses a grudge about her winning Maidenhead over him. They discuss her keynote speech in Birmingham, which deplored City excesses, the elite's 'narrow social and professional circles' and 'cutting out all the political platitudes about "stakeholder societies"' and agree it was full of nonsense. If she makes him her chancellor, which is the rumour, he will make her drop the ridiculous idea of putting employees and consumers on boards. Good luck being up against her on that one. I don't think it will be a match made in heaven if it happens.

12 July

H comes back from a leaving party at No. 10. He is sad and silent, and does not want to talk. He says it feels like a bereavement. Only hardcore Cameroons were there. Speeches all round, including one from Samantha. Dave says to H that he told Theresa she should keep people like Hugo and Philip Dunne because they are solid and reliable. He also tells her not to go near Fox and Davis, that they are trouble and have no following. But I really want Hugo to move on now. It's unlikely – very unlikely – that H will be offered anything, since T has already said she wants female parity in cabinet, and H won't move sideways. So, it's over and out, bar the promised knighthood. There is absolutely no indication where Theresa is going to place anyone. H puts his hand horizontal to his nose and says to George, 'The water is here, so how are you going to get out of this one, Houdini?'

Dave says to H, 'I have put in a good word with May.'

H replies, 'Thanks but I'm thinking of joining you on the back benches.'

13 July

Dave walked today. He will be sad, he will be worried about his legacy, of holding a referendum and all that will now follow. But I feel deeply he was right to make that decision, and this was reflected not only in the result but in the turnout. The time had come to renegotiate our position with the EU, and to give people the opportunity to have their say. Europe was shifting in ways that had become unacceptable to many: new treaties, talk of an EU army, more powers transferred. Yes, many of us, Dave included, would have preferred a reformed Europe, but it was not to be.

The referendum might be perceived as his failure, possibly his health reforms as well, but there are many achievements of which he should be proud: he turned around the Conservative Party after years in the wilderness and made it electable, with a win in 2015 which defied the commentariat; he presided over a coalition government at an extremely difficult time and in a way that united rather than divided the country. He made it possible for people of the same sex to marry. In my opinion, he restored Britain's reputation abroad whilst simultaneously putting the nation's finances on a more even keel, having inherited a disastrous fiscal crisis in 2010.

Above all, David is an honest, charming, fundamentally decent person, which is only too rare in politics. He is an uncomplicated family man and his achievements far outweigh his disappointments. On the whole, he played the cards he was dealt with integrity and intelligence and I believe history will judge him kindly.

But he has been a good friend to me as well. When in 2013 I felt my carefully constructed world was falling apart around me – H being a pig and always away – I remember ringing him up in a distressed state and he told me to just get in a car and come down to Chequers, where Sam and he slowly brought me back to life. I can hear him now, ringing up H to give him a severe ticking-off, with me smiling on in gratitude.

15 July

May Day saw Phil the accountant become Chancellor, Amber Home Secretary and Damian Green, an Oxford contemporary, at Work and Pensions. Fellow leadership hopeful Stephen Crabb, the Christian missionary, is off to spend more time with his family after sexting a nineteen-year-old. He's the bearded one who is also married, a devout evangelical Christian who disapproves of gay marriage but thinks it's OK to sext.

David Davis takes charge of the Brexit negotiations. I think this might work because he is such a headbanger, but it won't work if it's a trio (Boris, Fox, Davis): their egos are all massive and there will be almighty turf wars between the three of them and their departments. The Foreign Office is already pissed off that its power is being diminished.

As for Boris . . . none of us saw that coming. Ruth Davidson puts it best: 'Everyone deserves a seventh chance.' I'm not sure May hasn't put him there to destroy him.

H asks George if he is OK, which of course he isn't.

G: Yes, thanks. C'est la vie (if we can still use French)

H to D: Blimey, Baskets filling up fast with
Cameroon Heads

Dave: Davis, Fox, Ha ha

Everyone is really down, including my husband. I suppose there is always a small part of one that just hopes, prays. He knows that's it now: no cabinet for him. Gavin rings him to say as much. The most irritating thing on a day like this is how everyone rings you up, asking what you are getting, and you hear the disappointment in their voices when you tell them that's it. George is particularly miserable, he feels Dave has come out dignified and respected, whereas all the failure of losing the referendum has landed in his lap.

16 July

We are pumping mad. Almost everyone has been placed on Minister of State level, and still no word from Old Ma May, not even to sack Hugo. Just plain bloody rude to treat a senior minister that way. H rings Dave, who is doing the childcare while Samantha goes back to Downing Street to pack up. He sounds more exasperated than at any time that he was prime minister. Starts shouting at Nancy in the background.

'Don't clip her around the ear, you've already lost her once,' says H. 'I don't want to feel obliged to call the NSPCC.'

Dave also thinks it's rude of May to treat H like this. They have a rant.

A call to Richard Benyon. (The Cameroons are regrouping and

forming a mutual support group.) He says he saw Gove looking 'exceedingly refreshed' in the Lords with Boles and Maude, and asks if this is a regular occurrence.

Dom Raab has resigned (he thought he should go up, not sideways) and Anna Soubry's gone. (She was apparently offered a post under the legally ignorant Liz Truss and told Old Ma May that, as a barrister for fifteen years, she found her offer frankly insulting. All the Govites have been dismissed in one form or another – Morgan, Raab, Vaizey, Whittingdale, Boris. Theresa probably thinks she has drained the swamp, but we all think she is setting herself up for trouble. Too many good ex-ministers on the back benches now, causing trouble.

K furious about the complete dismissal of the Cameron legacy. She huffs and puffs about how they all rebranded the party and that May has not even got a democratic mandate, and how it was them wot won it. And how dare she be so dismissive of all the main players? They were there and for a long time, and there was a reason for that. She texts Hill and Timothy to congratulate them, but they do not respond, which is downright rude.

14:34: Even Tobias Ellwood, a PUS, has been told. He is staying where he is. H suspects there is a fight going on in the FCO to try to keep him.

14:52: Sacked! 'You know how it is, Hugo, I have to make way for some new people,' says the old boot. Siena is banging on the window to get into the car, so H, who doesn't want to chat with the new PM, puts the phone down. And to think he backed her – though I don't suppose that slime ball Gavin Williamson ever told her that.

We put a Looney Tunes picture up on Hugo's Twitter and write, 'That's all, folks.'

Friends start texting in. H sends one back collectively:

Managed to shout 'Viva Cameron!' before she got me with the final bullet!

Dave: Iron cross with oak leaf cluster. George thinks Panzer regiment reunion shouldn't be in the Commons.

Kate: Good for you

George: I wish her well . . .

Richard Benyon: FFS! This is all getting a bit silly. The fashionable place to be now is the back benches. I don't want to be anywhere near some of the dunderbrains she is promoting.

Pepe Meade: That's the way to go!! Abrazo

H replies:

> Now I can come and get my Order of the Aztec Eagle!
> Come and see us in London soon. Or I'll come to you.
> I need a haircut* – or perhaps not, as I have just been
> decapitated.

Henry Norreys: One day, that Mrs May, she gonna pay!

Alan gets H's old job. We don't in any way resent that. He suffered under the Cameron regime. He says he will be calling H for advice.

He will be vain, tetchy, primadonna-ish, but probably just as good.

Boris texts Hugo: 'We are very sorry to lose you and thanks for all your heroic work. They all seem to love you and rate you at the FO which is more than can be said for yours truly. B' It was a nice thing to do.

*

---

* A running joke between Hugo and Meade, who once as Foreign Minister arranged for H to have his hair cut in his garden in Mexico City, to the amazement of all their officials.

H comes down to Devon, defying the whip. He wants to send a message that he's cross. He talks to Anne Milton before he leaves; she also thinks that Old Ma May has been discourteous and unappreciative.

But really, he just wants to lie low for a while, have a good summer.

He is being asked to come back as chairman of CMEC,* which he has accepted. It will keep his hand in with foreign affairs, even if he is not in government.

I'm already down at Chaffcombe, cooking in the kitchen, waiting for him to arrive, when I am alerted by a constant hum, like a machine working in the distance. Something is definitely in the air. A vibration. A trembling. A commotion. I know what it is immediately: the bees are swarming. I go outside to double check and, sure enough, a big black speckled cloud looms above the house, shivering and twisting in helixes, threatening like a sudden turn of bad weather. I go back into the house and charge around it, lighting all the fires, and find the reconnaissance party nosing around in my bedroom wood burner. I quickly smoke them out and they pour back out of the chimney and travel west. Swarming, of course, is the process by which a new honeybee colony is formed, when the queen bee departs with a large group of worker bees. So, it's out with the old and in with the new, even at Chaffcombe.

17 July

Gove has gone into a nosedive, apparently, thinking he has lost all his friends, his income, his respect amongst party members. The old adage that all political careers end in failure has never felt truer. An account of his sacking came in the *Telegraph*:

---

* The Conservative Middle East Council, an organisation devoted to encouraging greater understanding of and ties between Conservative politicians and the Arab world.

'There is not going to be room for you,' Mrs May told Mr Gove. 'I have been talking to colleagues and the importance of loyalty is something on people's minds.'

[. . .]

'I'm not saying there is no way back or that you'll never serve in my government,' Mrs May added, 'but it would perhaps help if you could demonstrate that loyalty from the back benches.' Mr Gove, as always, was scrupulously polite.

'Thank you very much, Prime Minister,' he said, before turning on his heels. He had been in her office for as little as two minutes.

He walked the short distance down dimly lit corridors to his office where advisers were waiting for him and said: 'That's it.'*

1–4 August

Peace is not to last. There is a disgusting silly-season feeding frenzy over Dave's resignation honours list, which H is on. FURY AT DAVE'S GONGS FOR HIS CRONIES (that was the *Daily Mail*). HONOURS, THE STENCH GROWS (that was the *Daily Mail* the next day). TOXIC HONOURS NO ONE WANTS (*Daily Mail*, the day after). DAVE'S TWO FINGERS TO THE VOTERS (*Daily Mail*, the day after that.) Every day the bile continues, sending clouds over our Ibizan sunbeds and mostly at the behest of the top class warrior of them all, Paul *don't tell anyone I send my kids to Eton and have bought an estate in Scotland* Dacre, who is undoubtedly incensed by the flagrant oversight that he is not going to be ennobled himself. Clearly, he is propelled by his resentment over his cherished friend Gordon Brown's failure to land him one in 2010. But we think what really tipped him over the edge was

---

* Tim Ross, 'Revealed: The inside story of Theresa May's "Day of the Long Knives": Two minutes with the PM . . . and Michael Gove's fate was sealed', *Daily Telegraph*, 16 July 2016.

the Frogs giving a gong – the Légion d'honneur, no less – to editor of the pink sheets, Lionel Barber. (For what, exactly, the entire political class are not exactly sure.) 'LEGION DIS'HONNEUR' screamed the headline. The 'weapons grade social climber and name-dropper extraordinaire' has been given 'one of Napoleon's gongs in recognition of his newspaper's relentlessly pro-EU coverage'.

Poor desperate, dangerous Dacre, he has tried so hard all these years to bring resentment to the middle classes, to patronise women, to humiliate everyone in public life, surely, surely, they can dole out a measly CBE for his trouble?

Anyway, on he ranted, ruining our holiday, his paper trying to say that all the honours had gone to remain supporters. Pathetic, green-eyed monster rantings. In fact, the whole paper seems to be one long personal rant these days. 'Indeed, won't knighthoods for converts to Brussels such as Defence Secretary Michael Fallon, Chancellor Philip Hammond and former Foreign Office Minister Hugo Swire forever carry the taint of Judas's thirty pieces of silver?'

I don't know what all the fuss is about. Why can't Dave pack out the list with his cronies if he wants to? Show me a king who has not bestowed favours on his court. All these people worked tirelessly for nearly a decade to bring stability to government and showed a deep loyalty to their leader; it's completely natural and in order for Dave to want to reward them.

Gove has been spotted looking ill-shaven and rotund on the streets of London. Strangers have been warned (by *Private Eye*) not to approach him, as he may be dangerous, that he may be your friend and then try and betray you. The pics certainly show he has let himself go, but then unemployment can do that to a man.

Michael will be missing the power more than any of the others. But he is a great talent, an interesting man; he will bounce back, of that I am certain. Strong rumours are that he is being courted for the editorship of the *Sunday Times*.

26 August

Back from a stay with David and Samantha in Polzeath. They are both on good form, but Dave is still a little bossy. We travel over old ground (Gove, Hilton etc.). He is still cross but not sure how he is going to maintain it when Sam will be seeing Sarah at the school gates in September and he will be sharing the voting lobby with Michael. Sam and I agree that September is going to be tricky all round, as both of our husbands will be without their usual manic routines. H is already rearranging the cutlery drawer. D says he is still waking up at 6 a.m.

He tells us a nice tale of showing Old Ma May around the flat at No. 10 when he was still living there. Every room they peer into, even one with that gorgeous cupcake Florence playing, she gives her Medusa stare. Not for her Sam's *Elle Deco* style, clearly. Until she enters Sam's dressing room (and let me tell you, it was large!) and she sees her racks of shoes. Suddenly sunshine enters her soul.

I think I'm going to like it here. Just one question . . . we won't have to pay the bedroom tax, will we?

We all have a good laugh at the turf wars currently taking place in the FCO. Lots of I told her so, I told you so, that this would happen, from Dave. The three Brexiteer amigos only have a month or so to come up with a credible economic plan for post-EU Britain but already the storm clouds are darkening over Whitehall. Boris, who unbelievably is sitting in one of the greatest offices of state, seems to be spending most of his time batting away attempts at a land-grab by his upstart colleagues. In a leaked letter, the Fox, International Trade Secretary, has recommended that the moneymaking expertise of the FCO be relocated to his responsibility. The Fox believes that economic negotiation has to be the critical consideration in delivering the Brexit trade goals, a function he believes that cannot be properly filled by the FCO. He tells Bozza that he should therefore concentrate solely on 'diplomacy and security'. You can just see the mandarins now, leaping up and down on their red leather chairs in King Charles Street feeling their wedding-cake kingdom is under threat. But Boris is having none of it. Old Ma May puts out via Timothy that she is not best pleased with this internecine warfare.

Of course, the Fox is grappling with all the problems of a new department; how the hell is he meant to do it unless he gobbles up the FCO's commercial role, and in which H was a key player? Then again, most economic diplomacy is conducted through the embassy network and I hardly think Fox is going to set up a rival system and why would Boris even allow that?

Then there is DD, also struggling to set up a department, he also needs to carve chunks out of the FCO to make it work. He will need hundreds of key staff from key departments, which will be furiously resisted by the mandarins who will be protective and territorial.

H says unless Boris is careful he will end up with a much-reduced FCO, something H views with horror. At heart H will always be an FCO cheerleader and would like to see its role expanded rather than reduced.

Enter Alan, who hates Fox and hates Davis. And although he is not that fond of Boris, he will be determined his power base is not reduced. H speaks to Alan on his sun lounger in Marbella. 'Don't worry, Fox will be gone in six months,' says Alan. Harmony Hall, it isn't.

Even Phil the accountant is sticking his oar in. He has told Davis what is to happen to EU subsidies post Brexit. DD won't like that.

As Dave says, there was a reason he kept this mob at arm's length.

2 September

I have ended relations with the *Express and Echo* over what we consider to be their biased and imbalanced reporting which constantly favours Claire Wright. To be honest, we no longer need them as we can now put out our own content; in effect they come to us rather than we go to them, which is a big change from when we started in this game. What has happened to local journalism? It's very sad. The *Express and Echo* used to be such a good paper, but the last two editors have so diminished its seriousness. Talented political journalists such as Matt Chorley and Jason Groves all started their careers on local Devon papers, and they were a delight to deal with. The current political reporting just feels appallingly amateur and removed from the realities of governance.

The Champagne and Bubbles Ball, or the Bubblegum Ball, as we like to call it. This is sold to us as the Association responding to H's request to have more fundraising events. Had we only known they would respond in this way! I chain myself to the railings, pleading desperately for H to go alone, but he is having none of it: 'Get in the bloody car now!' We head off to the Woodbury Golf and Country Club, a hideous development originally owned by Nigel Mansell, the taciturn former racing driver. Luckily H's dinner jacket and trousers had arrived by courier from Bristol station, where they had ended up after Saffron had parted company with them on the train. H's rage went nuclear on hearing the news.

I am not the only one who doesn't want to go. The Bubblegum Ball has failed to excite or interest the good citizens of East Devon and numbers were low – very low – just fifty-two at the last count.

'Cheer up, you'll get to dance with everyone at least three times,' says Hugo in the car on the way there.

'I don't know how to ballroom dance.'

'Well, you should have watched more *Strictly* then.'

Smoothie-chops Darryl Nicholas, the youthful (and quite hot) former mayor of Exmouth, who would like to succeed H as the local MP and frankly the sooner the better from his point of view, is the MC, and a very funny one he is too. Think cruise-ship crooner between sets. Darryl's chaotic love life has settled down now and he has a buxom blonde Swede on his arm. According to his mother Cherry, he met her online. Apparently, she worked for the Swedish military in Afghanistan but has now settled down to a less demanding role in a shoe shop in Exmouth.

The band consists of two elderly moustachioed types who look bored and make frequent trips to the bar between numbers. Standard ballroom music, cha-cha-cha, slow waltz, samba, with a lot of electronic back-up, as the luminaries of the East Devon Conservative Association take to the floor, cream tuxedos and glistening red cummerbunds to the fore. H makes a short speech and later the loyal toast, where everyone stands except for the Elson sisters, who make a tentative effort by half pushing back their chairs, though without any great energy or enthusiasm and quickly give up on the effort. Terry Darville, the former hairdresser, who we like enormously, and who is now referred to as the Tin Man as his body is now entirely held together by metal, demands to lead off the dancing with me as he says, rather sarcastically, that he had never danced with a 'Lady' before. We seem to go around and around in circles until I am so dizzy I have to ask him to go the other way. At one point – and he has been waiting for his moment especially – he asks me what he should tell the good burghers of Exmouth as to why H got his knighthood. 'His number just came up, Terry, his number just came up in the lottery of life.' This was not the time or place to explain the tireless work H has been doing over the last six years and more for Queen and Country.

I am referred to as 'Lady Sasha' by one and all and H thinks my stock has risen immeasurably. I'm not so sure. 'Lady Sasha' is forced to dance with the astoundingly right-wing Colonel Peter Morrison from West Hill, who is a semi-professional dancer well into his late eighties and who must have cut quite a dash on ladies' night in officers' messes east of Suez. He moves me around the floor as if it is greased, leading the way through the half-crowded surface, parting couples that move too close. It's all in his wrist action, I think. I stare at his small eyes and his furred moustache, and I can tell that even in his dancing you can tell he is the no-nonsense type, the one who could shoot down an aeroplane and celebrate afterwards with a small sherry.

The inevitable raffle is conducted by Graham Liverton in a high camp manner, taking the opportunity to plug the Christmas panto in which he is an ugly sister. 'Oh no you're not!' chorus the tables. Darryl then announces there will be a further waltz. This news is met with some hostility by the band, who have made one trip too many to the bar. They shout back that they have already played the waltz and don't know another, and are not minded to play one anyway. We make our excuses and exit hurriedly, before things turn nasty.

But we do love each and every one of them. And it was actually good fun, for all its colour and characters.

5 September

Parliament back. David Davis statement. The chinks are starting to show. He tells those gathered that if membership of a single market meant having to give up control of the United Kingdom's borders, 'that makes it very improbable'. The spads don't like this, oh no, not one iota. They disagree, claiming that Mr Davis was merely 'setting out his opinion'. That saying something is probable or improbable does not mean it is necessarily a policy. These new kids on the block have no idea what they are going to be up against with Davis.

I ring H. He is utterly miserable. He absolutely hates the place. He sits next to Bernard Jenkin in the dining room, who moans about the honours list (not very tactful) and says how it has been abused by David. 'Like he did with your wife,' retorts H crossly. It's quite extraordinary how emotive the handing out of honours seems to be these days.

9 September

Peter Chadlington tells H that No. 10 has apparently been banned from any reference to Dave and George in discussions. The vindictiveness is out of control.

Meanwhile, K tells me Samantha is up early and out of the house, setting up her new fashion company and getting on with her new life, while Dave is left alone, taking the kids to school with no office or job to go to. He cannot be finding the transition easy. Suddenly she is the one with assistants rushing up, waving pieces of paper in the air.

As imagined:

Is that for me?

No, silly, it's for me. It's my time now. Go and shave that beard off, you look like the Gover. And get out of your dressing gown ... and get a job.

I've got a job.

No, you haven't.

Yes, I have, I'm an MP.

That's not a proper job.

19 September

K tells me that D had monthly meetings with Danny Fink* in preparation for his memoirs. Apparently, he has fifty-three hours' worth of digital conversations stored away on MiniDisc. They would meet for an hour in the evening, in the Downing Street flat or over dinner. When Danny presented the discs to him after his resignation, D said he didn't want to listen to them, but Danny persuaded him by saying, just take five away and make up your mind then. D was pleasantly surprised, not only by the emotions expressed but by the detail. Thank God he did it. If you don't record stuff in the heat of the moment, you might well lose it all. D, in relaxed persona, will have revealed a frank, humorous appraisal of events.

George and K are very cross that Dave has resigned as an MP. George particularly. 'He said he wasn't going to do a Blair and

---

* Baron Finkelstein, OBE. Editor and political columnist. Created a Conservative peer in 2013.

then he did one,' he complained. They are both cross with Feldman, who was in on the decision. They both bemoan the fact that he always gives bad advice.

20 September

Amber comes over for a kitchen supper while H is away in Devon fighting off protesters convinced that the NHS is in freefall – which of course it is. She feels, to me, like a rabbit caught in the headlights, but the new pressure clearly suits her, thinner and prettier than during the referendum campaign. I don't think it has yet dawned on her that an overwhelming responsibility has been placed on her shoulders. Hammond has said two things to her (both at the cabinet table): 'You have risen very quickly' and 'Have you noticed how you have now been placed above Boris in the pecking order?' She thinks Fox is nutty, DD is canny, Boris is trouble, Hammond is impressive. As for May herself, she is an island. She has had no discussions with her; Amber's communications are mostly with Fiona Hill, who is abundantly enthusiastic about Amber's elevation – so much so, Amber thinks she is the one that pushed for her.

She tells me she loves all the James Bond stuff, the MI5 and MI6 briefings.

But Amber's immediate concern is the number of potential inquiries that need decisions on whether they go ahead. Most of them she inherited from her predecessor, who kicked them into the long grass. Orgreave could slur the memory of Thatcher and the party won't like it. Another one is the Birmingham Six, and then there is the autistic boy accused of hacking into US computers and who is being threatened with extradition. Conflicting advice is floating about the place. I suggest she talks to May herself; she might now have some advice on which way to proceed, since she has first-hand experience of the cases.

We talk about grammar schools, but I feel she is repeating Kwasi's line – he is a keen advocate of anything retro and Thatcherite. Why should I be able to choose to send Siena to Cheltenham, she asks, and not let other people choose to send theirs to grammars. I don't get her line of argument (or his), since it's not parents who choose, but headteachers. Cheltenham, I say, is not really selective, as they take all abilities. Sending her there is about money, but that is my choice. Besides, the current education reforms mean that the parents select the school rather than the school selects the child, and if we improve the school system everywhere, as has happened in London, parents can do the same as I do without having to pay for it. It also means everyone benefits, not just a very small percentage.

And we talk children and clothes. I tell her she needs to remind her son Al who she is, before he gets splashed all over the *Sun* doing typical twenty-something things. Yes, she says, though maybe it was better his father did it.

She is wearing the same suit that she wore when she visited the French Interior Minister Bernard Cazeneuve.

'It's not that bad, is it?'

'It's a bit bus conductor, if you want my brutal opinion. Sorry!'

'But it's from Hugo Boss.'

'Well he was famous for designing uniforms, wasn't he?'

After a disparaging article about her dress sense, she got a call from Isabel Spearman, who said she was bringing over three outfits for her to try out the following day. I stressed it was a good idea to have a stylist. It is of course grossly unfair that such matters have to take up a female politician's headspace, but that is the nature of the beast – mostly the *Daily Mail* beast.

25 September

Craig Oliver's diaries are out. Craig is a former BBC pen-pusher and joint architect of one of the worst campaigns in living political memory. His diaries purport to tell us how it really was in

Downing Street, where he spent more time scribbling detailed notes for future economic prosperity – his future economic prosperity – than doing what he was employed to do, which was spin. Then this on the morning of the Brexit dawn: 'I suddenly retch harder than I have done in my life. Nothing comes up. I retch again – so hard it feels as if I'll turn inside out.' Too much information, Craig. K, Dave, G etc. tolerated him but were basically in constant mourning for the loss of that great working-class hot Tory Andy Coulson, who they all loved, worshipped, adored – and some even went further, or so it is said.

Of course, the diaries are entirely accurate and certainly worth a read. But the *Daily Mail* is really pissed off because, despite publishing the extracts, no one, and that means no one, defends the Cameron legacy and gets away with it. Dacre is now pinning quite a lot of his hopes on our new leader. I very much hope Old Ma May lives up to her sainted reputation, which has been completely embellished by the paper, but I somehow doubt she will. She must have promised Dacre a gong, so slavering is he these days.

Dave tells H he is seriously pissed off that the press is camped outside his house because of Craig's book. 'When is Dacre going to realise that I'm dead?' he says.

27 September

H has drink with Dave in Brinkley's.

He says afterwards that Dave is only half OK, that he has become lazy. The memoirs are not going swimmingly; he seems bored by the whole process of writing and so is speaking into a microphone, which converts it into text. He is not interested in any literary embellishment.

He tells H he went shooting with Tony Gallagher, and bagged so many partridges he had to have three injections in his back to ease the pain afterwards. This followed on from a riding trip with

Gerry Fox on Jemima Khan's estate. He does do all that exercise stuff to the hilt and is clearly producing a lot of adrenalin. We know from experience it's quite difficult to keep up with him.

He tells H that Sarah Gove is now going around saying to anyone who will listen that David brought forward the referendum to scupper Michael's chance at leadership.

'That woman clearly needs to be under full and permanent medical supervision,' says H.

Dave just says he is tired of the Gove spat and wants to move on.

Meanwhile, Samantha has been busy designing new interiors; apparently, she has bought so much marble for the renovation of their old house in Notting Hill 'that the heel of Italy has fallen off the map'.

4 October

Old Ma May is having a good conference. All disco glitterball heels and looking smug. A little too smug, I say, for one who has no mandate. But her speech was odd for a Tory. Lots of talk of a party that represents the working class of Britain. Lots of the usual kicks against toffs, the city and big business. Lots about returning to our roots, as the party of the ordinary, under-privileged people left behind by unfettered capitalism of the kind promoted by previous incumbents. A vision of a Britain where big firms are run by workers and where the state will intervene. When they stood up for a standing ovation, I couldn't help wondering whether my ears needed syringing or whether I had entered the wrong conference hall.

6 October

Amber calls. She is back from the conference and is facing a bit of a backlash from business after she told the conference that the

Home Office was considering requiring companies to declare the proportion of international staff in their workforce in a boost to British workers. She cited a company on her patch as hiring 'almost exclusively' foreigners except the company retaliated and said 75 per cent of employees were actually British. She is laughing on the phone in spite of feeling misled. She says the hacks are putting out the usual misinformation so they can create a story. The trouble is, the spads and even Amber should have seen around the corner on this one.

Then she tells me how her spads were despairing when her speech was to be pulled the day before she was to deliver it, and that she had to ring up Hill, who sorted it out with Theresa. So, who wanted to pull it? She is slowly learning to go to the top, and that there are many who will block her passage. She says my advice to go to Theresa direct and share her concerns was the best she had received since becoming a secretary of state. May seems to be bending over backwards to help her. I suppose because she cannot afford to lose her. But it might also be a sisterhood thing. Old Ma May has always been good at mentoring.

People ask me whether Amber will survive, and I honestly don't know. She has the stamina, but she is very raw politically. I did tell her that she needs to go submarine now, get a grip of her brief so that she is in control of it, rather than others, and so she can argue her point. It will take her a year. But I certainly get the sense that she is overwhelmed. Even Kwasi said to H that she was terrified.

She also tells me the dramatic news that Adrian (A. A. Gill, the critic and the father of her children) has cancer, tumours in his lungs and down his spine, that he has a year, possibly two at most. Whenever journalists came up to her to say how sorry they are to hear it, she just feels like crying. For all he did to her, she is still very fond of him. And he is a remarkable writing talent.

5 October

Benefactor dinner at Kew Gardens. I sit next to Marcus Agius, who has a love-hate relationship with Sir John, who was his boss at Lazard's. My father, in turn, has called him 'Wasserstein's butler' – Wasserstein was the American investment banker who was Chairman and CEO of Lazard's when they tried to strip my father, also a former chairman, of his pension. A loathed figure in the Nott household.

Marcus is full of philanthropy and goods deeds, but you can afford to be when you are married to a Rothschild. He is interesting when he says Sir John was useless with clients, and we go on to talk about George and whether politicians can make the transition into banking. He says it's usually a disaster because they come over all executive, guns blazing, when often that is not what is required. I say John Major does it quite well, 'Ah, but he just sits around the table, gives his spiel about world order and then leaves. He doesn't do any of the graft.' Basically, he is telling me he is just a show pony.

Henry Keswick is on my other side. He really is very unreconstructed. And not very bright either. He says he does not approve of Ruth Davidson because of her 'habits', and that he is very 'old fashioned' in that regard. Then he asks me about Devon. 'Who are your people down there?'

'Excuse me?'

'You know what I mean. Estates. Which estates?'

8 October

Jezza has had a cabinet reshuffle after being elected Labour leader. Now that he has such a huge mandate, he tells us he intends to put aside all the hate and bitterness of the past and is looking forward to even more vitriol and hostility in the future. Diane Abbott as Shadow Home will see to it.

13 October

Bump into Theo Rycroft in the street. He is the last of the Cameroons – not least by virtue of marriage to Sam's sister Flora – and he's still in No. 10. I ask him a few leading questions. He is instinctively discreet and professional but says Brexit is going to be a nightmare, very complicated indeed. He implies that Old Ma May is calling all the shots and that she doesn't care who knows it. He doesn't say it, but it all feels like Charles I: she is trying to rule without parliament. You can see it in the Commons. She lets the MPs ask the questions but tells them they have no right to decide on terms of our departure. To her Home Office mind, immigration is the key to her political fortune. And the only way to stop free movement is to abandon the single market. I have some sympathy with this. I can't see how Europe will allow for anything other than a hard Brexit.

Light relief from the downfall of Donald J. Trump in the presidential race for groping. All those women he sat next to on aeroplanes who suddenly felt his hand move under their skirts are coming out of the woodwork to tell us how it was for them. Not good. Not good at all. He kept telling us he needed to 'reach out' to women in America. And now we know he has done a pretty good job of it. Weirdly, one of his defences is that he learnt it from the best, Mr Clinton, who set a precedent in the White House for sexism, misogyny and adultery. Mind you, he's not wrong there. Welcome to America. And have a nice day. If you can, ladies . . .

Why won't Michelle Obama stand? She's the tops.

16 October

H and Siena share a father-daughter bonding trip to the O2 to see Justin Bieber. Somehow the saintly Sue has managed to wangle tickets for them. H enters an arena full of thousands of screaming teenage girls taking selfies, and all of whom see themselves as the first Mrs Bieber. He tells me later that the food in the box is surprisingly good, but Bieber is horrific; the show Vegas-like. H says that, rather curiously, he seems to go on singing when he clearly isn't; that he whinges about a football injury, and stretches and adopts yoga poses throughout this torturous performance. H's neighbour is also with his teenage daughter, and she has already been to see him earlier in the week. At the interval they exchange the usual pleasantries, asking each other what they do. H confesses rather embarrassedly to being 'in the House of Commons', at which he is asked if he is not permanently tempted to go to sleep 'on those green benches'. In the second half, Siena's crush launches into some homespun philosophy. He has clearly been in therapy. 'We can all achieve what we want to if we keep on trying' – H leans over to Siena and says, 'That means your GCSEs' – and 'we should all be different and how boring the world would be if we were all the same'. (More like how ghastly the world would be if we were all like Justin Bieber, H is thinking.) There are drunken shouts behind them, of 'Get on with it!' and 'Sing!' and Hugo's neighbour says 'he could be in the bleedin' House of Commons'. Bieber then jumps around on a trampoline and keeps on clutching his scrotum, which drives the girls, including our fifteen-year-old daughter, wild with excitement. He clearly has crabs. Oh well, at least this current infatuation is one up on the imbecilic Jamie Laing of *Made in Chelsea*, who we had to endure for quite a few years until we were delivered by the Bieber. Perhaps I am now officially a Belieber too – or maybe not.

19 October

Chaffcombe

I'm watching my farming neighbour, Mr May, churn up his fields with his plough, breaking up the stubbles left by the harvest. The soil is heavy clay, red, thick and obstinate like stirring a fruit cake mix. The colour is from the red sandstone that underlies the area and makes it the agricultural heart of the county; a strong begetter of tall grain. In the hands of this experienced farmer the field is willing, it knows not to struggle against the slope of his cut, it has tolerated him and his family for generations as they perfect the flawless line. This is their canvas.

I wonder how the Mays have kept their life so small and simple for so long; how have they managed to govern themselves against a tide of progress, to remain local, true to their soil? Theirs is the history of our island story. Now they belong to an extinction package devised by the economic architects of the EEC. They never called it 'elimination', of course, they called it 'modernisation'. They were trying to transform the peasantry into their own vision of a new social model. And it was not only the people they targeted but the land they worked and nurtured. This was the ambitious destruction created by Europe's Common Agricultural Policy – the annihilation of everything we truly hold dear: hedgerows, flora, fauna, small family farms like the Mays'. It promoted industrial farming and agricultural free trade, and has perhaps done more injury to the rural landscapes of Europe in fifty years than any other single law in the previous centuries. And the irony is that the eco-protesters hate Brexit, they march and they moan about how anyone who voted leave are racists and fools. They don't give a second thought to the Mays of this world. No, they actually think this life can be preserved through unaccountable bureaucracy and its friends in big business. They don't seem to care about the destruction, the cultural distinctiveness, the end of localism and democracy. And yet, what they really want is life how it was, simple and pure, the one that my neighbours refuse to relinquish, where the bees fly freely and the wildflowers grow.

The Mays just carry on ploughing, like in Brueghel's *Landscape with the Fall of Icarus*. They just harness the plough to their old tractor and drive it into the field before the weather changes. They wouldn't have time to stop and stare, or to listen to a commotion of wings or a lonely far-off splash in the water.

Their unintentional defiance against progress is really something to behold.

26 October

H has two days' shooting with Wafic and Rosemary. Having shot badly at the grouse earlier this autumn, he says he shoots as straight as he ever has done before and attracts nice comments, even from dead-eyed dicks like Archie Stirling.

Of course, H applied to be slipped both days, but the whips were having none of it. Nicholas Soames tells H he has a good source in the Whips' Office – which he maddeningly won't share, but H suspects Frank Field – who tells him when the Opposition won't be pressing for a vote, so he can slip away undetected by the wretched whips. So, there was no vote on the Tuesday. OK so far. But then H's whip starts texting him on Wednesday, during a particularly challenging drive, demanding to know if he will be present for the four o'clock vote as well as the seven o'clock. Nicholas tells H not to acknowledge or respond, but H feels he has to saying he cannot make the first but will be there for the second.

This elicits a huffy response that H will have to clear it with the Chief Whip or the Pairing Whip, Mel Stride. H sends him a long text saying he will never let 'his government' down if there is a knife-edge vote, but he cannot make the four o'clock. This is going to make things difficult with the whips, but H says he simply won't be used as lobby fodder and he intends to pursue his outside interests with vigour from now on. They will say, of course, that they only have a small majority, whilst letting their favourites and non-players off the hook. Too bad, H tells me later. And the simple truth is they have nothing to threaten him with and nothing to offer him, as he doesn't want anything from them anyway. It's clear a compromise will need to be reached. Sue says there is a lot of jealousy about H. Some feel he has always had good jobs, and now a knighthood to boot. Too bad. That's their problem, not his.

28 October

Juan Manuel Santos, the Colombian president, is coming on a state visit. Although he has just won the Nobel Peace Prize, he has not yet secured the agreement of his people on a referendum to approve the peace deal with the Revolutionary Armed Forces of Columbia (FARC). Alan Duncan has now rung H twice, a week apart, to enquire whether he has been notified that he is not to be in the official line-up to greet the president on Horse Guards, something H was not even asked to do when he was the minister with responsibility for that country. Alan maintains H was on the list until 'some official' noticed and had him struck off, apparently saying 'we don't want former ministers'. Alan, according to ... Alan, has insisted H is put back on it.

H tells Tobias (Ellwood) about this in the tearoom and asks him mischievously if he thinks this rings true, or the whole thing might have happened the other way round and Alan is terrified of it getting back to H. Tobias smiles enigmatically and says he will make discreet enquiries, but concedes H's suspicions are probably well founded. Though, as H says to me, 'I would not have wanted my predecessor around much.' Anyway, Sir Alan is very pleased that he and James, his husband, have got in on the state banquet and he crows that he now has two white-tie events this week to H. Again, he has forgotten that it was H who pushed him to insist on his attendance and not to take no for an answer. It all seems so bloody petty. Anyway Sir Alan, in his finery and KCMG bells and whistles, is going to have a good week. And quite right too, says H.

The one person who clearly dislikes Hugo is the revolting Bercow. In H's first Foreign Office questions as a backbencher he calls him reluctantly, then cuts him off mid-question. The chamber is aghast, but Bercow chunters to his clerks, pretending he'd thought H had finished his question. H just glares at him. Later he goes to the Speaker's Office and asks if it is possible for Mr Bercow at least to address him properly. They look embarrassed.

At the subsequent Prime Minister's Questions Bercow calls H – near the end, of course – and spews out 'Siiiiiiiiiiirrr Hugo Swire'.

H sees George Osborne in the chamber. He looks trim and well, but says he is finding writing his book extremely difficult. H asks him if they are going to have dinner. He says yes but it will have to be at the club of H's choice as he is no longer a member anywhere. H thinks he is keeping clean for a political second coming.

3 November

The *Spectator* awards, and it is universally acknowledged that GO gave the best speech of his life: 'There won't be much time for chit-chat, a bit like when Theresa and I last spoke ... '

Old Ma May retaliated, wearing a hard hat and hi-vis vest to accept Politician of the Year, before delivering a cutting put-down of Craig Oliver:

'I am particularly pleased to see Craig Oliver is here tonight. Sorry, *Sir* Craig is here tonight. I have to say, I understand that in his book about the referendum campaign, Craig says that when he heard the result of the referendum, he walked out of the office, he walked into Whitehall and he started retching violently. I have to say, I think we all know that feeling, most of us experienced it too when we saw his name on the resignation honours list.'

Ouch! Lots of score-settling going on there.

6 November

H is having a discussion in the tearoom about the Heathrow decision. Everyone's view is of course different. Benyon is sounding off. H says he is more adversely affected by the decision than anyone else, as planes will now spend an additional twenty minutes over his roof at Englefield, flying from the east to the west wing. Much laughter, and Richard saying, 'Fuck off, Hugo.'

*

Some weeks ago, Alan Duncan said en passant that he was putting H's name forward to be the Prime Minister's Trade Envoy to the Pacific Alliance, that being Chile, Colombia, Mexico and Peru. H thanks him but says he is not sure he would want to do it as he doesn't want to take on anything that might conflict with building a second career after parliament. What he didn't say was that, having been the minister with responsibility for, amongst other things, all of the Americas until July, why would he want to take on a much more insignificant role, such as this? Only last week he saw Boris in the lobbies; he scratched his head in his inimitable way, muttering, 'Ah yes, Hugo. Excellent. I've just signed off on something for you—', then rushed off before completing the sentence. And on Wednesday, during the Colombian state visit, the good Doctor Fox comes bouncing up to H in the chamber, excitedly saying that the announcement had gone down really well. 'What announcement?' H asks.

'The announcement I made during my speech in front of President Santos at the Mansion House business conference on Colombia: that you're the new trade envoy to the Pacific Alliance.'

'Well,' H replies, 'you're making another announcement now – and that's to me. As no one has discussed this with me, it's the first I've formally heard of it.'

He looks as if H has just punched him in the mouth and starts murmuring but no words come out. H fears this lack of joined-up government is becoming the hallmark of Mrs May's administration. But what to do now? Difficult for H to make a fuss, I suppose.

10 November

H has predicted for a while that the Donald would win. He thought people underestimated the visceral hatred of the Clintons and what people actually do when they are in the privacy of the polling booth, but I was wavering: would they really vote for a misogynist, racist bully with zero experience? Yes, they would.

There are now riots in the streets in America, flags burnt, effigies of Donald Trump hanging from poles and police in riot gear. It reflects a campaign unprecedented in bitterness and bile. But it also shows what a divided country it is. What a divided country we are too. What a divided world we live in.

There is a secret revolutionary side to me, like millions of others on this planet, that enjoys upsetting *Guardian* readers and Madonna, that doesn't think the groper will eat my babies or go hand in hand with Putin to bring on Armageddon, that maybe a businessman in the White House might just shake everything up for the better. But my other side thinks, is this 'self-made' bloke who actually inherited his wealth for real? And if he is, why can't he actually construct a sentence, and why insist that his rival should go to prison when he has about seventy court cases stacked up against him?

But my real reservation is that I'm not sure our democracy is working that well; and if it is, is it a sufficient barrier against political insanity? For too many people, the wrong answer has been given, so much so they are rising up and causing trouble. This is not new, but what is new is that they are behaving like mobs, not crowds, and they are able to do this because they can mobilise their anger through social media, Twitter, Facebook, et al. They can use phone-in shows. They have learnt the best ways to twist opinion polling to encourage agendas. People trusted people like my husband to make decisions, but no longer. Now they are angry with him and go public with it, and recruit followers. Everyone is a politician now. It makes it more and more impossible to govern. Trump will learn that to his cost. He will let people down, just as Obama did. No one can meet the people's expectations any more.

27 November

Back from a weekend in Ireland, staying with Ken and Brenda Rohan. Also staying were Julia Rausing and her husband Hans. Hans, aside from his great wealth, has a tragic backstory. His first wife, Eva, died of a drug overdose, and Hans, also an addict and unable to come to terms with her demise, hid her body in their house in Belgravia, until it was found by the police two months later.

Julia and I go back a long way. We were the girlfriends of two brothers in our late teens. Having never previously married, she is now as rich as Croesus and is busy, with Hans, doling out money from the Rausing Foundation to numerous worthy causes.

Julia tells Hugo she wants to get Hans a gong for all his philanthropic work, but H advises it would be best to lobby when he has UK citizenship. (The game is up for a lot of these non-doms, so they are applying fast.)

Hans is a curious creature. Clearly very damaged. Undistinguished. His conversation is simple, basic. We talk flowers, him purchasing a house by the sea, possibly in Cornwall, and Edinburgh University, as our children are there. He is very pleased his daughter has a new boyfriend, and clearly concerned his children will not be defined as victims of his own tragic life. When he sings a Swedish 'skål' song at dinner, it's as if he has spent two days willing himself to do it. Julia looks on beaming with pride. Brenda says he has come on in leaps and bounds, that a few years ago he would not even have been seen out in public, so great was his shame. He is totally dependent on and in love with Julia, who directs him at every turn; he is like an ebullient puppy around her.

H says many probably wouldn't give Hans the time of day if he wasn't a billionaire. But I'm more generous: I say he has woken up from a coma, so it's a little difficult to tell – all those years of arrested development due to his terrible addiction. He is now in catch-up time. Who knows what sort of man he would have been without the drugs?

It is a great love story, though. Truly, one to behold. Hans clearly is now at peace with himself and the world. It is really quite touching to watch.

29 November

The nutters have elected Paul Nuttall as UKIP leader. So that's appropriate, then. Our Nige looked delighted up on the platform at the Emmanuel Centre, congratulating the new leader. He was desperate to have it all sewn up, so he can get his life back/get his flight back to America, where the action is. The hyenas beamed side by side on stage. There is something really scary about that UKIP grin. More seriously, Nutty Nuttall has vowed to take on Labour in its working-class heartlands and could make inroads there, particularly as Citizen Corbyn's eye is off the ball, or in an Islington kitchen, or reading Emily Thornberry's tweets from the funeral of Fidel Castro (that nice man who proportionally executed more of his own people than Stalin). Hey ho and on it goes.

2 December

Drive down to Windsor for H's investiture with the girls. H is unusually nervous, but very excited. They never tell you who is going to do the honours, because if it's Princess Anne everyone complains and tries to switch days. H is most fearful of getting Andrew, although I'm not sure he does them anyway.

'I'm not kneeling down in front of that man. He might knight me with his todger.'

H manages to wangle us the best seats in the house, the girls and I just a metre away. The Queen comes in, a little frail but does her stuff as only she knows how. Asks the same question to anyone she doesn't know: 'And how long have you been doing this?' Then, when they say decades or something similar, she says 'Gosh', or

'Wonderful', or 'Have you really?' When H comes in, I can't hold back the tears. I'm so utterly proud. I don't know what they are talking about, but she suddenly comes over all serious with him, not the smiles everyone else is getting. Afterwards I ask H, but he is quite guarded, more respectful to the Queen than me, naturally, but basically it was about the Commonwealth. She started by saying thank you for travelling all those miles on behalf of the country, which is really nice because no one else has ever bothered.

10 December

A. A. Gill dies. I remember him vividly, giving the most emotional and loving speech at his wedding to Amber. Five years later, 'The Blonde' had moved into Amber's nest and taken everything, including her husband. Amber was left to raise two children under the age of three. It seems a cruel twist of fate that The Blonde will now have to do the same with her young children.

12 December

Just lovin' it. Trousergate. Nicky Morgan has told a newspaper that Theresa May's choice of a curiously shiny pair of leather trousers, which she wore for a *Sunday Times* interview and which cost £995, had been 'noticed and discussed' by her and other MPs. Owl-eyed Nicky said she had only ever spent that sort of dosh on her wedding dress. Old Ma May was not happy, not happy at all, particularly when her whole political philosophy is based on helping the JAMS – the just about managing. Morgan has paid for her candour; she has been disinvited from a meeting in Downing Street by Fiona Hill.

'Don't bring that woman to Downing Street again,' Hill told Alistair Burt.

Nicky Morgan then texted Hill: 'If you don't like something I've said or done, please tell me directly. No man brings me to any meeting. Your team invites me. If you don't want my views in future meetings you need to tell them.'

Ms Hill back: 'Well, he just did. So there!'

The spat is not only unprofessional, but troubling. It has echoes of Gordon Brown, the last PM to occupy a post without winning an election. That ended badly. Old Ma May needs to toughen up and develop a thicker skin, and she needs to remind her megalo-maniac staff who wears the trousers.

Meanwhile, over at Labour HQ, Jezza walks out of a Christmas knees-up when they start singing Blair's anthem, 'Things Can Only Get Better', on the karaoke.

20 December

From: 'TOWNSEND, Sue'
Date: 20 December 2016 at 12:21:41 GMT
To: Hugo
Subject: FW: Chaffcombe Manor Honey

This was forwarded by Alex – how do I respond?

-----Original Message-----

From: Howard Gale
Sent: 15 December 2016 13:55
To: Alex Hennessy (Sensitive)
Subject: Chaffcombe Manor Honey

Good afternoon Alex,

My name is Howard Gale and I am the chef to Mr Evgeny Lebedev.

Approximately a year ago Mr Lebedev attended a function at

Chequers and Mr Swire was also in attendance.

However the situation started I don't know how but somehow Mr Swire ended up giving Mr Lebedev a jar of his Chaffcombe Manor Farm Honey.

Mr Lebedev is a huge honey connoisseur and absolutely loved Mr Swire's.

Alas he has now finished the jar and I am wondering if it would be at all possible to somehow get another.

Does Mr Swire sell the honey or is it from a personal collection?

Thank you very much for your time and I look forward to speaking soon.

Cheers once again.

Howard Gale

Executive Chef
EL Private Office

23 December

Year end. And what a bloody year it has been. On top of everything else we have the Claire Wright agenda and, worse, the Corbyn agenda – you know, the one about the broken economic model, how neoliberalism only benefits the rich. They need to be reminded that it was only a year ago that the electorate actually voted, yes voted overwhelmingly for more of the same (Tory government) and actually less of the same (Brexit).

I'm a member of the right, I respect capitalism; I do not think its sole purpose is to foster greed, exploitation and abuse. And I don't know anyone in the Conservative Party who does either. But then storytelling is a powerful engine in politics, it shapes the facts and the myths, and weaves them into the fabric of the discourse, and whoever comes up with the best narrative wins the prize. It just so happens that for now, our narrative is the one the electorate is embracing.

*

I text David, to ask him and Sam to come and stay for a long weekend in May. Thought it would be nice for them to get away. I'm a bit annoyed by his rather grand reply: 'Very kind offer but Sam is flat out on business and Nancy's pony obsession make this rather difficult. I will come back to you again if diary eases off. I am now the not-busy one!!'

Meanwhile, George is all over the place: *Shall I stay, or shall I go?* Kate, who is in regular touch with him, thinks his time is up, that politics has moved on; his brand of neoliberalism is unfashionable, and by the time it comes back again there will be new players on the stage. We discuss Dave and Sam, and people's reactions to them (there has been a row with the Feldmans – what about, I don't know). We agree that the normal response, of sucking up, no longer applies, and people will no longer be treading on eggshells around them. Also, all the resentments, which have lain subterranean, might be surfacing for the first time.

G avoids H in the Commons. I say he is his own worst enemy: why does he do that? Maybe he is also finding it difficult, coming off his pedestal when everyone was so in thrall to him. Of course, he ruined many a political career and certain members will be feeling rather smug around him now. All of the Cameroons left on a strange high, excited by new episodes in their life playing out, but as time goes on not much excitement is emerging. The main players are certainly making money, but only as show ponies, and how long this will last is anyone's guess. Dave seems to be hiding out in the Cotswolds, riding horses and taking up gentlemanly pursuits again, but he can't be feeling very fulfilled.

As for H, he is slowly learning to adapt to a backbench life, and when I ask him whether he misses being a minister he says not at all.

2017

3 January

Sir Ivan Rogers resigns as our ambassador to Brussels, delivering a parting shot at Old Ma May's team for its 'muddled thinking'. The Brexiteers are seeing it as an act of naked sabotage by a supposedly neutral civil servant.

I ask Kate, who knew him when she was in No. 10.

'He was quite tricky to deal with. Everything was unachievable in his book. But to be fair, he was reflecting the Brussels view, which wasn't always what we wanted to hear. But, in the end, he was worth keeping on side: he is a very clever man. All this briefing against him is shameless and stupid, you can get away with this sort of behaviour in the Home Office, but not No. 10.'

9 January

Maria Strizzolo, a civil servant and aide to Robert Halfon, has resigned after being taped discussing how to 'take down' Alan Duncan, who has been critical of the Israeli government, with Shai Masot, who works at the Israeli embassy. Israel's ambassador, the appalling Mark Regev, has apologised for the involvement of an embassy official. They must be cringing with embarrassment, particularly since they consider their operatives, wherever they may be, to be a cut upon above the rest. Soames, Blunt, Duncan and H are not letting this one lie: Crispin has decided he is going to do an investigation into the Jewish lobby infiltrating parliament for the Foreign Affairs Select Committee. Soames rang last night, after the story had appeared on the front page of the *Mail on Sunday*:

'When Lady Swire gives you a deep-tissue massage, you can reflect upon what questions we ask in FO questions tomorrow.'

'Lady Swire is not giving me a massage. Lady Swire has just given me a salad and a glass of chardonnay.'

'If Lady Soames gave me a salad and a glass of chardonnay, I would push it away in deep disgust.'

10 January

In FO questions, H asks Boris to 'enlighten us on the thinking behind' why, in Israel, the British ambassador had been 'summoned formally because of the way the UK voted at the UN Security Council', but when a member of the Israeli embassy in London was 'caught on film conspiring with a civil servant to take down a senior minister in the Foreign Secretary's Department, the Chairman of the Foreign Affairs Committee and other Members of this House . . . the Israeli ambassador makes a couple of phone calls and all is forgiven and forgotten'. Boris coughed and spluttered, finding it all very uncomfortable. He then replied that the ambassador had made 'a very full apology' and the culprit was no longer working at the embassy. 'Whatever that person might exactly have been doing here, his cover can be said to have been well and truly blown, and I think we should consider the matter closed.'

Over in Israel, the possibility of a Palestinian state is becoming less and less likely. Benjamin Netanyahu says he believes in the two-state solution: bollocks he does. The trouble is, the world is watching and knows what he is up to – except, it seems, the Conservative Party.

16 January

David and George are in Davos, at the World Economic Forum. I would say this is not a good look for them at the moment. I mean, delegates pay nearly fifty thousand dollars just to be invited, and Brexit was a rejection of these elites. Maybe they have gone to shed a few tears while they clink their schnapps; after all, their era has come to a screeching halt. The problem with Davos is that it is a totally globalist forum, while electorates are turning national populist. The dichotomy is that one division heralds the coming of the world government and the other favours a return to national sovereignty. One is anti-American; the other puts America first. One is multilateral; the other is bilateral at best. One is about limiting growth and the other about bringing it back. These folk need to wake up: can't they see the ideological war has been lost? Globalisation is so yesterday.

20 January

Donald Trump will become the 45th president of the United States of America today. He will raise his right hand and solemnly swear to execute the office, and anyone who gets in his way, if he can. He will make America great again at the expense of every other nation on earth. He will protect jobs and Piers Morgan and Nigel Farage. But he won't put his hand on the Bible because he's a germophobe and he doesn't know whether God or Jesus or the disciples washed their hands after coming out of the bathroom and writing it.

25 January

Signal from MV *Titanic*, from Sir John and Lady Nott:

> We are making progress across the mid-Atlantic I'm in a flat calm sea. So far, we have not seen any icebergs or penguins. We are due in Barbados on Sunday, when we plan to sit under an umbrella on some beach. No sightseeing.
> We reckon the average age on this machine is between

sixty-five and seventy, which makes us the oldest on board; indeed a whole generation senior to the average, although there is ninety-year-old who is a permanent passenger. He says it is cheaper than an old people's home. True.

Miloska looks much better and sleeps much of the time. I think she is enjoying it but is adopting class superiority to most other passengers. I am more proletarian by birth and attitude than her.

I like the multiplicity of young grey-haired grannies who spend their lifetime cruising. Indeed, it is astonishing that the majority of the passengers seem to go on several cruises a year, which makes them much wealthier than us. Retired northern businesspeople mainly.

There are several retired policemen on board plus several retired military NCOs. Embarrassingly Miloska wants to talk about politics but it generates little interest among the other passengers. She is anxious to disclose some details of her husband's less than distinguished career, but I am horrified lest it be disclosed that I was once a politician. This would mean that we would be avoided when we sit at general tables for meals.

We have a comfortable cabin; the food is good and the weather on our balcony is already in the 70s.

In conclusion, the trip is going well so far and so long as we avoid adopting a superior attitude to our fellow passengers, we will get through the next three weeks in reasonable form. Love. Dad

29 January

May is in Washington and pictures are being beamed around the world of the Lady and the Trump. At the press conference he looked up at her, slobbering like an old hound. The problem for everyone, though, is that he's top dog in Washington. We thought it was quite the romance, a refined middle-class vicar's daughter and a stray mutt. We watched him grab her hand to walk out of the White House for their press conference, thinking this romantic adventure might just work, except it later emerged it was not a gesture of affection, but rather that he needed a soothing arm to negotiate a downhill stretch of path, so perhaps more the start of a slippery slope?

2 February

The big Brexit trigger vote last night. One GO turned up to give his views. George has been getting a bit of flak lately, particularly from the *Daily Mail*, for making money outside politics. As he got up to speak, all the Labour MPs were going 'Ker-ching!' Anyway, Boy George, who had wanted us to stay in Europe – because of the economy, stupid – is sticking to the line; he said he was concerned that immigration was being prioritised over the economy. 'I respect that decision,' he said, lying through his teeth, but warned of a bitter two-year struggle ahead. He is not going to drop that bone. He is hanging in there like an onlooker at an accident, waiting to jump in and be the hero. He sits next to H on the green benches afterwards. H mutters, 'What are all these bloody people talking about? What is the point of getting up and just repeating what the person before you said? Are you hating this place as much as I am?'

G replies: 'Look around you: everyone has been up at some point and then down at others.'

H asks him if he is getting any grief from the whips for missing so many votes.

G, in typical fashion, says, 'Not really. I tell them when I'm away. Besides, most of them are my acolytes.'

No one could say something like that except our George.

H tells him about a dinner he is arranging for Dave, where he is going to present him with a series of paintings of prime ministerial locations – Downing Street, Chequers etc. – by our great friend

Marcus May. A group of donors have pooled resources, both on the paintings and the party. GO is immediately put out: why, he asks, is he not getting a set of paintings as well, of Dorneywood and the Treasury? His reaction is telling. He has always put himself on the same platform as Dave, never one step below. In his eyes, he was prime minister as well.

Hugo receives a summons from Evgeny Lebedev to his flat in Portland Place (his other gaff is at Hampton Court), where he is greeted by the ubiquitous butler. Evgeny is running late. Obviously. Power play. They chat about bees. Evgeny gets nostalgic about his childhood and bee-keeping in Russia. They talk about Putin. He argues that although the Russians have done some bad things, we should be reaching out the hand of friendship to them. H agrees, but says Putin needs to change tack. Crimea he has banked, but he should desist from causing trouble in Ukraine, bullying the former Baltic states and tweaking NATO's nose; and then, of course, there is Syria. As they talk, H finds himself liking him more. He thinks he probably possesses all the clichéd Russian attributes: nostalgia, depression, introspection. H steers the conversation away from politics towards the honey and asks Lebedev if he is a hypochondriac. He laughs and says no, but he is interested in his health. He had his DNA analysed, and says it showed an unusual degree of tolerance for alcohol. Apparently, he can drink vast quantities without flinching. Very Russian. Anyway, he seems pleased with the honey, all three jars of it.

It's a pity H does not have the same level of tolerance when it comes to booze. This was apparently much in evidence at Nicholas Soames's birthday party at the Beefsteak. I couldn't go because I was bedridden with the dreaded lurgy. H arrives promptly, as requested, to be there before Charles and Camilla. A friendly pre-dinner chat with the Prince and quite good fun at dinner, with H sitting between a young Soames and his girlfriend. H drinks far too much claret, which is, as usual, very good, and gets over-excited.

The Duchess of Cornwall comes up to him after dinner, very friendly, and says, 'Congratulations on your elevation' in that rich, deep, gravelly voice of hers. For some unknown reason H replies, 'You mean my erection?' at which she looks nonplussed and beats a hasty retreat. What can he have been thinking? Quite mad. He will be banned from the court of King Charles for making lewd and suggestive remarks to his consort, and deservedly so. H has decided not to drink for the foreseeable future, to try to arrest what is clearly the onset of some sort of brain damage.

14 February

Chaffcombe

Slip down to Chaffcombe for a few days. Always something to mend, a builder to see. Even though the children have almost left the nest, the instinct to provide a shelter for my brood remains a strong one. Most nests are private and hidden, like Chaffcombe is, but the nesting of rooks is an altogether different affair. This noisy rabble takes over at this time of year. Today they are out repairing their nests in the treetops, etched against the sky like an inky line drawing. The male flies in with mouthfuls of mud or sticks and the female weaves it into the structure amidst much cawing by both of them.

There are many colonies here at Chaffcombe, each tree a village, each wood a town. These are hereditary grounds after all; they would have first come for their favoured elms, when this place was covered in them, then switched their affections after disease wiped them out. For rooks to desert a rookery has long been considered a bad omen for those who own the land, so I'm glad they are still here. Always good foretellers of weather to come, they are roosting at midday, which means rain is imminent.

18 February

Lunch with Amber. She is on good form, if still a little overwhelmed. We discuss the Calais refugee crisis. She bemoans how
fake news is being spread about the government's commitment
to child refugee resettlement. And she's right: the liberal left are
whingeing and wringing hands to salve their own cosy consciences.
I mean, the truth is we as a nation have behaved better than most,
we took in eight thousand children last year. The three thousand
who arrived unaccompanied and illegally have also been settled
here. Amber says she is concerned about feeding the traffickers,
that's why she prefers to take immigrants direct from the region.
Besides, she says there would be uproar from local councils if
new numbers were forced on them, they just wouldn't cope. Her
greatest scorn is reserved for Lord Dubs, who keeps comparing
the whole issue to the Nazi genocide and turning up with doe-
eyed young refugee girls for photoshoots on the steps of No. 10.
As Amber points out, the unaccompanied youngsters are mostly
not these girls, but young teenage men. Daughters, wives, sisters,
mothers, grannies are left in the camps.

What's it like, handling Old Ma May? It's all very difficult, she
says, like having a dragon breathing down her neck. Unlike with
other cabinet ministers, she knows and understands Amber's brief
intimately, so she watches her with a much more critical eye. She
says their meetings, which are few and far between, are agonising
because of her long pauses as she digests material. She has learnt
to grip the table so not to jump in and interrupt, which she apparently hates.

We go shopping at L. K. Bennett afterwards with my discount
card. I sweep up loads of options and make her try them on, but
she isn't really interested. We come away with two pairs of shoes
and a jacket. She's only half interested; it's more like trying to buy
a child a new school uniform before term starts.

28 February

To Dave and Sam for a curry supper at their recently renovated house in Notting Hill. They are in good form. Her business is taking off and Dave is making loads of money, and as a result says he has no interest in taking on a big public job like NATO, at least not now. Lots more time to chillax, put on weight and play the golf courses of the southern states of America, including Mar-a-Largo, where he was stunned by the narcissistic displays of the President. He says he couldn't believe how bling and tasteless it all was.

Dave is being billed as 'one of the most prominent global influencers of the early twenty-first century' by the Washington Speakers Bureau, who are flying him here, there and everywhere first class. He tells H he gets two plane tickets, and asks if he wants to come on a trip to play some golf in the States, as if H didn't have anything else to do. Which he doesn't, really.

As for all the dosh, he says every time he looks for a loophole to stash it away, he realises that George and he closed it, and laughs. He is dreaming of buying a house in Cornwall, on Daymer Bay, but still wakes up with a start, sweating about what to do with the NHS. He has only seen Old Ma May once and she was her usual frosty self, with lots of her trademark long pauses. He bemoans what a poor communicator she is. As for the book, he is not enjoying writing it, thinks it's going to be uninteresting. Of course, unless he is prepared to settle scores and wash his dirty linen in public it won't exactly fly off the shelves, and I doubt he will do that as he is too much of a gent.

On George, he thinks he should leave politics and I agree with him.

But below the bravado, one does feel there is a residue of sadness. He seems to have cut ties with most of the political Notting Hill set, maybe because of the humiliation he feels over his end. Is he motivated by money? Nope. Most of it is being mopped up by George anyway, who is showing Blairite skill in demonstrating how intensely relaxed he is about becoming filthy rich. What has Dave taken on? He says he is going to link up with some genome company in LA, but apart from that it's just chairman of Alzheimer's Research UK and the National Citizen Service, which have always been close to his heart and hark back to 'Big Society' days.

And he is still young. If he does have one big job left in him, what will it be? He has scant corporate experience. And even George's jobs are only really show pony ones. It's a mistake to think Dave is lazy, he is actually incredibly active – annoyingly so when you are with him – but it looks as if all that energy is being used for shooting, cooking, playing golf and taking his daughter riding; it's as if he has retired. He will bounce back in some form, but for now I think he is just a man having a well-earned rest.

6 March

Back from a stay with Lord Barker in Sussex, after a horticultural day course at Great Dixter. K8 (Katie Braine) also staying, with her dog Bunny. When H and I go to bed we chorus how sweet it is that Greg and George have gone to the trouble of putting some chocolates on our pillow, like in a hotel. But the odour is not very chocolatey. On closer inspection we discover it's definitely not chocolate. Hysteria erupts, everyone rushing into the room, saying *It's not my dog.* K8 blames Otto, Greg and George's dachshund, but his proud owners insist his legs are too stumpy for him to bounce up onto a bed. It becomes like Cluedo, Colonel Mustard in the billiard room, Otto on the white pillow. Greg asks everyone to recount their movements that evening. When we turn our backs for literally a second, K8 throws the hound onto the bed and says, 'There: look! I told you so. He can get on the bed.'

Sheets are changed. Windows flung open. Scented candles burned. In the morning, Greg comes in with a cup of tea and says Bunny had peed right in the centre of his bed, forcing him and George to sleep elsewhere.

The following day I go around to K8's – she lives in a palace designed by Philippe Starck, and spends half an hour in defensive mode: *my dog would not do that, he has never done that here, it was not me, etc., etc.* As I am about to leave, I notice Rocco, who had accompanied me, has deposited a great big turd in the hall and her Filipinos were desperately scrubbing the floor with disinfectant.

'Did your dog do that?'

'Yes, I think he did. He's never done anything like that before. I just don't understand it.'

17 March

Stone the crows: Boy George has been appointed the editor of the *Evening Standard*. And it's not even fake news. Personally, I think he will do it rather well. And, quite frankly, if he is not going to have power the political way he is, by hook or by crook, going to have it via the fourth estate. Is he going to build up an alternative powerbase from which he can take revenge for her sacking him? I wouldn't put it past him.

The picture of him addressing the newsroom, their jaws on the floor, is one to behold. Now even the staff are 'hacked off', it seems.

Rang up someone in the know. He wasn't asked by Lebedev, he asked Lebedev! 'It came like a shotgun-in-the-night moment.' Others have said he called Lebedev up to lobby for Matthew d'Ancona but then thought, what the hell, I might take this one myself.

22 March

A difficult and tragic day in parliament. An uneventful PMQs followed by a statement on new security measures involving airlines and laptops and mobile phones. There are to be three votes, starting at about 3 p.m., then H will head off to the station to join me in glorious Devonshire. But it is not to be. There is suddenly a commotion before the first vote: a plain-clothes policeman approaches the PM in the lobby and suddenly things move quickly and confusingly; everyone turns around, puzzled by the hullaba-loo. Suddenly Theresa is bundled out by lots of burly men; there is a lot of shouting and orders. *'MOVE! MOVE! MOVE!' 'OUT THE WAY' 'GET SOMEWHERE SAFE!'*

H is in his office, which is beneath the Speaker's Chair. Over the next few minutes the passage outside fills up with refugees. Sue shuts the door and they turn on the television to find out what is going on. There has been some sort of security breach. Someone is dead. Many people are dead. There is only one of them. There are many of them. H rings me in the car on my way to Waitrose in Okehampton. 'OK,' I say, perhaps a little too casually for his liking, 'keep me posted.'

Now they are in the Palace. They might come their way. Rumours abound. More people appear.

A woman comes to H's door, asking for admittance. Sue asks her who she is, and tells her to put her ID card under the door. She doesn't. Sue tells her to piss off. The woman then says she is pregnant. Still, Sue is having none of it.

'Sue,' H says, 'we should certainly let her in. I really don't want to read over my cornflakes about Sir Hugo, the Tory toff turning away a terrified pregnant woman, who subsequently gives birth outside his office with no offers of towels or water.'

Sue relents and opens the door to the multitude now gathered in the corridor, and many of them pour into H's small office in something resembling a tidal wave. It's certainly an eclectic group. A lady chef from one of the dining rooms; a bald man in a skull cap; Norman Lamont; Liam Fox; Dr Philippa Whitford, the SNP MP for Troon. Now *she* H is interested in. He asks if Eglinton Country Park, where lies the ruined castle of his Montgomerie ancestors, is in her constituency. She confirms it is but is clearly not interested in taking the conversation further. He also thinks it best not to bore on about his connections so he retreats; the SNP don't like to be reminded of their imperialist past and particularly not at the moment when the talk of another referendum is rising like sap in their bones.

But where is Toby? No answer on any phone. H feels suddenly responsible. He eventually rings. H tells him off as he would with Saffron or Siena in a time of crisis and accuses him of being adolescent and irresponsible for losing contact. He says he is fine and that Adam Holloway moved everyone quickly into his office. Being Adam, and a former SAS man, he has been expecting an event of this kind for some time and has spent most of his political career turning his office into Fort Knox. He can apparently host whole offices of people for months on end with water, food and no doubt sleeping bags and probably condoms; and, from Toby's cheerful voice, alcohol, most likely in considerable quantities. Sue is concerned that Toby has nicked the peach schnapps on top of the stationery cupboard, which she has been saving for a rainy day.

'If this isn't a rainy day, I don't know what is, Sue!' says H.

Sue then meanders through the gossip over to the TV and starts remonstrating with the reporter on Sky, who keeps calling New Palace Yard Old Palace Yard. She points to this, as is her wont, as evidence of yet another drop in standards. H says that in the scheme of things it isn't perhaps that important, but if she feels so strongly she should ring Caroline (Edmondson), who works for H part time and is the wife of Sky's political reporter Jon Craig. This she does and, hey presto, at the next mention they get it right. Sue looks satisfied and triumphant. It's women like her that built the empire.

The room is still filling up with refugees and is starting to smell like a cesspit that needs emptying.

H pops his head out into the corridor and invites an elderly man in a black Homburg, who is walking with a cane, to join him in his Noah's ark. He is very self-effacing and rather shaky. He sits in a chair and gets out the crossword. H asks him who he is. 'I am Lord Swansea,' he says rather doubtfully. It transpires that he had been attending the election for a replacement hereditary peer and has come in to Westminster to see how many votes he has got.

Norman, who seems to be coming and going a bit, returns to the office.

'I hope this isn't going to take long, I've got a dinner tonight.'

'I hope the first course isn't soufflé,' H says, which greatly tickles Norman, who waddles off to investigate matters. He returns later and asks if by any chance H has a corkscrew, and he hands him one. Triumphant, Norman disappears again and returns the corkscrew some hours later in considerably better form.

They are in the office for about four hours. H tells me he has developed Stockholm syndrome and has fallen in love with the Speaker. The truth is that it is very boring. Much shouting and screaming outside, with police dressed like extra-terrestrial warriors pointing machine guns around every corner.

And then it's all over. The noise. The killing. The carnage on Westminster Bridge. Tobias Ellwood, walking past the incident in New Palace Yard is told to *Move! Move! Move!* by the police but, being Tobias and prone to meander into other people's business, he instead gives a stricken policeman first aid. Pictures are immediately beamed around the world of Tobias, covered in blood, being the hero. This might just give Sir Alan Duncan, who has issues with him, a nervous breakdown. Good on Tobias, though. H wishes it had been him. He has longed for the headline Hugo, the have-a-go hero, but it will never happen. More likely Sir Hugo, the toff who turns away a terrified woman in the throes of childbirth from his warm, safe sanctuary. At least, Sue tells H, Philippa Whitford was asked what happened to her on Sky News, and she replied that she was royally entertained by Sir Hugo Swire in his office, so he may yet get a cul-de-sac named after him somewhere.

When he comes home, I ask him what he would have done in Tobias's situation. H says he's not entirely sure. I reply, 'I think you'd better put a first aid course on your to-do list.'

This is not to dismiss what a terrible human tragedy this was. The policeman who died at the gates of parliament would not have been armed, and therefore had no means to defend himself against a man with two very large knives and an insane religious dogma. If anything comes from this awful incident, one can only hope that the police who guard parliament are now fully armed with guns. After all, they are the first line of defence to our modern democracy.

27 March

I rent a tiny Landmark Trust property in the Rhiwddolion Valley. H has always dreamt of owning a croft, and this was as close to his dream design that one could hope for. My Christmas present to him: a weekend away from the rat race.

This remote area was once covered in oak forests, which until late feudal times provided cover for many lawless bands. Peace brought a clutch of homes, lived in by people and families who remained sheltered and hidden for centuries. Each stage of their development is marked in some way in the ground. Here you can see how farming gave way to lead mining, and then quarrying, as organised companies exploited the land with capital behind them. The decline of these industries brought depopulation leading to the eventual ruin of the buildings which the admirable Landmark Trust has now ably rescued. It is a highly romantic location, as quiet and isolated as it can get bar the odd roar from a far-reaching motorbike on rev. So isolated we have to leave the car on a Forestry Commission road and walk fifteen minutes up a track to get there.

All in all, we have a lovely weekend. Neither of us knows Wales and there is so much to see and do. We visit Plas Newydd House and Garden first, mainly to see Whistler's famous mural, which is stunning; H says it was always on his list to tick off. Looking at it, you understand why it was considered his masterwork. Commissioned by the Marquess of Anglesey in 1937, it stretches the length of the large dining room and portrays an imaginary and romantic coastal scene. The artist, by way of a signature, can be seen in an arcade, sweeping up rose petals; this is a reference to the fact that he fell in love with and was rejected by Lord Anglesey's daughter Caroline. Whistler meant to return to finish the painting after the war but was tragically killed in action.

Also fascinating were the extraordinary photographs of Henry Cyril, 5th Marquess of Anglesey – known as Toppy to his friends. Each snapshot is more flamboyant than the next. Toppy clearly loved raiding the dressing-up box. From an early age he had a fascination with the theatre, which nurtured a passion for jewellery, objects of vertu and costumes. He died young, of pleurisy at the Royal Hotel Monte Carlo, having worked his way through his fortune.

From Plas Newydd we drive all around the Anglesey coast – which is disappointing – before visiting the closest example of Xanadu I have ever seen in this country, the gigantic neo-Norman Penrhyn Castle. It's a real treasure trove, with intricate Celtic carvings, Chinese wallpapers, ornate plasterwork and such fascinating items as a slate bed made for Queen Victoria. But most impressive is the craftsmanship, in stone and wood, on stairwells and walls. Penrhyn was built on a fortune of slaves and slate and it is more hideous than not, but it's also inspiring in so many ways: for its ugliness, its grandeur, its ambition, its position.

The following day we do another trip on H's list: Portmeirion. It is everything you imagine it to be: a Legoland, a Disneyworld, a sweetshop, a TV set, a folly. It feels like a homage to a truant escaping the rigours of art and taste. That truant was its creator, Sir Clough Williams-Ellis, who suffered derision for its retrograde nature, for it being an exercise in pastiche or nostalgia, and yet you have to admire the vision and the pursuit of it. We see modern-day equivalents with Prince Charles's Poundbury development in Dorset. Places like this speak of defiance against the established order or the fashion of the day.

After Portmeirion we go to Clough's house, Plas Brondanw, which is as nice a family home as one can aspire to. Yew, evergreen oak, even a Chilean lantern tree in the garden, the greenness following the Italian Renaissance tradition dominates but there are occasional promises of spring colour in the tightly closed fists of the rhododendrons and the occasional daffodil. Exhausted, we conclude the day by visiting Bodnant Garden, which is in full flush of acid-loving plants. Horrible house, but the garden has become renowned the world over. You need time for it, which we didn't have.

4.5 hours back to London the next morning.

29 March

Gove has bought a house in Olympia. Clearly needed to get away from the place in Notting Hill, which is only a few streets away from Dave's. The sheer worry of bumping into him on a morning jog far too much. The Notting Hill set really is crumbling ...

Oliver Dowden,* in the lobby, tells H he is so sick of his wife's vegan cooking he was absolutely delighted when he came home and finally saw a ham and chicken bake in the fridge. He gobbled it down lustily. When his wife came back, she asked him where the dog's food had gone.

10 April

Putin and Trump have been getting their dicks out to prove which one is bigger. For onlookers it looks really – I mean *really* – scary. There has been an American rocket attack on a Syrian airbase, and Assad has retaliated. North Korea is also hotting up. I'm glad we are getting some chickens down at Chaffcombe. And water. And wood. And tins of baked beans.

---

* Conservative MP for Hertsmere since 2015. Previously special adviser to David Cameron.

19 April

Old Ma May has called a snap election. Funny, that. And after saying eleven times she didn't want one. Decided on a hill-walking holiday, apparently, when she was dehydrated, sweating, lost maybe; she can't have had a very nice time. The cynics are saying it's to exterminate the Labour Party, but they are doing a pretty good job of that themselves. On the steps of Downing Street, she told us she trusts the British people. I'm glad *she* does. There was a lot of I this, I that, but really she should have come straight out with it, rather like Erdoğan, and screamed I WANT MORE POWER AND I WANT IT NOW!

The thought of it fills us with dread. We had so hoped not to fight another one, but H doesn't have his ducks in a row to get out. Our compensation is that we spend a glorious May in Devon. The downside is that we have to take on Claire Wright again, with all her cronies spilling their bile about us. Of course she will walk it. Old Ma May, that is: Labour has no election slogan, no agreed key seats list and no campaign budget signed off. Watching Jezza will be like watching the walking dead. Poor Jezza, his chief goal had been to remain leader until the left had secured control of the party. That meant hanging on in there for a while yet, until the moderates in Labour HQ had been purged and replaced by Corbynistas. The Blairites must be dancing in the aisles.

And we're off: extended news bulletins; humans dressed up in chicken suits chasing politicians; Andrew bloody Marr, David bloody Dimbleby; Nigel Farage failing to get a seat . . . again (mind you, he might not stand: he could be going off to be Trump's diversity adviser); BBC bias (though Jezza seems to be suffering more on that front); purposeless debates based on wholly erroneous polls by worthless presenters. Perhaps Trump or Kim will start a nuclear war to take our minds off it.

20 April

George is standing down as an MP, and although, as expected, sadness swamps us, it's more about the curtain closing on an era. Power has always been a whore. Old Ma May has successfully sacked and humiliated all the Cameroons since taking over. She is backed by Paul Dacre, who she speaks to three times a week, and Michael Ashcroft, to whom she is also close. She wants her majority, and she wants it now. Fair enough, I suppose.

Kate is miserable, says she hates this brand of right-wing politics, and is dismissive about many members of the cabinet. Personally, I don't know what she's worried about; May is far more left than right. With G gone, K believes that the metropolitan, global, liberal brand of Conservatism (i.e. the one that never leaves London) is no longer alive and active. But I suspect it's more to do with the remain/leave argument, as everything is these days. I say politics is cyclical, that it's best to get Brexit over and done with, and then her style of politics can return. Which it will, probably via a new and reinvigorated Labour Party. Does she really want to drag it out? She concedes not. As for George, he is still capable of mischief; he is already threatening Old Ma May's brand of politics through his editorship of the *Evening Standard*. Menacingly and characteristically, he says he is going 'for now'. K is encouraging him to fight Kensington & Chelsea when the present incumbent steps down.

27 April

H has his election mug shot taken with Old Ma May. 'How was she?' I ask.

'Let's just say, she is not long on pleasantries. It was over in a second.'

2 May

A thank-you email from Sir John:

> Dear Hugo and Sasha. First to Hugo. Thank you so much for taking me to Northam. It was very generous of you to drive all that way. I much appreciate it.
>
> Second. Chaffcombe Palace. I must say to Sasha, in particular, what an interesting and rather unique manor you have created out of nothing special. I like the rather special drawing room and kitchen. Upstairs is still a disappointment because you refuse to carpet those awful floors. The house would be better insulated with carpets. But generally, I think you have done a marvellous job with the furniture and the environment. I like the idea of panelling if you can afford it. The sheep have greatly contributed to the land. The garden is outstanding and should not be enlarged. We were honoured to christen the annexe. It is very comfortable with an exceptional bed and furnishings. Next time I will use the conventional bath so I can lie back and avoid burning myself when I turn on the hot water in the copper bath. The kitchen is great and could do with two comfortable chairs and a standard lamp to make it a combined sitting room. I think you would save a lot of money on heating in the main Palace if you move to the comfortable suite in the winter months. In all, I think you have created something special but please set up a sinking fund to finance a new thatched roof which will hit you earlier than you imagine. Love Dad.

Another email, this from a constituent:

> Sir,
>
> I sincerely hope you will not be standing again.
>
> During your time as our MP you have been as much use as a chocolate teapot.
>
> Don't stand again!

*

H bumps into K at an Atlantic Partnership breakfast. She says Boy George is getting increasingly concerned that Evgeny Lebedev is going to use him to arrange his social life. She also says Dave has disappeared from view. She has not seen him for ages. She is surprised we are seeing him tonight.

Pre-poll round-up. Rachel Johnson flounced off to the Lib Dems last week; the oxygen of publicity can't have been getting to her head. Then, no sooner had she popped up, than Stanley emerged a couple of hours later to spout off about EU environmental laws. I don't know how that Jo Johnson copes with them all. On the Labour front Diane Abbott has a neural collapse on LBC when she couldn't cost out Labour's plan to introduce loads more police officers. And no sooner had it occurred than the hole that should have swallowed her up just got bigger and bigger, as she swung from a figure of £300,000 for the policy to end up quoting £80 million instead. It was a car crash. I mean, a real M5 full-on pile-up with dismembered hands and legs, brains spilt out all over the tarmac, kind of car crash.

Dave's handkerchief tree, which he planted in the garden at Chaffcombe, has been burnt by a late frost. It seems somehow poignant.

3 May

Dinner last night at Hertford Street, for Dave. The paintings by Marcus May were presented to him at the dinner. He was visibly moved. He is embarrassed about his £25,000 shepherd's hut, but says he was only being nice to the owner of the business, who had asked if he could have a pic – one of the hazards of modern-day political celebrity. How could he say no? It's typical of the man: he likes to please people, without seeing the consequences. As Sir John commented, the problem is that David will have no infrastructure now, so he's bound to trip up. At least he is now on alert. He has exchanged on a holiday home in Daymer Bay but is absolutely adamant we don't tell anyone. And at least the money is rolling in. GO texts H to thank him for pulling the dinner together. Says David is bowled over by the gesture. He offers to come down to Devon and canvass. H says thanks but no thanks.

Old Ma May has just come out on the steps of Downing Street to proclaim that the EU is playing silly buggers and she won't have it. Even claimed they were meddling in her election.

Of course, Kate and GO and Tony Blair and the Lib Dems are all under the complete misapprehension that a soft Brexit can be achieved. I tell anyone who will listen that the EU mob aren't going to give us anything. And if you want to know why, look no further than Mr Juncker: in his book, Britain will have to be made an example of, as a recalcitrant nation that steps outside the modus vivendi. He's doing everything he can to cling on to his own exorbitant power, even ignoring what most would consider warning bells such as new populist movements, in France, Germany and practically every other European country you can name. The man thinks it's more important to preserve his little technocracy than compromise or reform. So there you have it: as long we have him, we have no deal.

What we now know is that this isn't going to be about anything other than money. Exactly like every other divorce that ever was.

6 May

David gives a speech at the Oval, in his role as patron of the Rwanda Cricket Stadium Foundation. According to *The Times*, he seized the opportunity to thank the audience for getting him out of that shepherd's hut of his, and then went on to mitigate the purchase thus: 'I know Theresa talks about strong and stable leadership but I only heard the first part about getting a strong stable.'

That's my boy! Always could get out of a tight spot.

11 May

Claire Wrong is now up and running. First, the live streaming on Facebook of her announcement that she was standing. Then we had the crowdfunding. Then calling for people to sponsor and put up banners. Another announcement, for the creation of window posters to download from her website. She even has a campaign manager, who appears to be contacting anyone at the *Guardian*, the *Today* programme, *Channel 4 News* – in fact, anyone left enough to listen. They are pitching it as a David and Goliath contest to the news desks, which is hilarious, since she has well over five hundred helpers and we have one: Toby. She's good, though. She's energetic. She gets herself around social media nimbly. God! If elections are won and lost on that, we are fucking doomed. We still have the same bunch as when we first started twenty years ago, except now they are aged between eighty-nine and ninety-nine rather than in their seventies, which was already quite old. They really are analogue in a digital age and refuse to convert. Hugo is incandescent, as one of them put out an email saying where he was going to be on the campaign trail every day, except they sent it to la Wright herself! And guess who their role model is? Why, Old Ma May and her cronies at election HQ, of course, who think social media is just a gimmick, a passing phase, and that it demeans the strong and stable public image. Someone needs to tell those guys up there that, down here, platforms like Facebook, Twitter, Instagram and Snapchat are the main way she is getting her message across, and that young people don't actually watch party political broadcasts on television any more. And do you know why May's rejecting social media? Because she wants to play it differently to Cameron, apparently. Jesus wept. This is bad, really bad.

4 p.m. Candidates list in. Phew, Lib Dems standing, UKIP and Labour fielding . . . but also Peter Faithfull and a shiny new nutter, Mike Val Davies . . . I google both.

Peter Faithfull is standing for parliament, according to his election communication, because he believes Genette Tate, a schoolgirl who disappeared in 1978, was secretly buried in Aylesbeare churchyard. He feels that parliamentary privilege would permit him to talk about the case without fear of prosecution, and to conclude his investigation.

Next, I read an article about Mike Val Davies. Mike, it seems is bipolar, and a hoarder of newspapers. In fact, his home is so full of them there is no space for anyone to sit down. According to the article, Mike spends about £70 a week on newspapers, and is also partial to books, lots of books. His hoarding is apparently powered by his obsession with current affairs and history, which I suspect is why he wants to stand for election.

I think he has all the makings of a seriously good MP.

23 May

A major fuck-up on the issue of social care. Old Ma May springs a rethink on policy, mid campaign. Candidates like H are now having trouble on the doorstep. Of course, the blue-rinse brigade expects the state to pay for their social care costs, but May is now saying, pay for it yourself, ducky, through your property, which I reckon is pretty sensible, since the greys already own the wealth of this country, having ridden the property boom, and shouldn't be asking our kids, already laden with student debt and unable to buy a home, to cough up for them. Anyway, so tight a coterie does she operate in, no one knew about it, including the cabinet.

Hilariously, the decision came on Sunday night, with a decision to brief the *Evening Standard* the next day. News of the change was pitched straight at the editor, saying it was a natural policy evolution, except George didn't see it that way. Like any savvy editor, he ignored the nuanced briefing and tweeted of an impending U-turn. His paper then published the story on its front page, with the headline 'Strong and Stable? PM's Care U-turn Turmoil'. Don't think Boy George will be getting any exclusives in the near future. H is in despair!

31 May

Lots of cock-fighting at CCHQ over who is in charge of the campaign. YouGov are producing polling that says the Conservatives might actually lose. How can that be possible with that idiot Corbyn as the alternative? The pound has plummeted as a result. GO is pulling more legs off spiders by writing vile editorials such as 'Honey, I shrunk the poll lead'. I tell K to rein him in but she goes off on a tirade about how all of them, when they were in No. 10, were always being maltreated by the editors, and now it's Mrs May's turn. Yes, Kate, but we don't want Corbyn to get in, do we? Is George's vendetta against Mrs May worth that price?

Bercow has told Sky News he is going to break his promise to stand down as Speaker after nine years and will instead go on until 2022. As H says, if we have a majority there will be a huge army marching through the lobbies saying *Oh not you won't* . . .

1 June

Amber soldiers bravely on. Last night she stood in for Old Ma May in the seven-way BBC election debate, and cited the squabbling discord of her opponents as evidence of what a coalition will look like. She must have done well, as the *FT* is now tipping her to be the next chancellor. If May wins. Poor Amber lost her father two nights ago, and has also had to deal with all the Manchester bombing stuff. I text her to see if she is OK.

A piece in *The Times* this morning, following the YouGov poll, saying Hugo's is one of the seats that might go. Claire Wrong is going to do rather well, but well enough to beat us? I'm not sure. CCHQ is telling us there is no evidence of that.

David to H: How's it going? Are you enjoying yourself?

H: No. Fucking hating everything about this election and the independent candidate giving me a hard run. Maybe moving to Alcuzcuz [the house in Spain where Dave is chillaxing on another mini-break] permanently next week.

D: I'm sure you will be fine. Maybot has become rather wooden, it feels.

If May pulls it off, she really needs to take a long, hard look at her people skills and bring in ministers who have ideas, rather than relying on those of the Beard (Nick Timothy). Valuing loyalty over talent is not going to work for her.

3 June

The Marchioness arrives to canvass. I put up a picture of H and 'my mum' on Twitter. It gets eighteen hearts, which is big for H's account, and a comment pings in: 'Fucking hell mate! She looks younger than you!'

I don't canvass because I can't bear the aggression against H. I feel I could create an incident; H would have to unlock my teeth and hoist me away from my antagonist's ankle as the blood starts to surge.

The Marchioness gets the usual 20 per cent negativity on the doorstep, 'We never see him around here', etc.

'Well, he's been terribly busy, you know, flying around the world for the Foreign Office,' she replies grandly.

In the kitchen after H leaves for the day, she tells me she is very worried. That I must support him if everything goes wrong. Which annoys me, because it's not as if I haven't supported him our whole damn marriage and sacrificed quite a lot of my own ambition in the process. I say, 'Look, if he loses, settles the whole goddam question of leaving, but at the end of the day all I can do is cook him bacon and eggs. He will have to sort the humiliation out in his own head. It will be like a bereavement and he will, in time, get over it.'

As Kate says, everyone is just trying to land at the moment.

4 June

Another terrorist incident on London Bridge. Campaigning is suspended for a day, but the incident highlights Corbyn's historic support for the IRA and terrorist groups, and him being against a shoot to kill policy. The three jihadis were shot dead within eight minutes of the attack. He is fighting back by saying there should be more bobbies on the beat. But Theresa's typical approach of more sentencing, harsher sentencing, lock 'em up is not going to work. What we need to look at is stopping these fanatics before they go tonto, and that means looking at segregation, deprivation and how they create extremism. Oh, and the Israel–Palestine question, possibly, which inspires their anti-Western rhetoric.

Dave had real battles with her on this, and how she was counter-ing radicalisation when she was at the Home Office. Her snail-like handling of strategy infuriated him. It took more than a year for an expert panel to conduct a review into sharia law, and this inquiry has still not seen the light of day. Another plan to inspect madrassas has not been actioned, eighteen months after being announced. Meanwhile, the Home Office is still grappling with the very term 'extremism'.

5 June

The polls are narrowing more than widening. I like Sarah Baxter's analogy in yesterday's *Sunday Times*, of the story of Rip Van Winkle. The character in the illustrations looks exactly like Communist Corbyn. But, as Baxter points out, it's not Corbyn who has been asleep but us, or should I say innocent youngsters, who have not clocked the life he had before he had this one. And why would they? He has come down from the hills like the Child Catcher, waving such lollipops as free university tuition and lead-ing them off into a Neverland where there are no bills that have to be paid. I love fairy tales. And, according to the polls, so do others.

This from Hugo's whip:

> Hello all; hope you are well.
>   Two questions the Chief needs your clarification on: What are your mutual aid plans for tomorrow and how many are you taking?
>   Also, what are your mutual aid plans for polling day and how many are you taking?

Hugo's reply:

I am immediately dispatching three infantry divisions backed up by an armoured battalion and full air cover. I am only retaining a callow youth armed with a pitchfork (it's all we now have) to help me persuade my few remaining pensioners who haven't defected on account of our splendid manifesto to help me hold off the independent candidate from beating me, which some are now predicting her to do not least on account of the same splendid manifesto and excellent campaign with its highly effective precision bombing of my elderly constituents. Please pass on my best wishes and loyalty to all left in the bunker.

It elicits no response.

8 June

Election night: Sidmouth

We see the exit poll at 10 p.m. and audibly gasp. From then on, we feel we are being physically and mentally abused as the results come in.

We arrive at the count as soon as we think it's in the bag, although it's never over until the fat lady sings. I try to be friendly. Ray Davidson, the veteran Labour agent, offers me some champagne and I accept because I've always loved the old Labour lot down here. I tell him I think it's going to be his night, not ours. I go over to the Lib Dem candidate, who clearly knows by now that all her votes have been stolen by Claire Wrong. Again, try to be friendly. But she misjudges the moment and suddenly raises the issue of child benefit withdrawal for rape victims, and how H voted against it, so I plead my ignorance and beat a hasty retreat. I can't take much more confrontation, and there is so much hatred in the room already. My nerves are jangling more than normal, I think because I don't have an HRT patch affixed to my upper thigh as I usually do – I didn't have time to get prescription.

It is the early hours of the morning now, and our beloved long-time helper, John Humphreys, approaches and is whispering into Hugo's ear, 'Two gentlemen come to see you outside, Hugo.' John, a leading Mason, finds anything cloak and dagger quite normal. H does as he is bid and finds two of his constituents standing in the dark, dressed in identical suits looking rather like Gilbert and George. On closer inspection, he recognises one of them from an early point in the campaign, when he contacted Hugo with an offer of help. The man turned out to be a member of the Plymouth Brethren, who H has tried to help over some disagreement with the Charity Commission. The man had taken some leaflets, saying he would deliver them and that he and his Brethren would be praying for him. Now, he and another member are standing under a tree, asking H anxiously how things are going. He says not according to plan. They looked grave and then H added if they were inclined to pray for him, they should do so without delay and redouble their efforts. They assented and disappeared off into the night.

Inside, I turn to the *Express & Echo* liveblog to discover one of their journalists is writing that we are neck and neck with Claire Wrong. Incensed, I storm over to him.

'Why are you writing this stuff? You know we are not neck and neck.'

'I don't know. I haven't been in there.'

'Well, go and take a look, then. It's all of a metre away,' I say, pointing to the adjoining room.

'Oh, shut up and go away,' he tells me.

I'm now puce. Hormone-withdrawal puce. 'Don't tell me to shut up. Your newspaper is a disgrace. A complete disgrace. No wonder it's losing circulation and jobs.'

I storm over to H to tell him what has happened, and his chest expands four times, Hulk-like, buttons flying off, and he charges over to confront him.

'How dare you talk to my wife like that?'

The cub reporter looks mortified. He obviously thought I was just another nasty white middle-class Tory left out in the sun too long, not the Conservative candidate's wife. He apologises nervously to Hugo. But he is probably plotting his revenge in editions to come.

Next, there is a meeting with the returning officer, Mark Williams, to discuss the spoilt ballot papers. The candidates crowd around him.

'This one Claire? This one for you, Hugo. Yes? Agreed everyone? Ah, and this last one, Hugo, this is yours again, I think?'

Hugo looks at it and sees a poorly drawn penis in the box against his name. He turns to Claire: 'I hope my majority is going to be a bit bigger than that.'

Claire scowls and walks away.

The night wears on, until the result is finally announced. Wrong gets 21,270 votes, clearing out the Lib Dem stable; they only manage to pick up 1,468 and lose their deposit. Clearly a lot of tactical voting going on. Hugo has more votes (29,306), but the majority is down.

A camera crew ask for an interview but when we go in someone else is filming Ms Wright. 'Why are you here, Hugo? Can't you see I'm doing an interview?' she protests aggressively.

'It might have escaped your notice, Claire, but I have just been elected as the MP for East Devon, not you.'

I, meanwhile, am spoiling for a fight; saliva is gathering at the side of my mouth and starting to froth; I am chewing on the equivalent of the welcome mat, and head straight for her agent's jugular, launching into a diatribe about how can they possibly claim it was a clean fight? More of her henchmen and women start to circle me, denying all claims, but I am having none of it, and start jabbing my finger at them, I'm thinking, *clean fight my arse!*

9 June

A hung parliament. A fucking hung parliament. Well, that went well, didn't it. We went in with 330 seats and came out with 326. We have lost an election we didn't need to have. Where is our

Boadicea now? Crying all the way to the Palace, apparently, and trying to do a deal with creationists and anti-abortionists. Progress on Brexit? I dunno now. Talks start in eleven days.

The only highlight was Ruth, Queen of Scots, who managed to behead Alex Salmond and Angus Robertson. Crikey, if it wasn't for her we'd be living under the Bolsheviks, with ten refugee families moving into our house. UKIP have run for the hills and the Trots have nearly taken over the asylum, which is weird because it feels as if Corbyn has won by not actually winning an election. Schadenfreude from the Cameroons is at peak levels. DC vindicated, a bit, which is nice for him. Apparently as soon as the exit poll came in, all those expensive election gurus were not seen for dust. And that Lynton Crosby, what was he up to? All his scare stuff drove everyone the other way. And running a presidential campaign when you don't have a presidential candidate? Whose idea was that? And ... and ... and ... and ...

At least Rasputin's sidekick, Ms Hill, has gone. Even better, so too has that little squit Ben Gummer, who helped write the shockingly bad manifesto we all tried to sell on the doorstep and failed.

11 June

To think the Cameroons were drummed out of office for this. For bloody this.

12 June

Can you believe it: she is banging on about stable leadership again. Odd that, when she is only in office but not in power? I bump into George Bridges* in the park; I say that I don't know why they

---

* Baron Bridges of Headley, MBE. Created a Conservative peer in 2015. Variously a chairman of the Research Department and campaign director of the Conservative Party.

want to keep her on. Shaft her now. He agrees. I asked him about Nick Timothy, and he replies that even as a senior member of the Brexit team in charge of the Great Repeal Bill, he was completely excluded by No. 10. It was even suggested that he was being impertinent to ask to see things like the Article 50 letter! You just get this constant feeling that anyone or anything linked to DC is treated with disdain.

The new notion amongst pissed-off MPs is to rally around this cardboard cut-out until the time is right to plot a different course.

The highlight of yesterday was Boy George on the *Andrew Marr Show*, declaring with glee that the Maybot was 'a dead woman walking – it's just how long she is going to remain on death row'. When Marr asked what she told him when she sacked him, he lifted his upper lip into a curl and grinned: 'That I should spend some time getting to know my party.' H texts him: 'That must have been the best moment in your life.'

'Yes,' he replies, 'I have been waiting a while to deliver that one!'

Michael Gove is back in cabinet. Environment. Never known anyone who has less affinity with the countryside than him. At least he will be charge of policy to protect wheat fields from those running through them.

And there are the usual faux displays of loyalty. Boris, who is the clear favourite to win a leadership contest, leaking WhatsApp messages expressing loyalty and David Davis suddenly available for the airwaves; both are trying amusingly hard to convey that they are not on manoeuvres, which means they are. Their allies are already trying to shaft the other's respective leadership chances.

14 June

So many uncertainties on Brexit. What is in my crystal ball? What can I see? No Commons majority on anything, that's what I see. Shenanigans from the DUP, leading to a collapse in the arrangement. A Brussels offer that pleases no one. An all-out punch-up between those that believe in the principles of free trade, open borders and globalisation, and those that think it has all gone too far. I see Labour playing the political game, acting as refuseniks on any agreement made by a prime minister who already has her hands tied behind her back. I see a frustrated and tired nation watching weeks and months and years of deadlock. I see camps and corners. I see remainers successfully mobilising across parliament, getting a cross-party majority to stop Brexit after all. I see a second referendum.

16 June

Chaffcombe

Our linhay is badly in need of repair. It is a beautiful lofted, open-fronted wagon shed which is distinctive to the West Country, the hayloft known in Devon as the tallet. The rear and end walls are cob on stone rubble footings and the front consists of three oak posts rising full height to support the eaves and the crossbeams for the loft above. In the summer aromatic brown-green hay would have been tossed up by a farm labourer standing on a haycart below. The hay dried and was stored under the time-warped eaves, kept the cattle warm during the cold winter and Devon's notorious wet weather. It could also be fed into the hay racks underneath by tumbling it through gaps in the upper floor.

I stand under it now and look up at those worn purlins; some of them broken in two. At the far end, where the winter throws its weight, the cob has crumbled from the hurt of its recoil and a single golden ray of light is arrowing its way in, allowing the dust to dance in its stream. Two empty tea chests have been set high on the roof beams by the previous owners to house the barn owls and their droppings are evident. On the ground outside, a splintering of slate. The past remembered, if one steps off this fast-moving world for a moment and looks at the stones on the riverbed.

In my mind's eye I see a young man pitchforking the hay inside. He comes from Copplestone, and first came to work here in 1892, as a farm labourer. But an interest in politics is brewing inside him. He won't stay long at Chaffcombe; he moves to the Mays' farm at the top of the hill, then a year later he disappears. He moves to Bristol, where he works as a van driver and becomes involved in the trade union movement. His name is Ernest Bevin. He is to become, first, a trade union leader and from there a firebrand Labour politician, then Foreign Secretary in Attlee's government. When asked where he had been educated, Bevin said that he had gathered his knowledge 'on the hedgerows of experience'.

This, the nature of our colliding paths.

19 June

A glamorous dinner hosted by a Conservative donor and his wife in Belgravia. Amid museum-standard Old Masters, and political glitterati including the Astors and the Soameses, we sup on huge dollops of caviar and lamb washed down with delicious claret, 'for tomorrow we die!'

H jokes with William (Astor) that we will be soon renamed Brothers No. 34 and 34A in the farming cooperative, but that William will not be so lucky; he will get the pitchfork direct in the jugular for being a nasty landowner. But he says he'll have Lord Ali – the Labour peer and William's business partner – to protect him. No, H says, they always go for the capitalist turncoat scum like him first.

I ask Nicholas who he will back in a leadership election, and he says Rory Stewart.

'Rory!' I exclaim, half laughing. 'Rory the storyteller? He hasn't even been in the cabinet, Nicholas. Now is not the time to have an amateur. And what's more, he's an Old Etonian.'

'Nothing wrong with that, Sasha.'

Of course, Rory would be the Palace's choice. Clarence House's anyway, as he was tutor to Prince William and Harry, and the Prince of Wales is said to be completely captivated by him. And of course, Nicholas is Charles's best friend.

24 June

Back from lunch with Amber. Gossip first, about how stunningly bad the election campaign was. She said the cabinet were all on a train together down to the manifesto launch and everyone was asking whether any of them had seen it or not. Not one said they had. To think the election had already started. She said she partly blames herself, they all should. They all rolled over, they thought May was heading for a huge majority, she was scary and her people were scary.

How was your trip to Paris with her, I ask. 'It was OK,' says Amber, 'she likes me, but you can't talk to her like a normal person; she is just very cold.' Amber says she has no small talk whatsoever. I ask whether this means she is less phoney, more sincere. Probably, says Amber, but she says she is also cripplingly shy, and her pauses are agonising. Amber adds that she was lucky: for some unknown reason, Fiona Hill took a shine to her. She never suffered from their destructive arrogance and intransigence. But she adds that May lacks confidence – intellectual confidence – which was why she was so reliant on the gruesome twosome, Nick Timothy and Fiona Hill.

She is definitely going to stand. She has already seen GO, who will back her *(he's probably backing everyone at this stage, which is his way)* and Ruth Davidson, which is a coup. Her main problem is Brexit: she doesn't believe in it; she doesn't know how she can go out to bat for it.

'You don't. David Davis does. You set yourself up as the unifying candidate. You run what's left of this government as a gang of four until Brexit is over.'

We agree that she should keep her head down, silently seek out who will support her and look in control of her brief. Meanwhile

I will set up a supper with K, who can give her the ten-step plan of how to run a campaign and who the best players are to get involved. Suggestions for ops, press, etc. She needs to be ready to go if Theresa resigns.

After lunch we set up a WhatsApp chat, so we can talk freely. Hammond has asked to see her Wednesday, one on one. And Gavin shortly after.

A constituent rings up Sue about H calling for some steel street furniture to avoid a terrorist attack on the promenade along Sidmouth seafront. The constituent said that, taking into account the average age of the population, the death toll could run into the hundreds – i.e. they are too arthritic to do a quick dive into the sea to get out the way. Sue and I have a laugh afterwards: as if ISIS is going to target East Devon, for God's sake. The only real threat of an incident happening there is with a trembling pair of hands on the gears of an out-of-control mobility scooter.

2 July

Get K around to the 'Dungeon', our basement flat in Walpole Street, to discuss a potential leadership bid with Amber. K is superb, not least because she is highly experienced at this sort of thing and knows the players well. Amber is lucky to have the Cameroon crew on side. Listening to K, I really got an under-standing of how she ran Downing Street as efficiently as she did.

Over dinner of avocado, prawns and pasta, Amber laughs about the fact that she is unbelievably now part of the core team (with Hammond, Davis and Johnson). At a meeting last week about the public sector pay cap (Gove and Boris trying to remove it), Boris asked Hammond for £150 million for the NHS. Hammond just replied 'Silly boy,' dismissing him outright like a stupid child, but DD actually clipped the Foreign Secretary over the back of the head with his hand. Amber said it was extraordinary, and she was left rather shocked.

That's DD of the SAS for you, K and I chorused. Amber asks whether he is a shagger. K and I thought not. At one point he appeared to have a crush on Shami Chakrabarti, but it was more to do with both of them being anti ID cards than anything sexual. Amber is leaning towards reintroducing ID cards, and is going to sound it out with DD first. He might have changed his stance since Brexit.

'Have you told Kwasi yet?' I ask.

'Yes: he says I should definitely go for it, but he won't be supporting me.'

Again, we laugh.

Its agreed that Amber needs to focus on her conference speech, and to start having Sunday-night meetings with a small core team. She should vary locations. She needs to think about a) why she wants the leadership; b) what she would do if she got it; and c) who her key players are.

7 July

To Crosby Hall at its most magnificent on a balmy summer's evening. Moran looks older suddenly. Don't we all? He tells me he is spending a lot of his time powering up and down his indoor pool. Tonight was very much a DUP night; they were all out in force: the old UUP drinking, Donaldson and Foster, the Robinsons and the hard-line DUP not. None of the devil's buttermilk for them! Peter Robinson was a curious orange colour, as was Iris, fresh from a cruise. He is very deaf in one ear – H thinks he always has been – but he is on good form.

We talk much of the Conservative–DUP deal. H asks about the future of the UUP. Will they fold into the DUP now? Peter thinks probably not, but says they are finished. He is wryly amusing about the deal, saying he can't see what all the fuss is about. Supporting

Labour's legislation on twenty-eight-day detention cost Gordon Brown £1.5 billion, a third of which went to shore up Bombardier. So, Peter smiles, 'A billion to prop up a government for two years is cheap at the price.' H then asks Peter if he is going into the Lords. He thinks he will, but says he may have trouble with the Lords Appointments Commission, which seems to operate on rules of its own. Then, of course, he would be in the same boat as Moran.

I have a long talk with Arlene (Foster); she always bounces off H and me for intelligence on the new ministers. I give a run-down of Chloe Smith: 'over-promoted too early'.

'And Brokenshire?' asks Arlene.

'Loyal to May, but boring. Hugo calls him the Human Hedgehog.'

She agrees, calling them 'robots'. Both Arlene and (Jeffrey) Donaldson say it was impossible dealing with May on the deal, how indecisive she was on all the issues put before her. May was of course on the floor at that point, wondering whether she was going to survive after the election. It was not until Donaldson, Gavin and Arlene were locked in a room together that the whole thing was sorted out. They are both very grateful about the blog post I wrote calling out the borderline racism, which is being thrown at them.

At dinner, Theresa Villiers comes over and sits down; H and I are a little taken aback by how friendly they all are with her, and her with them. They obviously grew quite fond of her by the end.

Meanwhile, the Corbynistas are on the rampage. Corbyn even has an eight-point lead in the polls. Now it seems he is busily purging the Church of JC of the Latter-Day Saints of blasphemers and non-believers. Luciana Berger is the first to go – well, she is Jewish, and a woman to boot, and this lot are outright misogynists. The poor woman has just dropped a baby, and they were telling her to 'get on board quickly' or else, with a warning that she would be 'answerable' to the new kids in town.

2 September

I'm in a hysterical depression brought on by the dog, the husband, the children, the malfunctioning television, the washing, the washing machine and almost everything else. The listing of my grievances, and they are many, is broken by a terrifying noise outside in the street. Saffron rushes down the stairs, beckoning us to come and see what is making the tremendous noise. There, blinded by the light pinging off it, we delight in a Ferrari Spider wrapped in gold. Seated at the wheel is a swarthy-looking figure on his mobile. For a moment we think it is Peter Andre, the Australian crooner and ex-husband of the lovely Jordan. The number plate reads simply 'FIRYAL'. 'Hello, Firyal,' we say cheerily, and I add, 'Cor, what have you done to deserve this?' The man is rather shy and charming, and says he is a 'prize-fighter'. We congratulate him on his great good taste and H shouts, 'No arguments, Firyal!' as we wave him off in great cloud of CO_2 emissions, which we would normally curse and hiss and shout after.

We rush back inside and immediately google him. It transpires he is called Riyadh Al-Azzawi, and his car cost him two hundred thousand pounds, but the gold wrapping only four thousand; it seems a bargain to me. H says he might get the Jeep Cherokee done. Anyway, our new friend is quite something. He took up kickboxing when he was in his early teens, became Iraqi national champion six times and ultimately the British and then European titleholder. He is also a touch political, because he says he wants to re-unite Iraq through the sport. Now there's an idea that even Tony Blair didn't have. Worth a try, we think. After all, nothing else has worked. I only hope he is house hunting. He would make an ideal neighbour in these dangerous times and his car would certainly liven up this rather staid Chelsea street.

9 September

Are we watching another slow-motion car crash? All summer, Jacob Rees-Mogg has been touted as a possible new leader. Yes, really. The one who talks about his nanny, the one with six children with funny names, the one with crazy ideas that women who are raped can't abort, the one who is another proud alumnus of the most class-divisive school in Britain, the one who thinks it's OK to wear quadruple-breasted suit, probably with a watch chain, and to speak like a plum orchard.

All summer he has been touring TV studios to say it's a ridiculous idea. The No. 10 Gavins (Barwell and Williamson) are going mad. The only way May can kill him is by putting him in a job, but that will only happen if she were intolerably weak, the cabinet was useless and the party had finally given up any hope that it was pushing a modernising radical agenda, or that it was in a panic about how to stop the irrepressible rise of young Trots nurtured by the Labour Party. That's OK, then. He's probably heading for the cabinet in the next reshuffle.

14 September

H back in the House. Bumps into David Davis. 'How's it going?' asks H. 'You must feel you are under enormous pressure.' DD hunches his shoulders, spreads his fat squat nose further with a smile and replies along the lines of not really, I have a team of six thousand: they go in and do the negotiating and I go and have a cup of coffee.

(I'm thinking that's quite a comforting picture.)

'So it's all right, then? We can sleep at night?'

'Yes, it's all fine.'

H says it was rather like Siena coming home from school for the weekend:

'How was school?'

'Fine.'

'How do you feel about the headmistress being raped by an alien and giving birth to six hundred Martians, and you being sold into slavery at an ISIS auction?'

'Fine.'

20 September

It's bloody chaos out there. Boris does a Boris by marching everyone to the top of the hill with a Brexit article in the *Telegraph*, and then marches them all down again. Funny how it always happens in conference season. It's textbook Boris – single act of rebellion, 'accidentally' meeting hacks outside a lift or his house after a sweaty run, and claiming to be baffled by a media storm, before falling into line. He has been outraged at being excluded and at the briefings against him, according to his sister, who bumped into K, and this is why he is trying to force his leader's hand. Fair enough, actually. The cabinet, meanwhile, is still fighting the referendum as Rome burns. Old Ma May is powerless to stop the infighting. Even Hammond looks as if he will walk if Boris gets his way. Have we really left all this to these muppets?

Then there is Jeremy Heywood, the most Machiavellian of them all – after George's departure. He, like all his lot, is a remoaner, and he has clearly been trying to bring Bozza down. I wonder if he was responsible for the attack on Boris by Sir David Norgrove, head of the UK Statistics Authority, who challenged his use of the £350 million figure to save the NHS? Probably. It's got his fingerprints all over it; at least Boris's team thinks so. And why oh why is he not preparing for plan B? Most of the leavers are questioning the role of the civil service in seeking to shape the direction of Brexit. Yeah, and? Like they never meddle in anything or have their own agenda.

I WhatsApp Amber this morning: 'I'm despairing. The whole thing looks so fucking amateur from the outside. Changing speeches about the future of the country because of the whims and ambitions of cabinet ministers. It's a mess. And the Heywoods need reining in; they are also trying to control the agenda. It looks awful every way you turn.'

Amber: 'It's Brexit. We're all over the place because we disagree fundamentally – think it's impossible to please both sides so it's constant compromise.'

Me: 'It's bloody weak leadership, that's what it is.'

21 September

Invited to see Akram Khan's rather eerie modern take on *Giselle* at Sadler's Wells. The pas de deux was so beautiful it brought tears to my eyes.

Ed Vaizey there. He keeps saying to H and me we should have left; we should have left when we had the chance. I ask him who he would vote for in a leadership contest.

'Jacob Rees-Mogg, of course, because I really want the Conservative Party to go back to the eighteenth century.'

The Osbornes also there. Frances only half friendly. George doesn't come up and find us.

H says afterwards, 'I think I'd find it quite difficult calling George Osborne a friend these days, if I was asked.'

22 September

Lunch for the opening of the first Bahraini restaurant in London. It is conveniently near us, but of course we arrive late, to be greeted by a host of Gulf Cooperation Council ambassadors who have little else to do other than attend the opening of Bahraini restaurants. H and I are seated in places of honour, me adjacent to the smooth Egyptian ambassador and opposite the Kuwaiti ambassador, Khaled Al-Duwaisan, an old friend of H who is the longest-serving ambassador to the Court of St James's and has seen the likes of Hugo come and go a hundred times. H is opposite the

Bahraini ambassador and they have a good discussion about the GCC and the situation in Qatar. The freeze continues, but H gets the impression the GCC won't budge until they see some evidence that the Qataris are stopping their dangerous games, supporting terrorists and Salafists round the world. Al-Duwaisan smiles non-committally; Kuwait is not taking sides but are seeking to act as a mediator. Oman too will not get involved, and as usual are keeping their options open. Of course, they continue to play an important back channel role with the Iranians. HRH the Saudi ambassador arrives late, surrounded by his usual vast security detail. He tells H something truly amazing. The Saudis submit their usual list to get accreditation for the Labour Conference. There is a delay. Then the message comes back that no one from the Royal Kingdom is invited. This has never happened before. The Saudis are aghast, and soon the other Arab ambassadors show solidarity by refusing to attend as well. Even the head of the Palestinian delegation, who apparently has been trying and has so far failed to obtain a meeting with Corbyn, pulls out. As the ambassador says, if Labour become the government do they intend to have no bilateral relations with the Arab world at all? Incredible.

A latecomer is Baria Alamuddin, the glamorous Lebanese journalist who doubles as Amal Clooney's mother. Within seconds of sitting down she is apologising for her lateness whilst saying she has just flown in 'privately' to Farnborough. But as most of her audience have their own planes, and very possibly their own airports, they looked unimpressed. Indeed, most of them are under the illusion that Farnborough *is* London's airport. She then says she had been having a wonderful time in Morocco and how marvellous Lalla Salma was. I asked who Lalla Salma was and she looked pityingly at me and said, 'The King's wife,' as if I was some kind of dullard. I then congratulated her on having the bravery to wear white clothes. The ambassadors looked surprised, as normally they are clad from head to toe in bedsheets. A woman wearing white signifies the presence of a maid, and staff in general. You don't keep clothes looking white for long in the Dungeon, what with a distinct lack of staff, a genetic Nott resistance to getting any help, and Rocco the cockapoo. And that's before you climb into a filthy Uber. Anyway, this gave the glamorous Baria an opening to say how she had recently gone mad in Rome, buying a new wardrobe as she had been cooped up all summer with 'the twins on Lake Como'. These are the Clooney twins and soon there was much talk about George and Amal. She looked most pleased by this somewhat inevitable turn in the conversation.

5 October

Conservative Conference

Well, that went well! *Cough*. In fact, to put it mildly, it was the worst viewing experience I can remember in my lifetime. Showing now: *Nightmare on Conference Platform, brought to you by Strepsils, Olbas Oil and Ultra Chloraseptic*, a film so bloody terrifying I was torn between hiding behind the sofa or leaping into the TV to rescue her. And I don't even like the woman.

Just to recap: just as Old Ma May was telling us her government was prepared for every eventuality she is handed her P45 by a prankster from the media cesspit, then she is reduced to almost mute by a tickly cough, then the set collapsed behind her – or should I say the F fell off the wall. The edge-of-the-seat anxiety was made worse by her slurping glasses of water so that you then started worrying about her bladder; the cabinet up and down like yo-yos to give her some coughing space and drown out the phlegm sounds (or not, as the case may be); and an audience and a media with about 1 per cent interest in the content. It was the *will she or won't she get through it* emotion of it all. Then Hammond rushed forward with a boiled sweet, but the boiled sweet didn't come from the Chancellor's own pocket but a few rows back, so it could easily have been a cyanide pill from a Cameroon, for all we knew. It just felt like a political disaster, a tragedy playing out before our very own eyes. Here we all were, witnessing the physical disintegration of her premiership.

Amber calls from the car on her way back from Manchester. She said watching the frailty of her up on the stage was agonising, pitiful, tragic, but she is mostly seething about Boris's constant attention seeking. She confronts him in the green room before an interview: 'Half of my questions were about you! It's really irritating, Boris.' The big fat bouncy yellow labrador feigns surprise: 'Really, Amber? How awful for you. I'm so sorry.'

But Amber no longer needs to worry. Yes, he gave good oratory in Manchester, but the past few weeks have highlighted how he clearly is not a leader-in-waiting. All we saw was a stumbling politician hogging the limelight in a failed attempt to destabilise and replace a leader. End of. Halfway into my conversation with Amber she sighs heavily, as if she is on the floor: 'Do you know, Sasha, I just can't talk about him any more. I'm just too tired. He just dominates everything at the moment.' And I say back, 'You and me both.'

6 October

Von Schnapps has come out on the media about getting rid of the Maybot (so has lazy Vaizey). He says there are about thirty other MPs who want to shaft her as well ... But how many of the names he has got are his alter egos?* Just asking. He is not happy about the reaction: 'The plan was to do it entirely quietly.' Yeah, right. He is blaming the whips now. He always was an odd one. But the whips look like they have played a cleverer game and smoked him out. Then Gove on Radio 4, being loyal. I'm texting Amber furiously as he speaks: 'LIAR LIAR, PANTS ON FIRE, just trying to sound loyal because he has a reputation of being opposite.'

---

* Grant Shapps, Conservative politician accused of using the pseudonyms of Michael Green and Sebastian Fox. H coined the soubriquet 'Von Schnapps'.

'Gove saving his skin. As always, Boris pulls back from the edge . . . he's right on one thing – the party is oddly united around May,' she replies. *I'm not sure it is, Amber.*

'For now!' I text back. 'I've been through four of these and they are very fluid. It's the quiet backbenchers who bring it on. She's so wounded she might last a bit longer, but I doubt it. Stay loyal, which of course you will.'

I always find Amber so politically naive. Yesterday I texted her this:

Amber, the party is dying a slow death, it is what happens to all governments, they get tired, and no one listens any more. We are already there. BUT the opposition is appalling thank God. The only way you will do this is through IDEAS, NEW IDEAS. WE are just fire-fighting at the moment. All this housing stuff is crap, it's just tinkering. The problem is lack of supply not mortgages. It's planning. You will need a whole revolutionary vision of how you will change things. Solutions will win it for you. Find the cleverest people, experts not politicians necessarily, and for each problem find a solution. When your time comes this is what will win it for you, not the donors, not the MPs, it will be a vision of how you want to take the party and country forward.

K and I agree about Amber: we wonder how good she would be on the idea/policy vision thing. Dave apparently is of the view that the Maybot should stay; George – obviously – says no, she needs to go now. She can't do Brexit if she is weak. G is not backing anyone particular at this stage.

Shag, marry, push off a cliff: Hammond? Davis? Boris? Patel? Amber?

What a fucking mess.

If they could only coalesce around someone as a party and have a coronation, but there are too many competing egos and no talent to be seen.

*

Oh yes, a new board of trade has been formed by Liam Fox. Only snag is there is only one member on this board: Liam Fox.

According to David Davis, we are going to get a better deal without being a member. If I said to H, you are going to be a better member of White's if you are not a member, he'd say, 'What?'

9 October

Full jamboree down at Cornwell Manor in Oxfordshire, in honour of Kate and her twin sister Mel, hosted by Mel's partner Al Ward. A good three hundred people. Lots of residual Cameroons who have had banner headlines attached to them at some time or other, such as Charlie and Rebekah Brooks, Craig Oliver, Andy Coulson, Gabby Bertin, Andrew and Gaby Feldman but the two great men in Kate's life, as she calls them, are absent: one is on the political speaking circuit, the other Evgeny's panting lapdog at some overseas conservation project.

We stay, along with Thomas Strathclyde, Greg Barker and George Prassas at Hugo Rittson-Thomas's modest Notting-Hill-in-country manor, with its beautifully designed gardens; the highlight is an orchard with a deep carpet of red and pink cosmos. Cornwell Manor is also a beautiful house, which borders Bamford country. They are always trying to buy it off him, apparently. You would have thought they had enough already.

The party was fun, really good fun. Best moments included an absolutely surreal conversation with a female MP about how to achieve orgasm in our twilight age, with a good amount of detail about clitoral stimulation. An initially gentle conversation with a twenty-seven-year-old, who was surprisingly anti-Corbyn – it only clicked three-quarters through the conversation that she was

Jewish. This certainly became clear when she said that these days Palestinians only give birth to produce jihadist suicide bombers, and that all Palestinians should be deported to Jordan: *'They all have Jordanian passports, you know,'* and *'They should go. We won the war.'* I beat a hasty retreat, knowing there isn't going to be a Middle East solution any time soon. Then I have a laugh with Theo Rycroft, who's now working for Boris in the FCO, and then sit down with Jo Johnson, who asks me what I would do if I were Theresa. 'Sack your brother,' I reply, much to H's embarrassment.

Another faux pas in the morning when I notice our host keeps putting the lid back on the butter carton after every use at the breakfast table. 'That's so AC/DC,' I say. Afterwards, Greg asks, 'Why did you keep saying that? AC/DC means swings both ways. Didn't you mean OCD?'

10 October

Back to the Foreign Office for the launch of James Stourton's coffee-table book, *British Embassies.* H has long been an admirer of our embassies and a critic of how some have been pared back to the bone and others flogged off. Blair's lot saw them as elitist and merely B&Bs for visiting ministers, and it was not until Hague and Hugo were in the FCO did they regain some attention and respect. In fact, they opened quite a few more. With the approach of Brexit, they will be absolutely essential for bilateral diplomacy, so the plusher they are the better, quite frankly. Swings and roundabouts.

Anyway, H came up with the idea for the book and pressed it on Stourton; he felt the architectural range, built to adapt to different cultures but at the same time so uniquely British, needed documenting, particularly since it reflected our history of engagement with the world. The introduction acknowledges that it was H's idea and that he was responsible for the project's fruition by ensuring that James was given proper access.

*

H finally comes face to face with Theresa; the first time since she shot him in 2016. He is chairing the annual CMEC gala lunch at the Savoy. Ten colleagues have pulled out and he is incandescent with rage on behalf of the CMEC team who have worked so hard, and because each place costs a minimum of £120 a head. H finds out who the missing diners are and rings one of them, Johnny Mercer, leaving a message for him saying he may think he's so important he's going to be PM at any moment, but clearly he's got no fucking idea how to behave, etc., etc. At that moment, the great She Elephant is announced. H greets her and thanks her for coming. She is friendly and H finds himself warming towards her. He escorts her to the top table and makes a brief speech, saying the only sound of coughing the audience are going to hear in the room is the sound of CMEC supporters coughing up. The PM winces.

13 October

The West Hill harvest supper is well attended. H tours the village hall before they all sit down. People are friendly. He canvasses them on various options and the majority like Boris and want Philip Hammond sacked. Some want Jacob R-M to become PM immediately, and possibly succeed the Queen soon after that. This is Brexit country, after all.

H makes a long speech and answers endless questions, all predictable and the usual fears and clichés. The highlight of his evening is when Colonel Peter Morrison, who now tells H he is very pro Trump, makes a long-winded speech about the local press, saying how fed up he is with reading anti-Tory and, yes, anti-Hugo letters, and that we never get the other side. Our side. He wants to know what H is going to do about it. H asks for a show of hands from those who have written anything in support of the government, the party or him to the local newspaper. Out of about a hundred people, two raise their hands. 'There!' H says, rather triumphantly, 'They can't print what they don't receive.'

The Colonel looks deflated. Perhaps that has never occurred to him before. We rather hope he was more reflective when he was a leader of men.

29 October

The fallout from Weinstein is sending the ladies all into a twitter, or should I say WhatsApp groups. Everywhere you look new groups are forming to name and shame sex pests. The group everyone is getting most excited about is the Westminster one. Natch. Sex, power, politics and media, it was ever thus. Even Hugo's part-time secretary Caroline Edmondson is taking part; she's hit the front pages today, claiming Mark Garnier called her 'sugar tits' and asked her to buy sex toys for him.

Old Ma May is not best pleased, being a vicar's daughter and all that. She was never one for Westminster's late-night drinking culture. She's meant to be focusing on Brexit but now she has a full-blown sex scandal on her plate as well. According to the *Sunday Times*, she is getting weekly updates on the MPs' sexual peccadilloes from Gav, in a briefing that has been dubbed 'the ins and outs' chat. Gav is a terrible gossip by nature, so it all rings true. He's probably rather enjoying it, knowing him. I suppose Old Ma May fears the scandal could finally trigger her downfall; she needs to get a grip of it like David did with expenses in 2009. The *Sun* is saying there's going to be an emergency reshuffle. Which might be why Gav approached H to ask if he would come back. Not at same level, says H, and 'there are only a couple of jobs I'd do anyway'. Which is Foreign or Defence, which in the scheme of things is about as likely as winning £64 million on the lottery. Except the cabinet apparently has a few pervs, so maybe not that unlikely after all. Politics has always been about luck and gossip, not just talent.

How do I feel about it all? I think the burden of proof should be a little more than hearsay on a WhatsApp group. I mean, litigating in this area can be heated and messy as it falls between courtship flirtation and sex. Someone making a clumsy pass at a young woman is not going to stop, not even through mob justice. Looking back on my own younger days, the only person who always patted my bum on greeting me was one David Cameron. Mind you, he did the same to my husband at a state banquet and that pat went viral.

Sunday catch-up with the Home Secretary. We discuss the breaking sex scandal.

'How's it all going otherwise?'

'Nightmare. There is absolutely no plan on Brexit.'

'And Theresa?'

'Only interested in victimhood issues, like slavery, mental health, etc. Her eyes glaze over when Brexit is on the agenda. There is no political direction at all. Liz Truss and I were both saying how much we missed the Cameron regime.'

Amber now fears that there will be some a kind of deal. Labour will say they can't support it, then they will look like the party of In and will romp home with the voters. But, of course, Amber comes from a remain stance. I slightly question this theory, as many Labour supporters did actually vote for Brexit. She comes back by saying over 65 per cent voted remain. Still, on those numbers it would be tough for them. There is a story in the *Mail on Sunday* of her forming a dream team with Boris.

'The only way I would support Boris for leader is if the other candidate was Jacob Rees-Mogg,' she huffs.

31 October

The press is going mad on sex pests, thinking they have a new expenses scandal on their hands. They are buzzing around like blue-arsed flies. That little goblin Bercow is up and down in his seat, gripped by his own smug sanctity. (He should concentrate on what his wife is up to instead.) The Commons is being made to look like a bacchanalian tea party, full of sordid whiplashed old Tory fatties. Hogarth would have been inspired. The right-on brigade is also out in force; they that consist mainly of Greens and Lib Dims. I might care to remind them of the Lord Rennard shambles. Remember him, sweeties? MPs are bending over backwards to present themselves as holier than thou, which is odd because they are anything but. Old Ma May looks as if she wants to commit suicide. But that might be because Andrea Leadsom is taking it all on.

Personally, I can't see what all the fuss is about, and besides, many young women coming into the Commons are not entirely innocent in seeking out powerful men to have affairs with – I could name millions of them over the years. The trouble is, in this atmosphere anyone can say anything about anyone, but at least – unlike in the expenses saga – there has to be a modicum of truth in it. And whoever compiled the spreadsheet of forty MPs who are alleged to have behaved improperly or had carnal relations with colleagues can't even spell their names, which means they were probably sacked as illiterate researchers and are bearing a grudge. Lastly, office affairs, nebulous 'inappropriateness' and actual assaults are all being stirred into one sleaze pot, implicating a whole bunch of people whose actions were always consensual. Morally wrong, maybe, but not illegal.

H is convinced that the big sex scandals mainly revolve around gay sex anyway. Certainly, there is a rumour of a threesome and some peeing. But who is to say that Momentum are not active in this? I mean, Labour are far worse when it comes to misogyny. And they seem to be getting away with it.

The atmosphere is febrile. Hugo says to Sue yesterday, 'Sugar?'
Sue looks up crossly.
'In your tea, Sue. In your tea.'
Hugo assures me he has not partaken in any groping himself. Time will tell. He is at that age when he needs more of it and is getting less of it.

2 November

Driving down to Devon, the staggering news comes through that
Gav has been made Defence Secretary following Michael Fallon's
resignation. We are stunned. 'I don't fucking believe it. She's finally
gone mad,' I say. 'What did he do? Jam the chair against the door
and say, "It has to be me, Theresa, love. I'm young, untainted, your
most loyal, trusted servant"?'

3 November

The witch-hunt gathers pace. The faintly oily Charlie Elphicke
is next to be shot down. Whip withdrawn. Police informed. He
tweets: 'The party tipped off the press before telling me of my sus-
pension. I am not aware of what the alleged claims are and deny
any wrongdoing.'

And on the left we have Clive 'Get on your knees, bitch' Lewis
who allegedly grabbed a girl's bum at an event.*

I'd better keep a list, since this looks as if it is going to run and run.

7 November

Have set up an anonymous Twitter account called @torympwife to
vent my frustrations at this appalling government. H understandably
very nervous. I have told no one except Nicholas Soames, who gave
me lessons on how to use Twitter. Trouble is, every time Soames
retweets me I get hordes of followers. This week, when I was ranting,
he replied #shesonfirestandbywiththefireextinguishers.

I message him privately: 'Yeah baby, I'm hot!"
'You may be, but you are truly magnificent!!!!!!!!'

---

* An internal party investigation cleared Clive Lewis of groping a woman at
  Labour's 2017 conference.

'Every time you retweet me, I put on followers. Trouble is I've now got the media hound dogs trying to flush me out. Tight lips Soames please.'

'Standard onto me said I hadn't a clue but understood she/he comes from the north! My lips tighter than a lobster's bum!'

'xx I love lobster.'

'Moi aussi mon petit love antelope!'

*

Meanwhile, back at the ranch, Priti Patel has got herself wound up so tight in the Israeli lobbyist Stuart Polak's* web she is finding a whole bunch of other people have now moved in to pull off her legs. Including H, by pointing James Lansdale in the right direc-tion. Payback time for her sharp elbows in the FCO, it seems. Will May have the balls to sack her? What with Brexit, sex scandals, a botched election?

8 November

Priti Patel is on an eight-hour flight back from Africa to be sacked. Amber is in Washington and supportive texts from MPs are flying into her phone. She feels a little frightened by it all. Amber doesn't want to go for leadership this early if May falls. I am absolutely stunned by what Priti has been up to. It's almost as if she has been acting as a spy for another nation state.

24 November

Gove has been watching too much *Strictly Come Dancing*, appar-ently: Sarah thinks he's missing all the dressing up from his days

---

* Former director of Conservative Friends of Israel. Accompanied Priti Patel, then Secretary of State for International Development, on a controversial trip to Israel. Patel subsequently resigned from the cabinet.

over in Justice. I think it's more about him learning the moves – his manoeuvres to 'audition' for chancellor are in full swing. In cabinet, the Fox was spotted winking at colleagues, who were trying to keep a straight face. Even the PM has taken to rolling her eyes when he speaks.

25 November

Remembering last week's quick retail therapy with Amber: my L. K. Bennett discount card is always a winner when my girls are feeling depressed. She tells me in between shoe changes that the job sometimes gets her down. The pain of seeing and talking to crime victims, particularly young girls, wrenches her apart. She tells me she doesn't want the top job before Brexit. It's not for her under those circumstances. She says as much when Gove and Boles arrange a secret meeting with her. They are clearly up to their old tricks. You would have thought they learnt their lesson last time round but they just can't help themselves. The three of them agree there is no clear choice if May resigns tomorrow. Jeremy Hunt, maybe. But how desperate is that? Or are they laying the groundwork for another plan?

Amber and Boris also chat about leadership when they are together in Washington. He tells her he is full of regret he didn't stand against May. I suggest to Amber that he didn't have the numbers to beat May anyway. She's not so sure. He says something along the lines of 'I thought you were going to support me to run'. A replies, 'I thought you said you were going to support me, Boris.' Amber describes them all as boys playing games. Interestingly – and she has not told anyone this – Boris said that if she supported him for leadership, he would give her the chancellorship. But if it was a toss-up between Foreign Secretary and Treasury, she would take Foreign.

How much support has she in the party? She has Anne Milton on side, and those who are furious they have been overlooked by May – Nicky Morgan, etc. I roll my eyes. She says, 'I know, I know.'

She tells me the leadership campaign is called Operation Sunshine. We both laugh out loud. I'm not involved, but Kate has been helping her.

26 November

H and I take Amber out to dinner, to our local, the Surprise in Chelsea, to cheer her up. Her long relationship with Kwasi has been terminated. We both come home feeling she definitely hasn't got the appetite to be leader. Her heart isn't really in it. We are 100 per cent certain she is not going to stand.

28 November

Prince Harry has announced his engagement to the actress Meghan Markle. A mixed-race American divorcee. Times are a-changing. Even the monarchy has gone celebrity obsessed. The interview with them was like watching an episode of *The Crown*. Meghan has never done panto before; she might find it difficult, no longer swapping roles but having to stick to one permanently, albeit a big one. I came away humming *there'll be trouble ahead*. She's eating the redhead for breakfast, almost elbowing him out of shot. He is clearly not as clever as she is. At one point he becomes agitated, as if he is thinking she is stealing all the limelight: 'I think the question was for me!'

7 December

DD in front of the Brexit Committee yesterday; Hilary Benn asking the questions.

'Just to be clear, has the government undertaken any impact assessments on the implications of leaving the EU for different sectors of the economy?'

'Not in sectors,' says DD. 'The Treasury, of course, has an OBR forecast that has an implication, although even that is pretty crude. That is done from the average of all the external forecasts of impact on the economy and so on, so there is no systematic impact assessment.'

'The answer to the question is "no".'

'Yes.'

'The government have not undertaken any impact assessments on the implications of leaving the EU for different sectors of the British economy. There is not one, for example, on the automotive sector.'

'No, not that I am aware of.'

'Is there one on aerospace?'

'Not that I'm aware of, no.'

'Is there one on financial services?'

'I think the answer is going to be no to all of them.'*

It doesn't exactly fill one with confidence, does it?

15 December

The Maybot has suffered her first Commons defeat on Brexit. That bony, sanctimonious Frenchman Dominic Grieve tabled an amendment last night to her flagship EU withdrawal bill that gave parliament a right to a meaningful vote on the Brexit deal. He managed to corral eleven Tory MPs to join him in a rebellion, with the amendment passing by 309 votes to 305. The result was greeted with raucous cheers of 'We're taking back control!', and Labour MPs taunting and jeering. Last-minute promises by government ministers were dismissed as being too little and too late.

---

* Oral evidence: Department for Exiting the European Union Sectoral Analyses, HC 653, 6 December 2017.

Tory Boy Dominic Raab (he has stolen that crown from Matt Hancock) is even accused of 'smug arrogance' by one remainer rebel. H says it was all a whips' cock-up. The reaction by Brexiteers has been typically furious.

H talks to Amber in the lobbies. She must be secretly pleased about what's happened. 'It'll teach the government it can't just do as it likes,' she whispers to him. 'But Amber,' H replies, 'you *are* the government.' Sometimes I think she's still so amazed at being an MP, let alone Home Secretary, that she quite simply forgets, but such is her charm and amazing modesty, or is it do with her real views on Brexit?

Siena comes to dine with Hugo at the House. He asks her if she'd like to stay and watch the voting. She says she would, so up to the Strangers' Gallery she goes. She watches the MPs, some well known, some not so, come and go. Amber, her godmother, waves at her, but Siena is only interested in seeing, or ideally meeting, one person – that person being, of course, Jeremy Corbyn. She says that if she can get a selfie with JC (for the young, those initials seem to represent a new saviour) she will count that as her Christmas present. H's parsimonious Scottish blood kicks in, and after the penultimate vote he finds himself sidling up to the messiah in the lobby. H tells Jezza that if he complies, he will make a teenage girl very happy. This H concedes is not a very strong promise as JC makes every teenage girl happy, seemingly, just by his very existence. Jezza suggests they meet in Members' Lobby after the last vote. H votes quickly, runs upstairs and hurries Siena down. They rush pass the doorkeepers, who try to stop them because only MPs are allowed into the lobby during a vote and Siena is clearly not an MP, being sixteen and in a hoodie – though no doubt that will very shortly be the uniform in that place if the wretched Bercow gets his way. H grabs her by her hood and urges her to follow him quickly. Jezza is waiting for them, but he nervously says they can't take a photo where they are so they move through Central Lobby to St Margaret's Hall. Siena goes all sugary and almost flirty. There's a lot of 'Thank you *soooo* much' and then, having won JC over, she asks him to pose for the selfie while making some obscure gesture with his hand; a tribal signal to teenagers worldwide, no doubt. Jezza asks what it means and Siena – rather brusquely, to H's mind – tells him to 'just do it'. He seems a bit fazed by the whole episode, but can't be faulted on manners. He asks S how old she is. Sixteen, she replies, and adds, 'I'll be voting for you next time.' At this point the disapproving figure of Diane Abbott hoves into view and asks JC in a somewhat scolding manner, tinged with exasperation, what he thinks he is doing, before dragging him away.

Siena is overwhelmed, although apparently not by Jezza's hideous brown suit, about which she is disparaging, or his slight physical form. H informs her, 'We would call it svelte, being middle aged.' H asks her afterwards if she is really going to vote for him. 'Of course not,' she says, 'I was just being polite.'

Siena has sent the selfie to her friends and her stock has risen immeasurably. Her sister is green with envy and puts it up on the Instagram account of the Back Bench, her politics show on university radio, which gets a like from Jeremy Corbyn himself. Edinburgh Political Union's committee goes into meltdown. H and I think the whole thing is bizarre beyond belief. The man is just a muppet. At least H is his daughter's hero of the hour. So it was certainly worth the effort.

2018

8 January

It's all kicking off. The Maybot, for one full second, looked a bit stronger after she returned from her hols, and then bang, crash, wallop, her feeble attempt at a reshuffle goes horribly wrong. Her slow dance of political death takes another step forward. For now, Jeremy Hunt clings on, but rumours have it he was meant to go elsewhere. And so does Greg Clark, cling on, and he was also meant to go elsewhere (the staff were already doing a jig). Chris Grayling thought he was going somewhere because CCHQ told us he was via Twitter, and then he was told that, actually, he wasn't going anywhere. Andrea Leadsom, who the Maybot detests and was meant to be anywhere but here, also got to stay, and so did everyone else, basically – everyone apart from Justine Greening.

21 January

Dinner with Amber last night, and I have spent the whole day incensed by what she said. The long and short of it is that she is pretty certain the government will fall if May is pushed into a hard Brexit. And if that happens, she and her fellow remainers will team up and resign collectively. In my book, this is bordering on treason, particularly since she is in effect working to help Brussels, which clearly has drawn up a high-risk strategy to undermine the Maybot and exploit Westminster's political divisions with the sole objective of 'softening' Brexit. Amber's calculations are that May does not have a parliamentary majority in favour of pulling out of the customs union and the single market, and that Labour, via Keir Starmer (and Roland and Blair no doubt), are plotting to come out with that line. I did point out that Corbyn was a Brexiteer and might not curry favour with that idea, and nor would his northern seats. Amber is clearly piling pressure on May to choose between the hardliners and what she believes is the preferred option of remainers. Only this week she had a one-on-one with the PM, trying to persuade her to agree to free movement instead of the more phased one she favours.

'Do you want to overturn Brexit if you can?' I ask her.

'Gosh, NO!'

Really? Really, Amber? Or are you with Mr Tusk in coordinating a strategy to 'forgive and forget' if Britain changes its mind, while he hardens the EU line in talks to make the government's Brexit policy as politically toxic as possible?

But, in effect, if we go with a soft Brexit we are in a worse situation than being in the bloody EU. The public, in all their wisdom (which I think Amber is pretty detached from) will be outraged. What about Ireland, Amber says. Personally, I think Ireland will have to become united through mutual agreement, but she is horrified by that, not because she cares about the Ulster Unionist position but because it is a key sticking point. A weapon she can deploy.

All my close friends are urban remainers, so I never get into a discussion with them if I can help it. On the whole, I believe small is better, that people should govern themselves and that power should be reclaimed and localised whenever possible. I don't like the Greek, Spanish or Irish models, where people are thrown into the gnashing, salivating jaws of the bankers. I don't like the unaccountability of the whole thing. And I think we have gone too far down the hill to go up it again now.

H is in the House, and goes along to the Green Chip Dinner Club, which was set up to promote a Cameroon agenda by Greg Barker, H and others. Michael Gove present, and two other Secs of State, Matt Hancock and Damian Hinds ('perfectly nice but unimpressive'). H opens up the discussion, saying he bumped into Chris

Leslie in the Burlington Arcade laden down with shopping bags. Clearly embarrassed to see H while embracing such luxurious materialism, they soon got talking about the parlous state of the Labour Party. Leslie said it was ghastly and that everything was now coming to a head, not least on account of the party's notorious anti-Semitism. H told him they needed to move very quickly as Momentum was picking them off one by one. Leslie thinks they should wrap it up in a row about Europe, but H said they hadn't got time for that. He tells H they are going to announce something quite soon. H relays all this to the dinner but the general consensus was that they didn't think a new breakaway party would be formed any time soon because none of the moderates have any balls.

The conversation moved on to the subject of productivity, and as H made his contribution he could hear Gove mutter under his breath, 'Getting your butler to work harder, eh, Hugo?'

27 January

It's been Davos week. Now that Greg is heading up Oleg Deripaska's aluminium firm, he has developed a nice sideline in entertainment and has asked everyone he ever knew in politics to swing by a party he was hosting for his Russian oligarch boss and his cronies. 'Lots of dancing girls and caviar,' he tells anyone who cares to listen. In reality, it was a bunch of babushkas in folk costume wailing melancholically.

Dave turns it down, naturally, but as compensation offers Greg a quick spin on the slopes. In Dave's books this was probably the safest option; blizzard conditions, so goggles and bobble hats all round meant he could go incognito. Except one of his security men hurt his foot chasing them while skiing and the masks were off. Not that anyone noticed them anyway.

Since we are all watching *McMafia* on TV, everyone is a little jumpy. Even more so with the exposure of the Presidents Club, which last week had its annual bash at the Dorchester. Trouble was, it was 'men only', and the young hostesses were told to wear skimpy dresses and flirt with the men, who largely resembled carcasses hung up in an abattoir, and to not turn their faces away from the fumes of their halitosis when they nestle into their necks. Nothing wrong with a bit of slap and tickle said the organisers, who confiscated the girls' mobile phones and forced them to sign non-disclosure agreements, which just shows how naive they were, because why do you sign a document that works against you? These girls were then followed by an army of sex workers, all wearing red dresses to advertise their wares. The room was throbbing with testosterone of the banker, celebrity, CEO kind.

H, like all the men in my life, Sir John included, is a bit puzzled. They simply can't see what's wrong with chaps flinging themselves at scantily clad young girls who are being paid to be there. I mean, how else are they supposed to score, marry and keep the human race from going extinct?

Hugo wasn't at the Presidents Club dinner, although other MPs were, but that doesn't stop this new McCarthy-style atmosphere. Articles have now started to appear, usually written by female hackettes, about clubbing, British MP-style. Hugo is named in a *Politico* article listing said exclusive establishments and who frequents them, then in the *Evening Standard*: 'You can't move in White's or the Sublime Society of Beef Steaks without bumping into a Hugo Swire or Nicholas Soames.' His secret is out.

Pillow talk, and I quiz my husband as a journalist would, in case they get to him: 'So, darling, here is the question: what is the fundamental point in the argument against these clubs existing?'

He looks completely baffled by the question.

'Could it be that women are now part of the parliamentary process and should not be excluded from political manoeuvrings?' I ask him.

'Er, if you say so.'

'OK, I'm now going to media-train you in how to answer these questions. How do you think you should reply?'

'I don't want to sit next to Nadine Dorries in White's?'

'No, you can't say that.'

'My wife likes to know where we chaps are, or at least where we pretend to be?'

'Try again, Hugo.'

28 January

The *Sunday Times* insight team does another of its investigations, this time on Andrew Lansley, Peter Lilley and, yes, you've guessed it, Andrew Mitchell. All have been exposed as attempting to profit from a new cash-for-Brexit gravy train. The footage of Mitchell is excruciating. When H asks him about it all, he tells him he only went along to the meeting at the behest of the intelligence services. *Yeah, right.*

The papers are full of the Maybot's woes today: Brexit; the Pestminster sex scandal; a collective loss of faith in her abilities and the manoeuvrings of her aspirant successors; an interview with Trump, who said if he was PM he would do Brexit better and why doesn't she get on with it; her chosen successor's Gavin's snog with an office colleague when he was twenty-seven (yes, that's odd, that one, why legal letters are flying no one can quite tell). Her indecisiveness as to whether to boot the MPs out of the Commons so it can be repaired; her fear of letting Andrea Leadsom proceed with a new code of conduct for dirty old men in the Commons, because the dirty old men would drop a letter into the 1922 (and could get close to the number required for a vote of no confidence); the cancellation of a major speech on Brexit because both sides in the cabinet are lawless; her civil servant negotiator telling Eurocrats that she would be content to stay in the customs union or something identical to it, even after the transition period expires in 2021, which means she has entirely contradicted herself from her initial speech ... and so it goes on.

Of course, if she had been forced to flesh out where she stood on the single market, the customs union, the European Court of

Justice and paying into the EU budget during a proper leadership contest, it might not have changed any minds in the Tory Party, but it would have given her a mandate.

Meanwhile, the Chief Whip, Julian Smith, has told newly promoted ministers that they should not indulge in a tipple during the week if they want to keep their jobs, as he tries to impose new metrics for success. I mean, seriously, seriously, what the fuck are 'metrics'? Besides, you need to be an alcoholic to work for this mob in the first place.

Hugo groans, and tries to suffocate himself with a pillow. He can't take much more of this. And he's not alone: the more sensible and engaged MPs, are being left to ponder whether their future, their party's future and their country's future (in that order) would be best served by a change of leader.

H tells Greg on the phone that he thinks Gove might be back in the running for the leadership, much to Dave's annoyance.

'Really?' says Greg.

'Yes, really.'

'Well, you will be deported, then, as chairman of the Conservative Middle East Council.'

'To Guantanamo, probably.'

H comes down to Devon. On arriving at Tiverton Parkway and looking ahead to a full day in the constituency, the car doesn't start. We always knew it was a matter of time, his Jeep Cherokee is an old cart horse on its last legs. It also happens to be the most polluting diesel car in the country. Anne, his new Devon-based assistant, diverts from Plymouth in her car, which she says she bought with her last redundancy. H thinks she cannot have got much because it is the most basic car he has ever been in, but it's distinguished from his in so much as it actually works. At the end of the day she drops him back at the station to await the AA. A charming man duly arrives and they get talking. H says the car is left for long periods at Tiverton Parkway. Why, he asks. 'Because

I work in London,' says H. Doing what he asks. 'Parliament. I am the MP for East Devon,' H tells him proudly. 'Oh yes,' the AA man replies, head buried in the bowels of the car, 'I think I met the mayor of Tiverton once.'

29 January

A Westminster Hall debate on housing. H fulminates against volume housebuilders. Nicholas Soames supports Nick Herbert in criticising developers and inappropriate housebuilding in their part of the world. He is sitting next to H, who whispers congratulations on his principled stand and says that he is going to send a copy of his speech to Duncan Davidson, who started and retains a large stake in Persimmon, and that Nicholas can say goodbye to ever again being asked to Lilburn, Davidson's estate where he massacres grouse on a regular basis.

'You might as well put your guns away right now.'

Soames looks horrified and says he didn't mean Persimmon, and that they are an excellent company. 'Rubbish,' H says, 'they have some of the worst standards and you know it.' Soames snorts and goes into a grump, which is his way when challenged.

14 February

All is not lost. I read today that twelve new parties have been launched this year, and more than fifty last year. Alongside the usual 'save our hospital' effort and Citizens Against Mobile Phone Masts there are various pro- and anti-Brexit parties like United Kingdom Veterans. I particularly love the Rubbish Party, which was set up by someone called Sally Cogley; a supremely good effort on her part because, as *The Times* quips, she won just as many seats as other rubbish parties like UKIP.

Maybe two-party politics is over and the country wants to

embrace more coalition governments, hung parliaments and minority groupings holding the balance of power.

I won't hold my breath.

20 February

To Dave's last night. Boy George muscled in on the show – he probably heard the star attraction was a huge pot of caviar, but then again, he must have full access to the stuff day and night these days. As we smack our shot glasses down on the table, I say we are all Russians now and slap my thigh. There is lots of joking about Greg and his links to Oleg Deripaska, and when I say, hold on a minute, George, pot calling kettle black: you are being employed by the Russians as well, he says, 'Yes, fair enough, and worse: my owner's father happened to be the head of the KGB, London station.'

George says he's off to LA to accompany Lebedev to the Oscars party – Elton John's one, naturally. He declares he is a bit nervous because he won't know anyone there (more uncomfortably, no one will know him). I can't imagine two more socially awkward men going to a party together than them. He tells us the only people he has ever known in that world are the sexual deviants Kevin Spacey and Harvey Weinstein, and he is pretty sure they won't be pitching up this year.

I ask Dave which Russians are bribing him with the caviar but Sam interjects that actually it was a Christmas present from Lady Astor, who is in the money, having flogged OK-YA. We feel very honoured to be sharing it with them. Sam looks completely exhausted; a combination of jet lag, running a fashion business, two houses to do up, three children to look after. She's pale and fashionably thin. Mind you, I've never seen anyone mop up a tin of caviar as quickly as she did last night. She generously offers me some dresses if I'd like them, but I say I'm too fat for clothes at the moment.

The dominating conversation was of course Brexit. David and George still think it can be thwarted. Dave then went into a long explanation of how the Lords had only to delay matters by a few months, which would effectively block it. I became quite lost at this point; the political game-playing was way off my scale. Samantha wants a second referendum and Dave is OK with that as well, but I say, do we really want to prolong this agony, and won't we just get the same result? D thinks that there are at least eight MPs who will not vote for the final deal.

'Soames, for instance,' he muses. 'He surely won't support it.'

DC and George both think the irritating Anna Soubry is a heroine, a sort of anti-Brexit Boadicea, and she's gaining in popularity day by day. Funny this, because when they were in power they were slow to give her a job because they considered her completely barking.

Even now, G tries to manipulate H into causing trouble by not supporting a deal. Which is not H's current inclination at all. I just sit back and listen, increasingly depressed that they are still fighting the referendum. Of course, it's all tied up with their fall from power, an act that was mostly unanticipated; they are clearly still raw and coming to terms with their loss. Also, they can be quite male, and Bullingdon and clever, which always intimidates me.

H has also issued me with instructions not to get involved in Brexit discussions because of my views. I comply, as I'm not one to let off fireworks these days; I'm too old and unsexy to carry it off, and I don't want to appear as a crazed outlier in this group.

Ironically, one of George's favourite recruiting lines was always 'Do you really want to be on the wrong side of history?' As if this is the worst fate that can befall a man or a woman trying to climb the greasy pole. Looks like he didn't take his own advice.

We move on to May, and it is apparent in George's references to her how much he still loathes her. Almost like an obsession. In fact, if Shakespeare was alive he could write a whole play about it. George will do anything to bring her premiership to a bloody end. Interestingly, he has just had lunch with Gavin Barwell, May's

Chief of Staff. He's not impressed with Barwell's calibre but said 'at least he's human'.

'But why didn't anyone send someone like him along earlier to shut me down?'

Dave pulls it back to Old Ma May, saying he has heard from someone at the top of the heap, someone right beside her, that she has absolutely no intention of standing down. That she thinks she can run and run. Blast it! There we were, secretly hoping that, this being Lent and her being a vicar's daughter and all that, she might just decide to give it up, pack it in, say arrivederci. But it seems not, which maybe she sees as the ultimate sacrifice, and she's not far wrong.

Leadership next.

'Who would you vote for, George, if she goes?'

'Amber,' he says quickly.

Dave is not so sure, thinks she's a bit stiff and not really a Conservative, but that is not necessarily a problem. He bangs on about Ruth Davidson, who ticks all his boxes. G says there is some obscure constitutional point that would enable her to lead the party from Scotland or the Lords or her flat or in the bath ... again, I'm lost. But Ruth has told them it's not that she isn't interested, it's just she doesn't want to pick up the tail end of this dreadful government.

George thinks Gove is back in the running. The Camerons look despairing, but Sam concedes even she would prefer Michael to Corbyn.

There is a long discussion about Corbyn. George is convinced he can do it. H, Dave and I not so sure. G reckons twenty seats in London will go to him, and that 20 per cent of the vote comes from London. He reckons he is a real threat.

What is interesting is the list of MPs beating a path to D's door. Mark Pritchard, the energetic Johnny Mercer, etc.

There is no negativity about the baby-faced assassin Gavin, which is probably because they are both still linked to him. Hugo recently bumped into him in Green Park, flanked by two heavies.

'I've just been with the Boss' – Gavin's bosses change to suit the time of day. And Gavin – 'I think he'd make an excellent Foreign Secretary,' he told Hugo. H tries teasing D about this, but he is not to be drawn. Samantha says she'd support him if he wanted to come back in some way. And yet D has got everything he wants: an extension at Dean, the house in London done up and a house in his beloved Daymer Bay. He is not grand in that sense. When H asks him about getting a gong, House of Lords, title etc.he sounds genuinely uninterested: 'I'm really not into any of that stuff.' And we believe him. But I don't get the impression he dismisses the idea of returning out of hand. Of course, he would be mad to do so.

Jacob Rees-Mogg next. No one can quite believe he has gained such traction. There is a deep fear that if he goes to the member-ship, he could get the leadership. G is delighted that someone had written that JRM was 'a barmaid's idea of a gentleman'. It's a staggeringly good and accurate description.

After G leaves, D says his friend and former chancellor is like a caged tiger at the moment; that he is full of regret, feels he has cocked up. In response H says his name was booed at the 1922 the other day because of his disloyalty to Theresa, that he could never go back – the MPs loathe him too much. Dave sighs, 'Such a wasted talent.'

We order an Uber.

'You know, black cabbies still throw me rude gestures because I let Uber into this country,' Dave says.

I always come away from seeing my remoaning friends with a grey cloud looming over my head. I find I'm highly anxious at the moment, on all kinds of levels but mostly about the state of the world. I suspect this is based on news overload, which gives me a clear misperception of risk, anxiety, lower mood levels, contempt and hostility towards others, desensitisation and general depres-sion about the direction in which we are heading, and my deluded friends who are trying to stop us.

I think someone needs to tell me that we just live and then we die, and probably no one will ever notice what happens in between, and that I am bloody lucky to have had a comfortable ride.

21 February

The rather unimpressive Police and Crime Commissioner for Devon, Alison Hernandez, gave a radio interview in which someone asked about dangerous parking on pavements; she urged them to write to their MP. Hugo says, mercifully, they only got two letters, and dictates a letter back to Ms Hernandez:

> *Dear Alison,*
>   *I was rather surprised to receive a letter on the matter of inappropriate parking on pavements. I was further surprised to learn this was a result of an interview on the radio in which you urged listeners to contact their MPs to resolve this problem. May I point out that*
>   *a) You are the Police and Crime Commissioner*
>   *b) This is a matter for local authorities*
>   *c) This is not and never has been a matter for MPs and it is not good use of their time.*
> *Yours sincerely,*
> *Hugo Swire*

Sue, as usual, types it up muttering *I think I'll amend it slightly* ... This is how she handles Hugo: she just lets him rant and dictate. So, Hugo might start 'Dear Mr Smith, If that is your view, you can just fuck off', saying, 'I want you to send that, Sue. Make sure you do. I'm the boss, remember.' Sue again mutters that she will just amend it slightly. The letter that comes back for signing reads, 'Dear Mr Smith, Thank you so much for your enquiry about the EU. I note your concerns with great interest, and I'm most grateful for your letter.'

'Sue! That is not what I said.'

'Yes, but this is the letter you will be signing.'

Down in the constituency, it's the West Hill branch AGM and dinner, which means H does not get home until nearly midnight. Usual stuff. He sits through the dinner and then makes an indifferent speech, having had to listen to Colonel Morrison read out the Conservative Policy Forum report, or whatever it's called. H sometimes thinks, in the darkest moments of the night, that he may be dangerously right wing, but attending the West Hill get-together always cures him of such concerns. During questions, one member reads out, in a cross voice, some article, no doubt from that morning's *Daily Mail*, about Nick Gibb, the Education Minister, and an announcement about accelerated access to the school system for those who have suffered trauma abroad, most notably Syrians. The questioner pumps himself up like a mating cockerel and asks why it has been slipped out under the radar when 'everyone else is only talking about Brexit'.

H replies in his most oleaginous Sergeant Wilson manner that he thinks it is all rather a good idea if we want to integrate and assimilate these poor people into our society as quickly as possible, a reply which failed to elicit even a polite ripple of applause or nodded agreement, and H sits down again, not satisfying anyone's prejudices.

David Kohler, the chairman, tells H during dinner that they have Johnny Mercer coming to speak. He says it as if announcing the Second Coming is due to happen and soon, in West Hill. H mutters that Johnny is an enthusiastic young man but doubts he has what it takes, intellectually, to make a minister. This makes David cross: he clearly buys into gung-ho, *over the ramparts now, boys* Johnny becoming PM, and the sooner the better. DC told H at dinner recently that Mercer had asked to see him, and H told Johnny the following day that he knew he was trying to see DC. 'Did you diss me to him?' he asks. 'Of course I did, Johnny,' he says, half-jokingly.

'Well, things are going to have to change around here, really change in twelve months' time,' he replies in military fashion.

Saturday morning sees the Budleigh Salterton AGM, but mercifully no lunch afterwards. Jeremy Robinson, in the chair, kicks off by asking if everyone can hear him. There are no more than twenty of them in the hall. 'No,' comes a cry from the back. 'Can you speak up?'

'No,' says Jeremy defiantly. 'Do you want to borrow my hearing aid?'

The complainant falls silent. Lucky he didn't take him up on the offer as Jeremy is profoundly deaf so would have been rendered useless if he had handed it over. Jeremy asks for any apologies for absence. 'My sister,' says Jill Elson from the back. 'She'll be late as she's stuck in Tesco's.'

'On what aisle?' H contributes, to general sniggering. All goes well until Jeremy, the retired Budleigh Salterton solicitor, gets into a tussle with the treasurer as to whether the accounts have been audited or signed off. This goes nowhere, with the audience becoming increasingly agitated. 'Oh well,' says Jeremy, surrendering. 'I suppose it doesn't really matter that much.' H comes home saying he is terrified there will be another election soon. 'I just cannot face it.'

3 March

Chaffcombe

I retreat to Devon to meet Storm Emma head on: one of the worst snowstorms of recent years, which swept into Britain from Siberia two nights ago.

H is so annoyed I am having a nice time, he is determined to get down here. He struggles to Paddington in his Russian fur hat and snow boots, only to be told by the loudspeakers that someone in the Met Office is forecasting bad weather – not that there *is* bad weather, which there is, but that it is forecast, which in H's book means trains can still run. He sends a WhatsApp of him growling on the platform, looking like Captain Oates.

He manages to get a train to Exeter, after three cancelled ones, and decides he is going to walk for four and half hours to get to me – there is no branch line running, no buses or taxis, and Exeter is a ghost town. The likelihood of him getting hypothermia, slipping on the pavement and cracking his brain open, or getting buried in a snowdrift is pretty high, and illustrates how thick he can sometimes be. He is the type of person the emergency services want to kill rather than pick up. His retort is that the British are pathetic in weather situations: no one going to work, shops closed, panic buying. He says we need to demonstrate more of the Blitz spirit. He's right there. The Norwegians are having a good laugh at our expense, posting pictures of what snowy wastelands really look like.

Luckily for Hugo, he gets as far as Cowley Bridge (i.e. not very far), sees a beaten-up Mitsubishi four-by-four with VOLUNTEER written across it in large letters, and hails a ride. The driver is a Mr Adrian Boult, a site manager for Bovis by day. By way of introduction, H tells Mr Boult he is an MP, and that he will be writing to his local MP, Mel Stride, about what an excellent service he (Mr Boult) is performing in this inclement weather. This goes over Mr Boult's head; he just says proudly, 'My father is called Chris Boult. He's a parish councillor in Shobrooke and has just been appointed snow warden!' In his hierarchy of things, Mr Boult senior clearly scored much higher than the Financial Secretary to the Treasury, or Hugo himself. Which is about right.

Mr Boult carries on with his altruistic mission and picks up a pretty girl, and then a man with a huge onion-stuffed Subway sandwich jammed into his mouth. H looks at him sideways, and is tempted to tick him off for his anti-social behaviour, but decides now is probably not the right time to be grand.

4 March

'Oh, God, what have I gone and done now?' H moans.

Determined to kick-start our virtually moribund Conservative Association, he decides, most unwisely, to take matters into his own hands and host three lunches a year, with his name highlighted and the Association's underneath. This has caused deep upset: the thought of the MP interfering, etc.

Cherry Nicholas, who is organising the first lunch virtually single-handedly – lots of complaints but little contribution from others – suggests that some of the money raised was going to Hugo. Obviously, this is someone putting a rumour about. There's not much else to do when you have been retired for thirty years, I suppose.

Hugo thought he'd achieved a great coup in getting Amber to come to the first lunch. Although H was told he was not allowed to mention it on security grounds (ridiculous). They were only able to say the guest was a 'senior cabinet member'.

Naturally, H and others told everyone who it was, in order to try and shift the tickets. So far so good.

Then Amber texts to say that she is now also the Minister for Wimmin and had wimmin's questions that day and therefore can't do the lunch. Nightmare. We work on another date, and in the meantime H asks Arlene Foster to come. She accepts and H thinks he is on a roll. However, word leaks out that Amber has cancelled, so some who have booked tickets threaten to cancel too.

Tom Wright, a councillor from Budleigh Salterton and a former copper, was excited to be bringing the useless Police and Crime Commissioner Alison Hernandez, who has never met Amber and, with her sharp elbows, was determined to do so.

This was to be Wright's moment in the sun. On hearing Amber had pulled out he emailed Cherry, saying he wasn't coming. You couldn't make it up. It turned out he thought Arlene referred to Arlene Phillips, the judge on *Strictly*, not the First Minister of Northern Ireland, Arlene Foster. H rings Cherry to mollify her.

She says many may feel intimidated by Jeremy Robinson, but not her, as she's 'faced the bombs' before. H pretends to follow her train of thought but is quite mystified, though suspects she is talking about growing up in the East End of London during the Blitz. She says that at the last lunch one of Jeremy's friends, who in a Hyacinth Bucket way considers herself a 'cut above', had remonstrated that she didn't have the guest speaker, Johnny Mercer, on her table. 'Why should he be on your table?' asked Cherry.

'Because he needs someone intelligent to talk to,' replied Hyacinth.

'Are you suggesting I'm not intelligent? Because if you are, I suggest you have a word with my university, who awarded me an MBA at the age of sixty.'

The high-level politics continue. There is a row going on between Jill Elson and the executive committee, notably Alan Williams, the treasurer (and Toby's dad), who is behaving like Scrooge. The row is over a photocopier. It has been going backwards and forwards for four months. In the red corner we have Jill, who wants to buy a photocopier from a local outlet, and in the blue corner Alan, who wants to get one online, 'because you can get a service contract thrown in'. Complete deadlock. Jill doesn't think there is a need for anything too fancy as she has a friend called Reg who can 'fix anything that goes wrong' in his shed down the road. Alan says this is not a modern way to proceed. Eventually, H bought a bloody photocopier from his fighting fund and donated it to the Association. Three grand, all in. Just to stop the relentless bickering. I tell you, it's a war zone, East Devon.

15 March

H has quite an extensive list of directorships and chairmanships at the moment, but now we are entering a new cold war he has decided to add another one to his list. His new friend, Ian Tucker, fire and safety officer at the Palace of Westminster, came to see him this week and appointed him the fire and safety warden in his area.

Mr Tucker brought an associate along for the meeting; both were wearing high-vis jackets saying FIRE AND SAFETY OFFICER. H was suitably impressed and asked if he could acquire a similar jacket, but was told he would have to settle for an armband, which he is mildly disappointed about.

'OK, chaps, what area am I looking after?'

The two men go into deep discussion and consult their maps.

It turns out he is to be responsible for the two offices to his left. H did not feel this was sufficient for his talents and suggested an additional two offices further down the corridor. The fire officers say they are having trouble locating the occupants of these two offices, and H suggests that's probably because they are now cabinet ministers (Hands-on-cock and Sajid) and are a tad busy. They say they would have to consult their superiors, as this would be considered territorial expansionism. We don't do it like Russia in these parts. There are protocols to be followed.

'Can I just ask, what happens if I am not in my office when a fire breaks out?'

'Well, we wouldn't expect you to do anything in that scenario.'

Since he hates his office, and is never in it, I doubt his skills will ever be tested.

When the two men leave, Hugo puts on his armband and goes to the office next door, which is occupied by Nick Gibb's secretary, and introduces himself as the new fire warden.

'They looked frightfully impressed,' he tells me later. He looked almost as smug as when he was first made a minister.

How the mighty have fallen.

5 April

Corbyn attends an event held by Jewdas, the far-left Jewish group. You would have thought he would steer clear of such jollies, since his party is being accused of colossal anti-Semitism. But how could he resist, especially when they greeted him by chanting 'Fuck the police' and 'Fuck the Tories'. The hapless leader of the Labour Party accepted the invitation to their supper party, and arrived dressed in an anorak and bearing a bunch of beetroots from his own allotment. Jewdas has quickly seen this humble vegetable as a political tool and is auctioning the 'anti-capitalist beetroot' on eBay. *What can I bid?*

Arlene Foster comes to stay at Chaffcombe with her husband Brian, a PSNI officer. We discuss whether we should show them our pub, them being DUP and anti 'the devil's buttermilk', etc. As it turns out, they more than match us glass for glass, Brian getting more preachy and Presbyterian as the evening progresses: lots of talk about creationism and original sin and how love conquers all. I whisper to Arlene, 'Gosh, he should have been a preacher, not a policeman.' She sighs and says, 'I know.' I like Arlene heaps, always have. The dynamic was interesting, though. Brian completely dominated, and she was very respectful towards his views. She told me Old Ma May never asks to see her when she is London, she only deals with the Chief Whip, which is staggering when her MPs are propping up the government. Not even a courtesy cup of tea, apparently.

7 April

Sri Lanka

We are sharing a villa in Weligama with Greg Barker and lovely George P. We are really here to further Hugo and Greg's attempts to cover the roofs of this island with solar panels and construct much-needed energy from waste plants. This is H's latest Don Quixote tilt at making the long-promised fortune. I am not holding my breath. Now that Greg has become an international business-man, he and George have become susceptible to the finer things in life and only last a couple of days at the villa before decamping to the nearest Relais & Châteaux compound.

Then, last night, things really started to kick off following the US government's decision to place Oleg Deripaska on its sanctions blacklist. Oleg and Greg and Mandy del Son, who is another friend of the embattled oligarch, have hotly denied all the accusations, calling the sanctions 'groundless, ridiculous and absurd'.* As a British peer, Greg certainly adds a veneer of respectability to the EN+ conglomerate, one of Oleg's many companies. And of course Greg has built up a good reputation in energy and renewables from his time in government. Greg says EN+ is kosher and it is a public company, but the US is less convinced. They say Oleg and his merry men were involved in 'malign activities'. How much of this is really Trump bashing the Russians is unclear.

Greg rings in the morning and says he has to fly back to the UK – could H come over for breakfast? Greg picks him up from the hotel reception in a golf cart: 'Better get used to this, when we have to return the Porsche Cayenne.' But he's not really that worried and says he is already working on a cunning plan. Let's hope.

14 April

I email Saffron, in Edinburgh, a *Times* story about how senior British academics are helping Assad and the Kremlin win the propaganda war by claiming that the White Helmets faked a chemical weapons attack. Saffron comes back pretty quickly: 'Yep, Professor Tim Hayward was my tutor last term. An exceptionally boring man he is too. So boring, I never went to his lectures.'

'Any idea he was a potential psychopath apologist and conspiracy-theorist nutter?'

'Pretty standard up here, Mum.'

Fucking lazy lefty academics. I tell you, the thought of my

* Quoted in 'US sanctions on Russian oligarch Oleg Deripaska will reverberate around the world', *South China Morning Post*, 7 April 2018.

daughter's money propping up Professor Hayward's bonkers conspiracy theories sends me into a spiralling vortex of irritation. Though actually, I'm surprised she even knew him, since his crew has spent the year on strike for more pay. Only last week Saffron was marked down on an essay about North Korea, her tutor saying her suggestions were unrealistic – which is rich, considering her father, who had responsibility for North Korea in the FCO, gave her the non-sensitive information. These people have their heads in the clouds.

15 April

Fresh back from Sri Lanka, we attend the annual Saïd Foundation dinner at the Hurlingham Club. Reluctantly, as H is still suffering Delhi belly, or the Sinhalese equivalent, at any rate. I sit next to a retired judge, who first asks if he knows me, then follows this with a list of standard questions about children and school. I painstakingly answer, but neither are my favourite topics, particularly when the world is burning. At the end of this, there is a short silence, after which the judge repeats exactly the same questions. It is clear that the poor man has dementia. I turn to the other side, to speak to a man with a severe speech impediment, so conversation doesn't exactly flow.

H fares rather better on Wafic's table, sitting between his rather serious nephew and the wife of the newly arrived Lebanese ambassador, who apologises for being overdressed, but looks extremely alluring and glamorous. He's always had a thing for over-scented, big blow-dried Middle Eastern women. According to H, Wafic gets very animated; in fact, so animated that at one point a large chunk of fish shoots from the corner of his mouth and comes to rest on the Lebanese ambassador's wife's bosom. H tells me later that he is transfixed, and at a loss as to whether he should ignore it, draw her attention to it, or – his preferred option – take matters into his own hands and brush it off. However, this would also have involved taking the Lebanese ambassador's wife's right breast into his own hand and so, for fear of causing a diplomatic incident, he reluctantly decides that inaction is the only course open to him. Those years of FCO training are starting to pay off. A distinguished author comes bounding over, ostensibly to greet Wafic but takes the opportunity of staring down the cleavage of H's neighbour as well which was of course the motivating factor behind his visit. This causes much merriment.

16 April

Over the weekend, May, along with Macron and the chap over the pond, Trump, lobbed some missiles into a chemical installation in Syria as a warning that gas is not be considered a weapon of war. But Corbyn isn't convinced the Assad regime was responsible for the Douma gas attack, saying that Assad, 'or any other group' that carried it out, must be confronted with evidence. You couldn't make it up. He is also continuing to say that intervention in Syria should only be through the UN. *Which, if he hasn't noticed, Russia has repeatedly vetoed.*

How can anyone take this man seriously? The only people he seems to care about are the forgotten ones, such as the dispossessed from Chagos – he even came to see H about them in the FCO, probably because H was the only other person in politics, or the world, who had ever heard of them. But then that's the thing about Corbyn, isn't it? He looks at every situation and thinks, I'm going to do precisely the opposite of everyone else. I'm going to hold up my middle finger to all of you, and defy the whip an incredible 428 times. I'm going to be resolutely anti-British, support the IRA, take pictures of manhole covers, and give Diane Abbott a lift on the back of my motorbike through the unusual holiday destination of East Germany. Talk about wheel wobble. He just keeps throwing those bricks at the establishment – which is fine by me, because every time he does it, he is another step further away from becoming PM.

21 April

Amber is having her first real torrid time in politics. Apparently, that basket case of a department, the Home Office, has been threatening to deport people who came over from the Caribbean decades ago on the *Windrush*. Ostensibly, they had no paperwork. The news breaks just as the Commonwealth Heads of Government Meeting is at full flush, so everyone is in full apology mode. Except behind closed doors everyone is hopping mad, including Prince Charles, who is currently lobbying to take over the Commonwealth from the Queen. Mind you, he had his moments this week too, when he upset a woman of Guyanese descent, and on being told she was from Manchester, looked alarmed and said: 'You don't look it!'

Amber, naturally, was in the line of fire. I texted her to see if she's all right. There is a huge fuss about all the records being burnt, but I tell her it's bollocks, that she should check the National Archives. She thanked me for the tip and, and lo and behold the *Daily Mail* is now reporting that all the records can indeed be found intact in the NA. That I realised this before any of her officials means a) there is a plot to oust her, or b) the department is staffed by young, inexperienced, incompetent immigration officials. A combination of the two, most likely.

23 April

'I am not blaming anyone,' Amber tells the Commons, before blaming the culture of the Home Office, which she inherited (and who was the previous Home Secretary?) She unveils an emergency package of measures designed to end the crisis. H went in to help her. H said, 'Any attempt to lay any of this at the door of the current Home Secretary is plainly absurd and ridiculous,' and pointed out that there were examples of the Windrush problem as far back as 2000, under Labour.

She put her foot in it again today. The *FT* reported that she had recently boasted that the system for EU nationals applying to stay after Brexit will be 'as easy to use as setting up an online account at L. K. Bennett'. Linda* texts me, absolutely delighted: she couldn't buy this kind of publicity. There are winners when there are losers. Anyway, in the scheme of political gaffes it's pretty tame. Yes, she is detached from real people, probably because real people don't stand in front of a dispatch box after a cock-up, with the whole nation watching you on the Six O'Clock News.

24 April

Hugo in the Members' dining room queue, standing next to a large female Labour MP. They get to the pudding section.

'What are you having? The apple crumble or the fruit salad?' asks Hugo quite innocently.

'You want to be careful, casting aspersions about a woman's weight. It will get you into trouble.'

28 April

Amber had her worst day of her political career yesterday. We tweet each other throughout the day, with me trying to pick her up off the floor. On Windrush and immigration she said that she was scrapping the removal targets, which twenty-four hours earlier she had claimed did not exist. She had done so because she was explicitly advised by her civil servants there were no targets.

H and I put out a tweet on @HugoSwire: 'The Home Office is and always has been a dysfunctional department filled with large numbers of left leaning anti Tory civil servants who are prone to leaking. This is pure partisan politics and most intelligent people

---

* Linda Kristin Bennett, founder of fashion retailer L. K. Bennett.

can see that.' The Twittersphere goes bananas, particularly civil servant union reps and Claire Wrong's cronies, of course.

The actual truth is those people working in the Home Office actively brought down a Home Secretary. Amber tells me that one Hugh Ind, director-general of immigration enforcement, wrote her a memo saying there were no targets. Hence her confusion.

2 May

Following Amber's resignation as Home Secretary after 'inadvertently' misleading MPs, she is once again sitting proudly on the back benches. She's always been good at dusting herself down after a crisis. I'm also glad to see her in PMQs not sitting in sourpuss Soubry's remoaning corner, the favoured rebel location back corner right. Instead she was in 'Paintbox Row' near others like Damian Green, staying in the middle of the canvas as I suggested.

13 June

Two days of overturning the Lords amendments on Brexit.

H says, 'Nothing very unexpected in colleagues' behaviour over the last few days. The usual grandstanding, the same points made again and again, and puffball MPs posturing and pontificating. DD looked tired and slightly louche at the dispatch box, on which he leant as if he was ordering one for the road in the small hours, at the counter of some faintly dodgy bar.'

H says he keeps on finding himself next to Ken Clarke, who smells of stale cigars, the collar of his shirt flying off in alarming directions. H knows the world, and certainly his Eurosceptic friends, are watching, so adopts what he thinks is a neutral expression as Ken clearly takes pleasure in lazily undermining the government's position.

Division after division on Tuesday and Wednesday in the

stygian gloom of the voting lobbies. Richard Benyon tells H he nearly burnt his hand on a radiator, which was on full blast. The building is in such a state of collapse that if they turn off the lights, the ones in the Lords would probably go off too, as all the services seem to be interconnected and failing. It feels like a metaphor for this failing parliament. The Chief Whip, Julian Smith, just looks greyer and greyer as the days go on, but H rather likes him. Whatever deals he has done, he has bought time, and that is about all he can do at this stage. Kate Hoey and Frank Field vote with us. Soubry and Clarke against. The SNP stages a walkout, which is rather obviously orchestrated, and H shouts 'awaa with ye, ye wee jimmies' after them, which the Chief, himself from Stirling, is much amused by.

The Gover, in the lobbies as voting ended on the first night, says to H, 'I suppose you're off to White's?'

'Certainly not,' he says. 'Pratt's,' and walks off.

Gove still remains a possible successor to Theresa. H taking a constituent to see him later this week, on the subject of saving ... seahorses. 'No creature too small to defend or too big to fight for our Michael,' says H. That's particularly true at the moment.

14 June

Yesterday was always going to be busy. Kicked off in Chelsea and Westminster Hospital after a minor bleeding scare down below. The indignity and embarrassment of having to go through this dark-age process never decreases, in the main because of the two instruments of torture, the stirrups and the speculum, those two stalwarts of female internal exploration that never seem to get a design overhaul. So, there I am, legs up in the air like a handmaiden from Gilead, with a very large woman hunched over a small stool, looking up my *you know what*, and I, to lighten the atmosphere, say: 'Gosh, I'd never let a man do this to me.'

There is an awkward silence and then her nose lifts from the secret world of my internal organs. She fixes her eyes on me from between my legs and replies, 'I was a man.'

My muscles down there lock into what feels like a steel trap and the speculum shoots out of me like a Scud missile, flying through the glass panes of the examination room and landing in the lap of the piano player in the hospital atrium, where a lunchtime concert is in full swing . . . Well, nearly.

Then the nurse's face widens into huge smile and she says, 'Only joking, dear.'

We part friends.

Next stop was Alan and Jane Parker's Brunswick bash, where the tent alone cost twenty thousand pounds and no one was even in it. These people really do know how to charge their clients and pay themselves for the pleasure, and for what, exactly, I do not know. The old political gang there, all the girls – Gabby B, Kate, who now works at Brunswick, Flora (Sam's sis), Gaby Feldman, Frances O, Simone Finn. Most of them seem to be wearing Cefinn, Sam's label, even K. H says to Hugh Powell, 'Who is that foxy woman over there in the green dress?' (Also in Cefinn.)

'That's your hostess, Hugo.'

Anyway, we can't stay long. Another dinner to go to! On the way out I see David Macmillan, whose wife Arabella Pollen has just walked out on him.

Final leg. A private dinner for the prime minister of Sri Lanka, Ranil Wickremesinghe, and his long-suffering wife Maitree, hosted by Nirj Diva, the bombastic British MEP, self-appointed fixer and well-padded bon vivant, who is a booming, persistent figure in H's life.

H had seen Ranil earlier, at the Hilton Hotel, where he had just arrived from a private trip to Scotland that H had organised for him. So H has been tanked up since early evening and we are by now both nicely fattened by the delicious Brunswick canapés. As we walk into the Carlton Club, H turns to me with spaniel eyes and says, 'Sorry, this is going to be a very boring evening for you.

I apologise profusely in advance.' I don't go out very much these days, so he wants to make it nice for me.

It turns out to be anything but boring.

The dinner is for about twenty in an upstairs room. I walk into a wall of gammon (my new favourite word), meaty complexions indicating they are perilously close to a stroke. Around the table I go, and one after the other has that pink tone of stout yeomen, of high blood pressure caused by decades of harrumphing about 'political correctness gone mad', being defeated in arguments about the non-existent merits of Brexit, women getting the vote, and same-sex marriage. Or at least that was the overall look of the gathering. Hogarthian. You get the picture. So, I'm squeezed in tightly between Nirj and William Dartmouth (grandson of ostrich-feather fancier Dame Barbara Cartland, and son of Raine Spencer, stepmother of Diana, Princess of Wales), both of whom talk with their mouths full, with the inevitable consequences. I look down at the menu to see six courses, and groan internally. We are in for the long haul.

As the evening progresses, everyone is winding everyone else up. Michael Fallon and I are doing a pincer movement on Dartmouth, who is faintly ridiculous on all levels: a UKIP MEP, and a man so desperate to be taken seriously that he delivers his CV (Eton, Oxford, Harvard) before he even sits down.

When Dartmouth starts to speak, Hugo looks over at me and rolls his eyes in despair, which Dartmouth clearly notices. It is like winding up a clockwork toy; then H stupidly, and as it happens wrongly, corrects him about the proper title for the Sri Lankan ambassador, which causes a surge of blood to Dartmouth's face and something of a mini-explosion and he starts foul-mouthing Hugo to the assembled dinner guests. I stand up to end the dinner, and come over to H, who is talking to a new rising star of the party, Ranil Jayawardena, to say, 'We need to scarper NOW. That man is going to kill you.' We only manage to reach the landing when, sure enough, Dartmouth comes up like a human tornado and starts to release a cannonade of abuse at H: 'How dare you humiliate me like that, you jerk?' and continues in that vein, saying he is not fooled by H's legendary charm. There is an almighty scene. Hugo, who is highly inebriated and cowardly, seems more concerned by the gallons of spit flying onto his new Turnbull and Asser shirt rather than the headbutt that I fear may be about to be planted on his forehead.

I push Dartmouth into a corner to separate them. If he wants to have a bare-knuckle fight, he is going to have to do it with me. 'William, you are in public life, you simply can't behave like this . . . calm down,' I say.

'Your husband,' he booms back at me, 'is a fucking jerk.'

'Well, you tell him that privately. Just stop creating a scene: you are making a complete fool of yourself.'

'How dare he expose me like that, how dare he—'

'William, calm down.'

Someone takes over from me, because I am clearly inches away from serious trouble. H and I flee down the large staircase and lunge for the nearest taxi. When we get home, he conks out almost immediately, snoring in true gammon style.

My heart is racing all night from the drama of it all.

In the morning, H rings Nirj, who himself has a whole list of people to call because he has been told how offended they were by much that occurred last night. When they discuss Dartmouth, Nirj, who is obsessed by these things, just says, 'Yes, yes, but he is the tenth Earl, you know.'

20 June

Hugo comes home looking rather forlorn. None of his deals are coming to fruition. 'The trouble is, I'm really just a bed-blocker in the Commons. There are so many people who would kill for this job.' He concedes, however, he is enjoying it a little bit more, with this febrile atmosphere on Brexit.

30 June

Weekend with John and Suzy Lewis for the Chalke Valley History Festival. Also staying are John Witherow, editor of *The Times* (dangerously charming, like all good hacks), and one Michael Gove, who is speaking at the festival about Brexit. He is not with Sarah, but his son Will.

Gove is giving nothing away about the crunch lockdown at Chequers this Friday, tight-lipped as an oyster. But that is always the case with him. It's a game you have to play: you work out his positions on the board, and the easiest way to do that is by letting him ask you questions.

'What do you think the role of a Foreign Secretary is, Sasha?' and 'How can you be perceived as doing a good or bad job?' – i.e. has May offered it to him if he behaves, or is that the job he is now pursuing? His new line about supporting a Norway-style deal is throwing us a bit, particularly when he tells me that Old Ma May needs to change her red lines if she wants to keep the party together; by that he can only mean what Jacob Rees-Mogg is also suggesting: we shouldn't be in the single market or the customs union, and we certainly shouldn't be under the jurisdiction of the European courts. We have to remember Gove is an arch-Brexiteer. Of course, he has left the dirty work to JRM, who lays it down in a *Telegraph* article but, to be fair, is not bound by collective responsibility.

In another quiet moment I lead him down a blind alley. Did he think we were going to crash out with no deal? He said, 'Yes.' One moment he says the Chequers summit will be a 'fudge', the next he smiles when I suggest he should throw some fireworks into the room. Our suspicions are that he is going to let Boris fall on his sword, and he will get his job in true Gove assassin style. Getting rid of plastic straws might have street cred, but it's not a great office of state. So, my feeling is Gove is being at his most Machiavellian, promising stuff to both camps, which he even has the gall to tell me is the fundamental issue with Old Ma May. The problem is, whatever his motives – and they might be pure for once – you simply cannot trust him.

His son is much more forthcoming. Children of politicians can be mini-mes (JRM turned up at the festival with his son, who was wearing the same glasses and double-breasted suit). Will might well have been wearing a hoodie, but he was just as geeky-smart as his dad; you almost wanted to take the pipe out of his mouth and tell him to put down the *Telegraph* crossword. He sits between Hugo and John at lunch after Gove's platform debate and is quite illuminating about the motivations of his parents, which would be unfair to repeat here; out of the mouths of babes etc.

I have to say, Gove was excellent on the platform: eloquent, passionate, clever, he just won the debate hands down by putting everything in a historical context. At lunch I ask him about the Cameron feud but he doesn't want to be drawn; he is never quite sure whether he trusts H and me. He does say it's not his place to make amends; Cameron has to make an approach. His door is and always has been open. But rumour has it he is consciously going around trying to court the Cameroons again. George is in the bag; he has even rung up Kate for a drink.

Our conversation is broken by the arrival of Claudia Rothermere, looking like a character straight out of a Jilly Cooper novel in tight white riding breeches. She is her usual regal self. Barely acknowledges me. She invites Gove to drinks at Ferne that evening, and as the Wednesday Witch's employer he will be obliged to attend court. She then goes up to Hugo to say, 'Ah! Mark's brother!' which H is cross about, Mark being Hugo's brother. In retaliation H replies, 'Ah! Lady Thatcher's sister!' who Claudia is not close to, and who is married to Sir Mark Thatcher.

Our house goes over for drinks, but Hugo and I can't face it. All that showing off and sucking up. Apparently, Jonathan and Claudia come down from their bedroom halfway though, say their hellos and then disappear again. Thank God we didn't go.

10 July

The events of the last few days have been truly extraordinary. The Friday meeting at Chequers went well and the PM was applauded by DD and Boris, both of whom then went on to resign – though in Boris's case No. 10 had cleverly accepted his resignation before he'd had the chance to tender it.

Major panic all round. Was this the beginning of the end of the Maybot? As H predicted, Boris did in fact resign. He had no choice, especially after DD went. Gove, of course, has swerved again, siding with the PM in a masterful piece of political repositioning.

On Monday, H runs into Geoffrey Cox on the way to the extraordinary meeting of the 1922.

'They rang me,' he growled. 'The Chief Whip. He asked if I had any skeletons in my closet, to which I replied only a run-in with the Register of Members' Interests a few years back. They were going to offer me Steve Baker's job, but they gave it to someone else.

'Anyway,' he went on, chewing an imaginary cigar, 'I simply couldn't afford it. I reckon if I'd been a minister, I'd have chewed through a million of capital by now. I'm in the middle of a quarter of a million-pound case at the moment, as it happens.'

H asks him what he would accept, to which he said he might take Attorney General. He said he had been told they needed a lawyer who could understand the Brexit legislation, which now had to be handled by Robert Buckland, the Solicitor General. But politics is not like real life and the gods were smiling on Geoffrey that day.

During the 1922, Geoffrey, all Rumpole-style, rises slowly from his chair, turning to address the packed room as if it were a court-room and explains, succinctly and elegantly, why the European Court of Justice would no longer have a say over legal disputes in this country, and what a magnificent thing this was. (No one is quite sure if this is true or not, so lost in the maze is everyone.) The honeyed words fall from his lips and he resumes his seat and spreads his hands out on the table as he rests his case. Howls of

'How much has that advice cost us, Geoffrey?' and so forth greet his peroration, but the timing is perfect and the room is his. H says that in one stroke he undermined all the criticism of his outside earnings and lack of commitment to parliament. Gavin Barwell creeps up behind him and whispers in his ear. Minutes later, the Deputy Chief Whip Chris Pincher does the same. After a decent interval Geoffrey rises, quickly this time, and exits the room.

Of course, the news came through that Geoffrey had got it. H runs into him on Tuesday afternoon.

'I'm exhausted,' he tells Hugo. 'I've been up all night and I've already had to rewrite great tracts of the Brexit Bill – and all PRO BONO,' he booms.

H also runs into Gove in the lobbies. 'Ah, Sir Hugo,' he says, smiling mischievously.

'Michael, that was a magnificent swerve. It is a real pleasure to see a master at work. Just magnificent.'

'Oh, I don't think so,' he protests.

'I do.' And, grinning knowingly, they part company.

The *Evening Standard* says Gove was sounded out for Foreign Secretary, but politely replied that his fear of flying had precluded him from accepting it.

When I speak to K, she tells me all the political salons of London are talking about nothing else. What on earth is he up to?

11 July

Dominic Raab is now trying to sell a White Paper on our exit from the European Union. Of course, everyone is slowly cottoning on to the fact – leavers and remoaners alike – that it is a dog's dinner and will leave us in a far worse position than if we had actually remained within this totalitarian, piss-pot empire.

The Maybot is delighted to have got rid of the blond bombast finally, particularly after he told her that her plan for Brexit was a 'turd' and that even if she polished it, it wouldn't make a difference.

Then there was DD, who also flounced off, challenging her man Olly (Robbins) as he left. So, no surprises there then.

Theresa was not wrong when she said the cabinet was now split between those who wanted to remain and those who wanted to leave. So, we now have a mostly remain cabinet led by a remain PM. It's like the establishment are back in control after a coup and they are all telling us we are idiots. What relief she must be feeling that she no longer has to ride with the ideological investment in Britain leaving the EU.

But I wouldn't feel confident quite yet, Theresa.

13 July

H and I are all over the place on the White Paper: we don't know which way to turn. H rings Daniel Hannan,* who is his usual succinct and intelligent self; in fact, impressively so. For balance, H rings George Bridges as well. Both are of a similar view. Hannan explains everything to us, but the long and short of it is that he advises we should support the White Paper because no deal would be calamitous. However, he says we have conceded way too much, and this is about as far as we can go. If Europe pulls back, we must pull out. He says the closest similarity is the Swiss model and Switzerland is doing quite nicely, thank you.

16 July

8 a.m. on Monday morning, and it looks as if the White Paper is dead in the water. Old Ma May's veneer of unity, attempting to look like a paid-up member of both camps, is slipping as quickly as an ice sculpture in a heat wave.

---

* MEP for South East England 1999–2020. Columnist and activist.

17 July

I've never known such a febrile atmosphere since we have been involved in politics. Last night May announced she was accepting the amendments to her own plans, meaning the rebels were suddenly on the side of the government and the loyalists were the rebels. In the end she 'won' by just three votes. It's getting so topsy-turvy, it's difficult to keep up.

Well, I'm off to Devon tomorrow, where people are sane. Amber is speaking to the Association, so I need to go and make up a bed. At least we won't have many more days like this one for a while. Mind you, with Old Ma May's piecemeal approach anything could happen. Last time she went on holiday she got bored and called an election. If she hadn't done that, we wouldn't be where we are now.

Stepping aside from Brexit for a moment, we have a new sex scandal, involving H's former chief of staff Andrew Griffiths.[*] I should have guessed he was heading for the red tops: he was pretty flirtatious with me at a reception in Downing Street a few years back. I remember thinking, is this flattery and am I enjoying it? Or is this a bit OTT? He has been caught sexting two barmaids he called the 'Titty Twins'. Two thousand texts in three weeks, apparently, an average of around ninety-five a day, which must have been quite time consuming. The texts mostly concerned his desire to tie them up and whack them using his weapon of choice, the 'Spank Paddle'. He has subsequently had the whip withdrawn.

2 September

A long, hot summer. Siena goes with H to a refugee camp in Jordan to help teach English. A week in Cornwall, three days with Greg and George in Ibiza, then off to a house party on the sunny Costa

[*] MP for Burton 2010–19.

del Sol. The talk here, as everywhere, is all about the doom and gloom of Brexit. Divisions down the table are part of daily life now: Michael and Sandra Howard, who are also staying, are leavers; the rest, including our hosts, are remainers. The Prime Minister comes in for some serious slagging off. The Howards, H and I feel that as each idiotic move in the Brexit negotiations collapses, we become more and more suicidal, and blaming of the PM. We also agree this is a cabinet of chancers; that we are being governed by a bunch of people with such a shallow understanding of the processes we cannot hope to do anything other than fail. Now we are being led by people who run the country by announcements, tweets, ideas they can't possibly implement, it's what the *Spectator* calls the new 'bluffocracy'. It's not confined to politics, but is also prevalent in the media and civil service. Brexit has become the biggest bluffers ball of all time, an idea bluffed out by bluffers and rejected by bluffers, when of course no one has the faintest idea how the wretched thing is going to play out in the end.

Alan Duncan arrives with his husband James. There is an awful moment during dinner, when he completely lays into me in front of everyone on Brexit. Hugo is furious, as I have been issued with strict instructions to avoid the subject. But Alan just typifies the smug sort of remainer that I despise; I couldn't let him get away with it. People's Vote, support for a second referendum – it's all there in his soapbox repertoire. He is, of course, better informed than anyone, or so he thinks. What really gets my goat is his assumption that everyone who voted leave is pig ignorant. *Come on, you morons, it's back to the ballot box, and this time get it right.* Alan just looks at me as if I'm some Sally Bercow figure. I'm sad about this, because we all go back a long way in politics, and have a shared interest in the Middle East and foreign affairs. He took over from H, after all.

When I get back from Devon and have dinner with Amber, I get the same bollocks all over again, about how the people were lied to, and how they voted without the full facts having been put before them. She is particularly irked by Penny Mordaunt's threat during the campaign that Turkey would be allowed to join the EU. I throw back that it was the same from the other side, as she well knows.

What I really want to say to Amber is, I love you very much, but honestly, what are you up to? How can you think the EU is so damn marvellous, when you have been up so close and personal with its malevolent handling of negotiations with us? And Amber, if you want a Norway-style deal, with them issuing us with rules the whole time, maybe you should take a closer look at its bullying of countries like Poland, Hungary and now Italy, and they are inside the tent! And do you think it's right to be complicit in banging up Catalan nationalists, just because they challenged your hegemony? Don't you think the whole thing is falling apart anyway? Have you actually noticed the ideological battle between Macron and Salvini? Do you think Europe is actually happy about the popu- lation explosion going on in its backyard? But I don't say any of these things, because she's my friend and I want her to stay my friend, though our relationship is becoming increasingly fraught on account of our differing positions.

6 September

Anne Milton comes up to H in the lobby and has the usual leader- ship election chit-chat. She tells him that Nicholas Soames would make a good leader. H looks at her aghast. Soames is many things but leadership material he is not, he replies.

H then goes to a dinner of ex-ministers, and comes home saying he needs to find a tree and some rope. Boring beyond belief. He tells me how he feels utterly trapped by the institution and that he now loathes the establishment and wants to become a hipster, buy a Harley-Davidson, get stoned, have an affair and do everything he could possibly think of to horrify his constituents. He is in a slough of despond.

8 September

Some Nutt (yes, he's called that) is mouthing off about how, after centuries of pre-debate sharpeners, MPs should be breathalysed before voting. Surely, as a former government adviser he knows that MPs haven't a clue what they are voting for anyway, sober or otherwise.

9 September

Boris caught with his pants down ... again. Marina has had enough. Twenty-four years of living with a cheat and a breaker of promises has finally taken its toll. She has walked, and who can blame her. The new lady is Carrie Symonds, Conservative head of communications until she was asked to leave. I open my *Sunday Times* and there is a whole dossier of his misdemeanours, apparently leaked by No. 10. They are taking out the Brexiteers one by one, or trying to, and for what? May's Chequers plan? That's dead in the water – even Barnier has said as much.

But Boris for PM? The optimists in Team Boris – that will be Nadine – are claiming this morning that this litany of affairs is all part of a plan to get the bad news out of the way so it can't be used to damage him later. Not sure about that: he's more accident prone than calculating. But it is fanning the debate of how long the PM has left. She might get a stay of execution if she can persuade the Brexiteers just to get over the line, but after that she is toast, everyone knows that. Everyone except her. Meanwhile, the Brexiteers have shelved their alternative to the Chequers deal and are instead focusing their efforts on when to strike against their leader. This is not without risk, and they know it: if you are a sniper, once you fire the shot you give up your position. The alternative is a vote of no confidence, but that is also high risk, because if she wins it we get her for another bloody year. And if she loses, who knows who we might get. Boris? Hunt? Javid? Raab? Even Hancock might creep up on the inside.

29 September

H has been trying to work out what would really piss off Ms Wrong, as in Ms Claire Wright. 'I know,' he says to me, 'let's save Ottery St Mary Hospital.'

'That's a novel idea,' I reply. 'How are you going to do that when the NHS is in freefall?'

Ottery St Mary is Wrong territory, after all. It's front-line. We can't do anything Wright there, ever. And we certainly don't enter it without full camouflage gear, binoculars, a large hedge to hide behind and large doses of patience.

The thing is, she's got the whole place sewn up: local girl, councillor, lots of doe-eyed *poor humble me* stuff up against the Alan B'Stard-style MP with his offshore bank accounts and airline (wrong again), who is slashing and burning his way through local services, who never shows his face around the place (wrong again, Wright), the David of Ottery St Mary against the Goliath of the state, and so on.

I'm not saying she doesn't have a point: the NHS has indeed been closing community hospitals up and down the country, and she is Wright about the short-termism of this particular branch of austerity cuts, when the population is ageing etc., etc., but the problem down in Ottery St Mary is that she has been telling this poor fearful community that their hospital is going for nigh on ten years, and we have been telling the community (who don't listen because she is telling them it's all one big bloody conspiracy against them) that it isn't, because hell, if it was going to close it would have shut up shop years ago.

So H, thinking he needs to do something to counteract her false propaganda, invites the new Health Secretary, Matt Hands on Cock, for a visit. First to Budleigh Salterton Community Hospital, which with H's support has been transformed into a health and well-being hub, then on to Ottery. Of course Claire Wrong gets wind of it – tipped off by the local ITV reporter – and goes into full battle mode, turning up at the hospital with a few of her cronies. H, who has warned Matt prior to the visit about her possibly being the most strident and annoying female in the whole history of British opposition politics and best avoided, sees her coming towards them. Matt quickly pulls his spad by his tie into a dive, face-down, in the back seat of the car, leaving half his legs dangling outside the door as his driver slaloms around her and speeds off, ministerial blue lights flashing, despite all Ms Wright's attempts to hurl herself, Emily Davison-style, onto the ministerial bonnet.

Claire is outraged. Afterwards she rushes up to H, whom she detests, and starts running alongside him, the ITV camera following behind, à la Michael Crick. 'Did he give any guarantees, Mr Swire?' H, who is incensed that she refuses to acknowledge his recent elevation as a knight of the realm, considering him a product of a corrupt political system, just keeps replying: 'Did I say that, Claire?'

By the by, we have a cunning plan if this happens again. It goes something like this:

'Is the hospital going to close, Mr Swire?'

'Did I say that, Camilla?'

'My name is not Camilla.'

'And my name is not Mr Swire. So I'll call you by your proper name, Councillor Wright, and you can call me Sir Hugo. That way we will get along just fine – or not, as the case may be.'

Anyway, we think the whole thing has gone swimmingly and that we have trumped her completely until we view the media, which is all about her! We complain to the head honcho of ITV regional news, as we had given its political editor an exclusive about the visit, and some of the footage is taken down.

This just develops into another of Claire's conspiracies (on this occasion, the Wright one), generating even more material for her blog and social media. 'You can understand why Mr Swire and Mr Hancock will want this video deleted,' she writes in her blog, implying she and a 'dozen peaceable-looking residents' were utterly appalled by the shenanigans and that a pedestrian was practically mown down by a government car.

The thing about Claire is that she mainly campaigns to keep the status quo – hospitals, housing, planning – rather than presenting solutions to problems by way of a lucid and viable counter-argument to government policy. Everything is about feelings, pure 'muh feelings' emotionalism laced with a burning suppression of the underprivileged by Tory elites and spiced up with huge doses of cry-bullying passive aggression.

Sigh! And sigh again! Are we ever going to get shot of this woman?

3 October

The Conservative Conference begins. It kicks off as usual with the Maybot's interview with Marr. That went swimmingly. Not. Particularly after he accused her of personal responsibility for the death of a sixty-seven-year-old victim of the Windrush scandal. By the fade-out at the end, she refuses to indulge in small talk and death-stares him. And that's about as terrifying as it can get. Hammer House of Horror terrifying.

It's quite noticeable how some Tory activists are falling out of love with the slobbering golden retriever. Boris doesn't seem to notice or care, he arrives like a human tornado as per usual. This is his ground, or it was for a decade, the usual platform performance with a pile-up of metaphors. I actually thought he sounded quite passionate for once. But it wasn't to be his show, or his leadership bid. In the end, the glumbucket sashayed onto the stage to 'Dancing Queen' – someone in No. 10 thought that would be funny, after she got savaged by the media for a jig she did in South Africa a few months back, except that Brexit has clearly limited her own freedom of movement. She gave a good speech, avoiding the C-word (Chequers) and everyone was fooled, just for a minute or two, as she told us about the sunny uplands (I must be getting long in the tooth, don't all our leaders do that?) and how she was going to throw a huge festival, where we can all smoke lots of pot and go glamping.

And Boris retreated back to his humbug and head-scratching. Someone really needs to check him for nits.

16 October

Bercow is in trouble. But will it do for him? The new report into the bullying and sexual harassment in parliament came out yesterday, telling us all what we already know: that there is an unhealthy 'us and them' culture, with MPs enjoying an 'almost God-like status' that makes them feel they can behave how they like. There is a pattern: shouting, swearing, belittling, innuendo, sexual gestures, lewd questions about sex lives, suggestions they wear sexier clothes and make-up. But also inappropriate touching: hugging, groping, patting on the head, grabbing at breasts and bottoms, lunging for kisses. Those in charge (Bercow) are accused by one of the women who gave evidence of trying to 'cover up the traces' when complaints are made.

There is 'a collective ethos at the senior levels of the organisation, which sets the tone for a culture that permits abuse', and Dame Laura Cox, the author of the report, said: 'I find it difficult to envisage how the necessary changes can be successfully delivered, and the confidence of the staff restored, under the current senior House administration.'

Raab and Rumpole (Geoffrey Cox) are emerging as the two people in the cabinet who have sufficient intellect to take on the EU. When the Maybot's idea was put before ministers at their informal gathering on Thursday, they were subsequently rumbled by those around the cabinet table. An insider said it took Raab and Cox, both Brexiteers, to expose what was going on. Before the summer it was just David Davis and Jeremy Wright, but now an altogether sharper team is marking Olly Robbins's homework.

Whether a new plan B can be found remains the big question. This is on a knife edge.

18 October

Old Ma May said her piece before the EU leaders' dinner in Brussels last night, offering to extend the transition period by a year, before being booted out so the rest of them could get on with their turbot and beer and pan-fried mushrooms. As leavers and remainers erupted (not least over the possible £10 billion+ bill to extend), this morning she arrived back at the summit insisting it would only be for 'a matter of months' and might not happen at all.

H hitches a ride with Dave to Tessa Jowell's memorial. All of Labour royalty in attendance. In the car, Dave tells H that he wants a second referendum, which is quite odd, since so much shit is being poured on him for calling for the first one. Maybe he thinks they will cancel each other out and his reputation will be restored.

He urges H to ignore his constituents who are Brexiteers, as H isn't going to stand again anyway. He thinks he should try to help to stop the whole thing before it's too late, and go out and push for a second vote. H says nothing. Dave says he is very busy with this and that, but mostly with Nancy, who has inherited her mother's rebellious genes. I have to watch Siena on this front, so I know where they are at. Dave's book is out next year. I think he will find that all very uncomfortable. He won't be able to hide as he does now.

Inside Southwark Cathedral, H is seated in front of Evelyn and Lynn de Rothschild. Evelyn asks him who he is (H last saw him at the Atlantic Trust breakfast yesterday), and after a few words says they have so much to discuss they should get together. They exchanged cards ... again. H has quite a collection of Evelyn's cards, and Evelyn Hugo's, as they have the same conversation every time they meet. Lynn is friendly, but then suddenly leaps up as if stung by a wasp and rushes to the front of the cathedral virtually knocking down the bishop and associated clerics to reach one Tony Blair, to whom she stays glued until the service starts. A moving service, with an elegant contribution from Tessa's husband David Mills. The rest of her family included a handsome son, married to the daughter of Shaun Woodward and Camilla Sainsbury, and a very attractive daughter called Jess who is a lyricist and quite a well-known singer who told those gathered, 'To be loved like this since the moment we were born and to be her children is the single greatest privilege of our lives.' Blair gives an address worthy of Sir John Gielgud. Gordon Brown stares at his fingernails throughout.

2 November

The Times has obtained details of the extraordinary shenanigans at the Home Office, where officials completely failed in their duty to support Amber over Windrush and which subsequently led to her resignation. This morning, she told the *Today* programme that she saw the report in May and 'can't understand why it was sat on for six months'. She also said there had been a series of leaks clearly aimed to humiliate her.

Sajid Javid won't like this at all. Certainly, whenever H approaches him on this, he is evasive. He won't want anything spoiling his leadership bid, and the boss over at No. 10 wants to shut this down as she is implicated. She visibly grimaced the last time H raised it at PMQs. But Amber is delighted that Hugo pursued it with a Freedom of Information request.

14 November

The deal has landed. May calls the cabinet in one by one to stop them staging a coup. But first they are locked in a room and told to read five hundred pages in fifty-nine seconds, and they are told they can't take it home if they don't understand it and that there isn't time for questions. So there. Cabinet lasts five hours, with her saying Brexit means Brexit when it's perfectly clear this deal means nothing of the sort. Outside, Dracula – aka Jacob Rees-Mogg – and his band of mini-vamps are ready to draw blood: 'I personally bear no animosity towards my esteemed colleague, but if she lays her neck on the line ... well, I won't be able to stop myself ... '

Thank you, Count Jacob. Over to you, Kay, in the studio.

15 November

The Maybot is desperado to get her Brexit plan through and is now pleading openly with her party to help her. She uses a statement followed by a press conference to this end. Asked by a journalist if she was in office but not in power she insisted, 'No.' Asked if she regretted calling an election, she also said no. (Yeah, right.) And then we got a Geoffrey Boycott joke: he 'stuck with it and got the runs in the end'. OMG, what is wrong with this woman? With a vote of no confidence looming and cabinet ministers being urged to quit by leading Brexiteers, it's bloody chaos out there. Even Merkel has said she is not riding to the rescue with further concessions.

All my politico friends have spent the last twenty-four hours discussing what Gove is up to. What is his next move going to be? Like the rest of the Cameroons, May probably loathes him, first sacking him, then giving him the dead-end alleyway of the Defra job, which unfortunately for her he did rather well at. Apparently, they are always at loggerheads, but now he's suddenly come out in support of May's deal. Some say he was just being good-mannered, which shows how treacherous he can be. Because really, we all know he is as unimpressed with May's plan as everyone else. Then he told her he would only take Raab's job after he resigned if he could resurrect negotiations and cancel the planned EU summit on 25 November. She said NO WAY, JOSÉ. So he becomes petulant and says he doesn't want it anyway, and that he likes the world of carbon emissions and farm subsidies and greenie lobbyists because he is more likely to go to heaven, and we are all thinking, hang on a minute, wasn't he the leading advocate for leaving the EU and wouldn't this be his chance to secure that dream? Confused? You are not only one, dear reader. He told the Maybot all this minutes before she was due to face the cameras for her what-was-that-all-about press conference. When asked a question about him she looked somewhat shaken. His timing has always been impeccable.

I text Amber (she is about to be given Work and Pensions, replacing McVey), I tell her I'm pleased for her personally but concerned that May has replaced a Brexiteer with a remainer.

18 November

H calls together the East Devon Conservative Association executive to discuss the Brexit deal and Mrs May's future. As usual, the excuses come thick and fast, the most common being 'we are having people over'. About eight turn up. Jill (Elson) attempts to chair it by cutting people off mid-flow, saying, 'Let everyone have their say', before having her say again, which always refers back to the fact she was once, aeons ago, made redundant by Clark's shoes in Seaton. She attributes this misfortune to the ERM, interest rates, John Major, Maastricht, the weather, and almost anything else on her mind at any given moment. Lovely Lynn, her sister, says 'ordinary people' at the pub, etc., are complaining about cuts to the police, the councils, the schools. Jill then threatens to resign as chairwoman as she is not happy about the way things are going nationally, and hisses and fumes against Jacob Rees-Mogg, who she calls variously William (his father), Jeremy, James and Joshua. Tim Wood, who was an MP and doesn't let anyone forget it, talks about the problems during Maastricht, but it's more a reminiscence of once being in the whips' office. Jeremy Robinson can't hear and subsequently emails the absent Christine Channon (who has got it in for H at the moment) a totally erroneous version of events. Cherry Nicholas almost bursts into tears and tells some disjointed and incomprehensible story of her own family history, which H thinks involved the Nazis, Berlin, losing everything and, more recently, some incident involving a relation with a Canadian passport and the border with the US, although it was difficult to follow the full thread. Simon Card wanted to know what David Lidington's view was. On H asking the relevance of this, it was clear he simply wanted to highlight that he was on first-name terms with David from his Aylesbury days.

Jeff Trail, the current mayor of Exmouth and a former Royal Marine physical training instructor, has carefully written down his contribution, which he balances on his knee and reads out slowly and deliberately, as if he is running through the order of battle and we are his men, all seated around him, heavily camouflaged in the undergrowth. 'Right. The way I see it is this. The PM, Mrs May, is under attack. We need to deploy and reinforce her. She needs to demonstrate leadership, which we can back up with coordinated support.' Hugo is waiting for him to mention H-hour, and talk about air cover and artillery support, but he then veers off into fishing rights.

Each and every one of them then competed as to who was saying what to whom, and in which pub. It was a virtual tour of the drinking houses of East Devon, and all designed to show that they were regularly in touch with 'ordinary people'. Of course, everyone ended up none the wiser, but H has come to the conclusion that either they are all mad, or he is. And he thinks, on balance, it's probably him.

20 November

Lavish dinner at St James's Palace, hosted by Prince Charles as a thank-you to the Saïd Foundation for their charitable work in Syria, and a celebration of the Building a Better Tomorrow Appeal. The room is full of rich international donors. It is announced that the

Foundation has raised an extra five million pounds, which makes the guest speaker, David Miliband, lick his lips in gratitude. He is doing good work running the International Rescue Committee, helping Syrian children get an education and rescuing them from their war-ravaged country.

Before dinner we are all herded into a horseshoe to meet the Prince. H, who has grown the most revolting moustache to raise money for Movember, wonders whether the Prince will recognise him. When he comes up to H, he immediately baulks and points directly at his face.

'Oh, God! A moustache, Hugo?'

'You should see my wife's, sir.'

He rocked and rolled with laughter on cue.

When the Prince comes to me, he stutters, 'That moustache of Hugo's?'

'I know. He's been booted out my bedroom until it has been removed.'

He likes that. But then he would. He's a pro.

In the line to collect our coats, I joke with Rory Stewart. 'Better get your beauty sleep: you're probably on the news at six, seven, noon and midnight. I mean, it's not as if there is anyone else out there willing to sell her rotten deal. You will probably be Chancellor next week at this rate.'

'Yes, for a week,' quips his charming wife Shoshana.

21 November

Dom Raab texts H. 'Can we meet at 6 p.m.?' His office, according to H, is spartan and spare, like him. He is understandably cautious at first. After all, these are high stakes and he hardly knows H. But soon the atmosphere eases and they have a good chat. H tells him about the early days of the Cameron campaign; how the DD campaign got it wrong by bullying and intimidating, and it brought many people over to our side. Boris's team also got it wrong by promising jobs to people, and in the end that was what tripped him up. They talk about money for the campaign and he thinks he has it. They also talk about when and where and if. It is all very delicate, he says, as he cannot be seen to be doing anything, yet he has not only to remain in the game but also somehow show people who the real Dominic Raab really is. They laugh about him and Mrs Raab cooking spaghetti in a pristine Formica kitchen with their children as a potential photo op. He says he has always been given tough jobs but has a humane side, and was always asking to be able to show it. H said he was certainly perceived as being the Jason Statham of politics – he already knew about all the karate, etc. But, 'We need to get to the hinterland,' H tells him. Raab apparently has a small team, and he is going to speak to them and put them in touch with H. Let's see if he does. More interestingly, let's see who they are. H expects one or two surprises, says Mitchell may well be on board. *(Apparently not: Mitch is actually trying to get Raab to back DD.)*

27 November

H asks the PM in the House whether the Withdrawal Agreement backstop risks crossing over her own red lines that no new barriers with the union are created and whether there are circumstances in which NI could be treated differently in limited disputes which could end up being referred to the ECJ as arbiter. Her reply is shameless, that it would be an arbitration panel which would sort out disputes, not the ECJ. So misleading: in the current EU draft text it states that an arbitration panel may 'at any point decide to submit the dispute brought before it to the Court of Justice of the EU for a ruling ... The Court of Justice of the EU shall have jurisdiction over such cases and its rulings shall be binding on the Union and the UK.'

How can we trust her? The whole thing stinks.

4 December

The shit is well and truly hitting the fan now. Labour is pushing for Rumpole's legal advice on the withdrawal agreement to be published. Cox, for his part, coughed and blustered and boomed and basically said that publicly airing the flaws and weaknesses in Britain's future negotiations might not be wise. A vote today could result in him being suspended from the House of Commons. But more parliamentary shenanigans may be on the way. The lead-up to Christmas could be screwed – Scrooged, even – as parliament can pull all sorts of tricks out of the bag to keep it sitting, such as late-night committees and weekend sessions, or summoning officials to the bar of the House to be cross-examined. H doesn't think he will get a Christmas anyway because he reckons the Maybot will fall and then he will be running around trying to get Raab elected. He has now had two meetings with him, and with Henry Bellingham* and Nick de Bois,† who are both involved in helping run his campaign. H doesn't think they are particularly organised, unlike Amber, who is in full leadership-juggling mode.

Michael Gove asks to see H. Apparently the Chief Whip's idea is not to harangue, threaten and bully MPs to support Theresa but to get 'friends' to do it. Hence the Gover for H.

H goes in to see Michael, but he is with Robert Courts, Dave's successor in Witney. H waits outside, and then goes in as if seeing the headmaster. They exchange pleasantries. H starts by saying what a fuck-up it all is, how badly it has all been handled etc. M just sits there. They argue about the backstop. He says the Europeans don't want us to stay in, as it disadvantages them. Gove then tries to put their predicament in context and rather eccentrically and mischievously says, out of the blue, 'Imagine if you had married

---

*   Conservative politician. MP for North West Norfolk 1983–97 and 2001–19. Knighted in 2016.
†   MP for Enfield North 2010–15. Author of *Confessions of a Recovering MP*.

Jerry Hall.' (*Re the lock in, and how you get out of it, it's an analogy that comes from nowhere.*)

'I did nearly marry Jerry Hall.' (*Yes, darling, in your dreams. She only had a brief flirtation with you over a summer, which was designed to wind Mick up.*)

Later he concludes, carting out the Hall analogy again: 'So you'd have Jerry over a barrel.' (*Apparently by this he means we have them over a barrel on the backstop because they apparently loathe it, but if that is true why can't we drop it if they hate it so much.*)

'What makes you think I didn't have Jerry over a barrel?' says H, and they chuckle. *Ugh, men!*

They move off the subject of romantic liaisons and discuss the Union and the backstop. H goes on to explain he cut his teeth in politics as a Conservative and Unionist candidate and then was a Northern Ireland Minister. He tells Michael he passionately believes in the Union and questions Michael as to his own beliefs on that front.

'It's all hopeless. What do you think will happen next?' H asks.

'We need a new PM,' says Michael, looking at H searchingly.

'Yes, I agree.'

'Do you think Boris will get it?'

'I don't think he has sufficient credibility and support amongst colleagues.'

'So, who do you think will get it?'

'Dominic Raab. And maybe with you on the ticket?'

Michael feigns surprise.

'Your problem, Michael, is that you've pirouetted so much recently you've lost credibility. But you should run with Raab. But whatever happens, you'll be in the mix somewhere.' *Because he will make sure he is.*

They part as friends. 'I'm not your problem, Michael. You need to convince about a hundred others and you simply aren't going to do it.'

He didn't disagree. *Which is odd, because he has been selected by the Maybot to wind up the whole bloody debate in the Commons before the vote.*

Before leaving, H gets back to real politics and lobbies him on the problems one of his ninety-four-year-old constituents is having with badgers, who have turned her garden into something resembling Passchendaele. No one seems to be able to do anything about this dreadful situation. Leave the paperwork with me, M says grandly. 'Thank you,' H says, 'but I'm not trading my vote on Tuesday for you eliminating these bloody badgers.' Understood, says M.

Later Sue tracks H down and says No. 10 have been on and would he go and see the PM at 10.30 tomorrow? *(ERG sources say it's all current Privy Counsellors to spook them on the impact of no deal.)*

'No,' H says, 'I won't. She last spoke to me on the telephone when she sacked me in the summer of 2016. It's a bit desperate to want to win me over now. Too little, too late.'

8 December

So up she pops in parliament, with an emergency statement to say sorry folks, no can do, only to be drowned out by howls of laughter and derision.

You would have thought now was the time to get rid of her, but no, the letters don't seem to be arriving on Graham Brady's desk to make this happen.* It is quite extraordinary that after all the evidence laid before them, MPs still accept the May narrative of selflessly doing her duty to the nation.

Anyway, I have removed myself to Devon. I have found it rather difficult being around my cat-on-a-hot-tin-roof husband. Of course, no sooner do I drive away than my Westminster withdrawal symptoms kick in. I ring Hugo for an update on his leadership manoeuvres with Dom and he is dismissive, too busy to talk. I bollock him via a series of texts along the lines of *you would be nothing without me, I am your political brain, I am the one who first spotted*

---

* Sir Graham Brady, Chairman of the 1922 Committee, the parliamentary group which represents the Conservative Party in the House of Commons.

Dominic Raab, you do this every time when you think you are in the game, how dare you etc., etc.

He replies that he is not providing a running commentary and will call me at the end of the day. 'Fine,' I snap, 'make sure you do.'

He finally calls me after dinner but refuses to talk about the Dom meetings – he has had two today – in case anyone is listening in. He tells me that he has just come from a dinner with Jeremy Hunt, William Hague, Tim Boswell and Gary Streeter. The general consensus was that the train has left the station, that it is not about Brexit any more, it's about the leadership. They bitch about Bercow not being impartial during his time in the chair, thereby enabling the remain supporters with votes, debates and amendments. Geoffrey Cox is in a terrible state, one of them says: he has been in tears, apparently. His tears should have been of joy, since Labour didn't target him personally. But H says the most extraordinary piece of gossip he has been told tonight was that Corbyn recently gave an interview to the BBC, and while having tea afterwards asked the journalist who had interviewed him, 'So when are we on?', the implication being he is becoming somewhat forgetful.

12 December

H wakes me at 7 a.m. from London. 'Chocks away! The letters are in.' I turn the radio and TV on. All the usual suspects on the airwaves. Remainers supporting Old Ma May because they don't want a Brexiteer. Cabinet ministers supporting her publicly, but privately plotting. Matt Hancock particularly disingenuous. He is quite an actor, that one. But this prime minister is very difficult to budge. Her stubbornness, which is also her flaw, may see her through.

So why now? Everyone is fuming, that's why. The decision to pull the big vote, and her statement explaining it. Some wanted her to go ahead with the vote to demonstrate to Europe that we mean business, or just that there is no majority for any other plan. Others wanted her to lose, to shaft her finally. The cabinet is apparently completely split on whether she should be pressing ahead with no-deal planning or doing everything she can to avoid it. I reckon the reality was that they were only two letters short and then two more went in. But it's not the best timing. They should have waited until she had finished her tour of Europe to get concessions on the backstop. Now, she can say, and lie if needs be, that progress is being made when it probably isn't.

10.50 a.m.: H says the ERG think this contest has been manoeuvred by No. 10. If she does it very quickly, she gets the whole thing out the way in a day. Certainly, the timetable is all to her advantage. PMQs then a speech to the 1922 before the vote tonight. H forwards me a text exchange from Stuart, H's old researcher, who is now working at CCHQ.

'How are you going to vote, Hugo?'

'How I normally vote. I'm going to put a cross in a box.'

'That's very helpful. Can you at least let me know if anyone unusual is intending to vote against her?'

'All my colleagues are unusual, so probably not.'

'Thank you, Hugo, that is very helpful.'

Dave is also texting madly. 'You have got to support her. The alternative is a hard Brexit. A NO deal.' Well, he would say that, wouldn't he. He wants to save his own skin, and he is advising the PM twice a week. He is also trying, and has been for ages, to thwart Brexit. While I'm speaking to H, Gavin Williamson calls him.

Hugo tells him, 'I know you are wearing your old hat here, Gavin, but I have to say I was an early supporter of Mrs May and you purposely held my name back from telling her. [An old grudge rising to the fore here.] That woman has not talked to me, not a single word, since becoming leader. Why would I try to defend her now?' Gavin doesn't really try to persuade him.

'You can put a question mark by my name,' says H to Gavin, signing his own death warrant in terms of calls coming in, but ensuring no one will know which way he actually votes.

11.29 a.m.: I think she's going to win it. Groan. Amazing, really, if that's the case – it means most will vote for her, but then against her deal. Senseless.

1 p.m.: H says the mood is very much against her in the House but that she will win it, though she will come out very wounded. If a hundred are against her could she really go on, he asks me. He says Philip May was looking on anxiously in the gallery. Maybe he has said, OK, if it gets to this number we hop on a plane and spend Christmas in Madeira. My personal feeling is that she will win, but many who say they are supporting her will not do so when in the privacy of the equivalent of the voting booth.

H says he is having to dodge the journalist rats who are running riot: will you, won't you support her? I suspect Hugo won't support her, but he is not saying anything either way. Ultimately, it's his decision. But there is no love lost between them. I ask about the Dom campaign. Very relaxed, he says, everything slotting into place, but he acknowledges they are not so advanced as other campaigns. Which is probably a good thing. He or she who tries hardest, etc. But this is Boris and Dom's moment, they must know this is their best chance.

9 p.m.: 200 for her, 117 against.

17 December

I don't know if Brexit is making my husband even angrier than usual, but he is becoming increasingly like Victor Meldrew. I try to beat it out of him early in the morning by insisting he walks Rocco with me, over Chelsea Bridge and through Battersea Park, but it only makes things worse. Cyclists have their own lane on the road, but insist on riding down the bridge walkway instead, which to H is nothing less than a hanging offence. Every morning he plays policeman, shouting expletives, holding his hand up, blocking their path. Very soon he is going to stop a hoodie, who will by return slip a knife between his ribs. Worse, he might stop someone who works for the *Daily Mail*. He says he is going to start a new party, the PFPP (Pavements For Pedestrians Party).

I cannot exaggerate even slightly the resentment – nay, hatred – for the cycling fraternity my husband nurses deep in his chest. Like all his obsessions, there is something in it. Since Boris flooded the streets of London with those wretched hire bikes, rights of way have become the biggest unsolved political issue after Brexit. Running red lights. Sitting in the middle of lanes so you can't pass. Ignoring pedestrian signals ... the list goes on. Most of all, H hates what they wear. So bad is he getting, so close to making a citizen's arrest – but even nearer to being mown down, so I end up pushing him around in a wheelchair for the rest of my life – that I am forced to revise our route so his day can start on a calmer note.

18 December

Labour tries to call a vote of no confidence and fails.

H attends the last Green Chip dinner before the Christmas break. Afterwards, he travels back on the Tube with Rory Stewart. They spot Mark Marlesford* and H tells the story of their strange briefing years ago, when they went to Helmand with the MOD, as he knows it will appeal to Rory.

H and Mark had turned up at the appointed hour for the briefing. An officer went through the outline of the visit before handing over to a Sergeant Williams, who was to take them through the logistics. Williams squinted at a computer screen and very slowly outlined how they were to fly into Helmand, and where they were to be billeted, fed and so forth. He reassured them that they would be safe as they would be wearing body armour and helmets at all times and would not leave Camp Bastion other than on one occasion, when they would travel to the neighbouring camp, the rather unhelpfully named Camp Tombstone, to see the Afghan

---

* Conservative politician, created Baron Marlesford in 1991.

army being trained. Here the sergeant became nervous, squinted harder at the screen and said:

'Halthough you will be travelling hin han harmoured vehicle, you may well be what is called hinterdicted by what is the Taliban, which is what we call the henemy.'

Mark, who was struggling to hear, leant over to H to ask what was being said. H told him to be quiet, but that they may well be 'hinterdicted'. Mark looked surprised. Williams was by now in full flow: 'Hand I must warn you, gentlemen, that it is not himpossible that you will be habducted by the henemy.' He began to cough nervously. 'Hand that it is not uncommon for you, having been habducted, to be taken one at a time hand hanally assaulted.' Mark, straining to hear once again, asked H what was being said. 'Looks like we're going to be buggered, Mark.'

'Oh?'

'But,' continued the sergeant, 'what his himportant is that once you have been returned to the group, the rest of the group hembrace you, as you will feel dirty.' Mark, who was by this time looking a little alarmed, again asked H what was being said.

'Apparently, after we've been buggered we've got to gather round and hug each other.'

'Oh,' exclaimed Mark, 'it's like being back at Eton.'

Rory roars with laughter and says the briefing bears a remarkable similarity to his before he went to Iraq.

Chelsea is changing. Yesterday, en route to the dry cleaner's and weighed down by packages and suits, H was stopped by a man in a top of the range four-by-four who had simply stopped diagonally across the road. In a rather gruff Russian accent he said, 'Heathrow.'

H, being the gent, attempted to give him directions to the King's Road as a starter, but was cut off mid-explanation.

'No, Heathrow. I go Heathrow,' he repeated, this time with some force.

H tried again.

The man waved his hand at him. 'You have car. I follow you.'

H explained that he didn't have a car and was only going another few yards to the dry cleaner's and not to Heathrow, whereupon the Russki muttered darkly and shot off looking neither right nor left.

Sometimes we feel we are the only English people left in Chelsea, as it has become such a haven for the international super-rich.

19 December

H gives the girls dinner in the House. They love going there, and plead with him, 'Please don't leave politics.' Amber joins them. She has the glow of a new relationship; someone she was at university with, apparently. She tells them his wife left him a couple of years ago, at which Siena quips, 'Was he very boring?'

I'm avoiding Amber at the moment, so incensed am I by her trickery in trying to thwart Brexit. She is absolutely convinced that parliament will not let things happen, which is entirely naive. The executive can stop anything happening if they don't put anything before the House, which makes it impossible for Amber's cronies to lay down amendments.

Not long to go now before we say arrivederci, auf wiedersehen pet, au revoir to the EU. Still, everyone except me seems to be bound by apocalyptic fears for the future. But hey! What's this? It's none other than our very own Hands on Cock, who does not intend to get caught with his pants down and has been busy stockpiling drugs of the non-Notting Hill and Chipping Norton set variety. Matt is also cornering the international fridge market (coming to a hedgerow near you soon) to keep them in. It doesn't end there: rustbucket ferries are to be requisitioned and the government wants to turn what little remains of our navigable public road network into a giant car park where exhausted foreign lorry drivers can watch porn and no doubt blame their indolence on the tachograph, EU drivers' hours rules (Regulation (EC) 561/2006, if you are interested) or the working time rules (Directive 2002/15/ EC if you are still interested).

Personally, I think the deal is already altered and this is just all for show, but I might be wrong. The question is, how will the people react? If they are anything like my father, the stockpiling might get out of hand: Sir John still has masses of tinned frankfurt- ers left over from the last big scare, the one about nuclear winters in the seventies. We are not used to this, or even good at it. We have lived in the land of plenty for too long to not contemplate taking action.

The really good news is that some of the most irritating of our brethren have threatened to depart the party if no deal happens: Sarah Wollaston and Nick Boles say they'll be first out the door. H says he will be there to lock it behind them.

Also, according to *The Times*, Amber also kicked up in cab- inet: 'Just because you've put a seat belt on it doesn't mean you crash the car.'

I've been trying to tell my remainer friends the same thing for ages!

2019

3 January

I start the year in a Brexit rage. A rage directed towards my remoaner friends and the chaos they are causing to our reputation abroad, and to our status as an independent sovereign trading nation. When will it occur to them that they lost?

I know they feel the rejection keenly, but, guys and gals, you are really screwing the whole thing up by trying to de-legitimise the result. Just get over it. MOVE ON!

Only a complete idiot would try to predict what comes next, but here goes. Hopefully, we leave. No crash, economic figures fall but come back again, the remoaners are disappointed we have not gone back to the 1970s as they predicted. Alternatively, they get what they want, the second referendum is another dead heat and we return to bloody purgatory. A new leader is chosen, not a nutter (which rules out Gove, Boris, Williamson) and we have an election. Corbyn loses and Labour bin him. Or Corbyn wins and his revolutionaries overrun the Imperial Palace of Westminster. Richard Benyon has all his lands seized – we think this is why he is such a keen remainer – and we are all put to hard labour in the paddy fields in order to feed a starving nation, all the while dreaming of salad days of olive oil and feta cheese from Greece.

What will probably happen is the date of our departure will be delayed by that ridiculous excuse for a PM adding to the deadlock.

4 January

This is mental. The *Evening Standard* (editor: one G. Osborne) is now telling us we are going to get super-gonorrhoea if we leave the EU.

The pain or burning sensation will be the direct result of no deal. Apparently, our proximity to a borderless Europe makes a range of infectious diseases such as mumps, HIV, tuberculosis, bubonic plague and ringworm way more likely. Gosh! And it gets worse. We will also be short of Mars bars, and we must be careful looking up to the sky because a satellite might fall on our heads, according to the EU's Space Surveillance and Tracking Programme. And so it goes on. There will be no food, according to Michael Gove, so we are all going to be walking around emaciated like zombies, eating each other. Lorry parks will replace the hills and valleys of Kent. Medicines will be non-existent.

Reminder to self: bulk buy tins of spaghetti hoops.

Still, no deal is good for me: a new diet, new me kind of thing. I just need a gun to protect my hoard. Or I need to know where H keeps the key for the gun cabinet ... *which I don't, officer.* My only question is how does one go to Tesco and ask for a hundred tins of spaghetti hoops without raising suspicion?

13 January

Things are most certainly coming to a head this week, says H. A vote on Tuesday on the Withdrawal Bill, and as things stand the government looks to be defeated by a large majority. H has tabled an amendment – a resuscitated amendment that the Deputy Chief Whip, Chris Pincher, asked him to submit before Christmas and which now, much to everyone's surprise, not least H's, is referred to as the Swire Amendment. 'Perhaps that is how people find themselves part of history,' he says. 'Inadvertently.'

14 January

We are meant to be on course to leave the EU by the end of the month, but everything is going pear-shaped, even before the vote – a vote May is most definitely going to lose. MPs are running about with more cunning plans and amendments, including my husband. Rory Stewart, Gove's stand-in, is trying to be a snake oil salesman and failing miserably. Mind you, good on him, because there is no one else out there prepared to sell it. Whenever H passes him in the corridor he says 'Hello, Tariq', as in Tariq Aziz, the resilient apologist for Saddam Hussein. Rory takes it all in good humour.

15 January

H is doing a lot on the media as regards his amendment, which is designed to unlock the problem of the backstop. This morning, he is interviewed by the *Today* programme, and he cautions that the selection of his amendment is in the hands of the Speaker, and him alone. Come the debate, Bercow makes his selection. He does not select H's nor Andrew Murrison's, to which H is a signatory and which goes further than his in actually putting a date on which any backstop would expire. They are deeply annoyed by the little weasel's rejection because their amendments would have been helpful to the government. H leaves the chamber and is immediately rung by the *Mail*, who ask about events. H tears into the Speaker without holding back. The hack scribbles it all down and says, 'All off the record, I imagine?' 'Not a bit of it,' says H. 'Publish it all!'

H pops in and out of the chamber and assumes that he is not going to be called as a result, but towards the end of the debate a whip comes sidling up and says, 'You're on next.' H is only given a few minutes, in which he says how regrettable it is that his amendment and Andrew's have not been selected. Apparently, the Speaker mutters 'Stupid' under his breath. Par for the course. H goes on to say how it is with regret that he cannot support the government, but he rings me and tells me he feels distinctly uneasy as to whether or not he has called it right.

Then it comes, the vote that is, and wow! It is some defeat. H tells me on the phone that going through the lobbies with the entire Labour Party was quite an experience, one he had never had before, but it gave him the chance of a good chat with the Beast of Bolsover (Dennis Skinner), who is eighty-six. He had earlier, in questions, praised the NHS for replacing most of his body parts. H says he is well past it, but admires him for 'buggering on'.

My only hope is that all this runs down the clock till March – the only thing the old boot has said that I'm in favour of is that she won't pull the leaving date.

Though it's so utterly inconsiderate to orchestrate a drama in January when we are all trying to give up the booze.

16 January

H walks past the Foreign Office with Dominic Raab. 'Ah, our old haunt,' Raab laughs. They discuss details of the leadership campaign. 'You are so cool and unflappable,' Raab says. I think he is beginning to see H as a sort of Willie Whitelaw* figure. If only he knew how uncool and flappable he really is.

H has dinner with Dave and Sam at their house alone as I'm in Devon. Two hacks loitering outside. Dave has just had a colonoscopy, apparently, and says he has got a sore bum. Kate is there, and she and Samantha both look immaculately groomed and corporate, H says. Dave greets H by saying, 'I shouldn't have you here, you're an anti.' Samantha says she won't vote Tory again if it's a hard Brexit. H looks surprised that she had ever voted Tory anyway, and she concedes that she has never been a cheerleader for the party.

They discuss Brexit, of course, and the runners and riders post May. They don't like Jeremy Hunt because they believe his tack

---

* 1st Viscount Whitelaw, KT, CH, MC, PC, DL (1918–99). Soldier, Conservative politician and deputy party leader under Margaret Thatcher, to whom he became indispensable, leading her to remark that 'every prime minister needs a Willie'.

to the right is inauthentic and opportunistic. H raises Raab, and they all shriek. He patiently reminds Dave that, a few years ago, he had identified him as a likely future prime minister. H is genuinely perplexed by how much they seem to dislike him, as he says he has seen him be nothing but polite and courteous. It is all of course based on their remain stance; they see Raab as a rabid Brexiteer. The truth is they know next to nothing about him.

17 January

H stays in London for another day, in order to take DR to meet Michael Spencer, which they do at the private members' club George in the early evening. It's a typical Mark Birley joint, now owned by Richard Caring: discreet, tasteful, with paintings by David Hockney on the walls and an art deco downstairs bar into which Michael comes, filling the room, and gives H a huge hug and kiss, somewhat to Dom's surprise. Perhaps he is jealous. Michael is in ebullient form, alternating between being assertive and then reflective, all the time looking Dom in the eye, assessing him and weighing up the odds like the legendary City trader he is. Raab remains calm but speaks a bit quietly, so Michael has to keep leaning forward, which H thinks is good because it establishes intimacy.

Michael asks Dom about a probability on some issue and he replies 50 per cent. Michael says that's not a probability, so Dom ups it to 51 per cent. 'Oh dear,' says Michael, 'I can see you're not a mathematician.' Dom replies, 'No, I'm not, and Hugo warned me you were.' H leaves them alone for the last ten minutes, then speaks to Dom afterwards, from the train. He says he liked Michael and they got on. Michael texts H later and says he likes Dom too, and 'let's see how things go'. H will approach him for support on Monday.

23 January

H has been feeling a little strange recently, and has become suspicious of the breath freshener he has been using. At the same time, his glasses have been permanently fogged up as he can't lay his hands on his lens-cleaning liquid, but he has been too busy to do much about it. That is, until he locks himself out of his Commons office. Whilst waiting for Peter Fage to come over with his spare key, he squints at the canister of breath freshener under a strong light. It is at this point he discovers that he has been squirting lens cleaner into his mouth. A case of mistaken identity. He's lucky not to suffer the same fate as Mr Skripal. 'So, have you been putting ear cleaner in your eyes?' I ask him. 'Eye test, darling?'

24 January

H has been busy trying to raise money for the Dominic Raab campaign. He comes home saying, Dom this, Dom that; their relationship is becoming almost homoerotic.

'Be honest, Hugo, do you fancy him?'

'Yes, I can confirm I am in love. I am most definitely in love.'

I reckon it's the buff gym look that appeals to him; a body that contrasts greatly with his own. Raab is apparently always in the House of Commons gym – it's about the only place MPs ever catch sight of him these days.

'I think I might have to sign up,' H tells me.

'Well, if that's what it takes, then you do that, darling.'

I have been getting rather tired of Dom's catchphrase, which H repeats on an hourly basis: *train hard, fight easy*. But H excitedly tells me he now has a new one, which is apparently *you say, I do*. This came about in a taxi on the way to meet a potential donor, when H explains if any money is raised it has to come from the donor's wife, as she is a resident. 'The donor will probably want to host a dinner so you can meet her,' H tells him. A look of abject panic washes over Raab's face; he says he doesn't know what he would do about his children if he and his wife had to go out in the evening.

H puts it softly: 'You might need to get a babysitter, Dom.'

'OK, you say, I do, Hugo.'

They switch back to general chit-chat, then H says, 'You are not very country, are you? Much more urban.'

'I'm suburban, Hugo. I'm suburban.'

H comes down to Devon. Michael Spencer rings him and says he can't back Dom right now, but if things change he will be right in there. He has built a whole successful career on hedging, so he knows what he's doing.

25 January

Chaffcombe

Down on the farm, the equilibrium of the chicken house is being disturbed. Yes, it's not just the House of Commons that has disruptive members.

H couldn't understand why his egg production is falling. He asks Chris Cann, who is thatching the Bailiff's House, the building that is to become my office, to come and take a look at the hens.

'It's because half of them are not hens, they are cocks, Hugo.'

It seems there are three cocks in the coop and the poor hens are being shagged sideways, in between watching bouts of serious cock-fighting. Two of the cocks have to go. H, who has spent decades slaughtering birds on the estates of the British gentry, now can't quite bring himself to wring the necks of these two birds.

'I can't throttle a pet! It's not in me.'

'For God's sake, Hugo, don't be so wet. Just strangle it and then put it in a pot of boiling water and pull the feathers off. Then stick your hand up its arse and pull everything out, and put it in the freezer.'

I was brought up on a farm.

'I am not doing that, thank you very much. I have a different plan.'

'Which is?'

'I'll shoot them instead.'

'Fine. But do it humanely. And don't kill anyone else in the process.'

He gets out his .22, which he has been looking for an excuse to use since he bought it. He first tries to persuade Rob, our gardener, and the thatcher, Chris, to have coq au vin for their dinner so he can pass the responsibility for the massacre over to them, but neither are interested. So, with tremendous determination, he takes a deep breath, sweeps up his gun and advances on the chicken house as if it were a military campaign. Next, he releases all the chickens and withdraws behind the garden wall to take aim, watched by an increasingly sceptical Rob, and draws a bead on the very large white cockerel. Always having been an erratic rifle shot – both stalking in the Highlands and on army ranges, where he often scored a bullseye, but usually on his neighbour's target – he squints through the scope, squeezes the trigger and *BANG!* The cock lets out a shriek, leaps in the air and limps off as best he can. Unfortunately, next to him now lay a mortally wounded chicken, one of our best layers.

Rob and I just turn our heads and sigh knowingly to each other. 'Why does he always get it so wrong?' I say.

Infuriated, Hugo sets off after the cockerels, who he holds personally responsible for the hen's demise, and comes over all Rambo, spraying them with rounds and rounds of bullets. At least it was a clean, fast death. Trouble is, he uses so much lead he won't be able to put the chickens back into the food chain, even if he wanted to, so he throws them on the bonfire instead, which he and Rob subsequently can't light, on account of this patch of ground being the wettest in the whole of England.

'I know,' says Rob, 'why don't you try Burt over at the Railway Inn? He'll take anything dead and serve it up to his customers.'

Meanwhile, Jenny shows up. She is the mother of ten-year-old Leopold, who looks after the chickens and comes up on his bike after school every day to feed them.

I tell Jenny the sorry tale and she gasps. 'I hope Hugo didn't kill Lucky, Leopold's favourite.'

But it seems Lucky was not quite so lucky after all. The one who really was fortunate, though, was the local fox, who had three chickens for his dinner.

Anyway, harmony now reigns in the henhouse, so some good has come of it, and at least the hens don't have to put out so regularly any more.

5 February

Amber tracks me down. She tried to call last Sunday but I didn't pick up. It all went fine. We skated around each other's positions, talked about children first, then her new boyfriend. She gets really irritated when I ask her if he is marriage material and whether he has any money, which is a perfectly reasonable girlie question between friends in my book.

From what I can ascertain, her new Brexit tactic is a delaying one; she wouldn't tell me for how long because she knows I'm not in her camp, but it's irrelevant because all the power lies with the ERG at the moment, much to her fury. I try to tell her not to lump everyone who doesn't agree with her stance in with the ERG. I explain Hugo has deep reservations about the backstop as well and that there is a whole middle section of the party that thinks like him, and they are not ERG supporters. But Amber's position is so entrenched she can't see the wood for the trees any more.

She says everyone is utterly exasperated by May, that she simply doesn't talk to anyone. She listens all right, but gives no one, including her cabinet, any indication which way she is leaning – even her chancellor, who simply loathes her and she him. Amber says May is not leaning either way because she simply doesn't know what to do. We discuss how we are going to get rid of her, and Amber says it's impossible, that the cabinet is entirely split, and most have leadership ambitions so won't make the first move. Kate, who I speak to next, says it will have to come from the MPs, a group will have to say they won't back her budget, and then the men in suits, headed by Graham Brady, go and knock on her door.

My take is that it is down to the character of the woman; a woman who is incapable of leading her generals and her troops over the hill. She seems to walk blindly from one crisis to the next, never knowing where she will end up and what her next step will be. It just seems pretty blinking obvious that we can't possibly leave by March and that there will be another delay, and yet Old Ma May continues to insist the date will not be shifted.

21 February

First a bunch of Labour left Labour to form the Independent Group, citing the fact that they could not 'be part of a party that allows racism to flourish', and now our chief remain fundamentalists have joined them: Anna Soubry, Heidi Allen and Sarah Wollaston, who are accusing Theresa May of losing control to a hard-right group of Brexiteers. Personally, all I can think is good bloody riddance. One is a fruitcake and the other two were never conservatives anyway. Dave apparently tried to stop them via text, which is rich, because he and Boy George have been silently egging them on to cause all this trouble for two years. Oh God, to watch them in their press conference, all smug and self-important, all that starlight on them.

22 February

We go reluctantly to the AGM of the West Hill Branch, in their Führerbunker which doubles up as the village hall. A warm welcome, a glass of beer and then the AGM begins. Some deaths – inevitable – and one or two new members, and a self-congratulatory review of the social events and the small amount contributed to the Association's finances. Of course, the cost of putting on these events absorbs most of the profit, but in all fairness this branch is consistently the biggest contributor to the Association. Dinner and the raffle follow, but not before Colonel Peter Morrison has read out the report to the Conservative Policy Forum, which has apparently won not one but two special commendations from CCHQ. Pity the poor person who has to actually read this stuff, it's bad enough listening to it. This one starts off with an attack on the Germans and the French, with allusions to the last war, which many in the branch look back to with great nostalgia. After all, in those days you could at least tell your enemies and friends apart by their uniforms. So very much simpler.

H auctions off a bottle of House of Commons claret which is greatly reduced in value by him being asked to sign it, but anyway it sells for a respectable fifty pounds. He then speaks with clarity and conviction, and is firm about the Tory deserters, a second referendum and the need to get rid of May. He then pushes Dominic Raab as a good option, which is well received. Afterwards, the Colonel, who has always considered H to be the worst sort of wishy-washy pinko, comes up and declares that H is a new man, and how many have commented on it during the evening. This is, of course, because H was saying what they agreed with, but it is still quite encouraging. Perhaps they are going to push him to stand for the leadership of the party at the end of it all.

The usual stuff: some had difficulty reading out their part of the AGM report, some lost their way, and watching them vote for motions was excruciating as some were unable to lift their hands properly, others shook, and one man used one arm to help raise his other. Of course, all this is just around the corner for us, so I don't mean to scorn, but it is a portrait of our current membership.

24 February

Reading the Sundays yesterday, all I kept thinking was, is anyone actually up there in the control tower?

All this doom and gloom about no deal, and in comes the news that the world's largest sovereign wealth fund is taking a thirty-year bet that Britain will emerge from Brexit stronger outside the European Union, but no one was really listening, they were out bulk-buying for imminent food shortages.

Meanwhile, Labour officially comes out to support a second referendum in a bid to stop the haemorrhaging of members. Quite a shrewd move, considering half their MPs won't back it; second, it makes them look as if they are trying; and third, it won't get through parliament.

26 February

H and Bellingham go and have a man-to-man chat with Dom about skeletons in his closet as there is an increasing amount of background noise, presumably orchestrated by other camps. It's left to H to ask the hard questions. Raab C. Brexit looks appalled and utterly crestfallen by the questions, and H apologises but says they have to be asked so that they can be properly rebutted later on. H is back in love with him. Being the Dom campaign treasurer is taking up quite a lot of his time, but then H loves mingling with the rich. I think he feels that if he gets close, they will take pity on him and do an immediate BACS transfer. I tell him the rich get rich by not giving it all away, unless they are super-rich, and then they only give it away to causes to make them look even richer, and H doesn't exactly qualify as a good cause.

From the Commons, H goes to dinner with Spencer. A typical Michael dinner, according to H: a mixture of City types and a smattering of politicos, in this instance Kwasi (Kwarteng), Andrew (Mitchell), H and Tom Strathclyde. H sits next door to a man with a hoarse whisper, who says he is called Spiegel, and that he whispers because he damaged his vocal cords as a young man on the Chicago trading floor. H says: 'Ah, pork bellies,' remembering something he once knew about commodity trading. Spiegel looks at him, amazed, and asks if he is a clairvoyant as, yes indeed, he had started out trading pork bellies. They discuss their respective families and he insists on showing H a photo on his mobile of his latest girlfriend. 'Goodness,' H says carefully.

'Goodness what?' Spiegel replies, slightly testily, and then adds rather defiantly, 'She's Brazilian.'

'Ah yes, I see that, very pretty.'

'I know what you're thinking: she's too young.'

'No,' H protests feebly, 'it's not what I am thinking at all,' which of course is exactly what he is thinking, given that this man is in his mid-sixties and she in her early thirties, or so he maintained – twenties more likely, H thinks.

'Well, she's not,' he harrumphs and turns away. They did not speak much after that.

After dinner, H talks to Kwasi about the current situation. 'Amber's gone mad,' H says, and then they both blame Roland Rudd, Mandelson, Blair et al. There is no doubt that Amber has done herself considerable damage in the party. Moving on to the current situation, they both reckon that the Bill will go through if Geoffrey Cox's advice is good enough to convince the DUP. Only a few ERG diehards will want to out-union the Unionists, and if they acquiesce it's through. Cox will need to be very careful about what political spin he puts on the legal advice, citing Lord Goldsmith and the advice he gave during the Iraq War, which Blair ignored, resulting in the Chilcot inquiry. Dominic Grieve used to annoy the hell out of Dave, H tells Kwasi, because he always gave his legal advice straight and without the spin Dave wanted and needed for cover. Will Cox do the same?

Mitchell and H leave the dinner together. H asks about DD, who he'd previously said had discovered money-making and wasn't going to run in any leadership contest.

'But he looks as if he's lost some weight,' H says.

'Yes, that's why I think he will,' says Mitch.

H asks him if he will run DD's campaign. 'No fear – not after the last time.'

H does not necessarily believe any of this.

4 March

H takes Raab C. Brexit to meet some prospective donors at James Hambro & Partners. They are just about to cross Pall Mall when a car shoots past and H protectively pulls him back. Dom in turn recoils and virtually floors H; his animal brain default is self-defence, it's that black belt in karate he notched up in his youth. H thinks it's lucky Dom did actually remember who he was with or he would have been thrown to the ground, nage-waza style.

'I'm bloody not doing that again! His reaction was a bit OTT, if you ask me,' H tells me later.

Train hard, fight easy, Hugo.

H gets a text from Boris, asking him if he has some time to see him. He assents and trots off to his lair in Parliament Street. Boris's office is out of the way and very dingy, with an unloved and unlived-in feeling. H says to Boris that this is a great insult for a former Foreign Secretary. Boris calls it 'the whips' revenge'.

Boris quickly launches into his pitch, lamenting the fact that they have not spoken before, and asking about Dom's campaign. He says that he knows Michael Tomlinson and Henry Bellingham are involved, but asks who else. H says that he would not possibly expect him to say. Boris then says he doesn't think Dom can do it.

H tells Boris his problem is that he is divisive and that his Association members groaned at the AGM when someone got up and said Boris should be the next leader. Boris looks pained and keeps asking how many of them groaned, and why. He is curiously vulnerable and longs to be loved, and cannot understand it when he is not. H tells him that they were going to fight a clean campaign, then there is a 'but your camp did this', 'said this' claim and counter-claim, which is the nature of these things.

H subsequently speaks to Paul Stephenson, a key member of Team Raab. H says that it didn't appear as if Boris had any campaign infrastructure, that he is probably just muddling through, which he has done throughout his entire journalistic and parliamentary career. Paul says that he is repeating what did for him last time, allowing too many people to think they are in charge, only for them to fall out. Jacob is one, Lynton another; Carrie Symonds, the new girlfriend, is a third, and possibly the most influential. After all, it is she who sees him last thing in the evening and first thing in the morning – and several times in the night, I should imagine. Apparently, she has already let it be known that Lynton will be in charge 'over her dead body'. Boris's campaigns are always shambolic, rather like him.

12 March

It's 11 a.m. and we are waiting and waiting and waiting. Meaningful Vote 2 is tonight, and no one knows which way it will go. The Maybot is in cabinet as I write, hoping against hope the Brexiteers will be responsive to the assurances she gained in Strasbourg and that her deal will make it through parliament. Twitter is in overdrive. But the verdicts from the DUP or the Brexiteers are not yet in, they are waiting for the pronunciations of their 'star chamber'. Most MPs are also awaiting Rumpole's all-important legal opinion on the backstop, which is coming any minute. We think he is going to make a statement in the Commons. But the numbers are stark: 202 votes in favour versus 432 votes against last time around. He will have to be pretty confident for that many to do a U-turn.

6.17 p.m. Hugo tweets: 'I voted against the PM's deal in January. Whilst I believe this deal to be only marginally better, I believe it is the best deal on the table to deliver Brexit. The alternatives are too uncertain.'

6.30 p.m.: things are getting nasty on Twitter:

Useless Twat

bottled it

Free of principle then. Duly noted. Another one to vote out at the next election

You utter invertebrate

You just have to chuck the shite ones in the bin and you're golden!

scab

Melt

MPs' face a big decision tonight. Back riots or back riots. Remember the poll tax? This will be far worse if you ignore the publics instructions. . .wake up

You're being watched!

I text H: 'Your Twitter is going mental with anger.'
'That's fine, because I'm going mental as well,' he replies.
7.30 p.m. The government loses Meaningful Vote 2 by 149.

Addressing the Commons, May says: 'I profoundly regret the decision that this House has taken tonight.' The croaky voice, like its owner, scarcely there. Everyone was looking around for the stretcher-bearers in more ways than one.

13 March

Face-palm alert. Tonight was the vote on taking the no deal option off the table, which is a little odd to say the least, since the Maybot has done everything in her power to keep it on the table, to the extent of facing down rebels like Amber, warning it would undermine her whole negotiation. This was a free vote, probably designed so she could vote against herself, which means she is either a) a super-clever remain strategist (not!), or b) she has lost all control of her party and cabinet.

At 7 p.m., the vote on the Spelman amendment. It's 312 to 308 in favour, with nine Tories rebelling. The Maybot loses by a majority of four.

Then the vote on the final motion, as amended. The motion that opposed leaving without a deal. There was meant to be a free vote, but at half-past seven, as the vote was called, the Tory whips issued a three-line whip to oppose the motion. They are to vote against the idea of ruling out leaving with no deal. They are, in effect, now being told to vote to keep no deal on the table. Chaos, bedlam, pandemonium, commotion, uproar. The MPs are completely thrown. Which way should they vote, for fuck's sake! Some even went into the wrong lobby by accident; others did it deliberately.

Overall, MPs voted to reject leaving the UK without a deal, 321 to 278, a margin of 43. The vote is not legally binding but expresses the will of the House until an alternative outcome is legislated for. A result much greater than if the three-line whip had been executed. Another cock-up.

*

Grab an Uber and make my way over to Henry Bellingham's gaff in Stockwell for the lasagne supper for Raab C. Brexit and supporters. I have not met him yet, so I'm pretty curious. He is shorter than I thought, a supremely lean, toned specimen and extremely pleasant and polite with it. I can see why H has developed something of a man crush on him. I make him and his wife laugh about Saffron being the *oink* in the *Peppa Pig* song (my brother Julian wrote the music). But I come away not quite able to work out whether he is a real hottie or a bit nerdy. His wife Erika certainly didn't look sub-standard either. She smiles nicely, in fact they both do, but I get the feeling she is being swept up in a tornado that she doesn't really have any understanding of. My other impression of Raab is that he appears a little frightened, a little unconfident, which worries me because if he is up against big platform performers like Boris and Gove, he might just fall at the first hurdle with the members. His advantage, of course, is that he rep-resents a new beginning; he is supremely clever, young, full of ideas, and comes from a good classless background. His disadvantage is he has little name recognition or presence as yet.

Also there is Suella Braverman, who I like very much. The daugh-ter of immigrants from Kenya and Mauritius, state and independent and Cambridge educated, and a lawyer, she represents a newer Britain as far as the Tories are concerned. She is natural and confi-dent, definitely secretary of state material.

In fact, everyone there, apart from Henry and Hugo, represent a different type of Conservative, a new kind of Conservative. When Robert Courts stands next to his pregnant wife, I just see my younger self. Full of hope. None of the cynicism. Yes, this is a different crowd from the one we came into politics with, less silver spoon, more work your way up. That's a really good thing.

21 March

Apparently, it was International Day of Happiness yesterday. Although when Old Ma May took to the podium last night she looked anything but. In fact, she looked seriously pissed off. She told the nation – no hacks present – to one camera that she was asking for a short extension to Article 50.

The EU was not at all happy either. They don't want to give us any delay unless we first ratify the withdrawal agreement.

And actually, I'm not happy either. I'm down in Devon, the boiler is broken, the costs are escalating on the Bailiff's House, it's damp, and I can't sleep, and I can't do anything and I think I'm having a mini Brexit breakdown. I have switched off the news only to switch it on again. And my mother is not happy because Sir John is most definitely unhappy and is firing off rude emails to his old leave mates like Norman Lamont and being abusive towards them because they have announced they are supporting her deal. And Siena is not happy because she is coming to the end of her A levels and the pressure is getting to her. Saffron is happy, though, because I've just done her a Waitrose shop of rabbit pellets, which seems to be her current diet.

25 March

Chris Pincher, Deputy Chief Whip, rings H and says they need to get Dom down to Chequers but he is not answering his phone. Leave it to me, says H. Old Ma May, having fought off a coup attempt by the Gover and David Lidington earlier in the day, was now inviting the hard core down to try to flog them her deal . . . again. The nation is divided as to whether to give her points for trying or whether she is completely and utterly delusional, if not mad. So, here I am, watching the live footage of everyone arriving whilst also asking myself, do the ERG ever consider they might have an image problem, which is why they are so loathed? First IDS arrives in a Morgan, like Toad of Toad Hall. Next up is JRM with his mini-me sitting next to him in the Jag; his son is all tweeded up, with Harry Potter glasses. Then Raab arrives looking, well, like he usually looks: sweaty and just out of the gym, and wanting to kill people. And of course Gove, in a chauffeur-driven Range Rover. Boris comes in a car of the people, a scuffed-up Vauxhall or something similar, which mirrors his personal appearance. And Gavin Williamson is seen driving around in circles in a tank near Chequers, texting his boss to say he is just in the neighbourhood, and could he pop in for a cup of tea? People say owners look just like their dogs, and there is something in choice of car as well.

Anyway, it was quite a motley collection, a few Etonians, people called David, baldies and baddies. What was interesting was who wasn't there, most notably any women. Except one, but she doesn't count, despite being the PM, because she has totally lost the plot.

The upshot of it all is that the Brexiteers say they won't vote for her unless she quits, an invitation she declines . . . again.

26 March

In the lobbies last night, H comes up behind Mel Stride and Shrek (John Hayes), who are on the Gove campaign team.

'Hi, guys, how's the campaign going? Double figures yet? By that I mean two,' says H.

Shrek screws up his face and says, 'It's all very well having toffs in charge, it's all very decorative, but really . . . '

'Well, you did all right under Cameron as I recall, didn't you?'

On to the Green Chip dinner. A smaller group than normal, H says. Hancock, Gove, Rory Stewart, Stuart Jackson. Everyone going around in circles, no one knowing what the hell is going on. H tells me later that Rory went completely insane. He has apparently developed a serious twitch, as if a facial nerve is either malfunctioning or missing. Anyway, according to H, his eyes tightened, his face grimaced and he started pouting and portraying himself as some sort of saviour, as if some angel has stepped down from above and told him to save the people from famine and pestilence and fanatics. 'It's going to be Boris against me, and I'm going to take Boris down.' Implying he is the chosen one. The group tried to calm him down and told him this was unlikely, and that it would go to a Brexiteer, which seemed to come as something of a shock to him.

But that was the warm-up act compared to what Gove said, apparently. In an attempt to illustrate a version of the lesser of all evils of Brexit compromises he suddenly said: 'Rory, just imagine a jihadi broke into your house and the choice was either let the jihadi kiss Shoshana (Rory's wife) or something worse, which would you go for?' Everyone looks stunned. 'The point I'm making is that once you do one it is easier to do the other.' H told me that it looked as if Rory was about to thump him. It was left to Jackson to say, 'I think that is entirely inappropriate, Michael.' The Gover just looked surprised by the reaction. And there you have nutter Michael in a nutshell.

28 March

So, Ollie Letwin became PM for the afternoon (yesterday). This is the same Letwin that caused absolute anarchy in the Cabinet Office with potty ideas which were totally undeliverable 80 per cent of the time; the one who dumped parliamentary papers in a bin; and who once invited burglars into his home at 3 a.m. after they asked to use his loo. This is the man who thinks he can sort it out. Of course, anyone who knows Letwin knows whatever direction he takes, it will be the most difficult, indirect, uncomfortable, potholed, uphill, storm-tossed route possible. And yesterday he was true to form, taking hold of the parliamentary agenda and promoting sixteen – yes, sixteen – different options.

Except before that ridiculous vote there was a meeting of the 1922 at 5 p.m. And it was very packed and sweaty. Very, very sweaty, according to H. And at last, at bloody last, something indeed changed. She said she was going. Champagne corks popped, party streamers exploded ... well, not exactly. 'I know there is a desire for a new approach, and new leadership, in the second phase of the Brexit negotiations and I won't stand in the way of that.' And there was more: 'I am prepared to leave this job earlier than I intended in order to do what is right for our country and our party.' But the caveat was: you need to back my deal first.

30 March

Text exchanges between Benyon and H tonight:

Sorry to creep past Mark Francois' firewall but I was wondering if there was the smidgen of a chance of you supporting either of the 'softer' Brexit motions tomorrow? If you might, I, as a cheese eating surrender monkey would be delighted because (apart from the virtue of having some sort of Brexit in short order) I really want to get as many of us as poss to support them rather than see it get through with lots of Labour and just a few Tories. Happy to chat but if you get all technical with me, I will inflict a more tiresome advocate to answer any Mogg-like probings. Richard.

Hugo:

Monsieur Ben Yon

c/o Maison Petain

Rue de Vichy

Occupied Britain

Thank you. What I am looking for is the following:

1. See the quick removal of Madame May.

2. Avoid a General Election in which we would justifiably be vaporised.

3. Deliver somehow on what the people voted for in the

Referendum and on which WE stood for in the 2017 Manifesto.

4. Keep the party together.

5. Re-invent Conservatism and capitalism in the gig economy.

6. Take the battle to OUR ENEMY and win in 2022.

All these may be contradictory or impossible or both. I accept that. But I shall continue to try. In that regard I am prepared to look at anything in line with the above caveats. I have nothing particular to say about the likes of Boles, Letwin or Grieve, save to say they would have not fitted in the Grenadier Guards. And anyway, I have better things to do with my energies and time such as watch 'In the line of duty' which is about to start on BBC1 now.

As ever

Swire, Protector

3 April

Team meeting for the Raab campaign. The general consensus is that Dom needs some jokes. H says, 'I know one for the donors.'

'Yes, Hugo?' Wry smiles around the room. Most of them know it will be unsuitable.

Hugo tells Dom: 'You point to yourself and say, "Dom", and then you turn to them and say, "Non-Dom".'

4 April

Whoops, I've just seen a tweet that the House of Commons has been suspended because of a sewage leak in the chamber. The floods, fire and pestilence have begun. So has the tick-tock of the clock running down to freedom next Friday. A few hours later Uri Geller, he of spoon-bending fame tweeted: 'Yes, I did it @ HouseofCommons, I bent the pipes, and I won't apologise, you all deserve it! #brexit #startfromscratch'.

As it turned out, it wasn't a shitshow, as some have been calling Brexit, but a leak, which is perfectly normal for this place.

11 April

Britain is not saying goodbye to the EU tomorrow. The new departure date is Halloween. How fitting: it means this rocky horror show goes on and on, and if there is another extension, on and on again. It feels like Brexit is over. That the remainers have won. Old Ma May is going on holiday, and funny things happen when she goes on holiday, like calling an election, so we are all a bit nervous. H comes down to Devon. He has a death pallor and falls asleep in the sun almost as soon as he arrives.

Looking back at the EU summit, it is impossible to overestimate the sheer historic humiliation this PM has brought upon Britain. If she can't get a majority, she needs to make way for someone who can. But how many times has she been told that? Everyone has left for the recess in a state of depression. The only ones trying to stay upbeat are the leadership candidates. Raab has his first helicopter ride. H texts Nick de Bois: 'Did he enjoy it a little too much?'

'Yep!' comes the reply.

13 April

In *The Times* today, an interview with Rory Stewart: 'We need a standard bearer for the middle ground – it could be me.' And guess who's back to fill the political vacuum? Yes, Nigel Farage of the Garage. Up he pops, lights flashing, applause, usual stuff, mocking the elites, blah, blah, blah, slagging off the Tories. He's a good populist performer. Sigh! There he was yesterday, launching his new Brexit Party (his old one has gone too far to the right, even for him) in a venue of the people, a draughty metal-finishing factory in the West Midlands. But he's a natural, you can't take that away from him, no autocue, no notes, just good old-fashioned passion. Straight out the traps after the summit, and within hours nearly second in the polls. He offers people hope, but in reality he's just like the rest of us: he's a man without a plan for what Brexit means and how it's going to work.

I'm going to bed to read a book.

24 April

We finally think we have movement to boot out the old bat but find the 1922 is split down the middle about whether to change the rules. So, no change there then.

Meanwhile, the fragmentation of British politics continues apace. A press conference by the TiGs ... er, sorry, the Independent Party ... er, sorry, Change UK is called, with Serious Soubry elbowing everyone out the way to take the lead mike. She really needs to get a blow dry before she does these set pieces; her bird's nest hairdo just looked all mad professor. Only two months in and this burgeoning party is struggling with its brand identity. This could possibly be because it's the same old bunch of establishment elites, wanting to turn the clock back to the halcyon days of EU membership with the same old tired lines about a bloody people's vote. There was at least something new to announce: Rachel Johnson has apparently signed up, quite the coup! The thing is, if I were a hardcore remainer I would struggle with who to vote for, because it's quite a crowded field these days. There is Change UK, the Independent Group, the Lib Dems, the Greenies and the regionals, SNP and Plaid Cymru to choose from. But then, as Nick Watt, *Newsnight*'s political editor, put it, 'Isn't this all a case of the People's Front of Judaea versus the Judaean People's Front?'

H and I are increasingly concerned that we are going to be stuck sailing around the Greek islands with Nicholas Soames booming his remainer rebel views all over the Aegean. H tries to text him to see if he is accepting the Saïds' invitation this summer so we can come to a decision. He ignores H's texts. Then he cuts H in the dining room. Like all bullies, Nicholas does not like being confronted. 'Are you cutting me, Nicholas?' H asks him later. He splutters no and says that he is in a hurry to have dinner. H asks Benyon what's up with him. He replies: 'He doesn't like the fact that you are supporting Raab.' (Brexit's pin-up and all that.) And I'm sure he doesn't like the fact that Hugo's wife has views either.

25 April

Hugo is in White's, about to have dinner with DC, when his phone rings. It's Steve Willis, our builder/shooting friend from Devon, who is ranting down his mobile that the farmers are going mental, that H has to do something. H has to take the call into the telephone closet under the stairs and holds the phone away from his ear, Steve is so loud and cross. It's all to do with the ban on farmers shooting pest birds on their land without a special licence. The green blob, led by chiselled-jawed Chris Packham, have finally infiltrated Defra. People like Steve are going apeshit and say it's just the thin edge of the wedge.

H has a nice dinner with David. When they discuss the issue, he says, 'Bugger the farmers – what about people like me, who want to shoot pigeons out the window?' He thinks Gove, who is currently catering to the lobby groups in Defra, is certifiable. But we already know that.

He comes home saying Dave is looking lean and completely

relaxed, though he does concede he completely fucked up over Brexit. He tells H he doesn't want to do much more than he is doing now. A few jobs here and there, but otherwise chillaxing. Florence asks him, 'What you are doing today, Dad?' and he replies, 'Oh, I've got a meeting.' But she says he's a liar, and that she saw him watching back-to-back episodes of *Game of Thrones*. He loves his new house in Cornwall and is spending the entire summer there.

He is still very much pro-remain and says all cabinet ministers have backed May's deal and voted for it. He can't understand why the ERG hasn't come in behind. They discuss the leadership. 'Who would you vote for,' asks H, 'if you were in my position?'

'Hunt, probably.' But he adds that a lot of ministers who worked for him loathe him. David thinks it's probably Boris's for the taking. They discuss Raab. H goes through the options and Dave concedes he is in with a very good chance. He knows nothing about him other than that he promoted him. He was surprised to hear that some of the old Cameron donors were falling in behind him, such as carpet king Phil Harris.*

'Who would be the direct line to him?' Dave asks.

'Me,' replies H.

H asks Adam Holloway, 'What's up with Soames these days?'

'I don't know, I don't talk to him any more. I told him his problem is that he isn't the man he thinks he ought to be. Now, whenever I pass him in the corridor, I flick him a V sign and say, "Fuck off, Winston."'

It is not exactly Harmony Hall.

Another huge row has broken out over leaks from a meeting with Huawei. Spy chiefs are furious that the supposedly watertight

---

* Baron Harris of Peckham. Tory peer, philanthropist and educationalist.

meeting of the National Security Council appears to have fallen foul of Tory leadership jockeying. A senior Whitehall source warns: 'What this does is just undermines the ability for politicians to receive intelligence and candid advice.' A major inquiry is expected. The informed speculation is that it is Gavin Williamson. Hashtag anarchy. But Gavin seems abnormally bouncy if it was him.

1 May

May she stay, may she go. Mind you, no one has seen hide or hair of her for weeks now. They shouldn't hold their breath. A new study shows she is more evasive than her past three Tory predecessors as PM, answering only 11 per cent of her questions from Jeremy Corbyn. How she managed even 11 per cent is the talk of Westminster.

Meanwhile, the cabinet has been presented with two options, a second referendum or teaming up with Labour on supporting a customs union, which in effect is not Brexit. Both will end in calamity, of course. The government is up shit creek without a paddle.

Raab C. Brexit to H:

> Simon Keswick of Jardine Matheson offered me support at a Con Friends of Chinese event tonight. Geoffrey CB presided, so would have details

> H: OK. I know Simon. I'll call him

> DR. You know everyone 😉

> H: I don't know Beyoncé

> DR: Yet

2 May

H is in a meeting, giving Gove a beating on this cock-up with wild bird licences, when the news comes through about Rory's promotion and Soames virtually bursts into tears of joy and no doubt immediately starts texting the Prince of Wales. Gavin, however, is completely denying leaking the Huawei meeting, which, as H points out, he's not going to admit because he would be subject to a criminal investigation.

Dom is guest speaker at a breakfast at the Walbrook Club. Hugo sits next to Peter Palumbo,* who tells him its history, how it was built in the 1950s on an empty plot behind St Stephen's Walbrook by his father, the developer Rudolph Palumbo. The result is a success, but then of course Mark Birley was involved originally. Dom delivers a well-crafted and clever speech peppered, much to H's amazement, with some jokes and quips, which is encouraging. A big success, and H is approached afterwards by someone who wants to help but then says, inevitably, that he lives in Monte Carlo. On the way out, Jeffrey Archer approaches them in a conspiratorial manner and asks to have a private word. He made notes during the speech which he proceeds to run through in his usual bombastic way, interjecting that this is what he 'did for Margaret and for John'. He is impressed by Dom, which is good news.

   On the way out, H tells Dom that he's taking him shopping. He needs the uniform of the modern politician: plain shirts, strong single-colour ties, dark suits and good shoes. Then he doesn't even have to think about it. H feels on rather thin ground when he tells him this, as he is wearing a very loud Prince of Wales check suit and red socks, and looks like a bookie on the Curragh, but either Dom doesn't notice or is too polite to say.

   H congratulates him on the jokes. 'Ah,' he says proudly, 'they're

---

* Property developer and patron of the arts. Created a life peer in 1991.

coming in fast,' and produces from almost every pocket jokes that have been carefully typed out and laminated, as they are evidently going to be employed on numerous occasions.

3 May

The morning after the local elections. With 224 councils declared, the Conservatives have lost more than a thousand seats and Labour more than 110, while the Liberal Democrats have gained more than 530 and the Greens upwards of 130. UKIP, which is standing fewer councillors than in previous years, has lost eighty-five seats. The worst news for us is that the so-called 'independents' have taken control of East Devon. Claire Wrong is crowing from the rooftops because they are all 'her people' – by that, I mean of her left-wing persuasion.

6 May

Back from a bank holiday weekend with Greg and George. At Sunday lunch I sit next to the very well upholstered Sky News presenter Adam Boulton. He apparently knows me from years back, when he shared a flat with Carlo Gébler, Edna O'Brien's son, but I can't remember what I did yesterday, let alone thirty years ago.

Boulton makes no attempt to hide his remain credentials and is scathing of all Tories, particularly Raab, who he perceives as a ghastly 'right winger'. He says that the standard of today's politicians is appalling, and I suggest that it might be partly his fault, that good people don't go in because they want to avoid scrutiny from people like him, who are feeding a greedy twenty-four-hour news cycle.

Before lunch, I get a grilling from his wife, Anji Hunter, who is fizzing with character. She was Blair's Kate Fall, but with less power. She lays into me – nicely – for not having a career; she thinks that all women should have careers. I say, 'I was once a journalist . . . '

'But what are you doing NOW?' she barks back. It's always a weak point for me, particularly when they say something along the lines of 'I can see you would have done well in the workplace'. I tell her I never wanted to be 'out there', that I am actually a rather solitary figure. 'You don't come across as that,' she barks again.

14 May

H and Raab find a space in their diaries and head out for a shopping trip. H had to handle this carefully, of course, as he didn't want to come over as domineering or condescending, so he decided to sell Raab the Reagan line: 'If you look the part, you get the part.' He tells Dom that he needs to stock up now as he won't have time once he is at No 10. Dom reluctantly agrees: 'You say, I do, Hugo.'

So, they set off, Dom, Beth his spad and H, having blocked out three hours in the diary for this particular sartorial safari. H had it all planned but was inevitably told by the confident *I'm-a-spad-running-the-world* Beth that the shops H had suggested were totally wrong and that H was 'old' Conservative. 'After all, Dom, we have to remember Hugo is nearly sixty and his taste . . . Well, you know what I am getting at here,' she says, running her eyes up and down his Savile Row uniform. She informs the group that they will not be heading west to Lower Sloane Street, but east to megahipster Shoreditch. They wait ages for an Uber but H remains calm, while Beth has fun teasing him about his knowledge of Shoreditch.

It transpires Paul Stephenson, their main media/PR/marketing guru and everything else guy – and very nice to boot, according to H – has recommended a particular shop to Beth. On entering it H knows immediately it is wrong, but he sits quietly in the corner pretending he is on his mobile phone while Beth and Dom start to finger the goods. From the corner of H's eye, he can see rows of jackets with floral designs, one with Mappa Mundi not inside on the lining but unleashed on the jacket itself! He casts a discreet eye along a row of hanging suits each more garish than the next, some frou-frou, some luminous, so much so that he suspects not even Grayson Perry, or Sir Elton himself, would be seen dead in them. No, this won't do. It won't do at all for Dom's first appearance on the steps of No. 10, although it would certainly liven his image up a bit. Eventually they come over to H as a group and Dom says, 'Come on, let's go. Nothing here.'

'Why?' H asks innocently. 'Nothing in your size?'

Beth concedes they should now try Hugo's place, so almost an hour later, after a thirty quid taxi ride across London, they arrive at Oliver Brown in Lower Sloane Street. On the way there, Beth tells H that David and George got all their suits from Marks and Spencer, which H knows is not the case. Dom dives in, racks of suits are emptied and he goes off to get measured up. The fitter recognises him immediately and says that they used to make all the suits for David Cameron. 'Did he have them specially made?' says Beth with a furrowed brow. 'Well, we sort of did, really,' replies the tailor through the pins in his mouth. Beth looks irritated and H throws her a triumphant smile which she chooses to ignore.

They head into several more shops before returning to parliament drowning in bags, rather like Imelda Marcos in the January sales. H and Beth chuck Dom out of the taxi early so as not to be compromised, and then Beth and H, sweating like overladen mules, go in through separate entrances pretending they've just been on individual shopping trips. 'Well,' H says to Dom afterwards, 'in the unlikely event we are not successful getting you into No. 10, at least you'll win best-dressed backbencher of the year.'

16 May

The beauty contest continues, and the leadership campaign has not even started. Jeremy Hunt in the Commons, taking FCO questions. You could skid on the floor, it's so greasy. What is it about

Hunt? He has something of the head boy about him, the teacher's pet. Suddenly we are hearing about his interventions on defence spending, and a no-deal Brexit, swinging whichever way the wind turns. Oh, and pro-Trump to please the right wingers in the party. Do we really want such a goody-goody for leader?

And why is the human hedgehog James Brokenshire posing in his kitchen? It's not like anyone has ever heard of him . . . oh, OK, that's why. Because you only do the kitchen shot when you want to be leader. It's the *look at me, I'm normal* shot. Except that they never are – normal, that is. Brokenshire had two ovens, two ovens side by side. Of course, the article was a cover: he is a housing minister and he was talking about giving the young a lift up onto the housing ladder, but no one was listening because they were looking at those two bloody ovens of his. And that's not all: they also have two dishwashers. God, I dream of two dishwashers. Then he tried to laugh it off with another joke, even though we didn't get the first one: he tweeted a picture of him with Victoria sponge declaring, 'Amazing what you can rustle up! Maybe some more hot potatoes next! #twoovens'.

Ha ha, this is better than a spliff on a Saturday night.

It's all Raab's fault. He started it, all granite work surfaces and his and hers outfits matching the pastel blue tongue and groove. Raab thought the pictures were splendid, though, and they did look awfully nice as a couple.

But you think they would learn. Remember Ed Miliband had two kitchens. Nigel Farage's kitchen was a shoe box, probably because he was never at home and someone other than his wife was cooking him dinner. Gordon had an Ikea one he put on expenses and David resigned in his one at Dean, and Samantha spent huge sums of her own money having one installed at No. 10.

Maybe they should start moving the photo ops into the bedroom and slip open a few bedside drawers. Now that would really be interesting . . .

17 May

Hugo's and Brian Kingham's* dinner for about fifty donors. Raab is incredibly impressive on his feet, and I have seen some politicians in my time. A little nervous and sweaty to start off with, but he presents a true vision of what he believes in. He is strong on restoring discipline in the cabinet and on surrounding himself with a new and fresh team which will deliver Brexit. Long also on social justice and education.

I am half elated that at last there is someone I believe in but equally despondent because the membership is fixated by the flamboyance of Boris, who would of course be a car crash but is way ahead in the polls. What really comes across with Raab is his intelligence and experience with trade, business, law and foreign affairs, and of course Europe. You also get the sense that he would slice your head off if you didn't fall into line, which is quite a crucial characteristic if the Conservative Party is to survive this calamity and restore discipline.

Bellingham is trying to push both Hugo and me into accepting the post of Northern Ireland Secretary if Dom wins. 'Come on, Sasha, Hugo hasn't been in the cabinet yet.' I say absolutely not: Hugo will not be accepting anything, however big. We are done with politics. We have had enough.

When we come home, we hit the brandy and discuss what we will do if something is offered to him. Just as Bellingham is being sidelined, Dom has become increasingly dependent on H and now sees him twice a day. He will want him around if he wins. I think something drastic has to happen to Boris for that to happen, and we secretly pray the moment doesn't arise because it will upset all our carefully laid plans.

Hugo takes the Tarka line to Exeter after visiting the County Show, then on to London for John and Suzy Lewis's son's wedding.

---

* Serial entrepreneur, Tory donor and early backer of Dominic Raab.

On the train, he reads all the papers, which show Boris is way ahead in polls. He cuts out items for me to read about how to revive our sex life.

19 May

Amber rings.

I don't pick up, but text back: 'Amber, my darling, I'm so sorry, but I so fundamentally disagree with what you have been doing in politics and your approach to Brexit that I think if we had a "chat" it would go wrong. Let's wait until things calm down, or at least until there is an acceptance which way this is all going. XX'

23 May

Old Ma May resigned today. And I felt nothing, truly nothing, except a huge sense of relief.

'I will shortly leave the job it has been the honour of my life to hold . . . ' It was that word, hold, that did for her, as if she had dropped a Ming vase and was finally seeing the reality of the scattered pieces on the floor, and the cost of it all. The anguish started to flare in her voice. She had to push out the last few words before she pushed off back behind the black door. But before she went, she had a few words about compromise. 'Consensus can only be reached if those on all sides of the debate are willing to compromise,' she said. Was this the same woman who called an election, not to unite people around a single goal but to destroy those standing in the way of her plan? If she ever did compromise it was only to hang on to her job, and promiscuously so: she didn't care who she flirted with, as long as she got what she wanted.

26 May

Raab C. Brexit has a good interview on Marr. Lots of people ring and text H to say they are impressed, including Christopher Geidt, who is still plugged in to the establishment with a capital E. He asks H how Raab is going down in the parliamentary tearooms.

'Well,' H replies, 'it's our man or Boris. Boris dangerously far out in the field. We are nicely placed on the rails. All to play for.'

H speaks to DR afterwards, and congratulates him. It's the first outing of one of his new suits. 'There are only two people I need to keep happy, and that's you and Erika,' he tells H.

4 June

Trump press conference. May looked even more petrified than when Graham Brady went to see her. Trump is anything but predictable. He had already put out a rude tweet about the Mayor of London, even before landing on British soil. Then, at the conference, he goes and announces that everything is going to be on the table in any future trade deal, including the NHS, which sends a collective dagger into the heart of the nation. Raab C. Brexit quickly puts out a tweet, alongside Hands on Cock saying that it's not for sale which is a bit silly since the Americans are already getting their tentacles into our health system, such as owning private hospitals in London, including the one where the royal babies are tipped out. When asked about potential leadership candidates he says that Johnson and Hunt would both be good as PM but 'doesn't know Michael'. (A picture of Michael and him promptly goes viral.) He asks Hunt whether he thinks Michael will be good. And Alan Duncan is killing himself laughing in his waspish way (he's a Hunt man). There was a question about the protesters, and he replies it's all fake news, that in fact 'there were thousands of people cheering. Tremendous spirit and great love.'

Not from my daughter, who is somewhere near Trafalgar

Square under a huge balloon of President Trump in a nappy, listening to Jezza take the platform alongside former UK Muslim Brotherhood leader Anas Altikriti. Thank God they have shielded the Don from this nonsense. Next to Saffron is a loo paper sales-man with pictures of Trump printed on his product. Milk shakes are being thrown over non-believers because throwing milk shakes at non-believers is all the rage this year. Farage (banana and salted caramel) has had one, so has Tommy Robinson (strawberry); you are no one until you have been shaked, it seems.

I text her:

Can't believe you are falling for this Trump protest stuff. Of course, he's a terrible sexist sleazeball but America is our greatest ally, it's the office not the person we need to stay connected to. Your response is immature and not real politics.

'Your message is both predictable and pathetic,' she replies. *I'm not giving up so easily.*

He is also here for D Day celebrations when many Americans lost their lives to save our nation. Office not Person.

And again:

Enduring partners. Transatlantic alliance. Shared values of culture and justice and security. Office not person.

And again:

He is the guardian of our friendship. He stood by us during the Russian poisoning in Salisbury. In Syria he bombed ISIS alongside us and the French to get rid of that awful regime. We are now working through new challenges on cybercrime. Our economies are linked. 190 billion a year.

Finally:

Can't speak, out protesting.

Me again:

You don't change someone's mind by not speaking to them like Corbyn. You engage. That's politics.

(I send her ugly video footage of a Trump supporter being mauled by anti-Trump protesters.)
Me again:

Nice people you are mixing with these days!

'Have fun being on the wrong side of history,' she replies.
Text her a picture of the rubbish protesters left behind.

Thought you lot were into the environment? Could have fooled me. It's just all virtue signalling. Blame someone else always so you don't have to pick up the mess.

Bloody youth, always wrapped up in a soft duvet of idealism.

I know Trump is a filthy, racist misogynist, but he did say he was going to put us at the front of the queue for a trade deal. Everyone seems a little bit nervous of this which is baffling. It's all based on chlorinated chicken and chips, everyone seems to think this is a disgusting thing to trade in but what they don't realise is that UK consumers ingest far more chlorine in drinking water than they would eating a Kentucky Fried Chicken. In fact, UK salads are routinely chlorine washed. Remain ministers have spent far too long cosying up to European markets that are highly protection-ist, no wonder they are not interested in doing stuff with the US.

Personally, I'd like some of their cancer knowhow and machines in our NHS. And what's to be frightened of? Free trade is an exchange, a form of mutual co-operation that can only take place when both sides profit.

7 June

The leadership campaign is turning into the usual bunfight. Boris is way out front and H says Dom is languishing a bit. The team just aren't getting the numbers. But then the first attack hasn't started, let alone the heavy shelling, so anything can happen.

Boris's team, headed by the girlfriend, have him under very tight wraps and it's working, but he can't shy away from hustings and interviews for ever. In fact, next week he will have to show some leg. The maddening thing is that Dom's team have by far and away the best infrastructure and organisation, from the whipping operation through to press and fundraising – H's main area. H has raised a huge amount of money and he's still getting pledges for more. Of course, these pledges will only be turned into cash if Dom is one of the final two to go out to the membership. What is interesting about the campaigners is how all the respective teams know each other and the candidates. Some in the Raab team have in the past worked for Boris and Michael Gove. They have a camaraderie but do not let their friendships stand in the way of getting their man into No. 10. Things haven't got too dirty yet, but they will start to soon.

Hugo is struggling to get his party membership card, because without it he can't vote in the leadership contest. He has evidence of a standing order to show he is actually a paid-up member, but it is proving almost impossible as CCHQ have been inundated with thousands of people in the same situation. It is being blamed on Vote Source, the latest hopeless bit of IT used by CCHQ in a long line of equally useless experiments with 'modernisation'. Sue has been badgering Hugo's former researcher Stuart Pilcher, now at

CCHQ, who confesses that there is even a possibility that one of the candidates is not actually a member of the party. Sue promises not to tell anyone, and immediately tells Hugo. She makes him promise not to tell anyone, and H immediately passes it on to the team, but tells them to check that Dom is fully paid-up before using it. How magnificent it would be if it was Boris. Not impossible, although some think it is more likely to be Rory Stewart. All good stuff. Will Raab win? Looking more doubtful, but not impossible. It's still early days and much to play for.

9 June

Gove goes on Marr, and it's a disaster. He has been all over the papers for admitting taking cocaine. Trouble is, when he was Education Secretary he published a set of regulations on the prohibition of teachers for misconduct. Included in his list of offences that would lead to a lifetime ban from teaching was possession of class A drugs. An offence which he confesses to have committed several times. We had all the apologies and *I'm the adopted son of fishermen* stuff in mitigation. And he quickly dismissed suggestions he could be prevented from visiting the US as PM because of their ESTA form, which asks 'have you' or 'haven't you' on the drug question. He also denied it came up when he was vetted on becoming a minister, which H says is entirely plausible: he doesn't think that ministers are questioned in this way on taking up their office. Gove wriggled and squirmed, even the contrite lines didn't seem to work, and H and I squirmed with him. It was agony.

'I'd be fucked on this one,' H says.

'Well, darling, they say it's a middle-class habit.'

'Yes, I would say: I'm no expert on the habits of the middle classes. At our dinner parties, the butler passes around the cigars and port.'

'I think that would be worse than saying you took it.'

'How about: well, as an MP, I've never taken it, and I've been an MP for twenty years?'

'Better.'

'Or: I adhere to the principle of non-incrimination.'

'That immediately incriminates you.'

'I know: I've never taken it since becoming an MP, but don't ask any of my friends, my family, or my entire generation if they have.'

'Hugo, say nothing. That's the best line to take, other than the drug one.'

'No, I've got it! Ask me the question again.'

'Sir Hugo, have you ever taken drugs?'

'Five-one-zero-three-nine-four.'

'Excuse me?'

'Five-one-zero-three-nine-four.'

'What's that?'

'That's my army number, the only thing I'm trained to give under hostile interrogation.'

'Like I said, darling, best say nothing.'

14 June

H goes on Sky News. On the whole, I have encouraged him not to do any TV because he is not long on detail and he is very, very short on political correctness, which is always a concern for those that know and love him.

At one point he says to Adam Boulton, 'What is it with the Stewarts? They're always trying to set up alternative parliaments.'*

'But Rory Stewart is only trying to lead you across to the Methodist Hall in Westminster.'

'Well, if he was proposing to set up a parliament somewhere less wet, and hotter, I might follow him, but I'm not following him to the Methodist Hall.'

---

* The Stuart kings Charles I and Charles II established alternative parliaments at Oxford in the seventeenth century.

17 June

Boris a no show at the Channel 4 debate. In mitigation, it was Father's Day and he must have had a lot of house calls to make. But Bozzo's courtiers are doing a very good job of keeping him away from the electorate, in case he says what he really thinks. He was probably watching it with Carrie, enjoying the blue-on-blue blows. She will have been satisfied with placing nice puff articles, about how lovely she is and what a perfect First Lady she will make, with her ex-boyfriend Harry Cole in the *Mail on Sunday.*

Rory Stewart, who was clapped to the rafters by the supposedly floating voter audience, was at his tonto best. When it was suggested he didn't believe in Brexit he compared it to trying to 'cram a whole series of rubbish bins' into a larger bin, against his wife's advice. He wanted to say, 'Believe in the bin, believe in Britain.' To which those of us at home were thinking, this man needs to be sent to the bin, not filling them.

18 June

I am down a rabbit hole in the under-rooms of the Palace of Westminster. This is the ground zero, below the church, the burial plot, where worms wriggle.

The official who is showing a group of us around first opens a black door with a red sign: B62E. We crowd around. Discussion and dissection follow. We are looking at a riser, a void, apparently, except it is extremely congested, like an overstuffed broom cupboard but filled with services instead. Think Spaghetti Junction in a cupboard. It is part of a maze of inaccessible Victorian shafts through which services pass, but which could provide potential routes for fire, hell and damnation in a matter of minutes. It is why the fire safety team patrol the estate every minute of every day.

This is what years of untouching the untouchable looks like;

it's when the doctors stand at the edge of a patient's hospital bed, making notes, drawing up reports, diagnosing but failing to treat. It is a denial, a fear that any operation will just complicate matters. It is a story about dithering over repairs because of an innate dread that British politics will be changed for good.

Another door is unlocked; it opens onto the start of a labyrinth of passages and our guide switches on an LED light which illuminates the drama of rows and rows of pipes and cables, thousands of them running riot. Every wire seems to be pushing and scuffling and nudging for space, countless numbers run horizontally in silence, others thrum and tick. No one knows what many of them are for or where they are going; the layering is too thick to gain access. They just lie on top of one another, waiting to cause trouble.

We walk on through the tunnels, up and down steps, duck low-hanging pipes, pass red cages holding unit boards, go through smoke ventilation doors, pass plant rooms, step over puddles of water.

'Move quickly now,' he says suddenly, 'I don't know what that noise is.'

We stop in an underground chamber, surrounded by a different odour now. This is where parliament's shit gathers, in two giant cast-iron containers, before ejection into the drains. They have been here since 1888 and might fail at any time. It somehow seems appropriate, given what lies above.

Everywhere we go the signs of decay are prevalent. Turn right, turn left, and it's there. I become almost forensic with my attention. These scenes from the depths of the internal somehow make me feel as if I am studying the structure of the human body. The body's interior is not a thick soup or made up of meat-like flesh, it is, like this interior, divided into discrete organs with vital connections, blood vessels and nerves. Only when all the systems work together efficiently can health be maintained. Like all systems, skeletal, cardiovascular, electrical, sewage, they may all work as separate entities, but each is dependent on the other for physical and biochemical support. But the Palace is sick. Really sick. The immune system that protects it is being threatened by subversion from within; it can no longer defend itself. Defences and barriers are down. It is on the edge of collapse. It feels like a metaphor for our whole political system.

19 June

Raab is out. I don't sleep all night. The absolute fear of letting the Blond and his mistress, and his whole Kardashian family, elbowing each other out the way to get into the limelight, into No. 10 has brought on a bout of political melancholia. H and I, like everyone else, will now be shutting our eyes and holding our noses as we put our crosses in Boris's box. Because, really, no one knows which Boris we are getting: the clown, the journalist, the adulterer and liar, the sensitive one, the big-mouth one, the messy one, the clever one. Pictures have been circulating of his car, which is beyond sordid. What we won't be getting is someone who is manageable or trainable; Boris likes to shake things up, break the rules, take the speeding fine then speed again.

Good Boris likes getting rid of regulations, spy satellites (well, that figures, with all his shagging around), rights-first culture and reverse discrimination. Good Boris laughs at pomposity and grandiosity, so he was never going to like the European Union. He might have said 'fuck business' and caused an uproar, but really those two words were very telling. They weren't referring to business at all, but the holier than thou bodies that represent it. He will be the complete antithesis of what has preceded him: liberal, open to issues like legalising cannabis, tolerant of people's foibles and weaknesses. But Bad Boris, the Boris we fear, is the casual one, the one that can't be bothered to read spreadsheets, the one that misses deadlines, the one that makes everything into a joke, the one that trusts everyone and no one. We wait with bated breath . . .

26 June

I have slinked off to Devon to avoid the clusterfuck. My blues
are real; I am tired and tearful and want to hide under my
duvet. Not only are the children exhausting me, Walpole
Street is under scaffolding, the neighbours are repointing so I
have to wade through brick and dust, and H is a coiled spring
about his future, for when it all goes tits up, which it will.
In the meantime, the Maybot has been trying to empty the
Treasury coffers in a bid to provide herself with a legacy, which
has involved cramming three years' worth of domestic policy
announcements into three weeks (yesterday it was all about
new design standards for house builders). The chamber clears
whenever she turns up. Oh, and Mark Field lost his job as an
FCO minister after grabbing an eco-protester at a banquet in
Mansion House in the City of London. He was trying to protect
the guest speaker, Philip Hammond. Most of us wonder why he
bothered stopping her.

Before I left for Devon, H and I had a drink with Gove and Mel
Stride in the pub, and there was a general sense of gloom. Mel
had seen some poll that showed almost every Devon MP will lose
their seat to the Brexit Party. Michael was only really interested
in how the Carrie story is going to harm Boris. The following
night, H stays on with him after a Green Chip dinner. He clearly
is suffering from the wind-down and another episode of his
ambition being thwarted. He asks H what he should do, and H
advises him to go with grace to the back benches and behave,
and see what happens. Hugo says he is too much of a talent to
be ignored. Michael tells H that he is having a coffee with Dave
next week, which will be the first time they have seen each other
since their acrimonious divorce.

1 July

Boy George announces he is divorcing Frances after twenty-one years of marriage. It was a long time coming. Dave texts K to ask what is going on. She replies she has no idea. The collective Cameroon thinking, though, is that he is having a mini meno-pause, that he has decided to throw all his toys out of the pram and run off and become the head of the IMF or something similar, so he can be 'someone' again. He is apparently unimpressed by Dave's post-government career and doesn't want to end up like him. It's worth pointing out, however, that Dave does have a happy family life and is very immersed in it.

12 July

My ballot paper hasn't arrived yet so I might not be voting at all.

Holiday plans go from bad to worse. Siena goes on her leavers' trip to Crete, the post A-levels destination of choice. Malia is filled with bars selling petrol at one euro, bouncers, party cruises, vile drunkenness, tattoos, hangovers, sunburn, STDS and rivers of blood and vomit. I try not to imagine my beautiful, pure daughter is about to be initiated into a real-life version of *Love Island*. These over-cossetted private school children have absolutely no knowl-edge of real life, having been told for the last seven years how brilliant they are, and that they all will become prime minister if they try hard enough.

Anyway, we get the inevitable call that she has fallen down the stairs and is in A&E. I don't take it, because I've got Brexit depression and I've taken a sleeping pill. H comes into the bed-room, panicking.

'Deal with it,' I say, and the walls start vibrating from my deep snoring again.

'I wasn't drunk, Dad!'

'What, at two-thirty in the morning? Seriously, Siena, am I meant to believe that?'

She hobbles home on crutches, and we have to cancel the back-packing tour of the motherland, Slovenia. We also cancel Greg and George in Ibiza. Looks like it's the West Country for us!

14 July

OMG, Amber is on *Andrew Marr*, reversing so far up the drainpipe that my jaw clunks to the floor, as heavy as a drawbridge in a medieval fortification. On the programme, she is saying she accepts no deal has to be part of the leverage for negotiation, which as we know is the *de minimis* for being a Borista. I'd like to remind her that it was her earlier shenanigans, taking no deal off the table, that got us into this mess in the first place.

Alan Duncan and David Gauke have resigned, and also Margot James (I like her). So has Hammond, who has caused all kinds of trouble, saying he won't vote for his own government if it goes for no deal. Rory also due to pack it in, although he wasn't around much anyway: he's become a one-man travelling circus.

If Boris wins, which is anticipated, he will be left with a working majority of just one seat if the Conservatives lose the Brecon by-election next month. So, the odds that he will be the shortest-serving PM are pretty high. Another election could be quite inconvenient, especially since he has been so busy out shagging, divorcing his wife, not talking to his children, rowing with his girlfriend and pissing off his constituents, who claim they have to wait about nine months to see him. A wafer-thin majority there as well. No wonder he doesn't want an election any time soon.

24 July

Yeeeeeesssss! She's gone! The Maybot has gone! Hurrah, hurrah! All change at the top and bottom. BoJo elected leader, and Jo Swinson elected leader of the Lib Dims.

Then, yesterday, we had the MPs (including Amber) tripping over themselves to get into the cabinet, clapping until their hands burnt when it was announced in Queen Elizabeth Hall that the Blond had made it comfortably over Jeremy Oilslick. (Don't know why they are bothering: there is about two and half minutes left before an election has to be called.)

So, Boris told us that the sun was shining. Our future was assured. That he was going to prove to all the gloomsters and doomsters he is the booster-rooster who can deliver the goodsters. Deliver! Unite! Defeat! Dud? No! DUDE. The E stands for energise, apparently. He also said, in a conciliatory tone, that he knew that there were people in this very room, indeed even among his colleagues, who question the wisdom of what the Conservatives have done. *Yeah – and you're all the walking dead, because in twenty-four hours I'm going to get rid of all of you in my first reshuffle.*

The big shock announcement so far (today) is that leave guru Dominic Cummings has been summoned back into the fold as Boris's chief adviser. *The remain-loving civil service must be collectively fainting – the Guardianistas certainly are. It is the second hottest day of the year, and this might just finish them off.*

What a day! Even champagne socialist Saffron rings up and says it's as if a large, flat, grey stone has been lifted off the nation's head, and all the dull creepy crawlies in No. 10 are being flushed out into the daylight and the sun is finally shining again on the leave cause! Of course, this lot have no majority to do anything and there will probably be an election, but we will park that one just for the moment.

27 July

Reshuffle. And it was a cracker!

Cummings: Put in who you like, Boris, but there is no way any of them will have more power than me.

The spin was that the top jobs went to those who were born to second-generation immigrants. The interesting thing about that is they usually have a drawbridge mentality, which means they espouse reactionary politics and are the least progressive of the lot.

And it wasn't a Brexiteer big tent. Steve Baker was given a minor job and rejected it because of its 'powerlessness'. And Mark Francois wasn't even offered one. Cummings's hand, I suspect.

Raab C. Brexit gets Foreign Secretary and Deputy Prime Minister. So proud of H. He really did help put him on the map. There was a picture of Dom, sitting on his new desk in the FCO, and he looked so damn hot with his thin tie and tight white shirt, with his legs wide open. If I were a woman half my age . . .

Then we had Priti Patel, who was sacked for trying to unilaterally change Britain's policy towards Israel on holiday with Lord Pillock, I mean Polak. She's gone to the Home Office. The Count also in, as leader of the House. Marvellous. Chris Grayling gone, Fox gone, Boring Brokenshire gone. I mean, everyone *gone*. Penny Mordaunt sacked as Defence Secretary. Maybe he got confused when she said she wanted to remain . . . in the job.

Matt Hands on Cock still there, probably warming the PM's loo seat as I write, and Amber stays at Work and Pensions.

8 August

Up in London, our current Rasputin figure (Cummings) is sending rockets up the arses of anyone in range (spads, ministers, civil servants, the Queen, Dominic Grieve, probably Boris).

Thing is, we all know Cummings is stark raving mad (you just need to look at his blog) but we are hoping that his maverick, radical, lunatic streak is what just might, possibly, get us over the line. I discuss him with Dominic Lawson, who is down holidaying in West Penwith and who is an old friend. He tells me he is a genius, but he is so bloody rude to everyone, particularly politicians, that he is absolutely loathed by the establishment. His father, Nigel Lawson, had complained to Dominic about his abruptness and he was a prominent leaver and Sir John, who met him on several occasions during the Brexit campaign, also says he is utterly 'appalling'.

Down at the other lunatic asylum/snake pit, Mac the Knife (John McDonnell) pops up to say that if Boris doesn't go when they tell him to, he'll put Jezza in a taxi and send him off to the Queen to tell her they will form a government instead. (Just shows how out of touch they are – no one takes taxis these days, they take Ubers or public transport.) Trouble is, McDonnell has just told the SNP they can have another referendum, so the Queen is hardly going to agree to assisting in breaking up the union, and would she really want to hand power over to a bunch of Marxists?

20 August

It felt like the Last Supper. Well, the last interesting supper of our political lives, probably of our whole lives. When we left, it felt as if we were walking off into the sunset with the closing credits.

It was a small and select dinner at No. 10 (Fox, Damian Green and wife, Eddie Lister,* Mike Penning and wife, Danny Kruger† and Boris). I was in pride of place on the PM's right, but didn't behave in a particularly ladylike manner. This was confirmed today by Damian Green's secretary, who complained to Sue that I was shouting down

---

* Chief strategic adviser to Boris Johnson. Formerly chief of staff and deputy mayor for policy and planning during Johnson's tenure as mayor. Former Tory leader of Wandsworth Council. Knighted in 2011.
† Former speechwriter to David Cameron; awarded the MBE for charitable work. Boris Johnson's political secretary.

the table, telling my husband not to drink too much wine and not to put salt on his food, and that I was probably drunk. Not true! I had one glass of the white. I was only doing it on account of his blood pressure readings, which for the last two days have been telling us he is headed for the exit lounge. Sue tells me later that Mrs Green is a very good friend of Marina. Certainly, Boris looked very reluctant to engage with her, and just did the bare minimum to be polite.

Before dinner, I say to Danny Kruger that I have been trying to work out how the grouping came about. From the simple 'they are not on sun loungers in August and we need to keep them on side' to 'supporters of other leadership bids' and the 'cabinet-reshuffle disappointed', to 'endgame careers'. Kruger smiles; one of them was clearly right. As we all wait for Boris, we complain about the wine, and discuss how Liam Fox is writing a book about pandemics and how Green is still pretty bitter about being sacked by Old Ma May when there were far more dishonourable members of the cabinet playing tricks on her. And the inevitable when is the election coming conversation.

H is tucked into some room, telling Boris he's off at the next election but that he wants to get involved in a specific project after he has left the Commons. He puts it to Boris, who is enthusiastic: 'Let's do it, Hugo!'

The First Lady is a no show, she has pissed off to Greece, apparently, which disappointed H enormously. He had refused to wear his blood-pressure monitor, because he thought he might get to sit next to her, which would excite him so much it would send his reading off the Richter scale.

Dinner is amusing. Boris is about the best placement you can get. Cheeky. Flippant. Enthusiastic. Bombastic. Ebullient. Energetic. We have a good laugh.

I kick it off: 'You can't serve this food, it's disgusting. You'll never convert a remainer with this slop.'

'Cripes, it's not that bad, is it?'

'Goat's cheese and figs? The goat's cheese is three Dairylea triangles crushed together. It's inedible.'

'Here, Sasha.' He makes me a sandwich: a lump of butter, followed by a piece of rocket, a fig, because he thinks a piece of bread might improve it.

I accept. He stuffs in more mouthfuls and knocks back the cheapo plonk at an alarming rate. I look at his rotund build, thick, creased neck, pale, sweaty face, and characteristic dishevelled appearance; he looks back, as if he is working out if I'm shaggable or past my sell-by date. He'd probably do the same if a sheep walked in the room. He has definitely lost that *I've lost a lot of weight because I am committing adultery and my children won't talk to me and my girlfriend is hot* look. I reckon other things are on his mind and he has returned to comfort eating.

'Bloody hell, Boris, you only went and won it. How did you do that?' I say.

He tells me he is still pinching himself, it's as if it's all a dream. He can't quite believe it himself. I tell him I wouldn't have voted for him, and he asks me why. I say Dominic Raab looks a whole lot better in a tight white shirt. He looks half amused and half wounded. Boris needs to be loved at all times.

'You're related to Joe Strummer, aren't you?' he says with his mouth full.

'No, that's Hugo. His stepsister Lucinda was married to him—'

'Marvellous man, Joe Strummer, marvellous, I loved him.'

'In fact,' I say, 'Hugo has two claims to fame, that one, and the other is that he stepped out with Jerry Hall.'

Boris's jaw drops onto the table.

'Hugo ... and Jerry Hall? Never!'

He proceeds to shout down the table: 'Hugo! Did you shag Jerry Hall?' Everyone turns to look at Hugo, who is rapidly reddening. 'I can confirm there was a brief romance,' says H. The other wives look appalled by this unexpected turn in the conversation, as does Green, who looks particularly exercised, which is a bit rich. H turns back to Eddie Lister, quickly seeking a diversion.

Boris and I discuss briefly what happens next, and he clearly doesn't know. 'Prorogue,' I whisper in his ear. 'Yes, prorogue, I agree,' he whispers back.

'Just don't bloody tell anyone.'

'Yes, let it happen naturally, what?'

We talk about Amber. I say she is a dyed-in-the-wool remainer, and ask how will he reconcile that if she is in the cabinet.

He looks crestfallen. 'But I love Amber. Can't stand her brother Roland, though, he's a ghastly little man.'

There is a discussion about social care. Boris rejects Damian Green's idea of insurance. We move on to railway lines, HS2, which are good, which not so good, and moving freight through the Channel Tunnel, and extending broadband. He articulates a vision which is based on building: a sort of Victorian, grand project programme. He calls himself a 'Brexiteer Heseltine'. I mumble that I don't think Heseltine would find that very flattering.

'No, he absolutely hates me.'

He then shouts to Eddie: 'Let's get Hezza on side, Eddie. Bring him in.'

There is quite a lot of praise for George Osborne from Fox, Boris and Green. (Boris has been on the phone to the Americans, trying to persuade them to support George for the IMF.) David Cameron's name is not mentioned once throughout the whole dinner.

Boris is, in many ways, an island, a spinning, mad island. He gets by having very good people to do the work, and the detail. 'Cummings, he's an excellent chap, we have a really good team in here now.' The atmosphere is certainly different as you walk in to No. 10. Everyone is smiling, despite the fact they are on death row. And even though he is an island he seems, like Trump, to be much more in touch with the people and the provinces. I don't know what will happen to him, because events make politicians, but I have changed my view of him. Yes, he is an alley cat, but he has a greatness of soul, a generosity of spirit, a desire to believe the best in people, a lack of pettiness and envy which is pretty uncommon in politics, and best of all a wonderful comic vision of the human condition. He is not like any politician I have ever encountered before, and I have met many. You can't quite believe he is there. In that job! But he is and it's going to be a hell of a ride.

'I can't really sleep at night,' he says. 'It's all so worrying.'

He says he reads poetry every night before going to sleep and he's going to get a dog, which might help.

At the end of the evening, Eddie Lister is clearly dying to go home but Boris is having none of it, he is having fun and doesn't want to return to his boxes and empty flat and bed where he lies awake all night because of what comes next. He comes downstairs with us, and doesn't want us to go. David was always one for pushing you out the door, in quite a brusque way. For all his hinterland and hot young vixen and his agile mind, Boris just comes across as someone who is desperately lonely and unhappy on the inside.

30 August

Political dynamite. Boris has revealed his prorogation plan. We are all saying, it's cool, it's only four days, and he wants to have a new Queen's speech, but of course it's all tactics. Bercow was on his sun lounger and must have choked on his piña colada.

3 September

H nips off to No. 10 for a pre-session drinks reception.

H says there is a good vibe. Gallows humour? Amber beckons H over and asks, 'Is your wife speaking to me?' H replies that whilst I love her as a person and as a friend, it is probably best to wait until Brexit is resolved before seeing each other, otherwise there might be fireworks. Ridiculous to let politics come between friendship, but it often does, I'm afraid.

Amber asks if H has had a good summer and he replies archly that he has been busy watching the political pilates going on. Amber has demonstrated nothing but flexibility in her political principles and positions of late. H thinks she and Matt Hancock have reduced themselves in the eyes of most colleagues and that they now know it. Everyone is saying, why did Boris and Carrie get a puppy when they already have Matt Hancock?

She shows H her iPhone, saying a girlfriend had just sent her a photo of a typical reaction to current events. It is of H jumping over a hurdle at the Westminster Dog of the Year competition a few years back with his hair all over the place. She won't say who sent it.

H leaves No. 10 and there are messages on his mobile. An irate Dominic Raab asking where he is, as they are meant to be having dinner in White's together. Not an entirely good place to wait, I would say. H jumps into a taxi and rushes over there. Raab orders fish and no wine, as he has his first Foreign Office questions the next day. H orders grouse and large quantities of wine. They have a good chat, ranging over a number of things, and H offers him a lot of advice. Dom is thinking of moving into Carlton Gardens, the Foreign Secretary's official residence in London, but quite rightly waiting until after an election to see if we win, and secondly if he is reconfirmed in office. He says to H that the FCO are very pleased he is First Secretary of State. And that he thinks he has a Rolls-Royce team around him.

H tells him that he is not standing again. Dom says he is sorry but understands, that H is a young fifty-something and can make a go of something else while he has the chance. Soames and Benyon appear. Soames looks over in horror at Hugo and Raab C. Brexit and exclaims loudly, 'Oh my God, that's the limit!' which outrages Hugo, particularly on account of its rudeness, but also because he, Hugo, is in his own club and Raab is his guest, and someone who just happens to be the Deputy Prime Minister and Foreign Secretary, and a senior member of the party which Nicholas still professes to be part of. H tells Dom he must go over to their table when they leave, which he does, crouching at Nicholas's feet, and talking quietly and respectfully to him.

H sees Raab out, and then joins Nicholas and Richard. Richard is still wailing about the party having become the Brexit Party. H doesn't think he is going to stand again. Nicholas, who predictably is now saying how marvellous Raab is, says he won't either, but we suspect he will; he will find it very difficult to give up his elder statesman platform, particularly on Twitter. Though he might have the whip withdrawn for voting against the government. H drinks even more and has an excellent time. He returns home somewhat the worse for wear, to be heavily reprimanded by me.

'No more drink as of tomorrow, and the blood pressure pills start. That's an order.'

6 September

I have the very deep fear that Boris is losing this. But all the other options are bananas. Labour are saying they will negotiate a Brexit deal, have a second referendum and campaign against their deal for remain. The Lib Dems won't back an election because they want a second referendum, and if leave wins they won't respect it but if remain does that then ends it. The SNP want to stop Brexit and then leave the UK. All Boris, who is now a lame duck, can do is bypass the media and put his message out direct to the people, and all indications are that they are frothing with fury at the gate.

And if it couldn't get any worse for him, Jo Johnson commits fratricide by quitting his ministerial post, and his seat, bringing the grand total of exiting Tories up to twenty-two. When half your mates, and even your brother, do a runner and you are someone who needs to be loved, you are not having a good day.

Hugo has had two dinners in the House on two consecutive nights this week which just confirmed his intention to leave the place.

At the first dinner he sits next to Damian Green, and is careful not to reignite memories of the recent dinner at No. 10 where Green clearly thought Boris and I were out of control. H asks him what he thinks is going on. Hardly an original conversation-opener, but it is the only question anyone is asking around Westminster. He smiles with his thin lips and says that he has been told the whole thing is a set-up by Dominic Cummings and Michael Gove. Allegedly, Cummings, who is at heart a Gove man, is trying to create so much chaos and havoc that Boris is forced to resign. At that point, we all look to a saviour who can strike a more conciliatory note with Europe, who will reach out to those who have lost the whip and who is himself nervous about a no-deal Brexit. That man? Why, Michael Gove of course. Far-fetched, but not impossible.

The next night, Trish Morris* beckons H over and is her usual charming and chatty self. She introduces H to her dining companion, but he fails to catch her name or recognise her. What he does catch is her eye, and she his. A flicker of recognition crosses her face. H returns to his own table none the wiser and thinking no more of it. Suddenly there is a commotion behind him. Some old lags, including Greg Knight and Tim Kirkhope, are involved in an argument. The argument turns out to be with their neighbour, the unknown woman who he was introduced to earlier, who turns out to be the glamorous Baroness Mone, the bra tycoon. They have no idea who she is, and Greg is complaining about her being in the dining room for members. The argument gets more heated and Sir Paul Beresford has to intervene; he tries buttering up the noble Lady. Of course, what they don't realise is that she is a proper Glaswegian, and she gives as good as she gets. Better, in fact. She is cursing and getting redder and redder and is only just stopped from decking Greg Knight. Eventually, she is somewhat calmed, and leaves the room whereupon the boys' table take up their chuntering again. H said he would definitely have joined in on the Baroness's side, had there been a fistfight.

---

* Baroness Morris of Bolton, OBE, DL. A former vice-chairman of the Conservative Party and chairman of the Conservative Middle East Council 2010–15.

8 September

Absolutely apoplectic with rage. Amber resigns the Tory whip and leaves the government. She also says she won't stand again in Hastings, but will fight somewhere safer as an independent 'conservative'. Soames's seat being mooted.

> Greg to H: Is no one staying? Don't forget to turn off the lights when you leave.

> H: I may now have to stay to lead the party.

> G: I'm in. First sane idea of the week. Can I be your deputy from the Lords? We could do away with the manifesto and issue our favourite Sotheby's sale catalogue instead.

> H: Cabinet to meet for cocktails?

> G: Everyone needs a cocktail cabinet.

> H: Unless they are off their trolley?

> G: Talking of which, had you any inkling of what Amber was up to?

> H: No. Fucking disgrace. Orchestrated by Roland R and Mandy, I suspect. She was going to lose Hastings anyway. She signed up to the possibility of a no deal when she rejoined the cabinet. She has anyway lost all credibility. You will not agree of course.

> G: Well, I admire her for resigning from the Cummings cabinet, shooting the 21 was a deliberate act of civil war but to me it also looks like a mirror image of the way Boris and DD resigned (after a bit) from TM's cabinet.

H doesn't reply, but says to me with a long groan, 'I'm not going to have any friends after this. I think I'm just going to keep my mouth shut from now on.'

9 September

Battle lines drawn, swords unsheathed. H steps back into the breach for what may be some of his last days in parliament, and certainly his most dramatic. Boris has six votes to win and loses all of them, calling an election and the publication of the Operation Yellowhammer contingency plans among them. So, no election for the moment. The remainer coalition refuses to give him one as they are running scared of unfavourable polls.

Then Old Ma May's resignation honours list, which included a cricketer who had been prosecuted for domestic abuse (Geoffrey Boycott) and the usual backroom boys and girls of No. 10. The problem is that this lot of bag carriers failed in every task they were given.

H attends the third-term dinner. Everyone is telling Richard Benyon how sad they are at him standing down. H stays schtum, although Richard knows H is now also headed for the exit. Conversation moves on and Hugo reminds the doom-monger of the group, William Hague, that at one of these dinners a few months ago he had said how he'd looked at the situation from every angle and concluded that they were boxed in. William says, in his unmistakable lilting Yorkshire brogue, 'Ah yes, but then the box was made of caaaaardboard, mmmmmmm. Now it's made of metal, heavy metal at that.' And, warming to his theme, he says that now the box is in fact a coffin, and sits back, pleased with his analogy. They all speculate on what is going to happen or not going to happen. Because that's all they can do. Speculate.

H comes home at 1 a.m., tired and incensed, ranting about how he is going to make Bercow pay for his rudeness towards him.

'I absolutely hate, hate, hate, that place! I can't wait to leave it,' he tells me, before falling into a snoring coma.

12 September

Hugo attends the executive meeting of the Association to say he's off. He says not a single person thanked him for his twenty years' service. He comes home flat and emotional, and throws his hand up in the air and gives the Association the finger. I put out a tweet saying he's off, or something similar.

Claire Wrong can't believe her luck. If she had any dignity, she would have responded with something along the lines of *I know we had our differences, but* ... Instead she just says she 'stands ready to take on the issues'. Then we get the usual tirade of vile abuse from her supporters. She is completely deluded if she thinks she now has a clear run at the seat. I feel elated that we don't have to have anything to do with that cow again.

Curiously, one of the nicest tweets is from one of the Bad Boys of Brexit, Andy Wigmore: 'I like @HugoSwire he did incredible things for all @commonwealthsec countries especially #Belize and is a genuinely nice man – out of all the resignations, expulsions and retirements, he is the only one I am sorry about. Good luck for the future Hugo and thanks for all your help.'

In truth, he is already forgotten. East Devon has started the process of selecting a new candidate. Politics is a brutal business.

15 September

From David's book, which is now out: '[M]any of the arguments we had about politics were actually about logistics, rather than issues. Samantha worried hugely about how it would affect our life. Where would we live? How would we stay together? How much would we see of each other?

'She was right to ask all these questions: politics has been a destroyer of many strong marriages. For one person in the relationship it can become an obsession; for the other a duty, or even a burden.'

In my marriage, it was always the other way around. I was the obsessive, for Hugo it was the burden.

H says to me, 'What will we talk about when I leave politics?'

'We will still talk about politics. Until the breath leaves my lungs.'

'Oh, God. Will we? Really?'

16 September

I text K: 'Dave making a big mistake backing the rebels. He should be above the fray. He needs to keep his dignity and not take sides. The issue is too emotive to take part. I'm going to come down for his book launch after all. We can hold each other's hand.'

K: 'Boris cabinet full of people who voted against Brexit three times. Glad you're coming!!! Xx' *What sort of answer is that, Kate, for God's sake?*

Me: 'That doesn't mean Dave should wade in. He is an ex PM, like I said, he should be above the vulgar fray. I really think it's a mistake. And I say that as a loyalist and friend not as a Brexiteer.'

K: 'He hasn't weighed in. He's just been nice to them.'

Why, Kate, why? They have schemed and plotted with Labour and have made a Corbyn government more likely, and for the zillionth time what they voted for was not bloody Brexit, it was a trap to keep us in the EU, AND YOU KNOW IT! But of course I didn't say that, because most of my friends are dropping like flies, because of being on the other side of the divide on Brexit, and quite frankly I can't afford to lose any more.

18 September

We went to Dave's book launch last night, at the Conduit Club. What possessed the man? Overflowing with Tory rebels who have lost the whip: Antonia Sandbach, for God's sake. When was she ever part of the Cameron narrative? And, hot-footing it from the

Lib Dem conference, Sam Gyimah. I mean, what the fuck? There wasn't a single member of Dave's former cabinet there. Come to think of it, there wasn't a single Brexiteer, except Norman Lamont, natch, and me, and half a Brexiteer in George Bridges. It was staggeringly weird.

Of course, his No. 10 crew were present in thick numbers, and Boy George as well, relieved no doubt that he doesn't have to write a book because he featured so heavily in Dave's. K was there, and all those nameless faces who will spend the rest of their lives saying they worked in No. 10. Amber there, naturally. She tries to pull me over but I can only just about muster a smile back, and I head for the bar because I'm not sure how I'm going to get through this. I down a glass of vino in one and tell the barman to top me up, as if I am in the last-chance saloon, which I probably am. My last few minutes are devoted to getting my book signed by Dave. I slam it down in front of him and he looks up at me and blushes like a naughty schoolboy.

'Hello, Tory MP Wife,' and he smiles wickedly, because he thinks he knows I'm behind that anonymous Twitter account – which of course I am.

'Me? No, I just live amongst my flowers these days.'

'Yes, me too.'

He signs it, 'to Sasha with thanks for all the love and support', and he hands it back to me saying, 'Sounds as if we had an affair, doesn't it?'

And I'm thinking, I wish!

H and I go to the restaurant upstairs and have dinner with Greg and George P, who have just announced their engagement. No sooner have they sat down than they are racing though the index of Dave's book to see how many entries they have, which is virtually none, but Greg is smug because he has four compared to Hugo's three. There is a sticky moment when Greg attacks me for shutting Amber out, lecturing me about how I must separate my friendships from my politics. He doesn't think Amber has behaved badly at all, but then he is firmly lodged in the remain camp. I fight back. George kicks him under the table and H shouts at me to let it go. That apart, it was a fun dinner.

19 September

H, in his capacity as this year's president of the Colaton Raleigh & District Ploughing Association, attends the Ploughing, Fodder and Produce Show. He is there to hand out the prizes: open semi digger, open hydraulic, vintage tractor and trailer plough, Massey Ferguson class. In the fodder categories: three longest stems of maize (no roots), three cobs of maize off stem, sample of feeding barley, short ley, long ley, maize acreage. In produce: Victoria sandwich, lemon drizzle cake, cheese scones, boiled cider fruit cake, then chutneys and jams, and, for anyone who says they haven't modernised in four centuries, a category for the funniest selfie.

After a lunch of ham and coleslaw, H raises himself onto the podium. 'I just want you to know, looking at these hardened old tractors, that I myself, as of yesterday, have just bought a wonderful Massey Ferguson 35 X and I was thinking of coming and taking part in the ploughing match today, but given the apparent inability of politicians to do anything in a straight line at the moment I didn't want to leave the farmer with his field reduced to a series of crop circles.'

Farmer Trevor Glasper, a stalwart of the Branscombe area, comes up and they get chatting. 'Have you heard old Hugo Swire is retiring?'

'Yes, I do know that, Trevor, because it's me, and you have been speaking to me for the last ten minutes.'

23 September

Boris is in trouble again about a blonde ... again. An American blonde who has a dancing pole in her Shoreditch flat, which Boris made regular visits to. A spokesman said she was giving him IT lessons there and that it was all above board. *Software and hardware? How to turn him off and on again?* He is being accused of political impropriety after helping the woman's business when he was Mayor of London and there are further questions on why she accompanied him on several trips abroad. I don't know why everyone is getting so upset. Everyone knows Boris is a sex addict. In fact, in *The Times* this morning there is a whole article about how the brains of people like him produce unusually large quantities of oxytocin, 'a substance known as the "love hormone"', and they just can't get enough sex. Now we know what the root cause is maybe his new political poppet can send him off for treatment. Truth is, all this sex stuff is factored in with Boris. And this is just another one of those gotcha! Boris stories which we periodically read over our cornflakes.

27 September

I take a sneaky, guilty look at the appalling *Mail Online* and immediately have an attack of the vapours. Amber, stepping out of the Bible, polishing her halo, is now positioning herself as a unifying figure, should the PM be ousted. And guess who is helping her behind the scenes? One George Osborne, and I suspect that means *just call me Dave* as well. In a spinning vortex of outrage I say to H, 'I'm going to send her an email saying "Have you finally gone stark raving mad?"'

'No, you are not.'

I stop to think for a moment, and concede he might be right. 'No, I am not.'

H tells me that when he asked her whether Nicholas (Soames) was lining up his Sussex seat for her, the following conversation emerged:

'Oh, I know what your game is, Amber.'

'What's that, Hugo?'

'Are they going to give you the whip back?'

'It's not for them to give me the whip back, because I resigned.'

'I see. So you let Hastings select a new candidate, because it's a marginal, then you apply to have the whip back? And then look around for a safe seat?'

'Ha ha. Something like that.'

In the *Evening Standard*, she suggested Kensington was more to her liking.

Then Kate rings and goes off into her own vortex of outrage about how Boris is making the situation worse and that leadership is important and so is language and that he should watch that he isn't creating more division and that he needs to show respect for people who come from the other side of the argument and I'm holding the phone about ten centimetres from my ear and thinking *calm down, dear, calm down.*

Actually, I think everyone needs to calm down.

28 September

H texts the PM, cautioning him that some of those who have just lost the whip will continue to cause nothing but trouble even if he restores it to them, and advises against it.

Boris replies that the Surrender Bill has already cost us in Brussels.

29 September

The *Mail on Sunday* is claiming members of the French government helped remainer MPs draft what Boris now calls the Surrender Act and the same MPs are plotting to pass a second Act empowering John Bercow to ask for an extension to the Brexit deadline. H says to me, 'Those bloody corrupt Frenchies are at it again.'

He explains how Chirac didn't allow the French to join the coalition against Saddam, not because of some lofty anti-American principle (though that always plays well in France) but because

Saddam bunged him €5 million. He says it's difficult to remember a non-corrupt French leader at all. De Gaulle, probably? Certainly not Giscard, with Bokassa's diamonds, nor Mitterrand, a good lefty crook. And what of Sarko, with the alleged money from Gaddafi and France's richest woman, the L'Oreal heiress Liliane Berlinguer?

'Mind you, if I was married to the fragrant Carla I'd beg, borrow and steal to keep her in a good mood,' H says.

It remains to be seen if Macron passes the sniff test. Early days, I should have thought.

1 October

A wonderful exchange with Mark Francois in the Members' tearoom.

'Have you read David Cameron's book, Mark?' a remainer MP asks.

'I looked up F in the index and couldn't find my name, so didn't buy it.'

'Did you try looking under C?'

7 October

Twenty-three days to go until a possible no-deal Brexit, the Queen's speech is looming, the capital is under siege by a death cult run by middle-class hippies and still the same question is being asked: did Boris plug into Jennifer Arcuri's mainframe?

9 October

Boris treads over the dead bodies of Extinction Rebellion protesters (metaphorically, you understand) and describes the protesters as 'uncooperative crusties' who have 'littered the road', then delivers a rip-roaring speech at the launch of the final volume of Charles Moore's Thatcher biography. He goes on to describe the protesters as 'importunate nose-ringed climate change protesters' living in 'heaving hemp-smelling bivouacs'. No sooner had he done this than up pops another Johnson, Stanley, saying that he is proud to be 'an uncooperative crusty'. Managing Brexit must be a doddle compared to managing his family, who appear to have gone completely rogue on him.

10 October

Chaffcombe

H takes his new tractor out for a spin. He has got young Henry Greenhalf, our neighbour and an absolute whizz with agricultural machinery, to make up a box with lifting capacity that can be attached to the back of the tractor. He goes around the place picking up stones and rocks to fill in the potholes on the drive. He's feeling very manly as he chugs off happily down the lane in a checked shirt and a tweed cap, waving at me like he is in a drawing in a child's picture book.

He returns an hour later looking less than cheerful.

'What now?' I ask.

'I told Rob not to tell you, but you always find me out.'

'Have you broken the tractor already?'

He tells me that the vehicle nearly killed him because it has developed a propensity to buck. In fact, stone-collecting had become something of a rodeo event. Going up a steep slope, his beloved Massey reared up and he swung the wheel to the left and it came crashing down, nearly taking out my favourite magnolia. It took all of his riding skills, which are limited anyway, to hang on and not let the tractor end up on top of him. On his return to the yard he lost control again, and this time the tractor mounted a bank and he nearly buckled the front wheel.

I suggest it might be the link box, that it was not designed to be filled with heavy stones. It's simply the laws of balance: the weights make up the effort of the load and the two need to be equal at the same distance from the fulcrum. 'I know that, thank you very much, Sasha. I'm off to ring Henry to sort it out,' he huffs. It doesn't occur to him that it would be highly inconvenient for me to become a widow quite yet. Particularly as the life insurance I took out on him is about to run out.

Men!

11 October

Slowly reading Dave's book. It's a bit me, me, me and George, Samantha, me, me, the Queen etc., but when I listen to the audio-book I think it's actually a really good listen. Yes, it's his account, his take, his record, but also it explains quite succinctly how he came to make his decisions. It is not a political potboiler in any sense. H says that if my diaries were ever published, 'I will have to resign from White's, the Guards' Club, my regimental association, the Old Etonian Association, Pratt's and the Beefsteak, possibly the Country Landowners' Association, and almost certainly the Colaton Raleigh & District Ploughing Association.'

Now, that last one I'd be sad about.

15 October

The Queen's speech is probably one of the most bizarre in history. All ministers expect it to be voted down – which would be the first time since 1924. The Tories, of course, will accuse Labour of voting down support for the NHS, schools and police. Labour will accuse the Tories of being unable to govern. And so the merry-go-round keeps on turning. Also, much hilarity in the House today when Emily Thornberry heckled Raab after he claimed Jezza

wanted to withdraw from NATO, shouting 'Bollocks!' Bercow
tried to calm things down, but H ignored him and slung back the
accusation that the Shadow Foreign Secretary was being sexist
in her choice of language. Bercow half smiled, before putting H
back in his box.

16 October

We are all on tenterhooks, waiting to see whether Boris's deal is
going to work. An hour ago the DUP were saying they still had
significant differences with No. 10, the main issue being con-
sent, which they say is of chief importance to them in terms of
domestic politics. The ERG is suspiciously silent. The Lib Dems
say they won't support it, whatever it is; and no one knows what
Labour thinks, or if they do, they don't understand it. Some say
the EU are considering a five-week extension, but only for an
election or for the ratification of the deal. That would suit me.
Others reckon that Boris will write a letter asking for a delay
if there is no deal by Saturday. Steve Barclay says the PM will
'comply with the law and comply with the undertakings of the
court'. Amber is going around saying it's because they forced the
Benn Act that Boris is being forced to come up with a deal. Yeah,
right. What's she going to vote, I wonder, because now she wants
a second referendum.

17 October

Chaffcombe

I'm sitting in the Bailiff's House at my computer. I feel like
Rapunzel up here, or a big fat pigeon nesting at the top of a tree.
' ... *pause, take heed. Breathe. Just breathe and sit.*' Around me autumn
colours are beginning to show themselves. The ash is paling. The

big copper beech still fully dressed in its purplish radiance, but with lighter crimson tips where a tired sun catches its undersides. The red soil has been churned in the field outside my window, like a red velvet cake mixture in a mixing bowl. I love this rich soil of the Devon Redlands. There is something so pure about it, so honest and so full of experience. It connects us to the past and yet offers a future full of promise. And I love that its bricks curve around me in this newly restored building of mine, that '*someone made from living things from straw and hair and took the teeming mud salted with living things*'. All is quiet and calm down here. It is good to be alone sometimes so that even a wasp trying to get where it needs to go feels like a trespasser with its bombinating.

17–18 October

Boris has only gone and pulled a blinder in Brussels. In the words of Juncker, 'We haf a deal.' Beside him stood Bozza, looking like he had been dragged through a hedge backwards by a cuckolded husband. Clearly, picking the honeymoon suite with Varadkar in the Wirral worked wonders when the officials left the room. Even better, Juncker goes on to say, 'This deal means there is no need for any kind of prolongation.'

19 October

First came the highs, then the lows. H and I have gone straight to bed and pulled the duvet up over our heads. I am feeling particularly anxious, knotted up, cross about it all. The white-knuckle Brexit ride just got a whole lot wilder and we all feel like chucking up . . .

We got the girls tickets for the Saturday sitting, the first in nearly forty years. The last time, I was there, was watching my father, during the invasion of the Falklands. I remember it was a bearpit, the MPs were baying for blood, they wanted scapegoats for the shame brought on the nation; my father was an easy target. He just stood up and did his piece in front of a tsunami of abuse led by Michael Foot and his bellowing backbenchers. I felt desperately protective but helpless. As Alan Clark said in his diaries: 'Poor old Notters was a disaster ... The *coup de grace* was delivered by David Owen, who had spoken earlier. He forced Nott to give way and he told him that if he could not appreciate the need to back negotiations with force he did not deserve to remain one minute as Secretary of State.'

I wasn't going to miss another historic event.

It's interesting, being in the chamber watching the main players, which I haven't for a while. If you know them, you can tell by their body language whether they are excited, gloomy, who they are talking to, who they are not talking to, what the narrative is going to be. Amber sat in a very defensive position with her arms crossed, expressionless bar the occasional smile to the man in the upper gallery who is her current squeeze.

Theresa May was wincing, looking straight ahead of her. Maybe that was to do with sitting next to, on one side, Kenneth Clarke, and on the other the weed-addled, yurt-living crusties littering the streets around parliament. Actually, I think a quick puff on a bong and a strum on a sitar over on Lambeth Bridge might do her a world of good. It's already difficult to even remember now she was ever PM.

We go out for a coffee break and bump into Raab C. Brexit, who seems cheerful enough. He is busy with FCO matters, trying to keep that show on the road, including warnings to China not to mistreat the lawful and peaceful protesters in Hong Kong.

He is taking the credit for bringing over the Spartans to the deal earlier in the morning. I tell him he better get ready for the leadership if Boris loses his seat, but he says he might lose his as well if it's not sorted before the election: there is a big remain majority there and the Lib Dems are pouring in huge resources to snatch the seat off him. He is enjoying Chevening; lots of space to kick around a football with his boys, and he says Erika sends her love.

By the time we come back into the chamber, I know it isn't looking good. Then it comes out that the DUP are planning to back Letwin, and before you know it the government is defeated, 322 votes to 306 and 'super Saturday' is well and truly over. Only weirdo politicians could call something like this 'super Saturday'; most people wouldn't consider this a 'super' fun activity at all.

22 October

No surprises today. Bercow blocks Boris's renewed bid to initiate a 'meaningful vote' on his Brexit deal. JRM sets out a manageable timetable for Brexit legislation, ending in the Lords on Friday. But amendments are expected to flood in, with one in support of a customs union which would be deadly.

24 October

H tells me not to take Rocco to Battersea Park. He recently shared a taxi with our friend the Sexy Spook, and she told him of how two burly Russians with rottweilers followed her in the park where she was walking her dog, and how the Russkis deliberately unleashed their hounds. The rottweilers had a tug of war with her beloved mutt, leaving him with all his insides spilling out. He was in the vet's for six months and later died.

'Well, they clearly knew who she was,' I say to H.

'Yes,' he replies, 'and I expect we are meant to believe it was all coincidence. In fact, there are more Russian spooks on the streets of our beloved country than at any time, including the Cold War years.'

A sobering and not entirely comfortable thought.

25 October

No Brexit, no election and the budget is cancelled. But the Queen's speech got through! Crikey, Boris has now won three, yes three, whole votes. Brussels is waiting for Westminster. Westminster is waiting for Brussels.

This is deadlock of the deadlock of the deadlock. Corbyn just won't play ball, so Boris now says he's pulling the Withdrawal Agreement and will call for an election every day until the opposition weakens. People blame Cameron for the referendum, but he did something much worse than that: the bloody Fixed Term Selfish Act. He should have slapped a sunset clause on it.

Dear God, let us have a quiet weekend.

And it is a significant measure of our times and our Brexit fatigue to think even a general election will give us some respite. H says it's like not being able to leave the Hotel California.

27 October

H returns from Edinburgh, where he has been attending the Tertulias, the Anglo-Spanish get-together to which he has been enticed by his new friends the Brennans. This has historically been a pretty Labour-dominated event and H jokes that he feels like 'the only gay in the village'. H tells Dan Brennan* his story about Ian Paisley and the Pope's visit to Edinburgh. Dan follows up by saying he has twice passed out in the Lords in mid-flow, from heart attacks. On one occasion he rose to intervene on Paisley's wife Eileen, who had recently become Baroness Paisley of St George's. He later woke in St Thomas' to see the Big Man leering over him. 'Hello, Dan, howya doin',' came the famous voice, which could put thousands of loyalists on the streets at any time. Dan said he was

---

* Created Baron Brennan in 2000. QC and a member of Matrix Chambers, and a keen supporter of the Tertulias Forum, which promotes Anglo-Spanish relations.

feeling fine but was curious as to why Paisley, who he had never met, had come to see him.

Paisley's massive shoulders heaved in merriment and he said, 'I just wanted to come and shake the hand of the only man who has ever managed to shut my wife up mid-sentence!'

30 October

Finally, we have an election.

This morning Amber says she will not be fighting it. She had hoped to get the whip back after a meeting with Boris, but Mark Spencer, the Chief Whip, told her otherwise in a pretty brutal letter. He wrote, 'The receipt of the whip is an honour, not a right and as such it cannot be discarded or returned at will if it is to have any meaning.' What did Amber expect? Apart from ignoring the democratic mandate of the referendum and compromising our negotiating hand, she accepted a post in cabinet from Bozzie Bear, pledging to get Brexit done. Then she quits on the basis that Boris was not serious. Then he gets a deal. At which point she joined in with Oliver Letwin's tomfoolery in the Commons. To say H and I are disappointed by her shenanigans is an understatement. After all, we were the ones who encouraged her to join the Conservative Party, we were the ones who helped her passage using our political connections, and we were the ones who supported her when the shit hit the fan at the Home Office; she could not question our loyalty and friendship. But politics is a tribal business, and political parties, like armies, only function properly if loyalty and discipline are adhered to. In the end, she proved she was just too disruptive and as a result was ruthlessly cast out.

As for her fellow remainers, they are miserable that we are going to the polls before Brexit has been delivered. I'm not. It means we can tailor-make our own Brexit with a majority, and at the same time it stymies the Brexit Party as they can't moan about a bad deal and steal our votes. But it's going to be tough out there, and we might just end up with another bloody hung parliament. But my gut feeling is that Boris will do well, very well: the mood of the country is definitely with him at the moment.

I texted H yesterday, when the votes went through, because I know he will be feeling conflicted: 'You must not feel sad. You were never a political maniac boffin like Redwood, Jenkin, Cash, IDS, none of them could make the switch to business because they are too addicted, politics is a drug for them, it never was for you. You can now have a second life and freedom. You were the best FCO minister, but you don't want to go backwards. This is so the right decision, and that comes from a political junkie.'

He replies: 'How funny you are and how well you know your old husband. Just sitting here and was feeling a little maudlin but you are, as we both know, right. X'.

H returns to his office, where Sue is waiting for him surrounded by cardboard boxes containing all his memorabilia. Benyon ambles in. H tells him that Soames was in a state as he had to pack up thirty-seven years' worth of accumulated papers, etc., and that Serena had refused to have any of it at home in Sussex as all the barns were already overflowing. Richard slouches languidly in a chair with outstretched legs, and in resigned tones says, 'I really didn't know what to do with all my stuff either, as I haven't got an inch at home.' H roars with laughter and says, 'Richard, that is the grandest thing I think I've ever heard.' Richard practically owns the whole of Berkshire and lives in a palace with twenty-seven thousand rooms.

They then talk about going to head-hunters. H is sceptical about them. He found Virginia Bottomley – who they all go to, by virtue of her being a former MP – rather condescending when he went a while back. But not as condescending as she was to Benyon, apparently. La Bottomley asked where his skills lay and what he saw himself doing, to which Richard said he saw himself doing something cutting edge in life sciences, artificial intelligence or cyber security. Bottomley sucked on her pen, consulted his CV and peered over her glasses before responding that she wondered 'if there were any landed estates looking for a trustee'. Richard tells H he had never felt so small in his life. But then, on his second meeting, she was apparently considerably more helpful and impressive.

Benyon, like H, has mixed feelings about leaving the Commons. He has had the whip restored and would like to continue with his work on the Joint Intelligence Committee, but that would mean the Lords. It's possible, remarks H to me later, but Boris really does not owe him anything.

It's a tricky one, the *what next?* question. After all, what does an ex-MP have to offer? H was always dabbling in business throughout his career, but for the rest of them – at least the top tier – it's straight to the public-speaking circuit. The offers of sharing contacts? Those dry up pretty quickly, and no one is interested unless you are still plugged in to the people you have met along the way. Mind you, Derek Conway got to work for the Cats Protection League, but he can't have loved the moggies that much because he tried to get back into parliament as soon as he could, standing against H in the East Devon selection. And it's not only the humble MPs, it's the PMs as well. Lloyd George assumed he could be the editor of *The Times*, but ended up in his garden, potting flowers, only giving his name to a type of raspberry. He also donned druidical dress for a speech defending the national eisteddfods, the Welsh festivals of music and poetry.

The truth is, there is nothing so ex as an ex-MP.

1 November

When Soames is not loading his stuff into carboard boxes he is out there building his legacy. On Halloween he grants an interview to Laura Kuenssberg, in which he laments the decline in manners in recent years. He says the Commons is now 'a rougher, coarser place ... it's got very unpleasant'. For a small wee moment, I'm completely taken in by it, actually rather moved. Even Amber tweets: '"Always trying . . ."' Fabulous. A man who always stood up for what he believed in. And chided us all to do the same, with good humour and choice phrases.' But then I wake up. There is another side to Nicholas that can be quite colourful, particularly on his Twitter. Online, Guido Fawkes is quick to pull up some examples, such as calling Nigel Farage a twat on several occasions – but then there is no love lost, being at opposite ends of the Brexit debate – and he had to apologise after shouting 'woof woof' at a woman MP in the chamber. And then, after Adam Afriyie was caught plotting to bring down DC, Soames said he was a 'fucking disgrace to your party, your fellow MPs, your Prime Minister and your country' and a 'chateau-bottled, nuclear-powered cunt'.

His departure from the Commons might actually make it a less coarse, less misogynistic, less snobby place than it was when he was there.

6 November

Chaffcombe

Today Rob and I planted two trees donated by Extinction Rebellion, an English oak and a crab apple. (H actually stole the crab from Margot James.) Activists had placed hundreds of them, each with an MP's name on it, outside parliament. It was a good gesture, and one of which I approve.

I have planted the crab in stony ground near the water room next to the bore hole. It seems happy there, despite the thin and rocky soil; the roots will hopefully snake their way around the rocks and one day bloom with pale pink cup-shaped flowers, then turn bright with autumn fruits and richly coloured leaves. I am giving H a hand-crafted walking stick with a crab apple shaft for Christmas.

As we plant the oak I think about Westminster Hall, and its

great span of long-seasoned oak ribs. There was never a time when I walked through that hall and didn't marvel at what is one of the most remarkable wooden roofs ever made. How fitting to pick a tree that has such strength and one that is such a symbol of nationhood in Britain, like parliament itself.

I'm seeing myself under that roof now, looking up measuring my life against it, as in D. H. Lawrence's poem 'Under the Oak':

> *What thing better are you, what worse?*
> *What have you to do with the mysteries*
> *Of this ancient place, of my ancient curse?*
> *What place have you in my histories?*

7 November

H is in his last days in the Commons. In the tearoom he gets talking to Steve Baker, and asks him about the Brexit Party. He tells him that he and a couple of others from the Taliban Brexiteers had just been with Farage and Tice.* Fascinatingly, he recounts to H how they demanded two safe Tory seats as part of any deal. One each. Additionally, they both demanded to be ministers in the next government. Steve asked them if they were proposing a confidence and supply arrangement, or to be in a formal coalition. Neither, they said confidently. Well, how do you propose to be ministers in the government, then, he asked, at which point they apparently looked at each other, nonplussed, and were unable to answer. Says a lot.

Later, in the chamber, Sir Alan (Duncan) shimmies over to Boris. He has clearly lunched well and, according to H, actually flirts with the PM. H finds this strange, because never has anyone ever been ruder to and about their boss than one A. Duncan. But a story is also doing the rounds that Alan has done a deal with

---

* Property investor. Chairman of the Brexit Party since 2019 and elected MEP for the East of England at the 2019 European Parliament election.

Boris and is shortly to be smothered in ermine. Have the coronets really been ordered? Coats of arms commissioned? The portrait painters forewarned? H bumps into the PM shortly afterwards and teasingly says how pleased he was to see him getting on so well now with Alan. Boris's eyes become hooded, a thin, cold smile spreads across his lips and he looks at H and says, 'Ah, yes, of course, Sir Alan. Well, let's see . . . ' and draws a finger across his lips as if fastening them with a zip before smiling and moving off. H tells me he fears Sir Alan's ambitions are set to be dashed, but then in politics you never know.

'You never really know until something actually happens; or more often until after it actually happens,' says H.

H has commissioned a shell mirror from his old girlfriend Sophy Topley. It is for me, and for the bathroom at Chaffcombe. H likes the idea of having something by one of my predecessors, someone who was so much part of his life at one point. He often buys presents for himself under the pretext of them being for me.

He rings to tell me he has just been around to her flat to pick it up. He was early and she was in her dressing gown. H jokes that the last time he had been around to her flat he was there to belatedly remove the last of his belongings before Alastair Margadale, who she subsequently married and divorced, moved his things in. She was also semi-naked then, as she was being fitted for her wedding dress. That was about thirty-five years ago! H says they got on like a house on fire, naturally, and that her caustic Mitford wit is still very much in evidence.* She kept asking H to stay, although he was in a rush. H then congratulated her on her son Declan getting engaged to an Argentinian. Apparently Sophy likes her very much, but she doesn't speak any Spanish and they communicate through gestures. Declan then has to translate. The daughter-in-law-to-be is now having English lessons. On the first day the teacher told her

---

* The Lady Sophia Topley, née Cavendish, second daughter of the 11th Duke of Devonshire and his wife, Deborah Mitford.

class that they should raise their hands if they needed to go to the toilet. The d-in-law dutifully raised her hand: 'My boyfriend shay is no good sayin toilet!'

'Well, what does he suggest you say?' the teacher replied crossly.

'Leeeew!'

The Association have selected Simon Jupp to fight East Devon. H cannot help reflecting that when he put in for East Devon it was along with 395 others, who had all been approved through the Parliamentary Assessment Board and included two future prime ministers, David Cameron and Boris Johnson. H saw them all off and, after several knock-out rounds, won over 50 per cent of the vote on the final night. For a year he nursed the seat, stretching his bank balance beyond its natural boundaries (as he would throughout his political career), and was out and about meeting the community every weekend. Twenty years on and Jupp, Raab C. Brexit's media spad, is virtually given the seat without much of a competition. What does that say? An election is coming?

And yet, on the whole, the new candidates look diverse, with many more women and people from ethnic-minority backgrounds entering. I'm fine with this, as long as it's done by meritocracy rather than by the PR machine. Jupp comes from a much humbler background than Hugo as well, having worked his way up from being a sixteen-year-old cub reporter to working at the Foreign Office. The double-barrelled and privately educated are still there, but there is a greater fairness in play. And something else is happening: the death of the political tribe. In the past, if you had brown sauce with your sausages you voted Labour; if you holidayed in Tuscany you were New Labour or Conservative. But Brexit has smashed all those certainties and even the MPs are party-swapping. It is going to be the most interesting of elections and could lead to better MPs, braver politics and new ideas. It was time for H to go. To let others sow the seeds of change.

Later, early evening, and all H's suppressed emotion finally explodes in a conversation with his stalwart supporter John Humphreys. He suddenly bursts into tears as he is talking to him and has to put the phone down so he can re-establish his composure. I have only seen him do this once before, and it was when he came upstairs to tell me his father had died. 'Why Hugo, why now?' I ask, and H rather sadly replies, 'Because he said thank you to me, for being the MP, and no one has ever said thank you, and then I thought about attending his and David's wedding and I just felt immensely proud, suddenly, that I was part of a government that had made that happen.'

10 November

Chaffcombe

It has rained for a week, all morning, all afternoon. It seeps down through a low grey ceiling. When I venture outside it is over spongy, squelching, sodden ground. The old year is dying, and everything is frayed at the edges. All the flowers bar a struggling rose have gone. The days are shorter and colder. You can see how the dead squeeze into the world of the living in November: Halloween, bonfires, All Saints, All Souls. H is out doing his last Remembrance Sunday as a local dignitary. I say, 'But you are not an MP any more.'

'I know, but they still wanted me to come.' And of course it gives him a chance to wear his KCMG.

He has not missed a single Remembrance Sunday since becoming an MP. Nineteen of them.

The sun has come out, finally. I take a walk around the place while H is out and look at the silver birches, which have grown to great heights. My father gave me these trees when we first arrived at Chaffcombe. Back then they were merely whips. Today I look up at one of them; a thin show of bright yellow leaves on top of a tall lanky stem. It is bendy and thin, just like my father, despite his great age. Both belie how hardy and strong they actually are; I think it's the silvery-white bark and grey-green fissures that confuse.

My father has given and planted many trees in his lifetime. The last words in his political memoir read, 'Of one thing I am quite certain. I will have contributed more to life by planting trees, by nurturing the land at Trewinnard, and by preserving for future generations my home in Cornwall, than anything I did, or might have done, in politics, business or the army. What could anyone ask for more of life than that? So, I rest, content.'

I am buying sixty whips for Hugo's sixtieth birthday, so he can plant them around Chaffcombe. He doesn't want anything else.

In writing the poem 'Birches', Robert Frost was inspired by his memories of swinging on birches as a child in New England. The poem feels like a metaphor for politics as well: the swinger is grounded in the earth through the roots of the tree as he climbs, but he is able to reach beyond his normal life on the earth and reach for a higher plane of existence. Of course, the high plane of politics is appealing and wondrous, but one cannot avoid the return to 'truth' and responsibilities on the ground; the escape into another world can only be a temporary one.

To my father and my husband, both politicians, and for those to come, here are the poem's last lines.

> *I'd like to go by climbing a birch tree,*
> *And climb black branches up a snow-white trunk*
> *Toward heaven, till the tree could bear no more,*
> *But dipped its top and set me down again.*
> *That would be good both going and coming back.*
> *One could do worse than be a swinger of birches.*

12 November

8.35 p.m., and Chaffcombe is dripped in silver. A full moon is often thought a time of renewal, and with this beaver moon, it's time to tidy the space before the start of winter. It's named after the setting of beaver traps by colonists and Algonquin Native Americans. It seems appropriate that an election is happening under its watch.

We have decided not to go canvassing unless expressly asked by the new candidate.

17 November

Prince Andrew's interview with Emily Maitlis last night. A breather from the election, or was it a dry gulp? No one actually thought he was ever going to be clever enough to pull this off, and they were right. It was a televisual car crash.

24 November

What the Duke of York would call a 'straightforward shooting weekend' chez Drax; that is Richard Grosvenor Plunkett-Ernle-Erle-Drax, MP, at the Grade I-listed Charborough Park in Dorset. The grounds include a deer park and a chapel, with a folly thrown in as well. The estate is old, very old, and was listed as a manor back in the Domesday Book. Of particular interest to me was the eighteenth-century string staircase with its turned balusters and wreathed handrail, all intricately carved with oak leaves and acorns, but also the riot of wood above a door next to it, of carved trumpets, flags and thistles and the open mouth of a Green Man figure, the ultimate symbol of British heritage and defender of green spaces. Quite beautiful.

The house has been made incredibly comfortable by Elspeth Drax – come in, wife number three, please. She is a Norwegian interior designer, so rooms are atmospherically lit, and candles abound and cushions are plump.

Richard is something of a silver fox, with beautiful eyes and a lean physique, but he doesn't do it for me. It's his views. I mean, I consider

myself right of centre but he is off the scale. He's voted against pro-
portional representation (I agree on that one), same-sex marriage,
measures to limit climate change and a whole raft of human rights
and equality legislation, against a higher tax rate for those earning
over £150,000 (natch) and a bankers' bonus tax (double natch) – and
these are only the things he's voted against! He's voted for lower corporate taxes, lower welfare benefits, the 'bedroom' tax and to end
financial support for sixteen- to nineteen-year-olds. Anyway, you get
the theme. Oh, and he also voted against a 2016 amendment that
required private landlords to make their homes 'fit for human hab-
itation'. (But, as with all amendments, it would have been a Labour
trick to make people like Richard look exploitative. And to be fair,
local authorities already have strong powers to deal with this sort of
stuff.) His current best friend in the House is John Redwood, which
says it all. He is completely and utterly an unreconstructed, old-style
landed Tory, probably the only one left. When I mention I might try
to get Slovenian citizenship, he says why on earth would I ever want
to go to that miserable hellhole of a country? I ask him whether he
has ever been there and he goes silent, so I'm assuming he just thinks
it's a nasty foreign land full of Europeans and he wouldn't ever want
to go there.

At dinner we discuss his estate. How many acres has he got, I
ask. He is cagey and doesn't tell me, but I know it runs into the
many thousands. The wall around his estate is, after all, one of the
longest brick walls in England. H scolds me later in our bedroom:
'You never ask someone that question.'

H then goes on to tell me the story of being summoned, as a
former whip, to the shadow cabinet room prior to the 2010 election.
There he found other ex-whips all clutching lists of candidates who
they were being encouraged to nurture by the Chief Whip, Patrick
McLoughlin. This was around the time that DC reportedly told
JRM's sister Annunziata to shorten her name to Nancy Mogg, to
be in tune with the Cameroon modernisation programme. The
Chief Whip droned on about the importance of the election and
how they were to ensure the candidates worked around the clock.

Of course, this was completely fatuous as all candidates had long been mentored by others. At the end he asked if there were any questions. H raised his hand.

''ugo' intoned McLoughlin, in his broad Derbyshire accent, looking wary.

'Chief,' said H cheerfully, 'I have been given the following to mentor: the Honourable Jacob Rees-Mogg; his sister, the Honourable Annunziata Rees-Mogg; (titters) Richard Grosvenor Plunkett-Ernle-Earle-Drax; (laughter) and Nick King. My question to you, Chief, is should I ask Nick King to lengthen his name or the others to shorten theirs?'

The room dissolved at this point. The Chief Whip said, 'Bugger off, 'ugo,' and closed the meeting.

H also tells me how at dinner he was discussing *Downton Abbey*, and the scene where Lady Mary Crawley is about to be seduced by a Turkish diplomat (who then inconveniently dies on the job). Apparently, the Turk tells Lady Mary not to worry, that she would still be a virgin after what he is about to do to her. Richard tells H that this caused him and Elspeth sleepless nights, until it dawned on them that 'it could only mean one thing'. He wrote to his neighbour and friend Julian Fellowes for clarification. Yes, replied Julian, this was exactly what was meant. Poor Richard was deeply disturbed by it all.

27 November

Greg and George ring from the car on their way back from a smart shooting weekend in Norfolk. Apparently, George had machine-gunned any bird that came near him, and slit the throats of any survivors. Very Greek, which he is. Meanwhile, Greg was doing less well. Swathed in the latest and finest tweeds, cut to perfection no doubt in Savile Row, he was seen waving his gun at everything that moved and firing furiously at the slightest movement, but all to no avail. Distressed and embarrassed, he soon found himself out of sight behind a hedge in the last drive before lunch. With a flash of inspiration, he handed his steaming musket over to Tony, his driver. Tony, with his military background, hit every bird that came his way with astonishing accuracy. Greg quickly grabs the gun back, half impressed, half irritated, just before the beaters hove into view. His host was somewhat astonished by this remarkable improvement in his skills and everyone went away happy.

30 November

Hugo goes out canvassing in Budleigh Salterton for Jumping Jupp Flash, who tells H he is having a torrid time with Claire Wrong's followers. All his posters are being ripped up and the abuse on his social media has been so bad he has had to shut down his Facebook page. Join the club, mate. Except we had at least ten years to build up to our worst moments and he has had to jump straight in when they are running at peak capacity.

   She goes around saying that she is fighting a clean campaign. Maybe, but not all her supporters are. Worse, this time all the nationals are covering her story. It's the David and Goliath line as usual, but now she is considered to be the only independent in the country who might actually win a seat; *The Times*, the *Mail*, the *Guardian*, the *Independent* have all interviewed her. In the *New Statesman*, she gives a typically banal quote. 'I want to win now more than I've *ever* wanted to win – probably because it's more likely now that I can. I could never quite see myself winning but this time I sort of can't see myself not winning. All I can see is me giving a victory speech, but we'll have to wait and see.'

2 December

Christmas cheer: Labour's endless, unaffordable list of bribes continues apace. It feels like a closing-down sale. *Everything must go! Sanity, economic competence, the entire contents of the Treasury.* I can't remember the last offer: two hundred fags and a crate of Newcastle Brown? Labour have really missed a marketing trick here; instead of handing out leaflets they should have posted an advent calendar through everyone's door:

Dec 1: The railways

Dec 2: Chocolates

Dec 3: The utility companies

Dec 4: NATO

Dec 5: The state of Israel.

6 December

Hugo flies back from Hong Kong. He has become a non-executive for a large conglomerate that builds and places storage facilities around Asia. H has been tipped off that the Chinese will almost certainly be monitoring his every move. This is confirmed when he switches on his iPad and notices all his emails have been translated into Chinese. Some poor chap in a shed in Guangzhou is probably still reading them now, bored rigid by a stream of catalogues from Patek Philippe and various auction alerts, which are H's version of porn.

Meanwhile, on the election front Boris is refusing to put himself in front of master inquisitor Andrew Neil and there is a lot of hooha about it. But, I mean, why would you? A week before polling day? Why create a story when there doesn't have to be one? Calling him a chicken will be quickly forgotten when he bombastically bounces back into No. 10. And quite frankly why would you want to remind the nation that you are a congenital liar, an adulterer, a breaker of trust, a lover of buses and why would you want to answer difficult accounting questions on where the money is coming from for nurses, schools, hospitals, tax cuts, nuclear weapons, social care, police and your own love child. And we know Andrew Neil would ask him these things because last night he went on air and told the nation he would.

10 December

Remainer maniac menace Hugh Grant, the one who spent years campaigning against press freedom and who now wants to over-turn Brexit, the largest democratic vote in UK history, turns up in East Devon. Yes, really, there on Sidmouth seafront yesterday, surrounded by a bunch of mothy lefties from the Claire Wright cult. There they all were, taking selfies, waving Claire Wright manifestos, chuckling at his every word as more of the Jurassic edifice collapsed into the water behind them, which somehow felt symbolic for the whole remainer campaign which is becoming something of an old dinosaur itself.

Claire Wrong stood beside him in a blue bobble hat, cable knit white scarf and sky-blue coat, shivering and jumping on her toes with excitement, her eyelashes fluttering like two big butterflies over a summer meadow. And why is she holding a green cuddly toy with horns on it now she has a new mascot she can moon over and cuddle? Of course, the nice and mostly elderly denizens of genteel Sidmouth strolling the promenade would probably have trouble identifying Hugh Grant, and they certainly wouldn't have known him from social media as they don't use it. What they wouldn't know is that Hugh is in quite a panic about his children's future, and there he does have something in common with our current PM as there are quite a lot of them from different women. Anyway, they certainly wouldn't know he has a Twitter account where he actually goes a bit 'off road', retweeting quotes from Bozzo before adding his own spin: 'You will not fuck with my children's future.

You will not destroy the freedoms my grandfather fought two world wars to defend. Fuck off you over-promoted rubber bath toy. Britain is revolted by you and you little gang of masturbatory prefects.' I mean, if they read his stuff their false teeth would probably Exocet out of their mouths into the freezing English Channel.

But there Claire was, lapping it all up as if she were on set, starring in her own rom com. The best bit was the staged *Love Actually* kiss, where Hugh Grant was visibly bristling with discomfort. It would be fair to add here that I once sat next to Mr Grant at a charity performance of the Cirque du Soleil at the Albert Hall, and apropos of nothing he leant towards me, nuzzled his nose into my ear and whispered, 'Christ, you smell good.' And we hadn't even been introduced! I was at the point of total collapse after that as well, I can tell you.

What a pity he's just become another angry middle-aged man.

11 December

We are about to leave for dinner when a text comes through from Peter Fage, who is on the ground in East Devon helping Jupp: 'YouGov updated model of parliamentary seats comes out 10pm tonight. Best data and indicator ahead of polling day. Last one two weeks ago had us 47 CW 41. We won't comment on it and crack on, but I'll let you know what it predicts.'

Then it comes in: 'CON 47 IND 47'.

OMG, OMG, she's going to get it. She's going to bloody get it. We spiral into panic.

'It's all your fault,' I say. 'You didn't pass on the lucky rosette!'

'I couldn't bloody find it, Sasha, all right?'

He starts pulling all his desk drawers out, rifling through them in a manic attempt to find the elusive rosette, which has been handed down by each Conservative MP for East Devon to the new candidate. He's convinced Jupp will lose the seat because he hasn't handed it over. Truth is, Jupp refuses to wear a rosette anyway.

We get to Clarence House for a dinner in honour of Wafic. About forty of us. Drinks beforehand, with carrot sticks and dips and sausages; not very royal. Camilla charms all the men; she clearly still has it. She was, after all, one of the sex bombs of her generation and retains her smoky-voiced humour and naughty twinkle. The horseshoe of men around her are saying they are worried about the election result. H asks if she has her suitcase packed ready to flee. When Prince Charles comes up to shake my hand, I give a loud scream, because he squashes my chunky ring into my hand. 'Are you all right?' he asks. I explain it's the ring and I shake my hand to get the feeling back. 'It's from Cornwall, your estate. It's a Cornish shell, but it's not gold.'

'Not gold?' He looks surprised. H butts in, to say that now he has left politics he will give it the Midas touch shortly. *Very important for men to think they have branded their women with the correct jewellery.* They talk about the Commonwealth Enterprise and Investment Council, of which H is now deputy chairman, and then a bit about ocean plastics. I like Prince Charles and I think he will make an excellent king as long as he stays out of politics.

We dine under a portrait of the Queen Mother by Augustus John and surrounded by John Piper paintings of views of Windsor Castle, painted during the war and intended to serve as a record of the Castle in case it was damaged by enemy bombs. They are full of dark storm clouds, which somehow feels appropriate since we are only two days away from an election where a band of not so merry Marxists could take over.

The menu: double-baked cheese soufflé, roast turkey, then ice-cream cake and berry compote. From Premier Mode Ltd, Fawcett the Fence's outfit. He is there, ushering everyone around as usual.

At dinner, Prince Charles makes a very generous speech about Wafic – H thought he had tears in his eyes – and Wafic reciprocates. It was all quite moving. Wafic and Rosemary's ten-year-old grand-daughter beaming with smiles next to her father in a lovely red velvet dress. Wafic's story of his journey to the heart of the British establishment is down to both his extraordinary entrepreneurial ability and a philanthropic generosity that is unparalleled. He has built a business school in Oxford and rescued many children from war-torn Syria, among his many achievements. He is a good friend with a good sense of humour, and he deserves all the recognition afforded to him. And Rosemary, with all her grace and beauty, deserves recognition as well, for supporting him in all his endeavours.

Towards the end of dinner, I ask Alan Duncan how he is enjoying retirement, and if his diaries are coming out. He replies: 'What a good idea.' Then after dinner, his waspish husband James, who I have always been unsure about, darts over, all front fanged, and attacks me for being negative about Alan on my Twitter account. I say I can't remember anything too harsh, just a difference of opinion on Brexit, perhaps. But it's all a bit rich, as H tells me later, because Alan is at the time on the other side of the room, telling some Arab friend of Wafic that I'm leaden, with heavy Brexit views, and in front of my husband no less. Hardly the gallant behaviour of a knight!

13 December

What a night! My twenty-third wedding anniversary. And a landslide victory for Boris and Brexit. An overwhelming sense of vindication after swimming against the tide of urban remain, my friends. The story is of a red wall crumbling, the complete wipe-out of traditional northern working-class Labour support. Even Sedgefield, Tony Blair's former seat, red since 1935, turned blue. And there was more. Jeremy Corbyn quits. Jo Swinson loses her seat. The Brexit Party wins no seats. And, best of all: Grieve gone, Soubry gone, Gauke gone, Chuka chucked, Gyimah gone, Wollaston, Phillip Lee, Sandbach, Milton . . . all gone. Literally all the troublemakers. When it came down to it, voters did not like party-hopping democracy-dodgers. Bercow is practically crying on Sky News.

*

We started the evening in a complete state of nerves. The YouGov poll was not good, and in East Devon the amount of publicity Claire Wrong had received was unprecedented by anyone's standards. We put our glad rags on, and can't get it out of our heads that we are not going to an election count: this is literally the first time we haven't been to one since 1997. Instead, we head over to Scott's restaurant, where Michael and Sarah Spencer are generously throwing a lavish bash for their nearest and dearest. I sit next to the historian Niall Ferguson, and he is gloomy: he is talking about the successes of social media mobilising the youth vote and the latest YouGov poll. We discuss how our worst-case scenario would be another hung parliament, which would create an opportunity for a Labour–SNP–Lib Dem alliance, with a Marxist as PM. He's really shaking my confidence, being the brainbox he is; I had predicted a 30 to 70 majority and was confident Boris was going to sweep it, until now.

At 10 p.m., the exit poll says a majority of 86 and the whole room erupts; everyone is punching the air, banging the tables, the hedgies are ringing their pilots, telling them to switch off the engines of their jets. The pure and chemical thrill of it races through the room as fast as a narcotic running through veins. The waiters look on, amazed at the general hysteria.

At 10:24, H texts Dave: 'OMG!'

'Indeed. Good in lots of ways. End of Corbynism. End of Baker and Francois having power. Yippee,' he replies. But it's probably bittersweet for him. Boris has always been the personal competition. And now Britain will wake up to its first solid majority for many decades, and no Tory leader has done that since Margaret Thatcher in 1987. It might just be that Jeremy Corbyn has also produced something of a record himself, by precipitating such a calamitous defeat. But David should be proud; his achievement was just as great; he was the one that made the Conservatives electable after years in the wilderness. And the members of the tribe, those of us who slogged our guts out, day in and day out, should take this as a victory shared.

'Now Boris can be the One Nation man I believe him to be at heart,' says H.

'Agree,' replies Dave.

But H and I are still feeling somehow uncomfortable; we can't take the noise and the excitement amongst this mostly City fraternity and return home to watch it all unfold on TV. I look at Twitter and my eyeballs expand into two saucers; the exit poll is predicting a 96 per cent win for Claire Wright. I tell H, who just keeps saying, 'It can't be true, it can't be, on this Conservative swing?' But exit polls are usually right, I keep saying. We go to sleep because we can't bear to watch.

Saffron rings at 3 a.m. She is doing work experience for LBC and is at the Richmond count. She tells me Zac Goldsmith has lost his seat and stormed out in tears. I'm now awake. I text Peter Fage. He comes back, 'I think we have done it!' and then, not much later, 'We've had it confirmed, the exit poll was done in Ottery St Mary (her home turf) so gave her a 96% chance of winning. We are currently 4000 ahead.' I wake up H: 'Jupp's done it, babe.' I go back to Peter and I say I wanted to physically throw up when I saw that poll; he says he felt the same. Then he adds, 'A few days ago, we got Twitter private messages from Rylance (Lib Dems) and the Labour guy Dan Wilson who admitted they'd rather us win than her due to the level of abuse and trolling they'd been getting from her supporters.'

Lucille Baker, the area agent, tells us later that she was in the corridor leaning against a wall when Claire Wright swept past her, clearly aware she was losing, and that there was much drama, lots of slamming doors and unconcealed emotion. She certainly looked absolutely beaten as the announcement was made. And I do weirdly feel some sympathy for her. It just shows you can have the better campaign, but you don't necessarily win on the back of it. Claire always misunderstood two basic principles. First, to win, she would have to convert the Tory vote, and by supporting remain she was never going to do that. Second, campaigns rarely determine winners and losers, because voters pretty much know which way they are going to vote, which leaves the pool of unde-cideds relatively shallow. In the final analysis Claire is merely a campaigner, a good one, but her vanity superseded any rational take of the facts on the ground. It didn't matter how many streets she pounded, how many Facebook posts she put up, how many leaflets she put through people's doors, the basic psephology has not been altered in East Devon for a century or more; there is the Tory vote and there is the non-Tory vote, and where those votes fall has barely changed in that time.

Meanwhile the girls refuse to tell me which way they voted, but I think I can put myself on the line and say it wasn't Conservative. Saffron had Siena's proxy vote, and we suspect she went for the animal welfare party, which is another way of saying a curse on all your houses. When the results came through, H sent her a message on the family WhatsApp: 'Well, all the animals of Chelsea are very grateful for your support, Siena. They pass on their thanks.'

Late afternoon, and Boris is at the podium by the steps of Downing Street, next to a bushy Christmas tree, saying he will repay the nation's trust. He urges Britain to find closure over Brexit and he vows to work 'around the clock' to 'unite and level up' the country. One of his first calls is to Nicola Sturgeon, who has had a good war, to say he remains opposed to breaking up the union. This will most definitely be an area of confrontation in months to come. The job of rebuilding relationships with our friends, families and neighbours begins.

But back for a moment to Boris. This is Good Boris, lit up by the fairy lights like the true celebrity he is. Clever Boris. The one that won two terms as Mayor of London. The one who attained a landslide, breaking down old tribal loyalties. This is the Boris who won the leave campaign, defeating the serried ranks of the British establishment. The one that thwarted parliament which had been incited into rebellion by a remain Speaker. Boris, the political leader who ran a minority government and returned with a majority one. The seducer Boris, the one who secured a new deal from the European Union and brought Leo Varadkar on side. The ruthless Boris who recognised his obstacles to power and had the guts to withdraw the whip from twenty-one of his own MPs then ensured that every parliamentary candidate pledged to support his bill. How, Houdini-like, he escaped from the Fixed Term Parliament Act and got his election, during which he humiliated and marginalised the Brexit Party which could have easily cost him a majority. But most of all and throughout all of this he maintained his good humour and star quality. There are troubled times ahead but, on this day, this hour, this moment, he warrants praise for his political achievements, which are truly great.

17 December

Chaffcombe

A burning fireball of badness has been seen prowling the chicken house. Rob saw it first, then H a few days later. A day after that we found its carcass inside the linhay, lying against the wall. Close up, it looked as if it had severe mange. It must have been in poor health, because it's unusual to see a fox wandering about in the daytime, and in cold weather. It was clearly trying to find a warm place, such as the linhay. By then it was a death foretold of starvation and hypothermia.

I stare at it and find myself thinking about Corbyn and how he has been a parasite on the body politic since he first won the leadership of his party. How he infiltrated a party that was old and respected, and radicalised its new members. How he made it permissible for them to become nasty, racist, warring, to ignore any desire to show or promote social harmony. The trolling on social media was worse than in any other election that preceded it. It is

Corbyn who has rallied the young into supporting dodgy regimes, shared with them his disgust of our armed forces, encouraged them to metaphorically pull down Union flags because for him they represent imperialism. It is Corbyn who has separated them from the century-deep bonds that existed between party and place, and that is the main point: although he took to the urban centres and made them his strongholds, he didn't really belong to them, or to a country, a culture even. His whole political doctrine didn't come out of knowing places, it came out of the mind.

The red fox might be slain but the parasitism, that relationship where one feeds off the other, causing it harm, will stay until a political detox in the Labour Party can occur. When that happens, it will be ready to govern again.

28 December

Cornwall

West Penwith. A deep, leaden grey in the sky over a funerary landscape peppered with tumuli, cairns and quoits. A place which is as much about myth as it is about history. I am standing, in the very extremities of our land, beside the lichen-skinned Neolithic monument of Mên-an-tol. No one knows exactly why this mysterious holed stone is here on this moorland, with two sentry standing stones. It might have been an astronomical observatory, or the remains of an entrance to a chambered tomb, or part of a stone circle. Folklore has it that if you climb through it, it has curative properties, particularly for children. That you can ward off harm and see into the future. Is that why we are here?

Ever since I was a child, growing up here in west Cornwall, I always liked the texture of this landscape, the simplicity of it, nothing else but the human hand and heart coming together with the living earth. The way it reminds you of the shortness of things. When we wanted to step off the moving machine, we often came here, H and I, to this place. The moor takes away the voices shouting at you, the tug at your ankles, the guilt over inaction and choices made. It makes you look at its litter; the discarded standing stone belonging to a king who once stood nine feet high, a great warrior called Rialobran-Cunoval Fil, the son of Cunoval, slain in the battle of Glendhal moor, buried here with all his arms and treasures. Of small, ancient and lost communities, fallen-down walls, belief systems far from our modern world, and it tells you, through its own special melancholy, that the stars will still shine, the wind will still blow, the rain will still fall, and that new voices will articulate new ideas and that they will rise in the light and fall in the dark, but nothing will stop time unfolding.

And then we walk from Mên-an-tol across the moor to the engine houses of the Carn Galver and Ding Dong tin mines, ruined and lonely on the horizon, and know it's not just us that have struggled to leave our mark in this world.

Because, in the end, all we can ever hope to leave behind are shadows in stories told.

Acknowledgements

Mostly, to my husband, Hugo, a natural raconteur, whose stories and humour light up these pages. When I was merely flirting with the idea of publication it was super-agent Caroline Dawnay, ably supported by her well-organised assistant Cat Aitken, who took control of the steering wheel and pushed me into the back seat. Caroline is like a ripe peach: all soft and squidgy on the outside, with much empathy and passion, but her inner core is hard, professional, clever, experienced. To my parents for passing down those politically obsessive genes and everything else besides. To my amazing daughters, Saffron and Siena, who provided me with the millennial material, and to all the Cameroons for not mentioning me or barely mentioning me in their memoirs – this is payback! To Richard Beswick, Islington Man, who massacred the original text and brought my rantings and ramblings down to size. To Zoe Gullen's gimlet-eyed scrutiny. To the East Devon Conservative Association for their rolling criticism and support. To Sue Townsend, Hugo's long-term secretary, for her remarkable patience and loyalty. To the steady flow of political researchers who filed through Hugo's office, most notably Toby Williams, whose sense of humour thankfully matched my husband's, thereby avoiding any trips to employment tribunals. To Claire Wright, whose unsavoury supporters introduced us to social media trolling. To Rob Brealy, who keeps the show on the road at Chaffcombe, where I am now going to ground for the foreseeable future – no doubt to the relief of many!

Index

About the Author

Sasha Swire was raised and educated in west Cornwall, where her father, Sir John Nott, was MP for the St Ives constituency. She was a journalist on national and regional publications and in Asia before working as her husband Hugo Swire's political researcher from 2001 to 2019. She divides her time between Devon and London. This is her first book.

Credits

31 Roger Deakin, *Notes from Walnut Tree Farm*, ed. Alison Hastie and Terence Blacker (London: Hamish Hamilton, 2009)

81 Robinson Jeffers, *Roan Stallion, Tamar and Other Poems* (New York: Boni & Liveright, 1925)

145 'Our God is a great big God' by Nigel and Jo Hemming, © 2001 Vineyard Songs

200–1 Harold Macmillan, quoted in Ruth Winstone (ed.), *Events, Dear Boy, Events: A Political Diary of Britain* (London: Profile, 2012)

479 'The Blackbird of Glanmore' from Seamus Heaney, *District and Circle* (London: Faber, 2006)

480 'Cob' from Fiona Sampson, *The Catch* (London: Chatto & Windus, 2016)

481 Alan Clark, *Diaries: Into Politics 1972–1982* (London: Weidenfeld & Nicolson, 2000)

488 'Under the Oak', from D. H. Lawrence, *New Poems* (London: Martin Secker, 1918)

492 'Birches', from Robert Frost, *Mountain Interval* (New York: Henry Holt, 1916)